RISK MANAGEMENT

IN

HEALTHCARE

Second Edition

by

Dr Geoff Roberts

Witherby & Co. Ltd.
32-36 Aylesbury Street,
London EC1R 0ET

1st Edition 1996
2nd Edition 2002

WITHERBY

PUBLISHERS

© The Institute of Risk Management

Geoff Roberts

2002

ISBN 1 85609 225 9

Printed and Published by
WITHERBY & CO. LTD
32-36 Aylesbury Street
London EC1R 0ET
Tel No: 020 7251 5341   Fax No: 020 7251 1296
International Tel No: +44 20 7251 5341
International Fax No: +44 20 7251 1296
E-mail: books@witherbys.co.uk
www: witherbys.com

RISK MANAGEMENT
IN
HEALTHCARE

by

Dr Geoff Roberts

OTHER BOOKS IN THE SERIES

Business Finance for Risk Management
Business Organisation and Finance
Corporate Risk Management
Insurance, Non Marine – An Introduction
Liability Exposures
Local Government a Text for Risk Managers
Physical Control of Risk
Risk Control
Risk and the Business Environment
Risk Analysis
Risk Financing
Treasury Risk Management
Liability Risk and the Law

British Library Cataloguing in Publication Data
Roberts, Dr Geoff
Risk Management in Healthcare
1 Title
ISBN 1 85609 225 9

Foreword

In the 'new, modern and dependable' NHS, improving the safety and quality of care are now major objectives for all NHS care providers, on an equal par with activity and financial objectives.

Safety and quality go hand in hand. Safety is commonly regarded as the 'absence of unacceptable risk'. An organisation that pursues quality embeds sound risk management principles and processes into its systems and culture. Effective everyday management of unacceptable risk is an essential prerequisite for delivering quality.

As healthcare becomes increasingly complex, and available resources are stretched to the limit, managing risk has never been more important. The opportunities to be realised from effective risk management are potentially very significant.

In the NHS in England, for example, according to various research estimates:

- over 400,000 patients every year suffer potentially preventable harm attributed to 'medical error', resulting in over 34,000 avoidable deaths and prolonged hospital stay costs in excess of £2 billion;

- hospital acquired infections cost £1 billion per year – 15% of these infections are considered to be preventable; and

- claims for clinical negligence cost in excess of £400 million (and rising) and there are outstanding claims in the system amounting to several billion pounds.

Effective risk management protects assets, minimises financial losses, improves both the safety and quality of healthcare, and improves the health, safety and welfare of healthcare staff. In the NHS in England, this is reflected in the combination of the clinical governance and controls assurance agendas, where risk management is key to helping improve the NHS for the benefit of all who use and work in it.

This book is an essential publication for those interested in managing risk in healthcare. It provides very useful information on a range of relevant risk management issues, clearly and concisely. I commend it to you as a key reference text on healthcare risk management.

Stuart Emslie
Head of Controls Assurance
Department of Health

January 2002

Preface

In times of rapid change within the health services, any book on risk management cannot expect to reflect the latest additions to the compliance requirements on health services. Rather it should provide the framework within which a sound risk management framework can be understood and applied. That is the intention of this book.

For example, the National Patient Safety Agency is about to begin its work, although the detail of its activities were not available as this book was printed. Students will need to keep abreast with its developments through the website at:

http://www.npsa.org.uk

Web addresses, which should be regularly visited to obtain the latest updates, include:

the Department of Health at:

http://www.doh.gov.uk/dhhome.htm

the controls assurance support unit at:

htttp://www.casu.org.uk

and the clinical governance support unit at:

http://www.cgsupport.org

The understanding that is emerging of system failures which can result in harm, rather than harm only arising from the failure of individuals working within a system, is a major advance in recognising the causes of error. This understanding should allow for improvements in quality which are based on a systematic appraisal rather than individual blame. The challenge of creating 'low' or 'no' blame cultures in care organisations when mishaps occur is central to achieving improvements in safety.

The sharing of good practice also remains a challenging issue for organisational cultures. Examples of organisations that freely share ideas to improve services for patients can be found at:

http://www.geoffroberts.com

Students who need assistance are welcome to contact me directly through the website.

Dr Geoff Roberts   January 2002

Acknowledgements

I would like to thank the many friends, clients and colleagues who have influenced and contributed to this edition of *Risk Management in Healthcare*. In particular, Kim Donovan of the Controls Assurance Support Unit who made a significant contribution and gave access to her excellent thesis on organisations, Joe Holly who was co-author to the first edition, Eric Hodgson, Pam Lees and colleagues at Warrington Community Health Care NHS who are knowledgeable practitioners of effective risk management.

I would also like to thank Stuart Emslie, Head of Controls Assurance at the Department of Health whose encouragement and sponsorship made the updating of this edition possible.

Geoff Roberts
January 2002

Contents

1

INTRODUCTION TO RISK MANAGEMENT IN HEALTH CARE

It is the duty of each Health Authority, Primary Care Trust and NHS Trust to put and keep in place arrangements for the purpose of monitoring and improving the quality of health care which it provides to individuals[1]

1.1   THE NEED TO CONSIDER RISK ISSUES

Risk, the possibility of injury or loss, is common to all healthcare provision and permeates every clinical and organisational action. This pervasiveness is sufficient justification for making risk an essential concern of both clinicians and managers at every level. The cost of accidents, in both human and financial terms, only serves to highlight the significance risk can assume. In fact, managing risk in healthcare is so critical that it should be part of both operational and strategic thinking in every part of healthcare delivery. It concerns clinical practice, equipment design and procurement, personnel management, financial planning to name but a few elements of the service chain. A good understanding of how to deal with risk can mean the difference between the success and the failure of the single clinical episode and of the healthcare services as a whole.

Each year:

- 400 people die or are seriously injured in adverse events involving medical devices;

- nearly 10,000 people are reported to have experienced serious adverse reactions to drugs;

- around 1,150 people who have been in recent contact with mental health services commit suicide;

---

1   Health Act 1999 Section 18 (1)

- nearly 28,000 written complaints are made about aspects of clinical treatment in hospitals;

- the NHS pays out around £400 million a year in the settlement of clinical negligence claims, and has a potential liability of around £2.4 billions for existing and expected claims;

- hospital acquired infections – around 15% of which may be avoidable – are estimated to cost the NHS nearly £1 billion.[2]

Why produce a book on clinical and healthcare risk management at this time? In the light of the prevalence and potential significance of risk, one would expect the literature on risk management in healthcare to be vast and indeed it is in the narrow terms of clinical decision analysis.[3] Markedly less emphasis has been placed on the management of risk in the organisational, economic, legal and business context together with the clinical and other implications for healthcare. The Chief Medical Officer has indicated the need for an updated text on risk management in the NHS.[4]

Considerable attention has been devoted to risk in finance and risk pooling methods which has application to very specific aspects of health service resourcing. However, the focus has been on normative rules that guide financial institutional decisions under well-circumscribed conditions of mathematical market models. Risk management and work with patients and the work-places of healthcare staff together with the resources applied have yet to be squeezed into such models.

One-off accidents have also been researched extensively both in medicine and elsewhere.[5] However, few overall theoretical and practical guides to risk management in healthcare have been available in the UK.[6] The NHS Management Executive has published a

---

2 *An organisation with a memory* – Department of Health 2000 ISBN 011 322441 9

3 See, for example, Llewelyn, H & Hopkins (Eds.) A *Analysing how we reach clinical decisions* Royal College of Physicians of London, [1993] and Dowie, J & Elstein, A (Eds.) *Professional judgement: A reader in clinical decision making* Cambridge University Press, [1988]

4 *An organisation with a memory* – Department of Health 2000

5 See the *Journal of the Medical Defence Union* [1987 – 2000] and Bignell, V & Fortune, J *Understanding Systems Failures*, Open University Press [1984].

6 *To err is human* – Linda Kohn, Committee on Quality of Health Care in America, National Academy Press, 2000

handbook on healthcare risk management as an introduction to the subject.[7] This text provides a starting point for healthcare risk managers. The book synthesises thought on healthcare risk management and cuts across the multiple contexts and points of view in healthcare.

We hope the individual reader will gain a comprehensive understanding of the subject and make use of this book to gain access to a widely scattered range of materials for clinical and healthcare risk management. A further important aim is to allow healthcare risk managers to benefit from the insights of investigators and other practitioners.

The financial cost of damages awarded to patients of the NHS for clinical negligence in 1999-2000 is estimated to be £350 million. With the addition of legal costs and the opportunity costs of clinicians and health manager's time, the true costs may be of the order of £450 – £500 million. The total cost potential to the health service was stated in 2000 to be £2.8B.[8] The frequency and severity of clinical negligence litigation is increasing and various schemes are being devised to control the additional costs.

Furthermore, the Health and Safety Executive estimates that more than 5% of the NHS budget pays for the costs of non-clinical accidents to staff, patients and visitors.[9] On resource grounds alone, without considering the physical and psychological harm to the victim, families and colleagues, it is essential to reduce and control the impact of both clinical and non-clinical accidents. The millions of pounds given in compensation, though rightly given, is given to the few and it could be better spent on the healthcare of the many. In considering the management of these risks, it is necessary to define our concepts of risk, hazards, accidents and risk management.

Retrospective studies of hospital clinical records have shown substantial numbers of adverse events, resulting in harm to patients, occurs during inpatient treatment. 3.7% of hospital admissions in the Havard study resulted in adverse events in which 7% of the resulting

---

7   NHS Management Executive *Risk Management in the NHS* [December 1993]

8   Commons Select Committee – 2000

9   Health & Safety Executive *The Costs of Accidents at Work*, HSE Books [1993]

disabilities were permanent and 14% contributed to death.[10][11] Similar studies in Australia have identified adverse events in 16.6% of admissions, half of which were considered to be avoidable.[12] A small scale similar study in England in which 1014 medical and nursing records of former acute hospital inpatients demonstrated that 10.8% of patients experienced an adverse event of which about half were judged to be avoidable.[13]

1.2 DEFINITIONS OF RISK AND RISK MANAGEMENT; 'HAZARDS', 'ACCIDENTS', ETC.

"Risk" we have already defined as the possibility of injury or loss. However, the definition does not elaborate on what is meant by the components of the definition, i.e. "possibility" and "injury or loss". Different risk experts describe risk in different ways[14]. However, we believe that there is an underlying concept of risk which is used by them all. This concept of risk can be used across all the disciplines of healthcare services – from the operating theatre to the accountant's office; from the paediatric clinic to the maintenance of the boilers.

The variances in the understanding of risk in various contexts comes from the different emphasis on distinct elements of the concept. The difference in emphasis is the result of risk manifesting itself in varying ways in different circumstances. In medicine and epidemiology, risk is the chance of some adverse outcome such as death or the contraction of a particular disease. In business and economics, opportunities whose returns are not guaranteed are commonly described in terms of "risk".[15]

---

10 Brennan TA, Leape Ll, Laird NM, Herbert I, Localio AR, Lawthers AG et al, Incidence of adverse events and negligence in hospitalised patients. *N Engl J Med* 1991; 324:370-376

11 Leape Ll, Brennan TA, Laird MN, Lawthers Localio AR, Barnes BA et al, Incidence of adverse events and negligence in hospitalized patients: results of the Havard medical practice study, *N Engl J Med* 1991; 324:377-384

12 Wilson RM, Runciman WB, Gibberd RW, Harrison BT, Newby L, Hamilton JD, The Quality in Australian Healthcare Study, *Med J Aust* 1995;163:458-71

13 Vincent C, Neale G, Woloshynowych M , Adverse Events in British Hospitals: preliminary retrospective record review *BMJ*, 2001, 7285:517-519

14 E.g. Fischoff, B et al. *Defining Risk,* **Policy Sciences** [1984] Vol. 17, pp. 123-139. Hannsson, S O *Dimensions of Risk,* Risk Analysis [1989] Vol. 9, pp. 107-112

15 E.g. see Miller, R *Risk Management,* The Financial Times Business Information Ltd. [1984]

Our definition is imprecise as to how 'possibility' and 'injury or loss' combine with each other to determine risk. Risk has three critical elements:

- the potential injury or loss itself;
- the uncertainty of that injury or loss occurring;
- the significance of the injury or loss.

The three elements work interactively to present a risk. These elements also go to show why perception of risk is inherently subjective. As such our analysis should be useful to healthcare risk managers not only because it helps to clarify the focal concept but also allows them to bring the understanding and perspectives of various disciplines and people involved to the problems of risk management.

The rise of the consumerism in the doctor/patient relationship has, for many people quite rightly, shifted the emphasis from a paternalistic approach to obtaining a patient's consent to one which is much more participative. The doctor is expected to expressly refer to significant risks associated both with a particular procedure and the patient's own condition, if that makes a potentially significant change to general risks. Except when treated by statute under the Mental Health Act, the patient has a right to forego a recommended procedure or treatment.

Many measures and operational definitions of risk focus on only one of the risk elements. Such is the case, for example, when epidemiologists state that the risk of cancer is 20 in 1,000,000 in some population. It is an indication of uncertainty associated with the particular injury or loss. This does not necessarily contradict measures that focus on other risk constituents, say, an insurer's view that providing coverage on a £200,000 house is riskier than providing coverage on one that costs £80,000. They are alternative measures of distinct elements of risks.

The significance of the potential injury or loss is also important in its interaction with the other elements. This illustrates why risk is an inherently subjective concept. What is considered a loss is peculiar to the person or group involved and its chance of occurring. For instance, the chance of being admitted to one hospital may be a relief to one person but a threat to another who associates it with the workhouse.

In the domestic environment we can agree with our partners that our nine-year-old daughters should be accompanied to school a mile away on the basis of reducing different risks. One risk would be the danger of traffic, another the danger of abduction. Even though the probability of the latter is very much less than that of the former, the significance of abduction for some far exceeds that of the traffic accident. This difference in the personal perception of risk has a profound impact when considering the moral, legal and political dimensions of healthcare risk management. It can also give rise to charges of "irrationality" in the allocation of resources for the reduction of risk.

This analysis has an effect on how we view an accident or a hazard, but their definitions are far simpler. An accident is the event or series of events which actually produced an injury or loss. A hazard is a physical condition which has the potential of inflicting injury or loss such as the trailing wire or the broken packaging in sterile supplies.

The definition and role of risk management in healthcare emerges from all these definitions. Risk management may be defined as the process whereby an organisation anticipates the potential for injuries or losses and acts to avoid those injuries or losses before and/or to ameliorate them after they occur. In one sense, therefore, risk management may be seen as part of general business planning and control activity. In another, there are clinical overtones to the activity in that the injuries or losses may flow from the clinical processes themselves. Both require a level of technical expertise to identify the circumstances providing possible injury or loss-producing circumstances and to measure the possible costs and benefits of a risk reduction exercise.

1.2.1 The special place of risk management in healthcare: different perceptions

Our analysis of the concept of risk underpins our approach to risk management within healthcare. It also allows the risk manager to understand "Why healthcare risk management?" The significance of any risk can be viewed from a range of positions which themselves interact. These positions are:

- moral
- political
- legal
- professional
- economic

1.2.1.1 Moral perspectives

Broadly speaking, moral thinking takes two general paths, the teleological and the deontological, in answering the question "What is the right thing to do?" The teleological approach usually defines 'right' in terms of the good produced as the consequences of an action. Utilitarianism[16] is the most prominent form of teleology which calculates the probable results of performing various actions relevant to a situation and to choose one that will maximise the ratio of benefit over harm produced.

Deontology defines 'right' by considering intrinsic features of an action, largely independent of its consequences. Three main concerns of the deontologist are:

- fulfilling one's duties in a situation;

- respecting the rights and autonomy of others (regardless of the consequences);

- treating others with equal justice.

Broadly, we are advised to respect everyone's capacity to determine and pursue his or her goals, never treating people as mere means or tools to our ends.

The potential for moral conflict on the bases of these two general approaches is enormous. The risk manager will be aware that most people deploy both approaches in debate in different contexts and sometimes in the same context. The use of resources demands in terms of efficiency, economy and equity that the maximum number of people should receive care and treatment from the health services. The clinical imperative is likely to be more deontological especially in terms of fulfilling a duty in a situation and respecting the rights and autonomy of each patient.

The risk manager cannot be expected to resolve a centuries old debate. The risk manager can best assist in acting as an under-labourer in the process of decision-making[17] by:

---

16. *Business Risk Management* Ritchie and Marshall. Pub: Chapman and Hall 1993

17 See Candee, D & Puka, B *An Analytic Approach to Resolving Problems in Medical Ethics,* Journal of Medical Ethics, pp. 61-70, vol. 2 [1984]

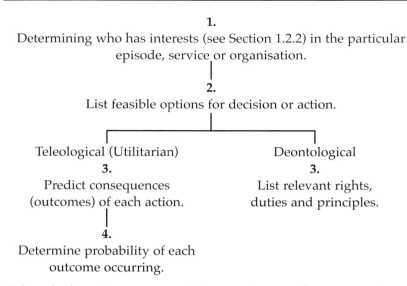

1.
Determining who has interests (see Section 1.2.2) in the particular episode, service or organisation.

2.
List feasible options for decision or action.

Teleological (Utilitarian)
3.
Predict consequences
(outcomes) of each action.

Deontological
3.
List relevant rights,
duties and principles.

4.
Determine probability of each
outcome occurring.

Although the risk manager will be involved in the debate, the key decision-makers are likely to be others for the most part. It is not solely up to the risk manager to determine the basis of valuing each outcome, for example, or establish the validity of the rights-claim of any of the parties which are the next steps respectively in utilitarian and deontological decision-making.

1.2.1.2 Political

The political (and sociological) context in which risks are perceived and managed must also be considered. The political will operate both within and outside the immediate healthcare environment. Allocation of resources to reduce particular risks will be a policy issue as the various parties to events will have different perceptions of what risks are important as well as there being different political motivations and cultural backgrounds.

Research shows that there are major discrepancies between the risk assessment of experts and non-experts. However, it cannot be assumed that non-experts are mistaken and decisions about risk should rely on the formal assessments of experts. A contrary conclusion can be drawn from our analysis above, since formal risk assessments could ignore factors which 'lay' people find important. It would be foolhardy for the risk manager to base decisions only on formal assessments. Risk managers should be aware of others perceptions – patients, managers, general public, clinicians – to risk at three levels:

- the probabilities and costs of potential outcomes;
- familiarity with the situation that produces the risk;
- the perceived degree of control a person or group has in affecting the outcome.

1.2.1.3 Legal

In practice, it will be the legal context which will have the most direct and noticeable effect on the conduct of healthcare risk management. Legal rules and regulations together with professional conduct rules and practice standards constitute the regulatory framework for both health services and risk management itself (See Chapter 2). This is a complex area. Because there is often such a dearth of quantitative data that a statistical modelling approach requires, measuring risk stochastically, cannot easily be adopted. Process tracing methods have to be developed and their compliance with the regulatory framework becomes crucial.

There are two main parts to the legal context:

- professional negligence law;
- statutory regulation of the workplace.

Professional negligence law with respect to medicine and related professions deals mostly with two types of error:

- negligence in practising medicine (malpractice)
- negligence in informing patients prior to a medical intervention (informed consent)

Statutory law and associated regulations define and set out the principles for the conduct of business in relation to environmental hazards to staff, patients and visitors

1.2.1.4 Professional

The professional contribution to risk control is central to the successful impact of a risk management programme. Contributions are needed not just from nursing and medical staff, but from all professional groups who contribute to clinical care. Significant contributions have been made through national audits such as the Confidential Enquiry into Maternal Deaths and the National Confidential Inquiry into Perioperative Deaths and Confidential Inquiry into Suicide and Homicide by People with Mental Illness. Increasingly, the Audit Office studies offer a forum to contribute to the sharing of good practice and utilisation of facilities.

The recognition by the Royal College of Surgeons that introducing new techniques – 'Keyhole' surgery – without adequate training leads to inadvertent harm to patients has led to the introduction of a structured training programme. What is surprising is that despite the forseeability of these complications if operators are inadequately trained, the risk is not managed prospectively.

1.2.1.5 Economic

The increasing interest in the economics of healthcare provision is set to have an incremental impact upon the safety of healthcare. In particular the payment of damages to patients can only impact on the system by diverting moneys from patient care.

The impact of the compounding effects of year on year increasing efficiency will impact upon the priorities by healthcare providers. The safety of patients and the efficacy of treatments must become central to these priorities.

1.2.2 The extent of risk factors

The effort to determine risk in healthcare needs the definition of healthcare process and what/who is involved. This may necessarily include:

- patients
- staff
- clinical process
- care environment
  - space and physical surroundings
  - equipment
  - buildings
- business processes
  - personnel
  - financial

  - information
  - planning
- non-staff
  - carers
  - relatives and friends
  - contractors
  - general public

Consideration of risk is therefore should clearly not be confined solely to individuals, but needs to be embedded in the system of healthcare delivery.

1.2.3 What risk management in health care involves

1.2.3.1 *Strategic risk management – "Doing the right things" –*

relationship to business strategy and planning the healthcare process

1.2.3.2 *Operational risk management – "Doing things right" –*

relationship to clinical management and general management

1.2.4 The healthcare environment (task environment characteristics)

1.2.4.1 *The organisational environment: provider/commissioner split*

The establishment of the provider/commissioner split in the health system provides additional opportunities for risks to arise to both parties and those whom they are supposed to be serving – the patients. The risks may arise from differences in intent, timescales and provision of resources.

The primary method of reducing risk in this area must rely upon shared values, good communications and a shared vision for the service, but political imperatives may deflect either party from its intended direction. Examples of this may be found in the direction of funding from service development to the maintenance of certain levels of waiting lists. Acute mental health provision and practices may be highlighted by an act of violence by a patient upon a member of the public. Missed cases of child abuse will have an adverse effect upon the reputation of both health and social services.

The development of Primary Care Groups and Primary Care Trusts as commissioners of healthcare poses additional risks for provider Trusts.

These arise from natural fluctuations in demand that will be particularly acute where large-scale epidemiological models of health needs are applied to much smaller units represented by smaller groups. In these situations the model of contracts for service provision needs to be carefully assessed so as to counter the potential for error arising out of the 'statistics of small numbers' effect.

1.2.5 Central fund for clinical negligence
Clinical Negligence Scheme for Trusts (CNST)

The establishment of NHS Trusts as corporate entities placed upon them the burden of compensating patients who are the subject of clinical negligence. This risk is by its nature capricious. With the development of a mature market of clinical negligence claims, a Trust with an exposure to obstetric claims could easily find itself with many millions of pounds payable in compensation in any one year. These risks to the stability of healthcare provision have resulted in the establishment of a financial risk pooling scheme for Trusts, the Clinical Negligence Scheme for Trusts, (CNST).

The CNST scheme is under the control of a Special Health Authority, the NHS Litigation Authority. Trusts are able to join the scheme as members. The subscription was initially being assessed by broad criteria including the type of clinical activity, income and the claim excess chosen to be paid. The excess level is at the choice of the Trust with the minimum level of excess determined by the Trust income. The scheme is developing and will allow for discounts for Trusts demonstrating a structured risk management programme. Future subscriptions will need to reflect individual claims experience.

The CNST is examined further in Chapter 5 (5.5).

1.2.6 Links to quality

Risk management programmes are directed towards the prevention of loss and the limitation of damage when loss has occurred. The methods used for risk identification, assessment and management do not differ significantly from those used for successful continuous quality improvement programmes. Risk management and quality improvement may be considered as different parts of the same spectrum of effort to improve quality within organisations.

'Just-in-time' management methods, which have been adopted so successfully in Japan, rely upon a detailed knowledge of work processes and the key components of each stage of the work process. The performance or safety of such a linear process, P, is a function of the state of knowledge of certainties, C, and uncertainties, U.

Expressed as an equation the risk manager may wish to consider the proposal:

$$P \, f \, C, U$$

The performance or safety performance of a working system is a function of the knowledge of the reliability of the component elements.

These elements include people and all other components of the working system. The concept has been reinforced in the process of system re-engineering to promote efficiency. In practical risk management terms it underlines some key questions – what do we know about a system of care and its safety, what have we assumed about the system of care and apparent safety? **Building out assumptions of safety and replacing them with an explicit expectation of safety is central to effective considerations of risk and risk management in healthcare.**

1.3 OPERATIONAL RISK MANAGEMENT IN HEALTHCARE

1.3.1 Multiplicity of healthcare processes

- characteristics of individuals/groups in decision processes
- qualitative and quantitative dimensions of information and information systems
- basic quality required of information systems that information is accurate, relevant and timely

Risk management decisions are actually special kinds of decision problems which in healthcare have other complicating considerations. For example, in a clinical decision problem, the clinician must select an action with the intention of providing outcomes at least as satisfactory as those that would result from any available option. When this goal is achieved the decision has been successful; otherwise it is a failure. Thus, a "decision problem" is the challenge of making a successful decision. In risk taking, risk is one – but only one – significant aspect of the available options. This is because implicit in risk decisions is the question "How much risk is acceptable?"

In isolation, there is no such thing as an acceptable risk because, by its definition risk should always be rejected. The reason an option containing risk is not rejected, is that other considerations, including attractive benefits, may be considered above any additional negative features. For instance, a surgical operation that tolerates a potential subsequent disability may be acceptable to a patient because it also has the advantage of removal of pain and longer survival. The role of risk therefore is that of one kind of negative feature that might characterise a decision option.[18]

1.4   SIGNIFICANCE OF RISK

Risk managers and the 'man in the street' may both assume that the more significant the potential losses in a situation, the greater the implied risk. This is not necessarily so. The significance of the loss can be affected subjectively in two ways. Reference outcomes can easily differ from one person to the next. Thus an outcome that is a loss for one individual might well be a gain for another. For example, a termination of a pregnancy complicated by the need to perform a hysterectomy would be a very significant loss to a woman intending a later attempt to carry a successful pregnancy, but little loss to a woman who considered her family complete. But even if two individuals both consider the same outcomes as losses, there is still room for differences in the significance of those outcomes to each individual, differences that have a bearing on the risk.

Often potential outcomes are quantified, say the number of discharges or wrong drug administrations. Typically, greater magnitudes are preferred to lesser ones or vice versa. For example, a hospital prefers more discharges to less, but wants the lowest possible mistakes in drug administration. On the other hand, there are also existing quantified outcomes for which some intermediate amount is most preferred, amounts of fluoride in drinking water being an example. For any given quantified outcome, although loss significance is greatest for either maximum, minimum or intermediate amounts, there can still exist important differences in loss significance from person to person (or group to group).

---

18 Some might question the critical assumption that risk is negative and something to be avoided. Expected utility theory and decision analysis allow for *risk indifference* and *risk seeking* behaviour, but in healthcare risk management or medicine these behaviours may seem unethical.

1.4.1   Uncertainty

Every concept of risk requires that there must be uncertainty about the outcomes of a prospective action. If the outcomes are guaranteed, there is no risk. However, various risk conceptions differ in precisely how uncertainty affects risks. At least four roles can be identified for uncertainty:

- risk as uncertainty;
- uncertainty about loss categories;
- uncertainty about which losses will occur;
- levels of uncertainty.

"Risk as uncertainty" means that risk is said to exist whenever the outcomes of an action are not assured. Economists often use this concept of risk when they refer to any prospect with no guarantee of returns as a 'risk'.[19] Risk as uncertainty is the risk conception implicit in many discussions of risk-taking within decision analysis.

Uncertainty about loss categories is when decision-makers typically are unable to anticipate every significant outcome category. Situations differ in the extent to which potential outcome categories – and therefore possible injuries or losses – are apparent. The riskiness of those situations increases with the uncertainty about what might be the categories of losses.

Sometimes the locus of uncertainty about loss categories resides in the alternatives themselves. Take the case of public hazards. The newness of a technology is often seen to be a significant contributor to its riskiness. In fact, a new and untried technology is inherently risky partly because no one knows what kinds of losses it might produce.

In other circumstances, the uncertainty about loss categories is a reflection of the risk takers naiveté. Consider the professional risk analysts whose task is to unveil the myriad ways a proposed project conceivably could turn out badly.

---

19 In order for this viewpoint to be consistent with the notion of risk as the possibility of injury or loss, the worst potential outcome must be less attractive than the reference.

1.4.2　Injury and Loss

Implicit in the concept of injury or loss is the notion of a reference (or reference outcome). The reference is the focal outcome that is taken away or denied. Any outcome that is preferred to the reference is a gain; one that is less preferred is an injury or loss.

1.4.2.1 Multiplicity of loss and injury

There is a multiplicity of potential outcome categories – and thus classes of loss – that are possible in risk situations. Market researchers have recognised this idea for some considerable time and is also incorporated into the way general and special damages are calculated by the courts. However, in healthcare, the losses a prospective procedure might produce can fall into the categories shown in Table 1.4.2.1.a.

Two important ideas are implicit in the notion of multiplicity. The first is that, all other things being equal, the greater the number of distinct

Table 1.4.2.1.a.

LOSS/INJURY	EXPLANATION
Physical/Psychiatric	The patient/employee/visitor is physically or psychologically harmed.
Emotional	The loss affects the patient's self image or self-concept.
Financial	The patient loses money. The provider loses money and sustains opportunity costs.
Social loss	The results affect the way others think about the patient or reflects badly on professional competence and reputation.
Market	Affects way the general public thinks about the provider. GPs refer elsewhere.
Time	Wastes patient's time and causes inconvenience because must be re-admitted, repaired or replaced.

losses that are incurred, the worse off is the organisation or person. The second is related but separate. Options exist in the numbers of significant outcome categories they entail, for instance, floor covering which is relatively straightforward, versus information systems, which are more complicated. Again, all else being the same, we might expect that the potential for consequential losses – and hence risk – increases as the number of significant categories increases.

1.5 CAUSES AND TYPES OF ERRORS AND ACCIDENTS

1.5.1 Types of Errors

An examination of the different types of error which may occur is necessary for an understanding of the causes of mistakes which occur in healthcare.

1.5.1.1 Type I Error – Omission

A type I error is typically due to an act of omission. This may involve the failure to comply with current regulations or statute or to fail to comply with current professionally accepted practice.

The basic cause of type I errors is lack of knowledge. A common example is to fail to carry out an investigation where it was indicated, as may happen in the Accident and Emergency Department.

Type I errors thrive in departments characterised by inadequate training and supervision. Personnel working in departments may positively contribute to the likelihood of error through failure to keep up to date with recent advances in their subject.

1.5.1.2 Type II Error – Commission

Type II errors are acts of commission, that is, an act is committed which should not have been. An example is the blood vessel may be inadvertently lacerated at operation through a type II error by the surgeon through lack of concentration.

Underlying these types of error is a lack of commitment or consideration for others involved in the healthcare process.

Type I and type II errors may be differentiated by a simple case of needlestick injury in a laundry worker. In case of the laundry worker sustaining a needle stick-stick injury, the act of commission is the member of staff leaving the needle in discarded laundry. The act of omission is by the laundry worker in failing to look for needles. A different mind set is required to make each error.

1.5.1.3 Type III Error – Unawareness

Type III errors arise from a faulty specification of the nature of a problem which leads to real solutions being adopted to deal with wrongly identified problems, rather than incorrect solutions to real problems. These errors may arise from a lack of understanding of the assumptions made or a lack of knowledge or consideration of the consequences of a decision. Type III errors are most easily recognised to have occurred where the management of the service fails to understand the true nature of a problem which it intends to address. Often this results from inadequate research.

An example of a type III error is a radiotherapy unit where leakage of radiation occurred through the fabric of the building during the treatment of patients. This posed a threat to passers-by. The response of the management was to erect a sign stating "Radiation Hazard – No Loitering".

A further example is the removal of hand washing facilities in wards as a result of the fear of Legionnaires disease outbreaks in hospitals and as part of modernisation of the ward environment. Legionella bacteria thrive in tepid hot water. Ward sinks provided tepid hot water. Removing the sinks was thought to be a pro-active and preventative measure to reduce the threat of the spread of Legionnaires Disease. As a result (partially) of this action, the incidence of hospital acquired infection rose to an annual cost of up to £1B per year. This rise in cross infection and the emergence of drug resistant bacteria, coupled with a lack of teaching of medical students in basic hygiene measures now poses a major problem for the health service.

The author has spoken to a group of 200 graduating medical students who were about to take up duties on wards and operating theatres. Less than one third indicated that they had been taught to clinically wash their hands as part of the medical course.

Omission – Commission – Unawareness

1.5.1.4 *Factors related to errors in medication prescribing*

In a study reported from the Albany Medical Centre in 1997,[20] medication errors with the potential to cause patient harm were studied over a twelve-month period. The following is a direct quote from the published abstract:

The results showed a total of 2103 errors thought to have potential clinical importance were detected during the study period.

The overall rate of errors was 3.99 errors per 1000 medication orders, and the error rate varied among medication classes and prescribing services. A total of 696 errors met study criteria (i.e., errors with the potential for adverse patient effects) and was evaluated for a likely related factor.

The most common specific factors associated with errors were:

- *decline in renal or hepatic function requiring alteration of drug therapy (97 errors, 13.9%),*

- *patient history of allergy to the same medication class (84 errors, 12.1%),*

- *using the wrong drug name, dosage form, or abbreviation (total of 79 errors, 11.4%, for both brand name and generic name orders),*

- *incorrect dosage calculations (77 errors, 11.1%), and*

- *atypical or unusual and critical dosage frequency considerations (75 errors, 10.8%).*

The most common groups of factors associated with errors were those related to:

- *knowledge and the application of knowledge regarding drug therapy (209 errors, 30%);*

- *knowledge and use of knowledge regarding patient factors that affect drug therapy (203 errors, 29.2%);*

- *use of calculations, decimal points, or unit and rate expression factors (122 errors, 17.5%);*

- *and nomenclature factors (incorrect drug name, dosage form, or abbreviation) (93 errors, 13.4%).*

---

20 Lesar TS; Briceland L; Stein DS JAMA, 277:312-7, 1997 Jan 22-29

CONCLUSIONS: Several easily identified factors are associated with a large proportion of medication prescribing errors. By improving the focus of organisational, technological, and risk management educational and training efforts using the factors commonly associated with prescribing errors, risk to patients from adverse drug events should be reduced.

1.6   TYPES OF RISK

Risks are the chances that hazards may produce an unfavourable outcome. The control of risks therefore requires the management response to be appropriate. The response to hazards may be conveniently categorised to aid the consideration of the different management coping and response mechanisms which are necessary for each type.

- First Order (primary)
- Second Order (secondary)
- Third Order (tertiary)
- Fourth Order (quaternary or market)

An example of the approach to the risk of fire and security problems in a hospital is given in Table 1.6.a.

1.6.1   Response to First Order or Primary Risk

First Order or primary risks result in direct damage potential. The primary response to risks is preventative and immediate damage limitation. For fire risks it includes the safe design of buildings with compartmentalisation of roof spaces, the use of fire doors, alarms and smoke detectors, the clear marking of fire escapes routes and the use of fire retarding materials. Alarms should be tested regularly. Flammable liquids and medical gases need to be safely stored and, as with flammable materials, should be stored away from sources of ignition.

All staff need regular fire training which should include being shown the nearest fire exits and the evacuation route when starting work in a department. Evacuation routes should not receive the ventilation outflow from another part of the building to control smoke. Beds in areas where patients are not ambulatory should contain fire sheets to assist with evacuation and staff should be trained in their use. Practice

Table 1.6.a. AN APPROACH TO FIRE AND SECURITY RISKS

Hazard	Response			
	Primary	Secondary	Tertiary	Quarternary (Externally imposed)
Fire	Controls fire – fire alarms, fire brigade and patient evacuation.	Make building safe and restitution costs. Where do we treat patients if the premises are damaged?	Adverse publicity – Public Inquiry, Inquests. "I don't want to go to a hospital which catches fire."	European or Government Directive on fire control.
Security	Restrict access.	Note theft.	Repeated thefts – "easy pickings".	"Maternity units must review security."
Insurance Status (not insurable in the NHS).	*Insurable.*	*Insurable.*	*Not insurable.*	*Not insurable.*

evacuation should be performed on a regular basis, especially from areas of high dependency.

Outside the NHS, primary risks may be partially covered by insurance, but an examination of necessary precautions and training shows insurance to be only a small part of the business answer. The NHS risk pooling scheme is intended to cover most primary risks.

1.6.2 Response to Second Order Risks

Second order risks arise as the direct consequence of the outcome of first order risks.

With the fire extinguished and the patients and staff safe, the secondary response needs to be initiated. Although this risk is partially insurable, the major part of the organisation's response should be covered in effective contingency planning. Questions to be addressed include which patients are most in need of treatment, where they will be treated, and the effect the fire will have upon the ability of a healthcare provider to meet its contract. Does the contract with the healthcare purchaser have a *force majeure* clause to cover the contingency and business interruption?

Commercial insurance research shows that second order risks can have a financial consequence of four times the first order cause.

1.6.3 Response to Third Order Risks

Third order risks arise from the indirect consequences of first and second order risks.

Adverse publicity can colour the attitude of the patient population for years after a fire, particularly where patients have been injured or died. The positive element of "image and Trust" held by the public of the provider is essential for long-term success. Inquests and Public Inquiries will mean that a hospital or other healthcare provider is exposed to these risks. A policy of openness adopted at an early stage is the most effective means of dispelling public disquiet at events.

1.6.4 Response to Fourth Order or Market Risks

Fourth order risks are the societal consequences of first, second or third order risks. Market risks arise simply from being in the particular business and are not within the direct control of the healthcare provider. An example would be the sudden announcement of new fire regulations either as a national or European standard or by way of government intervention resulting from public disquiet at first, second or third order risks. At best, market risks are a diversion and distraction from carrying out routine business. At worst they materially add to the cost of undertaking business.

To an extent, market risks can be predictable and may arise from a failure to undertake basic common-sense practice. An example has been the urgent requirement to review security in maternity units which followed a well publicised kidnapping from a unit. A preventative approach to risk management cushions against this type of risk through the systematic examination of work processes.

In mental health, the notoriety attracted by certain client groups from well-publicised and tragic cases has markedly altered the approach to continuing care in the community.

1.7 CAUSES OF ACCIDENTS

1.7.1 Active Risks

The traditional view of the cause of accidents has to look at human error, whether in aviation accidents, train accidents or in health. Whilst the direct cause attribution to 'human error' of clinical accidents may provide an easy solution to identifying the source, there is little evidence that supports this as a method of reducing future injuries and misadventure.[21]

1.7.2 Latent Risks

Latent risks within an organisation are central to the consideration of a system approach to risk management. These start with management responsibilities, and organisational risks which are discussed further throughout the book.

Accidents in healthcare rarely have a single cause. Research in anaesthesia has shown that a single episode of patient harm can result from the summation of up to eight different adverse events. This means that relying upon identifying just the basic cause of an accident

---

21 *An organisation with a memory*, Department of Health- 2000 – ISBN 011 322441 9

is unlikely to demonstrate the likely causes of recurrence. Reason[22] describes these factors as latent risks – 'accidents waiting to happen'.

One view of the causes of accidents, which has wide acceptance in the nuclear and aviation industries, is the 'Swiss cheese'[23] model. Ideally, all the defences against mistakes, which separate hazards from losses, should be intact. However, where they should be intact, they are full of holes – like Swiss cheese. When the holes align, a hazard can easily cause the journey to become a mistake.[24]

How does this relate to actual practice? Imagine three slices of Swiss cheese representing the three checks undertaken on a patient undergoing an operation on their left knee. The checks are carried out on the ward, when they arrive in the operating theatre suite and by the anaesthetist.

An example of what risk in practice can mean – the chances of the wrong operation – a lottery for hospital patients?

For this example, assume that the error rate in checking a patient for an operation at each step is 1%. This rate may not be unexceptional. When the checks are carried out thoroughly and independently at each stage, the risk of having the wrong operation is $10^{-2} \times 10^{-2} \times 10^{-2} = 1 \times 10^{6}$ or 1 in a million. Is this an acceptable level of risk?

Take the situation where the ward staff are busy and distracted, the operating reception are also busy and think that the ward staff will have checked, and the anaesthetist is distracted by a call to the recovery room – so adequate checks are not performed. The risks of a wrong operation transform to $10^{-2} + 10^{-2} + 10^{-2}$ which equates to a 1% chance of having the wrong operation. This represents a 1,000,000-fold increase in the risk of inadvertent harm through clinical practice. Is this an acceptable level of risk?

If four steps of checking are introduced, perhaps as an intended additional safety measure, the rates of errors in the process producing the wrong operation will vary between $10^{-2} \times 10^{-2} \times 10^{-2} \times 10^{-2} = 1 \times 10^{-8}$, or 1 in 100 million chance of error for the 'safe' hospital or ward, to the same 1% error rate where checks are not correctly performed. By

22 Reason J *Managing the risks of organisational accidents* Ashgate. Aldershot 1997

23 op cit

24 *An organisation with a memory* Department of Health- 2000 – ISBN 011 322441 9

comparison, the chance of winning the national lottery is stated to be approximately 1 in 14 million. What should be accepted as a tolerable level of risk?

The pattern of risk behaviour is not frequently taught as part of the medical and nursing curriculum, which perhaps explains why health workers do not always consider the consequences of errors and slips in their practice. **Part of the challenge to effective risk managers is to redress this shortfall.**

1.7.3 Basic Causes of Accidents

The basic common causes of accidents may be summarised as:

- Poor Housekeeping
- Substandard Practice
- Physical and People
- Unsafe Practice
- Unsafe Conditions

1.7.4 Underlying Causes of Accidents Job Factors Which Increase the Likelihood of Error

1.7.4.1 Inadequate work standards

Risks arise from lack of training and supervision. The culture within an organisation can predispose it to errors. This can be typified by a 'make do and mend' approach or an organisational apathy characterised by the statement "we have always done it this way". At one hospital patients were brought to operating theatre with stretcher poles protruding from covers on the trolleys. The explanation was that this prevented injury and discomfort to the patient. At the same time a number of members of staff received injuries from the poles!

1.7.4.2 Inadequate equipment

Inadequate equipment for the job in hand can increase the risk of error considerably. Inadequate, or the absence of acceptance testing may mean that equipment may unexpectedly fail during use. For example, poor housekeeping and inadequate out-dating of sterile equipment will increase the opportunity for inadvertent harm. Modern sterile equipment is marked with both the date of sterilisation and expiry. Equipment manufactured prior to 1988 may have only the date of manufacture marked. Sterility is guaranteed for five years. Any equipment with only one date marked is therefore past its shelf life.

1.7.4.3 Inadequate maintenance of equipment

Lack of planned preventative maintenance increases the likelihood of equipment failure. The maintenance of equipment between patients can be an important method of preventing cross-infection. This is particularly so with anaesthetic gas tubing which has been used for patients with pulmonary tuberculosis.

1.7.4.4 Abuse, misuse or failing to check equipment

Incorrect configuration of equipment and misuse increases the risk of patient harm through failure of the piece of equipment. A real example involved the failure to check anaesthetic equipment prior to a simple procedure on a young boy. By doing so the anaesthetist failed to detect that the anaesthetic bag contained a foreign body – the end of a needle sheath. During the anaesthetic, the sheath moved through the tubing before becoming lodged in the boy's trachea. The obstructed airway was not spotted immediately and the patient sustained irreversible brain damage.

1.7.4.5 Inadequate leadership or supervision

The maintenance of inadequate work standards invariably flows from poor standards of leadership and supervision.

1.7.5 Personnel Factors Increasing the Likelihood of Error

1.7.5.1 Lack of knowledge

Poor personnel selection which may arise because of an assumed level of knowledge which does not exist. This may be simply a failure to test the typing ability of an applicant for a secretarial position. At a more serious level there may be a failure to examine the depth of knowledge of a locum, particularly in anaesthetics, prior to the clinician undertaking a session at short notice.

1.7.5.2 Inadequate physical capacity

An employee may be asked to undertake duties for which he/she is not physically suited. A frequently occurring example involves the lifting of patients in operating theatres. The rapid departure of other staff at the end of a procedure often leaves the anaesthetist and assistant to move the patient from the operating theatre table.

1.7.5.3 Inadequate mental capacity

Health workers are not immune from developing illnesses such as pre-senile dementia or alcoholism. A mistaken sense of protection for a colleague may disguise the early detection and treatment of conditions which impair the clinician's ability and insight.

1.7.5.4 Mental or physical stress

Health workers subject to or responding to excessive stress may be more prone to errors of judgement. It is the responsibility of those providing leadership and supervision to detect and respond to stress levels. All units should have in place peer review mechanisms through both audit and clinical supervision.

1.7.5.5 Improper motivation

Most notably in recent times the cases of Beverley Allitt and Harold Shipman have highlighted the dangers health workers can pose to their patients through deliberate acts aimed at harm. Although the Beverley Allitt case was stated at the time to be the first identified case of a nurse deliberately harming patients; other such cases have since been reported.

The motivational 'wild card' in clinical risk management will remain one of four significant challenges which need to be considered and addressed whatever risk control methods are considered. The others are elemental (weather, electricity, gas) risks, technological risks and biological risks. (Personnel recommendations of the Allitt Inquiry are given at the end of Chapter 6 (6.8).)

One simple example of an elemental risk presented on a Saturday morning at a children's hospital. The operating theatres, with attached intensive care unit, had recently opened to much acclaim. The surgeons needed to operate on a very sick child to carry out a thoracotomy for a lung abscess. Whilst the child was in the anaesthetic room, a manhole cover in the room ruptured its seal and the room filled to a depth of three feet with fresh sewerage within two minutes. The operation was cancelled and the child transferred elsewhere. The ICU was closed. The theatres were out of action for some considerable time. The cause was simple. During building work, the existing drains were insufficiently checked and became blocked with the heavy rain on the Friday night. The back pressure in the drains caused the manhole cover to blow.

Risk managers and the public may sometimes wonder whether such lapses in working systems are caused by participants leaving their thinking brains at home. (BAHJ – Brain at Home Jobs)

The repeated occurrence of large-scale medical negligence problems caused by the unawareness phenomenon leads to the concept of an OFTEN mode for errors. This is represented by:

Obvious
Failure
To
Engage
Neurones.

1.8   PEOPLE AS RISKS

Research on the causes of people as risks of producing untoward events in undertaking their job shows:[25]

Error Producing Condition	Effect on error rate (times more likely to commit error)
Unfamiliar with task	17
Time shortage	11
Poor human/system interface	8
Designer/user mismatch	8
Irreversibility of errors	8
Information overload	6
Negative transfer between tasks	5

25 J Williams, *A data based method for assessing and reducing human errors to improve operational performance* 1988 ed. IEEE Forth Conference on Human Factors and Power Plants, New York IEEE 200-231

Misperception of risks	4
Poor feedback from system	4
Inexperience – not lack of training	3
Poor instructions or procedures	3
Inadequate checking	3
Educational mismatch of person with task	2
Disturbed sleep pattern	1.6
Hostile environment	1.2
Monotony and boredom	1.1

This may produce interesting, if unwanted, changes in risk producing care environments. Using this research, a junior doctor may be more likely to commit an error by 1.6 times if their sleep pattern is disturbed to see a patient. By decreasing the hours worked by having a locum doctor to stand in, who is then unfamiliar with the task or patient, the error rate is likely to be ten times (17/1.6) higher.

1.9 MANAGEMENT RESPONSIBILITIES IN THE PREVENTION OF RISK

Healthcare providers and commissioner management have clear responsibilities to prevent and control risks. The extent to which it is able to do so is related to its abilities in the following areas:

- planning;

- organising;

- leading;

- controlling.

Any provider should be able to clearly demonstrate all of these elements. If it is not able to do so, it is inevitable that unforeseen risks will arise in the organisation. These risks arise primarily from:

- inadequate managerial standards and education

- inadequate managerial control;

- inadequate management programmes and review.

Accident investigation, as well as preventive audit, needs to look at each of these areas in a systematic and thorough manner.

1.10   ORGANISATION RISKS

Primary risks arise in health organisations through an inadequate knowledge base in decision-making. Decision making for NHS Trusts whether in primary or secondary care implies choice and judgement. Additionally, for quality and equity, decision-making requires consistency of the process.

To minimise the associated risks in decision-making, choices need to:

- be explicit, evidence based, communicated, understood and owned by the participants and stakeholders;

- be informed;

- be planned;

- reflect the Trust or Health Authority Board strategic intentions in addressing the health needs of the population served.

An aid to informed decision making which covers these points is given in Figure 1.10.a.

Figure 1.10.a. QUALITY CHARACTERISTICS OF NHS PROVIDER AND COMMISSIONER DECISION MAKING

Be informed:

Knowledge of Market Needs	Knowledge of Market Preferences	Knowledge of Available Resources
1. Demography Health needs identified	1. Working with patient and carer groups	1. Use of staff knowledge through business planning
2. Commissioner identified needs for patients and carers	2. Working with GPs PCGs, PCTs and other professional groups	2. Use of Board knowledge
3. Involvement of doctors and other healthcare professionals – provider identified needs	3. Aware of opportunities and changing preferences	3. Financial control and contracting, both in the NHS and private sectors
4. Researched based best practice	4. Market intelligence – drugs, technology, etc.	4. Research Grants acquired and applied

Be planned:

Strategic	Business	Flexible
1. Local – Commissioners with patient involvement	1. Information from users HImps, JIPs	1. Reflect changing needs
2. Local – Board with patient involvement	2. Information from other providers	2. Reflect changing resources
3. National Targets NSFs and LITs	3. Board agreement and ownership of plans	3. Encourage increasing resources
4. Future statutory, consumer and professional requirements, WHO and EEC	4. Formal systematic risk analysis of required performance and outcomes	4. Business opportunities are explored and developed

Reflecting the Board Strategic Intentions:

Quality	Accountability	Communication
1. Operational decisions devolved to the lowest effective level	1. Operational decisions devolved to the lowest effective level	1. Seeks advice from and consults with individuals and organisations working in partnership with the Trust
2. Monitor standards and seek to improve	2. Appropriate training, including budget control	2. Clear lines of communication, including Team Briefings
3. Policy of openness	3. Acknowledge achievement	3. Board involvement
4. Purchaser/ provider agreement on Standards	4. Assist when there is a shortfall in performance	4. Simple, timely and effective communication
5. Advocacy schemes for patients and carers		

2

THE REGULATORY FRAMEWORK FOR HEALTHCARE RISK MANAGEMENT

2.1 INTRODUCTION

Every person providing or supporting the delivery of healthcare services has a duty to behave lawfully. A key task of the risk manager is to ensure lawful behaviour, despite the increasingly complex regulatory framework. Risk management requires an understanding of the regulatory framework for:

- managing compliance with different statutes, regulations and rules in order to prevent or limit damage;
- structuring the implementation of a risk management strategy within a quality service.

The complex interweaving of civil and statutory, professional and patient standards, rules, regulations and expectations in the delivery of health care has evolved together with the health services ability to identify, to assess, to prevent and to alleviate injury and disease. Some of the laws apply solely to the specific actions of individual practitioners. Others lay down powers and duties beyond the range of individual action such as the National Health Act of 1977, Health Act 1999 (which imposes a statutory duty of quality) or the Public Health Acts of this and the nineteenth century. More and more laws directly increase the rights of patients. For example, patients have greater access to their health records through the Data Protection Act 1998. The Hospital Complaints Procedures Act 1985 provides a statutory framework for patients to express their dissatisfactions and to have them investigated and to receive an explanation.

These and other statutory provisions have been paralleled by the development in case law. As the science and technology of medicine have advanced, so have professional guidelines and regulations for practice changed to reflect those advances. These developments, particularly in recent years, have been within a climate of increasing demand for more effective and efficient healthcare delivery reinforced by pressures to involve patients in the decision-making process. The direct involvement of patients and their representatives has now been formalised in the NHS plan which will have the most important and significant impact upon the delivery of services for patients.

2.2 THE THREE INFLUENCES (ELEMENTS) OF THE HEALTHCARE PROCESS

It is usual to consider the impact of the law in terms of legislation and case law. In terms of healthcare risk management the most useful distinction is in terms of compliance with:

- statutory requirements
- professional requirements
- patient standards and delivery of services.

As will be discussed in the following, it is in compliance with these that risk management contributes to preventing or reducing damage prior to potential mishap and to limiting damage after an actual mishap.

2.2.1 Statutory Requirements

The statutory requirements are laid down in legislation, as Acts of Parliament and subsequent Statutory Instruments. The statutory requirements on which the risk manager must seek compliance can be usefully divided into:

- those which apply to the general carrying out of service delivery such as the Health and Safety at Work etc. Act 1974 and subsequent regulations and the Occupiers' Liability Acts of 1957 and 1984.

- those which apply specifically to the delivery of healthcare such as the Medical Acts 1956, 1977, and 1983, Health Act 1999 and the Nurses, Midwives and Health Visitors Act 1979.

2.2.2 Professional Requirements

Professional requirements underpin the assessment of professional liability and medical negligence. The requirements on how practitioners should behave are established through decided court cases but rely on the practice and research of the professions. Rules and guidelines are set down not only through case law, but also through bodies such as the General Medical Council, (GMC), the Royal Colleges, the United Kingdom Central Council, (UKCC), the Board of the Council for Professions Supplementary to Medicine and the College of Physiotherapists, and through the circulars of the Department of Health. The UKCC is due to be replaced by a Nursing and Midwifery Council, NMC, to regulate nursing, midwifery and health visiting.

The NHS plan sets out three key tests for regulatory bodies:

- be smaller with much greater patient and public representation;
- have faster, more transparent procedures, and
- develop meaningful accountability to the public and the health service.

The plan also calls on the GMC to 'explore introducing a civil burden of proof and making other reforms that genuinely protect patients'.

The GMC's document *Good Medical Practice* (1995) sets out the duties and responsibilities of doctors under seven general headings:

- good clinical care
- maintaining good medical practice
- relationships with patients
- working with colleagues
- teaching and training
- probity
- health.

Under reform proposals, doctors will require to be revalidated every five years to remain on the medical register. Details of the GMC and the latest guidance are available at *http://www.gmc-uk.org*

2.2.3 Patient Standards and Delivery of Services

The delivery of healthcare is increasingly responsive to the rising expectations of patients. These expectations are expressed not only in higher standards of outcome but also in the quality of process. In risk management it is useful to distinguish, as far as one can, that part of the regulatory framework which impacts directly upon the patients real and perceived concerns, and the ways she may wish to express dissatisfaction. Such standards, as set down in, for example, the *Patients' Charter* and the mechanisms which allow for expression of dissatisfaction, for example, through the Health Service Commissioner, are key to the implementation of risk management, not just in terms of personal injury but also for business and market position.

The establishment of local Health Improvement Programmes (HImPs) and the monitoring of services against established targets will pose additional challenges to healthcare providers, whether in primary or secondary care.

The key areas which have been identified for the performance of the NHS and quality improvement have been identified as:[1]

Health improvement

to reflect the over-arching aims of improving the general health of the population and reducing health inequalities;

Fair access

to recognise that the NHS's contribution must begin by offering fair access to health services in relation to people's needs, irrespective of geography, socio-economic group, ethnicity, age or sex;

Effective delivery of appropriate healthcare

to recognise that fair access must be to care that is effective, appropriate and timely, and complies with agreed standards;

Efficiency

to ensure that the effective care is delivered with the minimum of waste, and that the NHS uses its resources to achieve value for money;

---

1   HSC 2000/023 – *Quality and Performance in the NHS* July 2000

Patient/carer experience

to assess the way in which patients and their carers experience and view the quality of the care they receive to ensure that the NHS is sensitive to individual needs;

Health outcomes of NHS care

to assess the direct contribution of NHS care to improvements in overall health and complete the circle back to the over-arching goal of health improvement.

Consumerism and patient expectations

The rise in the number of complaints and claims can be expected to continue to escalate because of the social trend of increasing consumer demand and the higher propensity of the general public to make recourse to civil or statutory law if expectations are not met. Consumerism should not be an unwelcome development for it can provide a measure of, and an inducement to, improving quality of healthcare. It is the role of the risk manager to balance compliance with civil and professional regulations, statutory provisions and patient standards. Ensuring compliance in practice helps to raise standards and in the event of mishap helps to establish:

- whether legal requirements have been breached;
- how the effect (on people, finances, public image and so on) of the mishap can be limited;
- how compensation is appropriately awarded.

As such, it contributes to quality management.

2.2.3.1 The Patients' Charter

Introduced in 1992 as part of the UK government's Citizen's Charter initiative, the Patient's Charter proclaims a number of rights of citizens, some national standards of service against which local health authorities will be assessed, and the expectation that additional local standards will be published and pursued. Most of the 'rights' have been established for many years but the Charter now tells patients that they are guaranteed and promises investigation and action if they are denied.

2.2.3.1.1 The Patient's Charter Rights for every UK Citizen

1. To receive health care on the basis of clinical need, regardless of ability to pay.

2. To be registered with a general practitioner (GP)

3. To receive emergency medical care at any time, through their GP or the emergency ambulance service and hospital accident and emergency departments.

4. To be referred to a consultant, acceptable to the patient, when their GP thinks it necessary, and to be referred for a second opinion if the patient and GP agree this is desirable.

5. To be given a clear explanation of any treatment proposed, including any risks and alternatives, before the patient decides whether they will agree to the treatment.

6. To have access to their own health records, and to know that those working for the NHS are under a legal duty to keep their contents confidential.

7. To choose whether or not they wish to take part in medical research or medical student training.

8. To be given detailed information on local health services, including quality standards and maximum waiting times.

9. To be guaranteed admission for treatment by a specific date no later than two years from the day when a consultant places the patient on a waiting list.

10. To have any complaint about NHS services – whoever provides them – investigated and to receive a full and prompt written reply from the Chief Executive or general manager.

Of course, an investigation of failure to attain one of these rights may provide little comfort to the person who has struggled for months to register with a GP or who has been the reluctant subject of a medical student's attentions. The Charter does not entitle patients to compensation for inconvenience, humiliation or pain incurred while waiting for service. Compensation remains the last resort in the cases of medical negligence.

The publication of some national standards against which health authorities are compared might be seen as a clear incentive to get a limited number of things right first time – assuming they can control their performance in these areas and the penalties for failure outweigh the costs of success. As many of the services are sub-contracted to quasi-independent NHS Trusts, or occasionally private contractors, this control loop is far from straightforward.

The first nine national standards of service which the NHS has been aiming to provide since 1992 are:

1. Respect for privacy, dignity and religious and cultural beliefs.

2. Arrangements to ensure everyone, including people with special needs, can use services.

3. Information to be given to relatives and friends about the progress of treatment, subject to the patient's wishes.

4. When called, an emergency ambulance service should arrive within 14 minutes in an urban area or 19 minutes in a rural area.

5. When attending an accident and emergency department, patients will be seen immediately and their need for treatment assessed.

6. When attending an outpatient clinic, patients will be given a specific appointment time and will be seen within 30 minutes of it.

7. Operations should not be cancelled on the day patients are due to arrive in hospital. If, exceptionally, an operation has to be postponed twice, the patient will be admitted to hospital within one month of the second cancelled operation.

8. A named, qualified nurse, midwife or health visitor should be responsible for each patient's nursing or midwifery care.

9. A decision should be made about any continuing health or social care needs that a patient has, before discharge from hospital. Appropriate services should be arranged and agreed with patients.

It is intended that local health authorities and providers will in turn establish, publish and pursue local standards covering an increasing number of activities.

An important example of the increasing voice of patients as consumers has come with the reaction to 'do not resuscitate policies' operating in Trusts where the patient played no part in the process or decision not to resuscitate. The political response has been to require that:

Every hospital must implement a local resuscitation policy, using as a basis the guidance produced by the British Medical Association, Royal College of Nursing and the Resuscitation Council (UK).

Chief Executives must ensure that:

- their Trust has an agreed resuscitation policy in place that respects patients' rights;
- that a non-executive Director is identified to oversee the implementation of the policy;
- that the policy is readily available to patients, families and carers;
- that the policy is subject to audit; and that
- implementation of the policy is regularly monitored.

What may seem extra-ordinary would be that it could ever be considered good or adequate or humane to exclude the patient from the process of making a decision that they were not to be resuscitated.

The author would appreciate hearing of further examples, typified by the failure of medical ethics at Alder Hey Children's Hospital with the failure to inform parents that their child's remains returned for burial were incomplete, with organs retained at the hospital, and as controversially, the Bristol Children's cardiac surgery, and the repeated large scale failures of cervical cytology screening.

2.2.3.2 *Complaints*

Complaints and complaint procedures are covered in detail in Chapter Five.

2.3 PROFESSIONAL LIABILITY

The focus of healthcare must be the patient. The ultimate breakdown in the healthcare process is when the patient is subject to avoidable damage in some way in or by the process itself. Damage causes a profound effect on the patient, on the patient's family and friends, on staff morale and on the trust the public has in the health services. The economic impact can also be extensive in terms of both actual and opportunity costs. It is important therefore that the basis on which an action for negligence can be brought against a healthcare provider or individual professional is understood.

Negligence is about breaching a duty to use reasonable care and causing an injury to another. A legal definition was given in the *Blyth v Birmingham Waterworks in 1856:*

Negligence is the omission to do something which a reasonable man, guided upon those considerations which ordinarily regulate the conduct of human affairs, would do, or doing something which a prudent and reasonable man would not do.[2]

Compensation for injury as the result of the action of a healthcare provider or practitioner is usually pursued through the civil law although negligence may be punished in the criminal courts. To mount a successful civil action for compensation the plaintiff has to establish *on the balance of probabilities* three key elements:

- a duty of care was owed to the plaintiff by the defendant; and

- the defendant must be in breach of that duty by falling short of the standards required by law; and

- there must be a causal link between the action or omission of the defendant and the damage sustained.

The corollary to these elements is that it must have been reasonably foreseeable that a careless action or omission would have caused the damage and that some damage has been sustained. Therefore, not all actions or omissions in the treatment of patients are necessarily negligent.

2.4 DUTY OF CARE

- the healthcare professional

- the health provider

- the commissioning agency for healthcare

Except where a healthcare practitioner comes upon the scene of an accident,[3] there is very little to dispute in the duty to of care owed by a

---

2   Blyth v Birmingham Waterworks [1856]

3   A healthcare practitioner, who comes across the scene of an accident and does nothing or walks away, may be considered to be acting unethically. However, they could not be prosecuted for crimes of manslaughter or assault nor could they be sued in a civil court for negligence. The practitioner can only be held responsible if there is some **special relationship** with the victim.

healthcare practitioner to their patient. Almost by definition, someone who is regarded as a patient has a duty of care owed to them. The duty of care arises for the healthcare practitioner not only because of foreseeability and proximity but also because of the special relationship between the practitioner using her skills and knowledge on or on behalf of the patient. The practitioner "owes a duty to the patient to use diligence, care, knowledge, skill and caution in administering the treatment. No contractual relationship is necessary, nor is it necessary that the service be rendered for reward".[4]

In the NHS, corporate health providers have a vicarious duty of care to patients. They can be held liable for the actions and omissions of their employees in the course of their employment.[5] It has long been agreed that institutional healthcare providers owe a direct duty of care identical to that of individual health practitioners.[6] Therefore, the liability of an NHS Trust hospital, for example, is dependent upon the breach of duty on the part of the individual employed healthcare practitioners. From the aggrieved patient's point of view, the practical issue becomes who pays and how he/she should plan and pursue the claim.

The perspective of the aggrieved patient is especially important for the risk manager. A healthcare provider may be primarily and even exclusively liable for its failure to institute and maintain a safe system of healthcare provision without there being fault on the part of any healthcare practitioner.[7] This issue arose in the *Wilsher v Essex Area Health Authority* case where a house officer inserted a catheter into a vein instead of into an artery of a child. The registrar, who was asked to check the procedure had been done correctly, also failed to notice the mistake. The child was over-oxygenated because of a misleading blood/oxygen reading. The trial judge observed:

"In my judgement a Health Authority which so conducts its hospital that it fails to provide doctors of sufficient skill and experience to give the treatment offered at the hospital may be directly liable in negligence to the patient … I

---

4   Per Hewitt CJ, in R v *Bateman* [1925] 94 LJKB 791 at 794.

5   *Gold v Essex County Council* [1942] 2 All ER 237 and *Razzel and Snowball* [1954] 3 All ER 429.

6   Cassidy v Ministry of Health [1951] 2 KB 343

7   Wilsher v Essex Area Health Authority [1986] 3 All ER 801

can see no reason why, in principle, the Health Authority should not be so liable if its organisation is at fault."[8]

This judgement leads to difficult questions of distinguishing between policy and the level of resources determined by the government and Parliament and operational decisions made at provider level. It is important for the risk manager, in such circumstances, to ensure and to show that resources even within imposed restrictions are competently managed. It may not be possible to identify and establish individual negligence where healthcare professionals are lacking the equipment required for the tasks a provider has contracted to undertake or where the number of patients exceeds the number that can reasonably be treated at any one time.

There is also the danger that the courts may be prepared to accept a lower standard of proof where the allegation is against the provider institution rather than an individual healthcare practitioner. If the individual healthcare practitioner can show compliance with a recognised and properly accepted procedure, then a claim will be unsuccessful. In the complex operational arena of a healthcare institution or clinical setting, demonstrating compliance will be more complex.

2.5   STANDARD OF CARE

Once a duty of care is established, the appropriate standard of care must be determined. Only then can it be established if the action or omission fell below standard. Although the required standard of care is determined by the courts, much consideration is given to practices of the various professions. A judge will rule on what is an appropriate standard of care in the circumstances on the basis of what a reasonably skilled and experienced practitioner would do.

In the Bolam[9] case, the judge said:

"A doctor is not guilty of negligence if he acted in accordance with a practice accepted as proper by a responsible body of medical men skilled in that particular art....Putting it the other way round, a doctor is not negligent, if he is acting in accordance with such a practice, merely because there is a body of opinion which takes a contrary view."

---

8   Ibid.

9   Bolam v Friern Hospital Management Committee [1957] 2 All ER 18

This test of reasonableness was further applied in the case of Bolitho.[10] The case involved an allegation that a paediatric registrar had failed to attend a child with breathing difficulties and that had the registrar attended they would have intubated the child and by taking that action would have prevented subsequent brain damage. The case was rejected in the House of Lords. The case provided a valuable examination of the role of an expert. The five Law Lords unanimously held that a judge must not simply accept the view of a medical expert. Judges have to be satisfied that an expert has weighed up the risks and benefits and reached a "defensible conclusion". Lord Browne-Wilkinson stated:

"The use of these adjectives, responsible, reasonable and respectable all show that the Court has to be satisfied that the exponents of the body of opinion relied upon can demonstrate that such an opinion has a logical basis. In particular, in cases involving as often they do the weighing up of risks against benefits, the Judge, before accepting a body of opinion as being responsible, reasonable or respectable will need to be satisfied that... the experts have directed their minds to the question of comparative risks and benefits and reached a defensible conclusion on the matter".

The defendant will be tested against the standard of the practitioner in his particular field of healthcare. A person who professes to exercise a special skill must exercise the ordinary skill of that specialty. The Sidaway[11] case added that the test that the practice accepted as proper by a responsible body must "rightly" be so accepted in the view of the court.

Not in all cases will the courts accept an established practice. In one case[12] where a patient was burned by a physiotherapist during a course of treatment, the physiotherapist was found to have been negligent. This was so even though the physiotherapist warned the patient according to the Chartered Society of Physiotherapists' advice. The court found the warning to be inadequate to safeguard the patient. It will be interesting to follow developments in relation to the use of 'evidence based medicine' where it conflicts with the opinions of 'a responsible body of medical men'.

---

10 Bolitho and others v City and Hackney HA 1993; 4MLR 381

11 Sidaway v Board of Governors of the Bethlem Royal and Maudsley Hospital [1984] 2 WLR 778

12 *Clarke v Adams* [1950] 94 Sol Journ 59913 Op. Cit.

The specialist is expected to achieve the standard of care of the reasonably competent specialist practising in that field. The more skills a practitioner possesses, the higher the standard of skill expected. However, he/she is not required to attain the highest degree of skill and competence, only a reasonable level of skill within that field.

That inexperience does not provide a defence to an allegation of negligence was also confirmed by the *Wilsher*[13] case. The standard of care is objective, paying no regard to the shortcomings of the defendant. The *Wilsher* case held that the trainee or learner must be judged by the same standards as more experienced colleagues. The house officer in the case was found to have discharged the standard of care expected of him because he deferred to the registrar, not because he was inexperienced.

A patient's right to complain is not limited by the chance she was treated by a less experienced practitioner than a patient coming the next day or in the next bed. If it were otherwise inconsistency could be introduced in healthcare processes, contrary to risk management principle offered in Chapter 1 and allowing inexperience to be proffered frequently as an excuse and defence.

The duty of care also includes the duty to prevent self-infliction of harm. In the case of *Selfe v Ilford and District Hospital Management Committee*,[14] the HMC was found negligent because the duty of those in charge of the patient included the duty to avoid self-harm which was foreseeable. The judge was highly critical of the ward organisation in this case which allowed Mr Selfe to abscond from the ward and seriously injure himself although he was known to be a suicide risk and required continuous observation. The case also demonstrates that the health provider has a legal duty to establish and maintain a system of safe working conditions. Again questions are raised for the risk manager relating to the allocation and use of limited resources especially with regard to staffing levels.

2.6 DISCLOSURE OF RISK AND CONSENT TO TREATMENT

Patients should be asked their consent before embarking on treatment, because they have a right to determine what is to be done to their

---

13 Op. Cit.

14 Selfe v Ilford and District Hospital Management Committee [1970] 114 Sol Jo 935

bodies. The concept of seeking and giving of consent before clinical interventions is a basic principle in civil law, and good standards of healthcare practice have been constructed around the principle. This general principle refers to capable adult patients, but there are exceptions in regard to:

- children;
- the mentally disordered;
- the unconscious.

"In essence a consent is legally valid only if certain conditions are satisfied. This means that in any particular case a [practitioner] must satisfy himself that any consent obtained from his patient meets these conditions. At their most general they are:

i. *the patient must be legally competent (i.e. capable of consenting);*

ii. *the consent must be freely given;*

iii. *the person consenting must be suitably informed."* [15]

Consent must be 'real' i.e. in Kennedy's words the patient must be "suitably informed".[16] Furthermore, "once the patient is informed in broad terms of the nature of the procedure which is intended, and gives her consent, that consent is real."[17] The consent must be given to the procedure which is intended. A doctor, for example, who has received permission for a Caesarean operation should not go on to sterilise the patient. In some cases a practitioner, acting in good faith may take an operation or procedure further than consent permitted when a further condition is discovered for which surgery or a further procedure is thought necessary or desirable. It is necessary therefore to ensure the consent form is properly structured.

More information and detailed current guidance on consent is available on the Department of Health web site: *http://www.doh.gov.uk/consent.*[18]

---

15 KENNEDY, I *Consent to Treatment: The Capable Person* p.52 in Chapter 3 of DYER, C (ed.) "Doctors, Patients and the Law" [Blackwell, London 1992]

16 Op cit. note 13.

17 Chatterton v Gerson [1981] QB 432

18 Reference *Guide to Consent for Examination or Treatment,* Department of Health, 2001

2.6.1 Medical Treatment and Consent – Children

The primary control for giving consent for a child's medical treatment rests with those who have parental responsibility. Where the child has achieved sufficient age and understanding to give informed consent, the child's consent is required and in certain circumstances may well override the consent of those with parental responsibility. A particular example arises for dental treatment where the child's consent must be obtained at an age usually much younger than 16 years.

The final decision about who gives consent in a particular set of circumstances usually rests with the medical practitioner, but referral can be made to the Courts to resolve any dispute.

Section 3 of the Act enables a person with care of the child, but not with parental responsibility, to give consent to emergency treatment in the event of an accident. This provision allows a carer to make routine decisions about consent for medical treatment, provided they are in the interest of the child and provided that the decision is not likely to be controversial. If it is known that the parents may object, or if there is a choice, an application may be made for a specific issue order under Section 8.

2.6.2 Consent Form

Consent does not always have to be written or explicitly obtained to be valid. It can be inferred from the clinical situation: opening a shirt for a chest examination or presenting at a casualty department as 'a walking wounded'. However, a written consent is strongly recommended for any procedure or treatment carrying any significant risk or side effect including anaesthetics, surgery, certain forms of drug treatment, such as cytotoxic drugs, and treatment involving ionising radiations.[19]

2.7 PROOF OF NEGLIGENCE

In all clinical negligence cases:

- the burden of proof lies with the plaintiff

- the standard of proof is based on the balance of probabilities

- the burden of proof is greater because the allegations impair

---

19 NHS Management Executive [1990] *Guide to Consent for Examination or Treatment.*

the standing and reputation of the healthcare practitioner or provider;[20]

- a practitioner is liable only if he/she falls below the standard of a reasonably competent practitioner in her field.

The plaintiff, therefore, in most cases must establish:

- the accepted practice was improperly implemented

or

- no reasonable practitioner would have acted in the way the defendant did.

If the defendants depart from accepted practice the burden of proof shifts to the defendants to justify the departure.[21] The risk management response is to ensure that practitioners record not only the procedure, but also the reason for using that procedure. A review of practice by clinical audit would also examine the circumstances in which departure from the accepted procedure was justified.

It might be that this shift in burden may be considered a variation on the maxim *res ipsa loquitur* (speaks for itself) applies. A plea to this maxim has the practical effect of shifting the argument on negligence to the defendant. The defendant has to explain how the matter in hand (*res* or the event) could have occurred in the absence of negligence. A simple example is where an operation has been performed on the wrong side. If the plaintiff is unsuccessful in the plea, the argument can still be continued to prove the case of negligence on the balance of probabilities.

The concurrent requirements for a successful plea to res ipsa loquitur were established in the case *Mahon v Osborne*[22] in which a swab was left post-operatively in the patient. For res ipsa loquitur to be successful the following need to apply:

- control over the relevant situation, environment or events rested solely with the defendant;

---

20 Hornal v Neuberger Products Ltd [1957] 1 QB 247. *Huck v Cole* [1968] 112 Sol Journ 483, CA

21 *Clark v Maclennan* [1983] 1 All ER 416

22 *Mahon v Osborne* [1939] 2 KB 14

- the event would not have happened unless the person in control failed to exercise due care.

Not every instance of injury is sufficient in itself to make a plea of res ipsa loquitur successful. In *Fish v Kapur*[23] the patient's jaw was fractured during the extraction of a tooth, but the plea of self-evident negligence was refused. In this case, the plaintiff was unable to get expert advice that a broken jaw does not occur in the absence of negligence.

2.8 PHYSICAL AND PSYCHOLOGICAL HARM

2.8.1 Causation

As has already been seen, the burden of establishing negligence rests with the plaintiff. The courts will ask "but for the negligence would the injury to the plaintiff have occurred in any event?" In medical negligence cases the cause of the mishap may be difficult to pinpoint for a variety of reasons including:

- only indirect evidence, e.g. epidemiological, may be available;

- the pathology may be multifactorial;

- not all factors may be ascribable to the negligence of one person;

- the pathology may be slow in development;

- there may be a pre-existing condition.

2.9 MANSLAUGHTER AND GROSS NEGLIGENCE

In some cases in which there is a fatality, alleged carelessness or momentary recklessness may appear so great that charges of manslaughter are made. Such a process would be initiated by the Crown Prosecution Service after investigation by the police. Such cases are rare but there have been a number of cases in recent years. The concept of "involuntary manslaughter" was raised in the quashing by the Appeal Court of the conviction of two doctors on a charge of manslaughter because of an intrathecal injection of vincristine. Vincristine is a drug used for chemotherapy in the treatment of certain

---

23 *Fish v Kapur* [1948] 2 All ER 176

cancers. It should be given by intravenous injection. Given by the intrathecal route, (in the spinal cord space), it is neurotoxic and invariably causes major neurological problems. It is almost invariably fatal.

2.10 EMPLOYERS' VICARIOUS LIABILITY AND NHS INDEMNITY

If a practitioner is employed then the employer is "vicariously liable" for the practitioner's actions and can be also be sued, if the practitioner is negligent in the course of employment. In an NHS facility, if the patient can identify the person who was negligent, he/she can sue that person and also the employer. Where the patient cannot identify a specific member of staff who was negligent, but all staff responsible for her care were employed by the NHS Trust or Health Authority (HA), then the Trust or HA is necessarily vicariously liable for whoever may have been at fault. In *Cassidy v Ministry of Health*[24] the court found that a patient's injury was caused by negligence and that all the staff involved were employed by the NHS. Therefore, there was evidence of negligence against their common employer. The employer may also be liable directly to the patient in that it failed to provide an adequate and safe service.[25]

Under the NHS indemnity scheme, which came into effect in January 1990, Health Authorities assumed responsibility for the handling of all negligence cases including payment of compensation and costs. After April 1991, Trusts took responsibility for such cases. The final decision on whether to settle a case rests with the HA or Trust. Where a practitioner feels that his/her interests are distinct from those of the HA or Trust, although this may be taken into account by the authority, he/she has no right to contest the claim. However, with the agreement of the plaintiff, the HA or Trust and the court the practitioner can be separately represented.

2.11 LIABILITY IN CONTRACT

Medical negligence cases arising from NHS practice are not usually framed in contract law. Usually the plaintiff will not have paid for the practitioner's services. Where the patient is fee-paying there is

---

24 Op cit. note 5.

25 Op cit. note 6.

undoubtedly a contract between him/her and the practitioner. In private practice the payment of a fee or consideration establishes a contract that the practitioner will provide a service of a reasonable standard. Where a patient is a private patient there is an additional contract in respect of the accommodation and nursing arrangements. Whether an action is taken in contract or tort, the practical problems for the risk manager and any one else involved in respect of causation will the same.

2.12 STATUTORY REQUIREMENTS

The very business of delivering healthcare has a great number of legal implications. Numerous statutes impose responsibilities. It is the risk manager's task to ensure that the Trust or HA complies or is moving towards complying with each of the regulations.

2.12.1 Duties of Employers

In their position as employers, Trusts and Health Authorities have considerable responsibilities for those they employ. Employed people have extensive rights, violation of which could lead to an award against the employer in the industrial tribunal or in the civil courts. Employment law[26] is a huge subject and it will usually be the province of human resources specialists within the Personnel Department.

The main provisions of the Employment Rights Act[27] are to bestow the following rights:

- to have particulars of the terms of employment within 13 weeks of commencing employment including who is employing whom, date employment began, hours of work, holidays, sick pay, pensions, length of notice either side, job title and, where there are 20 or more employees, disciplinary procedures;

- to have itemised pay statements;

- to join and take part in trade unions;

- to have time off work to perform various public duties;

---

26 employment law/procedures references see also chapter 6
27 Employment Rights Act 1996

- to have minimum periods of notice;
- to have a written statement of reasons for dismissal;
- not to be unfairly dismissed;
- to redundancy payments;
- to statutory sick pay;
- to time off for ante natal care;
- to return to work after having a child;
- to statutory maternity pay;
- not to be discriminated against.

2.12.2   Equal Opportunities Legislation

2.12.2.1 Sex Discrimination Act 1975

The Sex Discrimination Act (1975) makes sex discrimination in employment unlawful. The Act defines five types of discrimination:

- direct sex discrimination
- direct marriage discrimination
- indirect sex discrimination
- indirect marriage discrimination
- victimisation

Direct sex or marriage discrimination

Direct sex or marriage discrimination arises where a person treats a woman, on the grounds of her sex, or a married person on the grounds of their marital status less favourably than they treat, or would treat, a man or unmarried person (or vice versa).

Indirect sex or marriage discrimination

Indirect sex or marriage discrimination is the application of a requirement equally to both sexes or married or unmarried persons, which has the effect of excluding considerably more women than men, (or vice versa), or married persons than unmarried persons, unless the requirement can be shown to be justifiable irrespective of the sex or marital status of the person to whom it applied.

Victimisation

Victimisation is defined as discrimination against a person, e.g. disciplining or dismissal, as the result of a person asserting their rights under the Sex Discrimination or Equal Pay Acts.

Sex discrimination by an employer is not unlawful where the person's sex is a Genuine Occupational Qualification (GOQ) for the particular job e.g. for reasons of decency or privacy. It is important to note that physical strength or stamina is not a GOQ.

Positive Action

An employer may encourage women only or men only to apply for jobs which in the previous twelve months have been done solely or mainly by members of a particular sex. However, any appointment must be made solely on the grounds of merit.

2.12.2.2 Race Relations Act 1976

The Race Relations Act defines two types of discrimination – direct and indirect.

Direct Racial Discrimination

Direct Racial Discrimination consists of treating a patient on racial grounds less favourably than others are or would be treated in the same or similar circumstances.

'Racial grounds' means any of the following:

- colour
- race
- nationality (including citizenship)
- ethnic origins
- national origins

Segregating a person from others on racial grounds also constitutes less favourable treatment.

Indirect Racial Discrimination

Indirect Racial Discrimination consists of applying in any circumstances covered by the Act a requirement or condition which, although applied equally to persons of all racial groups is such that:

- a considerably smaller proportion of a particular racial group can comply with it

- it is also to the detriment of the person who cannot comply with it

- it cannot be shown to be justifiable on other than racial grounds.

Victimisation

Victimisation is defined as discrimination against a person, e.g. disciplining or dismissal, as the result of a person asserting their rights under the Racial Discrimination Act.

Exceptions

There are certain exceptions to the Act, e.g. where the employment in question is for the purpose of a private household, or where being of a particular racial group is a genuine occupational qualification.

Positive Action

Positive discriminatory measures are allowed by the law to encourage applicants into particular areas of work where people from a particular racial group have been absent or under-represented within the previous twelve months, e.g. by providing access to training for members of that particular racial group.

2.12.3   Disability Discrimination Act 1995

The Disability Discrimination Act 1995 (DDA 1995) applies to employers who have more than 15 employees. The Act makes discrimination related to disability unlawful. Implementation of the application of the Act has been incremental.

The areas covered by the Act are:

- education

- housing – buying or renting land or property

- employment

- access to goods and services

- public transport.

In employment all aspects are covered including selection, undertaking the job, promotion, career development and redundancy or dismissal. Additionally the employer must take such steps as it is reasonable for him to have to take to prevent a disadvantage to a disabled person.

2.12.3.1 Disability

Disability is defined as "A physical or mental impairment which has a substantial and long-term adverse effect on a person's ability to carry out normal day-to-day activities".

Physical or mental impairment includes sensory impairments. Hidden impairments are also covered (for example, mental illness or mental health problems, learning disabilities and conditions such as diabetes or epilepsy). People who have had a disability within the terms of the Act in the past are protected from discrimination even if they no longer have the disability.

2.12.3.2 Reasonable Adjustments

From 1 October 1999, where a service provider offers services to the public, it has a legal duty to take such steps as it is reasonable for the service provider to have to take in all the circumstances of the case in the three situations described immediately below. This duty is referred to in this Code as the duty to make reasonable adjustments.

The duty to make reasonable adjustments is a continuing duty. Service providers should keep the duty constantly under review in the light of their experience with disabled people wanting to access their services. In this respect it is an evolving duty, and not something that needs simply to be considered once and once only, and then forgotten. For example, technological developments may provide new or better solutions to the problems of inaccessible services.

Section 21 refers to a service provider being under a duty to take such steps as it is reasonable, in all the circumstances of the case, for it to have to take in order to make reasonable adjustments. The Act does not specify that any particular factors should be taken into account. What is a reasonable step for a particular service provider to have to take depends on all the circumstances of the case. It will vary according to:

- the type of services being provided;

- the nature of the service provider and its size and resources;

- the effect of the disability on the individual disabled person.

However, without intending to be exhaustive, the following are some of the factors which might be taken into account when considering what is reasonable:

- whether taking any particular steps would be effective in overcoming the difficulty that disabled people face in accessing the services in question;

- the extent to which it is practicable for the service provider to take the steps;

- the financial and other costs of making the adjustment;

- the extent of any disruption which taking the steps would cause;

- the extent of the service provider's financial and other resources;

- the amount of any resources already spent on making adjustments;

- the availability of financial or other assistance.

A service provider must comply with the duty to make reasonable adjustments in order to avoid committing an act of unlawful discrimination. A disabled person is able to make a claim against a service provider if:

- the service provider fails to do what is required; and

- that failure makes it impossible or unreasonably difficult for that disabled person to access any services provided by the service provider to the public; and

- the service provider cannot show that such a failure is justified.

2.12.3.3 Direct Discrimination

Direct discrimination occurs when a person is treated less favourably for reasons of a disability e.g. failing to shortlist a disabled person on the assumption that they would be unable to undertake a particular job.

2.12.3.4 *Victimisation*

The Act defines discrimination as the victimisation of a person who has asserted their rights under the DDA 1995.

Exceptions

There are certain exceptions to the DDA 1995 where service providers can justify discrimination. These are:

- health and safety
- legal consent
- protecting the interests of others
- reasons of greater expense (for small businesses)

2.12.3.5 *Equal Opportunities Definitions*

Prejudice

Prejudice occurs when a judgement or decision is made on the basis of little or no factual information

2.12.3.5.1 Stereotyping

A stereotyping is a characteristic, which may apply to one or more of a group, and which is applied to all members of the group.

2.12.3.5.2 Discrimination

Discrimination occurs when someone treats another person less favourably than they would treat someone else based on their prejudices.

Direct discrimination consists of treating a person on racial grounds or on the grounds of race, sex, marital status or on the grounds of disability less favourably than others.

Indirect discrimination consists of applying a requirement or condition, which although applied equally to all, is such that a considerably smaller proportion of a particular group can meet the requirement and that the requirement cannot be shown to be reasonable.

Institutional discrimination is the collective failure of an organisation to provide an appropriate and professional service to people as a result of their diverse needs. Institutional discrimination can be seen in processes, attitudes and behaviours which amount to discrimination through unwitting prejudices, thoughtlessness and stereotyping which disadvantage minority groups.

2.12.3.5.3 Bullying

Bullying can be defined as offensive, intimidating, vindictive, malicious, insulting or humiliating behaviour, abuse of power or authority which attempts to undermine an individual or group and which may cause them to suffer stress or cause stress related illness.

2.12.3.5.4 Harassment

Harassment is any form of behaviour that one person finds unacceptable and offensive and which is not reciprocated.

Racial harassment is targeted unacceptable behaviour motivated by racial intolerance affecting the dignity of women and men at work.

Sexual harassment is unacceptable and unreciprocated behaviour which is sexually motivated and which affects the dignity of women and men at work.

2.12.3.6 Duties of Occupiers

The Occupiers' Liability Acts 1957 and 1984[28] set down what is expected of occupiers of premises in terms of members of the public who use those premises. The responsibility owed depends on whether the member of the public is:

- a person invited or permitted to be on the premises by the health services (e.g. a patient);

or

- a person not so invited or permitted, either expressly or implied (e.g. a burglar)

A 'duty of care' is owed to the first category – visitors – and is defined as:

---

28 These Acts are not applicable in Scotland and Northern Ireland

"... a duty to take such care as in all the circumstances of the case is reasonable to see that the visitor will be reasonably safe in using the premises for the purposes for which he is invited or permitted by the occupier to be there."[29]

Consequently, an occupier must be prepared for children to be less careful than adults. However, the Act does not forbid the contracting out by the occupier of the responsibilities by for example a disclaimer notice. It is the Unfair Contract Terms Act 1977 which puts significant limits on the extent to which any business, using a disclaimer notice for example, may avoid their obligations:

"A person cannot by reference to any contract term or to notice given to persons generally or to particular persons exclude or restrict his liability for death or personal injury resulting from negligence."[30]

Liability for loss other death or personal injury, such as damage to property, can only be contracted out of if the term or notice in question is reasonable. Even warning a visitor does not necessarily absolve the occupier of all responsibility. The warning has to enable the visitor to be reasonably safe.

There are special provisions for independent contractors such as electricians, plumbers and so on. The Occupier's Liability Act 1957 states that an occupier is entitled to expect that an independent contractor in the course of his work will guard against any special risks ordinarily incidental to it. An occupier would not reasonably expect an electrician to undertake his work in wet conditions.[31]

2.12.3.6.1 The Health and Safety at Work etc. Act 1974

The Health & Safety at Work etc. Act 1974 is the primary legislation covering the requirement of employers to provide, as far as is reasonably practicable, a safe environment for their employees. The legislation also imposes a duty upon the employee to take reasonable

---

29 Occupiers' Liability Act 1957, Section 2(2).

30 Unfair Contract Terms Act 1977, Section 2(1)

31 The case of *Roles v Nathan, Roles v Carney* [1963] 2 AER 908 CA is often cited where two chimney sweeps were asphyxiated by fumes whilst sealing a sweep hole. They had been warned on several occasions by an expert employed by the occupier. It was held by the court that sufficient warning had been given and also that the danger was a special risk which was part of their work of which they could be expected to appreciate and guard against.

care and to participate in the implementation of safe working practice. The following examples are of the extensive regulations and Acts which contribute to underpinning efforts to provide safety.

The Management of Health & Safety at Work Regulations

- Safety Representatives 1977

- First Aid 1981

- Dangerous Pathogens 1981

- Reporting of Injuries, Diseases and Dangerous Occurrences 1985

- Ionising Radiations 1985 / 88

- Control of Substances Hazardous to Health 1999

- Electricity 1989

- Noise 1989

- Genetically Modified Organisms 1992 / 93

- Work Equipment 1992

- Workplace 1992

- Personal Protective Equipment 1992

- Manual Handling Operations 1992

- Display Screen Equipment 1992

The Factories Act 1961 and The Offices, Shops and Railway Premises Act 1963
Consumer Protection Act 1987
Data Protection Act 1998
Specific healthcare Acts

- Mental Health Act 1983

- Notification of Diseases

- Misuse of Drugs 1971

- Access to Health Records 1990

- Access to Medical Reports 1988

- Registration of Nursing Homes 1984

2.13 CORPORATE GOVERNANCE THROUGH CONTROLS ASSURANCE

Section 2.13 was written by Kim Donovan RGN, RM, MA

Research Fellow, Controls Assurance Support Unit

2.13.1 Background

Until the 1990's the term Corporate Governance was not widely discussed. In 1992 the Committee on the Financial Aspects of Corporate Governance (Cadbury Committee), established by the London Stock Exchange and the accountancy profession, defined it as 'the system by which companies are directed and controlled'[32]. Corporate Governance requires a management Board to be properly constituted so as to be capable of controlling the risks faced by their organisation in the pursuit of their objectives and taking actions to minimise these risks. This requires the Board to ensure that all internal systems, which control the activities of the organisation, are working effectively and the Board to take responsibility for those systems.

The importance of Corporate Governance in the UK has been fuelled by public and governmental concern over a number of corporate failures, such as the Robert Maxwell Pension Fund Case, where the weakness of Corporate Governance was clearly a contributory factor [33] and a concern that systems could possibly remain inadequate. The Cadbury Committee was set up to address some of these issues, as there was a perceived low level of confidence in financial reporting and in the ability of auditors to provide the safeguards required[34]. This Committee identified three fundamental requirements for good governance in organisations, comprising: internal financial controls; efficient and effective operations and compliance with applicable laws and regulations.

A number of reports sought to build on the work of the Cadbury Committee including Greenbury, Hampel and Rutteman who all progressed individual elements of its recommendations. In September 1999, the Combined Code was issued by the Institute of Chartered

32 The Cadbury Committee Report: Financial Aspects of Corporate Governance (1992) Burgess Science Press. UK

33 Charkman J (1995) Keeping Good Company. Oxford University Press. Oxford. P248 - 249

34 Charkman J (1995) Keeping Good Company. Oxford University Press. Oxford. P249

Accountants in England and Wales, providing Corporate Governance guidance for directors of UK incorporated listed companies. This code brought together all the elements, extending reporting requirements to cover the whole system of internal control, not just financial, and recommending that the system of internal control be 'embedded into the operations of the company and form part of its culture'[35]. The Combined Code modifies Cadbury in that it requires organisations to 'conduct a review of the effectiveness of the system of internal control and report to shareholders that they have done so', rather than report on the effectiveness of the control system. This review of controls includes financial, operational and compliance controls and risk management.

2.13.2   Corporate Governance and Internal Control

Internal control encompasses the 'resources, systems, processes, culture, structure and tasks that, taken together, support people in the achievement of the organisation's objectives'[36]. An effective system of internal control provides reasonable assurance that the company will not be hindered in achieving its objectives by risks that are foreseeable.

In addition to an annual assessment for the purpose of making its public statement on internal control, the board needs to continually monitor its systems to ensure that decisions are made effectively on the risks it faces. The Combined Code states that 'effective monitoring on a continuous basis is an essential component of a sound system of internal control. The board cannot, however, rely solely on the embedded monitoring processes within the company to discharge its responsibilities. It should regularly receive and review reports on internal control'[37].

The Board plays a vital role in the organisation's success. It needs to provide employees with the necessary skills, knowledge and information in order to work within and monitor the control system. This will require the board to continually communicate its objectives as

---

35 *Internal Control. Guidance For Directors on the Combined Code.* The Institute of Chartered Accountants in England and Wales. September 1999. P3, P7.

36 *Guidance for Directors. Dealing With Risks in the Boardroom.* The Canadian Institute of Chartered Accountants. Criteria for Control Boards. August 1999. Annex A, P9.

37 *Internal Control. Guidance For Directors on the Combined Code.* The Institute of Chartered Accountants in England and Wales. September 1999. P 8.

well the risks, in order for everyone in the organisation to work in harmony towards the achievement of the same goals.

2.13.3   The Value of Corporate Governance

The perceived value of Corporate Governance has two aspects. The first relates to the organisation having the ability to achieve its objectives. It is believed that foreseeable risks can be minimized and that, if bad things do happen, a well-governed organisation has the ability to rebound more quickly. The second relates to the belief that organisations with good governance will perform better over time[38].

Corporate governance also provides a means for setting priorities for resource allocation. It is believed that 10-20% of annual turnover could be identified as loss, with a significant proportion potentially being capable of relocation.

2.13.4   Linking Corporate Governance to Controls Assurance

Controls Assurance is a process designed to provide evidence that NHS organisations are doing their 'reasonable best' to manage themselves in order to meet their objectives and protect patients, staff, the public and other stakeholders against risks of all kinds. It is based on best governance practice, which includes a requirement for organisations to conduct a review of the effectiveness of their systems of internal control and report to stakeholders that they have done so. NHS bodies are similarly required, through Controls Assurance, to provide an assurance statement within their annual report which addresses this condition.

In order for NHS organisations to sign such a statement, there must be a clearly defined system of internal control. The NHS Executive have assisted this process by providing a control framework, which consists of the following overleaf in Figure 2.13.4.a.

Self-assessment is at the heart of the control framework and includes not only an annual review for the purpose of making a public statement on internal control, but also incorporates continuous monitoring. Self-assessment represents the belief that cultural change and continuous improvement are more likely to be achieved if they are

---

38 Putting A Value on Board Governance. The Mc Kinsey Quarterley 1996. No. 4 P 170 - 175

Figure 2.13.4.a – CONTROL FRAMEWORK FOR CONTROLS ASSURANCE[39]

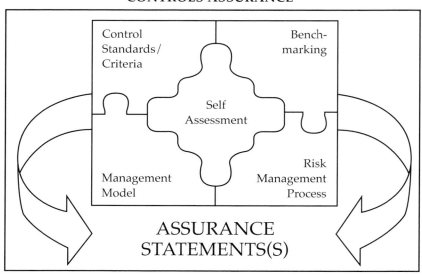

driven by professionals assessing their own work, rather than by third party auditors judging compliance and taking punitive action. A range of management tools exists, providing a systematic approach to self-assessment. Figure 2.13.4.b describes the management model developed for Controls Assurance.

2.13.5 Utilising Standards for Self-Assessment

A number of key Controls Assurance standards relating to organisational control and risk management have been developed, which reflect potential areas of significant risk i.e. those which potentially threaten the ability of an organisation to meet its objectives. Control criteria within these standards are arranged into the elements of the management model (accountability, processes, capability, outcomes, monitoring and review and audit).

Each standard includes:

- a statement of the standard, supporting rationale and key references

- key control criteria which set out the control objectives. These

---

39 HSC 1999/123 *Governance in the New NHS*

Figure 2.12.4.b – CONTROLS ASSURANCE
MANAGEMENT MODEL[40]

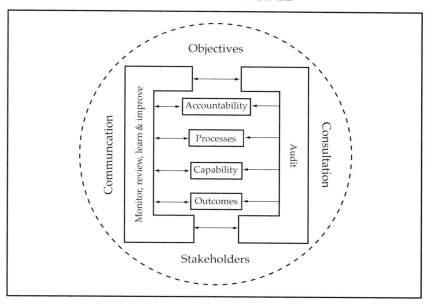

are arranged into the elements of the management model (accountability, processes, capability, outcomes, monitoring and review and audit)

- the source

- background guidance

- examples of verification

- possible links to other criteria

Each criterion is weighted based on 1) level of importance (i.e. statutory, mandatory or voluntary requirement) and 2) difficulty in achievement. This is not an assessment of risk, as it purely acts as a tool to enable benchmarking and evaluate improvement. Having undertaken a baseline assessment the board can evaluate the risks faced by the organisation. During the self-assessment process, the point at which compliance becomes about risk is when the percentage of compliance with a standard is analysed. For example, if an organisation is 80% compliant with a standard, Controls Assurance is

---

40 NHSE (1999) *Guidelines for Implementing Controls Assurance in the NHS.* Guidance for Directors

concerned about the 20% non-compliance and what this means in terms of risk. Without this simple intellectual step, Controls Assurance ceases to be about risk and remains a compliance exercise.

A fundamental assumption behind Controls Assurance is that all statutory and mandatory requirements represent a risk of some kind. Similarly, good practice guidelines provide options for dealing with potential risks and, therefore, compliance with standards and risk management go 'hand in hand'.[41]

The control standards / criteria are output driven, which is a 'results focused' approach. Whilst they provide examples of the input measures needed to achieve the output i.e. policies produced or personnel employed, their design focuses on what the organisation actually achieves. This is consistent with the use of 'RADAR' logic which consists of Results, Approach, Deployment, Assessment and Review.[42]

The process of self- assessment enables organisations to measure and improve their performance. Weaknesses or control failings can be identified, actions prioritised based on an assessment of risk, measures developed to minimise risk and monitoring arrangements implemented. In addition, the board's annual assessment should consider the scope and quality of management's ongoing monitoring of the system of internal control.[43]

In order for NHS organisations to provide evidence that they are doing their 'reasonable best' to manage themselves so as to meet their objectives and protect patients, staff, the public and other stakeholders against risks of all kinds, supporting documentation must be provided which will enable independent verification of the assurance statement.

2.13.6   The Key Elements of Internal Control in the NHS

Controls Assurance is based on the principles of Corporate Governance, which is essentially about good management practice. It focuses on a system of internal control, which enables the board to be

---

41 NHSE (1999) *Guidelines for Implementing Controls Assurance in the NHS*. Guidance for Directors

42 *The EFQM Excellence Model Changes*. Http://www.efqm.org/imodel/changes1.htm

43 *Internal Control. Guidance For Directors on the Combined Code*. The Institute of Chartered Accountants in England and Wales. September 1999. P 9.

continually made aware of and manage foreseeable risks. The system of internal control in the NHS incorporates financial and organisational control in addition to clinical governance.

In order for directors to make key decisions, adequate information is needed on the nature and extent of the risks faced by the organisation. Continuous monitoring and annual assessment are, therefore, vital components of the control system.

The NHS system of internal control depends, critically, on three fundamental aspects:

Accountability (who is responsible to whom, and for what?). This includes not only NHS organisations providing assurances to the general public but also assurances being made to Parliament by the Chief Executive of the NHS Executive.

Assurance (declaration by an accountable officer that the organisation, or part, is meeting its objectives)

Audit (independent verification of the assurance)

The NHS system of Controls Assurance takes the requirement to report to stakeholders one step forward, as it focuses on the need for NHS organisations to provide objective evidence and independent verification of the assurance given.

Controls Assurance provides a firm foundation of financial and organisational controls, which will provide reasonable assurance that the NHS will be able to meet its objectives, providing an environment in which patient services can flourish.

2.13.6.1.1 Note

This work was undertaken by the Controls Assurance Support Unit, Keele University, which is funded by the Department of Health. The views expressed in this publication are those of the author and not necessarily those of the Department of Health.

The Controls Assurance web site is at http://www.casu.org.uk. The Department of Health Controls Assurance web site is at http://www.doh.gov.uk/riskman.htm.

2.14 THE INCREASING REGULATORY FRAMEWORK

2.14.1   Formulating a Risk Management Response

As the regulatory framework in health care becomes increasingly complex, the risk manager will need to continually refine the tools available to ensure that the organisation complies with current requirements. These are discussed in detail in Chapter three. When new requirements are introduced, it is helpful to carry out an impact analysis.

The essential parts of an impact analysis are to establish a current baseline of how the organisation complies with expected standards or procedures, to compare these with the required standards and to define the 'gap analysis', which requires to be met.

Key questions:

- where are we now? (baseline assessment)

- where do we need to be? (standard compliance and performance)

- how do we bridge the gap? (action plan)

To adequately meet these challenges requires:

- adequate stakeholder contributions and participation;

- promotion of ownership of the problem;

- direction of effort;

- marking success in meeting requirements;

- acknowledging achievements;

- signing off when completed;

- adequate board level reporting.

The impact analysis of potentially significant change requires:

- identification of the source and extent of the risk;

- identification of the timescales available;

- short timescales —> high pressures, high level of uncertainties

- longer timescales —> lesser pressures, more opportunity for certainty

- identification of ways to make up the difference;
- resources
- people
- expertise
- financial
- identification of ways of measuring success

See Figure 2.14.1.

Figure 2.14.1 – EFFORT/RISK MATRIX – ORGANISATIONAL CHANGE

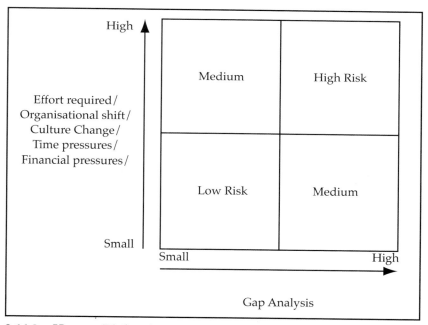

2.14.2   Human Rights Act 1998

The Human Rights Act 1998 came into effect in October 2000 and provides for a form of incorporation of elements of the European Convention of Human Rights into English law.

2.14.2.1 Fundamental Principle of the Act

The fundamental principle of the Human Rights Act is that it is unlawful for a public authority to act in a way which is incompatible with a convention right, unless primary legislation gives the public authority no choice.

Proceeding under the Act must be brought before the end of one year from the date that the act complained of took place.

The Act does not end the right of individuals to petition the European Court of Human Rights in Strasbourg, but provides that domestic remedies should be exhausted first.

2.14.2.2 Key Areas to Address

The challenge for the NHS and risk managers is to ensure that three key areas are addressed:

- clinical practice;
- commissioning;
- human resources.

Chief Executives have a duty to ensure that all staff (including contractors and independent or private providers of their public services) are made aware of the duty placed on public authorities by the Act.

2.14.2.3 Relevant Convention Articles

Article 2: the right to life – e.g. challenges to decisions about the distribution of health care and financing of treatments;

Article 3: the right not to be subjected to inhuman or degrading treatment or punishment;

Article 4: Slavery and forced labour;

Article 5: the right to liberty and security of the person – mental health;

Article 6: the right to a fair and public hearing – e.g. disciplinary and professional hearings;

Article 8: the right to respect for family and private life, home and correspondence – e.g. confidentiality of health information;

Article 9: the right to freedom of thought, conscience and religion;

Article 10: the right to freedom of expression;

Article 11: the right of peaceful assembly and to join a trade union;

Article 12: the right to marry and found a family;

Article 14: the right not to be discriminated against on any ground in relation to the enjoyment of convention rights

2.14.2.4 Areas for Particular Attention

The risk manager will need to assist in a continuing examination of the following areas:

- employer/employee relations;
- detention of voluntary mental health patients;
- mental health review tribunal conduct;
- do not resuscitate policies;
- consent to treatment – including refusal by older children;
- standards and regulation of residential care;
- decision making processes;
- policies on the conduct of procedures and guidelines;
- hospital and personnel security;
- allocation of resources.

In particular, all existing and new policies will need to be read and interpreted in the light of the organisation's responsibilities under the act. It will be a safeguard under due diligence if the fact that this has taken place is explicitly stated in each policy.

2.14.2.5 A Risk Manager's Checklist for Decision Making Relating to the Human Rights Act

Which article under the Act is relevant to the decision?

Is the legitimate aim of the decision set out in the Act?

What is the legal basis for the decision?

Is there a 'pressing social need' for the decision?

Is the decision proportionate to the rights and legitimate aim?

Will the act of decision discriminate against any individual on any ground?

Further information is available at:
http://www.doh.gov.uk/humanrights/

2.14.3 Clinical Governance

Clinical governance is the system of steps and procedures adopted by the NHS to ensure that patients receive the highest possible quality of care. It covers, among other things, how staff treat patients, the level of information provided to patients, their involvement in decision-making, the provision of up-to-date and well supervised services, and the prevention of errors and accidents.

Key elements in clinical governance are:

- demonstrable accountability, both individual and corporate;
- demonstrable leadership;
- improving the quality of care;
- developing and maintaining appropriate professional skills through active and monitored lifelong learning;
- auditing progress with regular board level reporting.

All NHS organisations are required to have a clinical governance programme in place. A recognised programme has the following aims and characteristics in Figure 2.14.3.1.[44]

Purpose:

to work towards achieving agreed objectives outlined by the organisation to enhance the quality of patient care. To enable staff to continuously develop their skills through recognised professional development programmes, individually tailored to meet individual needs as well as the needs of the service/organisation.

Characteristics of the programme:

- clear objectives;
- defined timescales;
- recognised teams of people, with appropriate skills;
- implementation process;

---

44 *Steps Towards Clinical Governance* NHS Executive 1999

Figure 2.14.3.1

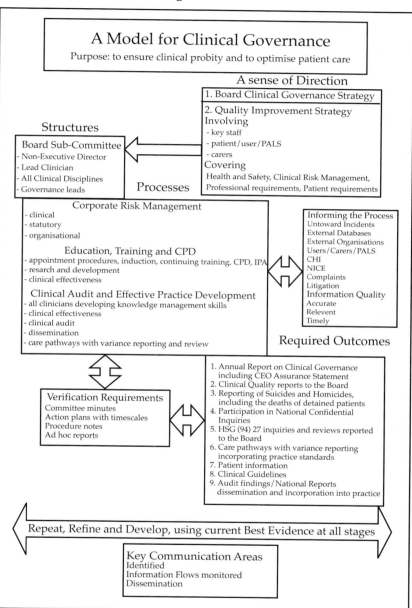

- facilitates change within the organisation;

- ongoing monitoring;

- corrective action plans.

2.14.3.1 *Principles of a Clinical Governance Programme*

Clear objectives are needed for:

- the development and Implementation of continuous quality improvement programmes within the organisation;

- relevant timescales associated or required for successful implementation;

- any relevant costs identified.

Forward planning – there should be a programme plan established, agreed and supported by the organisation, which can be monitored and controls clearly outlined.

Sound decision-making – The organisation needs to be managing the programme and making the appropriate decisions along the way, cognizant of the programme objectives, in line with the usual needs of the strategic direction of the organisation.

A potential framework for clinical governance is shown in figure 2.13.9.1

2.14.4 Commission for Health Improvement

The Commission for Health Improvement (CHI), is an independent body created by the Health Act 1999, to help the NHS monitor and improve the quality of clinical care provided throughout England and Wales. It started its official work in April 2000.

CHI functions at two levels: national and local.

The Commission's national role involves advising and guiding the development of clinical governance principles, and monitoring and reviewing their implementation across every part of the NHS. Locally, it is responsible for overseeing and assisting external inquiries and investigations into individual NHS bodies, or services; and independent scrutiny, or review, of clinical governance arrangements.

The most prominent aspect of CHI's work is a rolling review

programme. This will involve visiting each NHS Trust, Health Authority and primary care group/Trust (England) or local health group (Wales), once every four years. In each case, CHI looks at a broad cross-section of services, examining the management, provision and quality of care services. Review teams contain a mix of doctors, nurses, managers and lay people, ensuring that pressures and sensitivities unique to any particular group are understood.

The aim of the Commission is to improve standards of care by focusing on the experience of those using the NHS as a way of restoring public confidence in the NHS

The Commission carries out a rolling programme of clinical governance reviews. This is the first time a thorough and extensive review has been undertaken within the NHS. CHI aims to provide a catalyst and impetus to encourage NHS staff to seek excellence.

Under the terms of inspection under the National Plan, the CHI, together with the Audit Commission, will inspect NHS organisations every four years. In addition, organisations rated as 'red' under the government's system of 'earned autonomy' will be subject to more frequent, two yearly CHI inspections. 'Red' organisations will be those who are failing to meet a number of the national targets. Criteria will be set nationally, but assessed by regional offices with independent verification by CHI.

There will be significant financial disadvantage in being a 'red' organisation. Access to a share of the NHS Performance fund will be held by the Modernisation Agency who will control access for 'red' organisations.

The government will also continue to use its powers to send the Commission into those Trusts where there are serious and urgent concerns about clinical practice or patient safety.

The Commission's management structure comprises a Board, with 13 commissioners, with a Commission Chair. There is also a Directorate with seven departments: Policy & Development, Medical Affairs, Nursing, Information and Clinical Governance Reviews, Communications, Human Resources and Finance and Corporate Governance

2.14.5 Some Risks to the Work of the Commission for Health Improvement

Duplicating the work of other review groups.

Allowing individual reviewers to pursue their own interests.

Raising expectations about what is achievable in the short term.

Making comparisons between Trusts, health authorities, practices and PCG/T / Local Health Groups without rigorous statistical analysis.

2.14.6 The National Institute for Clinical Excellence

The National Institute for Clinical Excellence, NICE, was set up as a Special Health Authority for England and Wales on 1 April 1999. It is part of the National Health Service, and its role is to provide patients, health professionals and the public with authoritative, robust and reliable guidance on current "best practice".

The guidance covers both individual health technologies (including medicines, medical devices, diagnostic techniques, and procedures) and the clinical management of specific conditions.

2.14.6.1 Citizens Council

With the National Plan a Citizens Council will be established to advise the Institute on its clinical assessments. It will complement the work of the NICE Partners Council that provides a forum for the health service and industry to comment on the work of NICE.

It is likely that the Citizen's Council will be a committee of the board. The Council will be composed of representatives of the general public. It is likely that the Council will advise the Institute on those clinical priorities with respect to appraisals or technologies where value judgements are necessary. The Council's terms of reference, membership, and the way in which members will be chosen will be the subject of further discussion between the Institute and the Department of Health.

It is not envisaged that the council will have a role in setting the Institute's agenda, nor will it be involved in determining the scope of the Institute's appraisals or guidelines.

2.14.7 Health Improvement Programme (HImP)

The development of a Health Improvement Programme was first set out in the Government White Paper on the NHS, 'The New NHS, Modern, Dependable' in December 1997. It stated that:

The HImP is the local strategy for improving health and healthcare and modernising services. It covers the population of a Health Authority and its purpose is to address:

- the most important health needs of the local population, and how these are to be met by the NHS and its partner organisations through broader action on public health

- the main healthcare requirements of local people, and how local services should be developed to meet them either directly by the NHS, or where appropriate jointly with social services

- the range, location and investment required in local health services to meet the needs of local people.

The HImP is the vehicle for achieving national targets such as those set out in the public health White Paper, *'Saving Lives – Our Healthier Nation'*. It is also seen as the means to deliver locally agreed targets.

Health Authorities lead the development of the HImP in collaboration with the rest of the health community, partner organisations and local people. It will monitor implementation by the health community and others, and will also decide on and be required to ensure the delivery of the health components.

Working together in partnership to develop and implement the HImP is key to its effectiveness. The HImP belongs to the whole of the local community and must, therefore, have the widest possible involvement, from all the health agencies, local authorities, voluntary sector bodies, community groups, business and others. In the statutory sector this is underpinned by duties of partnership and all public sector agencies are expected formally to sign up to delivering their contribution to the HImP.

More integrated services will be achieved through the medium of joint investment plans for continuing and community care services, and moves towards pooled budgets, lead commissioning and integrated service provision.

The key to the HImP is to clearly define objectives based on prioritized health needs and to ensure delivery. Here, important areas such as co-coordinated workforce plans, information and information technology plans and estates strategies will need to be an integral part of the HImP.

The HImP gives new impetus to local action to improve health and tackle the determinants of health such as unemployment, education, housing and community safety. All local plans, for example the Housing Investment Plan, the Local Agenda 21 and Education Action Zones will contribute to health and be integrated with the HImP to combine and add more force to local action for health.

2.14.8   The NHS Plan[45]

The NHS Plan, issued by the Department of Health in 2000, will have the most significant effect on the format of delivery of services for health. Its starting point is that the NHS is a 1940s system operating in a 21st century world and that it has:

- a lack of national standards;
- old-fashioned demarcation between staff and barriers to improve performance;
- a lack of clear incentives and levers to improve performance;
- over-centralisation and dis-empowered patients.

Pooling the resources of health and social services under new agreements will be an important part of the funding arrangements, forming Care Trusts to commission health and social care.

2.15 NHS CORE PRINCIPLES

The NHS plan states that the core principles of the NHS are to:

- provide a universal service for all based on clinical need, not ability to pay;
- provide a comprehensive range of services;
- shape its services around the needs and preferences of individual patients, their families and their carers;
- respond to the different needs of different populations;

---

45 The NHS Plan – Cmd 4818-I Department of Health July 2000

- work continuously to improve quality services and to minimise errors;

- support and value its staff;

- work together with others to ensure a seamless service for patients;

- help keep people healthy and work to reduce health inequalities;

- respect the confidentiality of individual patients and provide open access to information about services, treatment and performance.

- Public funds for healthcare will be devoted solely to NHS patients;

2.15.1.1 Setting Priorities and Developing Standards

The Department of Health will, with advice, set national standards in priority areas. These will be in three forms:

national standards for key conditions and diseases through National Service Frameworks (NSFs). NSFs have been produced for mental health and coronary heart disease and will be followed by a National Cancer Plan, for older people's services and diabetes. Further NSFs will be developed.

clear guidance on the best forms of intervention and treatments from NICE. The work programme for the NICE will be increased as a result of the plan. A key aim is to improve consistency of approach.

a limited number of national targets. These will include shorter waiting times, the quality of care new services to help people remain independent and efficiency.

The techniques described in this course book will enable those concerned with risk in the health sector to maximise the opportunities to gain improving quality of care for patients in a complex and changing care environment.

3

RISK MANAGEMENT METHODS

"I keep six honest serving-men
(They taught me all I know)
Their names are What and Why and When and
How and Where and Who."[1]

3.1 INTRODUCTION

A risk management strategy and programme is a sign of a commitment by a healthcare organisation to quality and excellence. A risk management programme represents another step toward making that commitment a reality. The methods and concepts of risk management are well known and the benefits of successful risk management have been demonstrated by a number of healthcare organisations both in Britain and abroad. Most of the methods are adapted from analytical methods generally used in research, commerce and industry. Risk management is now widely acknowledged as an effective strategy for improving healthcare and clinical performance which offers rewards for patients, providers, purchasers and staff.

3.1.1 Requirements

Risk management constitutes a strategy for improving healthcare delivery and performance through the commitment of all staff to reducing risk cost-effectively through the continuous improvement of services, of health care processes and of the people involved. It requires:

- defined risk management policies and healthcare objectives;

- an organisation structure to promote communication, change and risk reduction;

---

1 Rudyard Kipling – *Just So Stories*

81

- defined processes for the continuing delivery of risk assessment and prevention;
- training for all staff;
- motivation to secure professional and staff commitment.

The key to continuing success through risk management is the effective implementation of methods that translate the concepts of risk management into real performance improvements. These methods can be applied organisation-wide and their effects are organisational, managerial, clinical, technical and personal. They need to be tailored to the specific needs of the organisation. The application of the methods should also bring together leading research with current best practice in the field of risk management. Applying the concepts and methods detailed in this book will enable the building of a risk management culture within an organisation.

3.1.2 The Need for Change

Healthcare services face a number of pressures for change:

- the NHS Plan;
- increasing patient expectations;
- competitive pressures in a managed market;
- increasing professional and staff expectations;
- continuing pressure on internal costs;
- higher service performance demands from government;
- compliance with clinical governance requirements;
- compliance with NICE recommendations;
- fulfilling HimP expectations;
- rising levels of complaints, claims and litigation;
- patient satisfaction surveys showing weaknesses and negative perceptions;
- clinical research and the development of 'evidence based medicine' indicating areas for improvement.

The NHS, in common with healthcare systems throughout the world, has undergone major management and cost-led change in recent years.

Experience suggests that involving and empowering professionals and staff in contributing to risk management will achieve further change and performance improvement most successfully.

The NHS Controls Assurance Unit has promoted the Australian / New Zealand Risk Management Standard 4360:1999 Risk Management. This promotes a holistic, generic and non-prescriptive approach to risk management in an organisation. The risk management overview of the AS/NZS 4360:1999 approach is shown at figure 3.1.2. (1). A stepwise adaptation of risk management in healthcare is shown at 3.1.2.(2) where risks are identified in terms of concerns and perceptions, prioritising risks, developing a strategy, identifying a management response and monitoring actions and implementation.

3.2 THE RISK MANAGEMENT APPROACH TO QUALITY

Eight Dimensions

The traditional view of quality implies that:

- improving quality and reducing risk is expensive;
- a 'reactive' organisational culture is set up;
- 'acceptable' levels of risk or quality become institutionalised;
- employees are at fault for errors;
- errors or accidents are removed by inspection and checking.

The risk management approach to quality, on the contrary, means that patient requirements are met and that:

- quality is, at worst, cost-neutral;
- a 'preventive' culture is developed;
- the aim is to become 'error free' via continuous improvement and risk assessment;
- the process ensures that mistakes are minimised.

The application of the risk management methods underpins the strategy and leads to:

Figure 3.1.2 (1) – RISK MANAGEMENT OVERVIEW FROM AS/NZS 4360:1999)

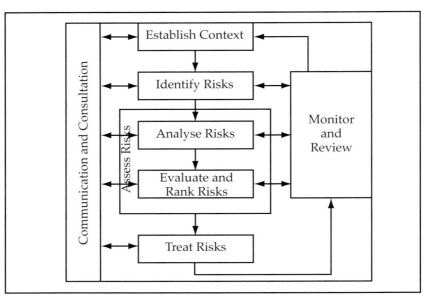

Figure 3.1.2 (2) – RISK MANAGEMENT APPROACH

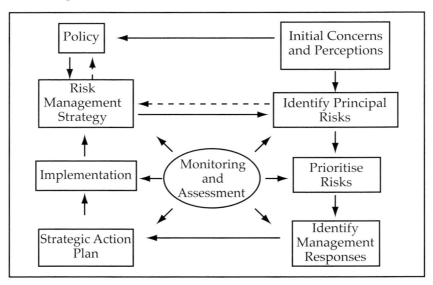

- a fuller understanding of risks, expectations and priorities;

- a better understanding of the capabilities of the organisation;

- delivering the service which is expected as effectively and safely as possible;

- being efficient, as well as effective, in meeting agreed requirements and in reducing risks;

- continually seeking to prevent accidents and improve performance.

The objective is the safety of the patient, staff and visitors and to satisfy the requirements of the patient at the lowest cost. Both organisational and patient requirements have seven dimensions of quality and performance which require examination and correlation:

- continuity;

- consistency

- controls;

- compliance;

- communication;

- contingencies;

- co-ordination and cohesion.

3.2.1   Continuity

CONTINUITY of care between health care episodes means ensuring that the procedures for both routine and emergency handovers of patient care, both within and outside the acute care setting, are sensitive to the patient's treatment needs and the health professionals information needs.

3.2.2   Consistency

CONSISTENCY of patient care provision implies ensuring equity of access to a high standard of care and that all staff are up to date in terms of induction, continuing training and skills. Staffing levels and skill mix should be consistent with the agreed levels of provision necessary.

3.2.3   Controls

CONTROLS in care should be in place and relate, for example, to:

- management structure and systems;
- operational planning;
- health and safety procedures;
- security and access control;
- waste control.

"'Control" comprises all the elements of an organization (including its resources, systems, processes, culture, structure and tasks) that, taken together, support people in the achievement of the organization's objectives. Control is "effective" to the extent that it provides reasonable assurance that the organization will achieve its objectives reliably. Leadership involves making choices in the face of uncertainty. "Risk" is the possibility that one or more individuals or organizations will experience adverse consequences from those choices. Risk is the mirror image of opportunity.' [2]

3.2.4   Compliance

COMPLIANCE should be maintained and continually updated with agreed standards set by:

- *statutes* such as The Health and Safety at Work etc. Act;
- *professions,* externally by e.g. the Royal Colleges and registration bodies, and internally by local professional groups through the clinical governance agenda;
- *organisational* through e.g. the Patients' Charter and performance standards.

3.2.5   Communications

HIGH QUALITY COMMUNICATION with, and with the agreement of, the patient is essential. In order to develop and achieve the first six dimensions, good inter- and intra-professional communication, especially through health records, is also essential. Communication is central to the financial success of both health commissioners and providers.

---

2   Guidance for Directors – *Dealing with Risk in the Boardroom* – Canadian Institute of Chartered Accountants Toronto, August 1999

It is important to understand the rapid increase in communications lines which are created when a number of organisations or individuals work together. The number increases according to the formula:

$$N = \frac{O^2 - O}{2}$$

where N is the number of communication lines or channels and O is the number of organisations.

Example:

No of organisations or individuals	5	10	15	20	25	30
No of communication lines/channels	10	45	105	190	300	435

See also 5.2.2.1 for the Ombudsman's view on communications.

3.2.6   Co-ordination and Cohesion

CO-ORDINATION AND COHESION of effort result from the application of a sound risk management strategy which identifies board level responsibilities and reporting by a risk management committee and which specifies a common approach to risk management throughout the organisation and its activities.

3.2.7   Contingencies

CONTINGENCY measures should be in place in case of uncontrollable, especially external, untoward events occurring:

- externally e.g. Major Accident (MAJAX), sudden influx of casualties;

- internally e.g. unforeseen shortages of resources or skills, infection control failure;

- elemental e.g. fire, flood or utility failure.

Within these seven dimensions, healthcare risk management is a natural part of health professional and staff commitment to quality patient services. It is a natural extension of professional and staff involvement and teamwork, innovation and ethical behaviour. By committing itself to these eight dimensions of healthcare risk management, a healthcare organisation will set itself standards of excellence that will enhance the quality of patient care and the economy of health care.

3.2.8 Linking the Dimensions for Quality and Risk Management – Threat/Risk Analysis – Developing a Risk Register

Individual threats or risks to an individual or organisation can be summarised as potentially arising from the following areas (acronym BC TEMPLES):

- **Biological**
- **Cultural**
- **Technological**
- **Elemental**
- **Motivational**
- **Political**
- **Legal**
- **Economic**
- **Social**

The source of the threat may be:

- **Internal**
- **External**

The 'vectors' for transmitting the threat or risk may be:

- **Human**
- **Organisational**
- **Environmental**

Predicting the likelihood of an impact will be based upon the knowledge of the process and predictability of events. This was referred to in Chapter one at 1.3.3.

The performance, quality or safety of a linear process, such as providing episodes of care, P, is a function of the state of knowledge of certainties, C, and uncertainties, U.

Expressed as an equation, the risk manager may find this helpful:

$$P f C,U$$

Increasing the knowledge base of the organisation, both of its own processes and the application of therapeutic methods, reduces the uncertainties of outcome. The use of extreme values to consider a response to a set of circumstances can be important. For example, in the first six hours after the Hillsborough Disaster there were 1.75 million attempted telephone calls to the Sheffield telephone exchange; 250,000 were actually handled by the exchange.

The areas of potential impact on the individual or organisation may be:

- **Reputation**
- **Financial**
- **Quality/Performance**
- **Legal (including litigation and/or prosecution)**
- **Injury (to patients, visitors or staff)**

which should be assessed for severity, prioritising and acceptability by the board risk management committee. An example of an impact matrix is shown at figure 3.2.8. The interpretation of the words describing the effects of impacts on the organisation is a matter of choice for the individual organisation. Experience shows that the most important effect is when the board decides and owns the concepts.

Contingencies for these threats and impacts need to be developed (see SIMULATION for iterative learning and implementing techniques) which encompass:

- **Controls**
- **Compliance**
- **Communication**
- **Consistency**
- **Continuity**
- **Co-ordination and cohesion**

and which are based on using these key questions:

- **Can it go wrong?**

- **What can go wrong?**

- **How can it go wrong?**

- **How do we stop it going wrong?**

- **What do we do if it goes wrong?**

- **How much resources, time, money, manpower and expertise are available to deal with the effects?**

Having identified threats and risks with full consideration of potential root causes, the risk manager is in a position to compile a risk register. This should include the date that the risk was identified, the risk itself, the impact that realisation of the risk would have on the organisation, the likelihood and score, the risk owner, what action needs to be taken to mitigate the risk, what residual risk remains and the continuing monitoring action required. An example of a risk register is shown at 3.2.8 (4).

3.2.9   Management Methodology for Quality

The traditional and established view of a quality management cycle is based on a plan, do, check and change iteration. This established approach can easily be adapted to encompass specific identified risks. This approach is illustrated in figure 3.2.9.

**Figure 3.2.9 – QUALITY MANAGEMENT CYCLE
(PLAN → DO – IMPLEMENT → MEASURE AND ASSESS → CHANGE)**

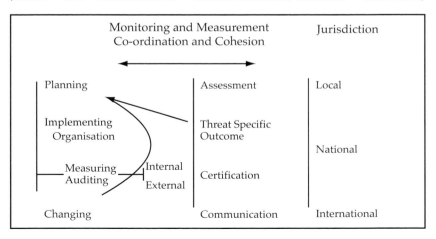

Figure 3.2.8 (1) – WORKING CONTINGENCIES

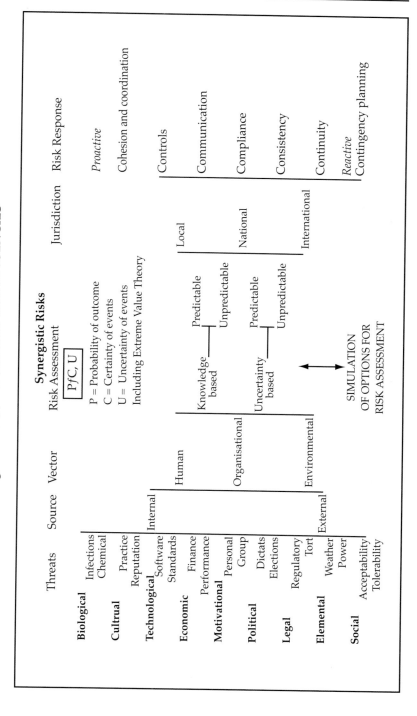

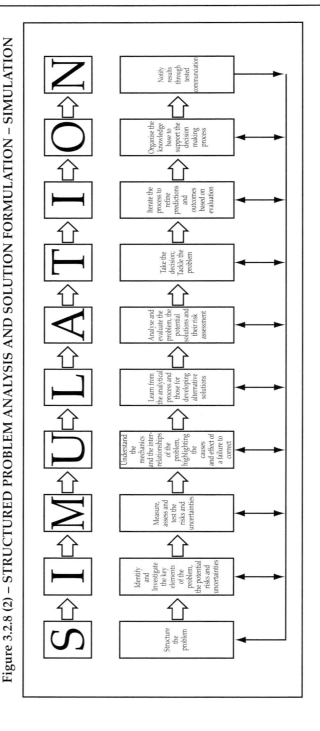

Figure 3.2.8 (2) – STRUCTURED PROBLEM ANALYSIS AND SOLUTION FORMULATION – SIMULATION

S → I → M → U → L → A → T → I → O → N

Structure the problem

Identify and Investigate the key elements of the problem, the potential risks and uncertainties

Measure, assess and test the risks and uncertainties

Understand the mechanics and the inter-relationships of the problem, highlighting the causes and effect of a failure to correct

Learn from the analytical process and those for developing alternative solutions

Analyse and evaluate the problem, the potential solutions and their risk assessment

Take the decision; Tackle the problem

Iterate the process to refine predictions and outcomes based on evaluation

Organise the knowledge base to support the decision making process

Notify results through tested communication

Figure 3.2.8 (3) – EXAMPLE RISK IMPACT MATRIX

Impact Area	Consequences				
	Insignificant	Minor	Moderate/ Significant	Major/ Severe	Catastrophic
Financial loss or impact	£1k – £10k	up to £50k	up to £250k	up to £500k	over £1M
Safety/Injury		Verbal abuse Up to 3 days absence	RIDDOR reportable accident Long term recovery	Unexpected death of a patient Permanent disability	Multiple unexpected deaths/injuries/ infections
Reputation			On going adverse local press comments/local action groups	Adverse reaction from specialist commissioners	Multiple failures leading to loss of reputation
Legal			Civil action – defensible	HSE prosecution – no defence Criminal prosecution for abuse	Failure to meet registration requirements Registration tribunal
Quality and performance		Failure to meet internal standards	Repeated failure to meet internal standards Failure to meet national performance	Intermittent failure to meet professional standards and/or statutory requirements	Sustained failure to meet national professional standards and/or statutory requirements

Figure 3.2.8 (4) – EXAMPLE RISK REGISTER

Risk Ref	Risk Description	Risk Type	Impact	Likelihood	Score	Responsibility	Mitigation Action	Residual/ Contingency	Monitoring

3.3 UNDERPINNING THE RISK MANAGEMENT APPROACH

The successful application of risk management methods requires:

- management commitment;
- organisation-wide observation and measurement;
- promotion and recognition;
- ownership of the risk management approach;
- team building.

3.3.1 Management Commitment

Risk management requires managers to demonstrate consistency of purpose and long-term commitment. Risk managers should:

- demand and assist continuous improvement;
- obtain professional and staff involvement in the risk management process;
- establish risk management as a service priority;
- organise for risk management.

Because risk management requires the commitment and creativity of professional and staff, role models – clinical, technical and managerial – must be identified and teamwork developed. Common definitions and language of risk need to be adopted and embedded within written risk management policies. This is assisted by common processes for delivering, measuring, managing and improving safety and risk assessment, and by common risk management education and training.

3.3.2 Organisation-wide Observation and Measurement

Risk improvement programmes depend on the use of performance measures and supporting measurement systems. Risk management requires that teams take ownership of their services and measure their own performance. Therefore, all professionals and staff should:

- understand measures and performance criteria which apply to their activities;
- establish the application of measures and criteria for the

people, patient services and management processes within their activities;

- measure their key outputs and process;
- record and analyse untoward events against agreed criteria;
- use measurement as a guide to risk management and process improvement.

Again, common education and training in skills and knowledge is required.

3.3.3 Promotion and Recognition

Risk management requires the promotion of awareness of initiatives and their integration into day-to-day activities to acknowledge the importance of safety. It is underpinned by:

- effective communication within and between specialties and staff teams;
- empowering teams to identify risks and realise improvement opportunities;
- recognition, both formal and informal, of achievements;
- personal development of all employees.

3.3.4 Ownership

Risk management becomes embedded in day-to-day activity by the acceptance and ownership of the approach by professionals and staff. It is they who will integrate risk management effectively in all practices and procedures, and ensure effectiveness cross-functionally and between specialties. To embed risk management within the organisation, practices and procedures must be developed that have:

- demonstrable capability to reduce risk;
- features designed to prevent untoward events;
- in-process measurement and corrective feed-back mechanisms;
- compliance with standards and criteria;
- optimisation throughout the patient treatment cycle.

3.3.5 Team Building

Risk reduction has to be achieved by individuals and through teams. Risk management emphasises the importance of team building because of the following benefits:

- teams make better use of individual expertise;
- teams produce better ideas than individuals;
- teams involved accept the required changes;
- the team approach results in less time being taken;
- team building develops individuals.

Successful team building is based on the following key principles:

- recognising a team leader;
- agreeing objectives;
- constructive interactive behaviours;
- personal space for innovation;
- involvement;
- consensus;
- recognition of achievements.

Reaching consensus is an important element in team working because it builds ownership of group actions and outputs, but does not remove the risk manager's role in managing risk reduction. The key contributions to reaching consensus are:

- agreeing objectives of the discussion;
- listening to and testing understanding of everyone's point of view;
- concentrating on areas of agreement;
- trying to obtain any missing information;
- recognising that differences of opinion can be beneficial if motives are right;
- if voting is unavoidable, use it to clarify reasons for disagreement;

- pressure of time can focus agreement, so set a deadline for decision if appropriate.

Overall risk management leads to the continuing improvement of services, processes and people. It is a cyclical process which encourages innovation within the organisation and comparison with best practice externally. This cycle provides a structured process for implementing and realising identified improvement opportunities, and should be used in conjunction with the range of analytical tools and techniques described below.

The risk manager provides the means of ensuring the process change optimises the overall patient care, promotes ownership of the change and recognises the interdependency of functions and specialisms. The process also enables commitment to risk management to be translated into a series of actions through which people at all levels can review safety. These steps make risk management concepts a reality and enable the risk manager to achieve the resulting benefits.

BOX 1: Inter-active Behaviours Analysis

Inter-active Behaviours Analysis (BA) is a tool to help team members improve the way in which they work together. It is one among many such tools, though it is of particular use in making all types of meeting more productive in terms of output and more useful in building strong and creative group relationships. The method was developed by the Huthwaite Research Group as a system of describing and classifying oral behaviour of individuals working together in groups. The purpose of the technique they developed is to identify the oral behaviours that support effective teamwork and team results in varied circumstances and applications. The research identified eleven groups of behaviours in four categories that can be analysed and used to improve the effectiveness of teams. There are many other team-building techniques and a surfeit of handbooks detailing their use.

3.4 COST AND MEASURES OF RISK

Resistance to implementation of risk management methods is often expressed in terms of cost. It is therefore necessary to have a cost framework in mind to be able to justify risk management. Costs can be broken down into the following three categories:

- *cost of compliance* – i.e. the cost of activities which are designed to ensure that practices are updated to statutory, professional and organisational standards;

- *cost of non-compliance* – i.e. the cost of activities which result from failure to comply with those standards;

- *opportunity costs* – i.e. the cost of lost opportunities to improve cost effectiveness or limit the damage of an accident.

To facilitate analysis these can be broken down further into six categories:

compliance   –   prevention costs;
                     –   appraisal costs;

non-compliance– internal failure;
                     –   external failure;
                     –   exceeding standards or requirements;

lost opportunities–   the cost of missing out

The six categories of cost can be defined as:

1. *Cost of prevention* – costs of activities that prevent accidents from occurring such as training, risk awareness programmes, planning and risk reduction teams;

2. *Cost of appraisal* – costs incurred to determine compliance with practice standards such as inspection, checking and auditing;

3. *Cost of internal failure* – costs of correcting accidents or poor performance such as repeat operations; treatment changes after poor diagnosis; surplus, obsolete or out of date supplies;

4. *Cost of external failure* – costs of complaints, claims and litigation;

5. *Cost of exceeding standards* – costs incurred providing information or services which are unnecessary or unimportant or for which no known requirement has been established e.g. redundant documentation, unnecessary tests or recalls, 'defensive' medicine;

6. *Cost of lost opportunities* – loss of existing or potential patient contracts from failure to deliver services at the required standard.

Introduction of a healthcare risk management can expect:

- an initial increase in prevention and appraisal costs;

- a reduction in the other costs
- improvement in the cost of lost opportunities takes considerable time to become significant.

Reduction in the costs of risk management will be achieved through:

- improved service design, planning and implementation;
- improved process capability;
- improved skills and motivation.

There will be, in addition, cost reductions over time through the learning and experience curves as prevention and appraisal becomes better known.

3.4.1 Risk Management Measures

The risk management process uncovers eight generic ways, in addition to the cost of the process itself, in which the results of work can be measured:

failures – expectations or specification not met;

reworking – correction of work required;

waste – materials, equipment etc. thrown away;

repeats – work done again;

backlogs – work behind schedule;

lateness – work after agreed time;

surplus – work, supplies or equipment not required;

attitude – work delivered in the wrong way.

Within this framework of costs and measures, the opportunity for using structured methods can be realised and the improvement opportunities identified. The methods provide an opportunity for every member of staff – professional, technical, administrative and ancillary – to contribute to the development of innovative improvements focused on the safety of patients and others. It provides a framework for:

- improving the service by removing the causes of accidents and untoward events;

- ensuring solutions are not jumped to before they are analysed;

- maximising the performance improvement;

- implementing improvements that eliminate errors through prevention processes;

- improved use of resources

- improved motivation;

- reduced inter-departmental conflict;

- reduction of waste;

- more time to manage the healthcare process.

3.5 A METHODOLOGY FOR RISK MANAGEMENT

The risk management approach is a cyclical one of constant updating and improvement. There are six interacting parts in this process, in each of which different tools and techniques can be used. Any tool or techniques described below can be used in any part of the cycle. Nevertheless, certain tools and techniques are used in some parts more than others. The parts of the cycle are:

Identify and select the untoward events to be addressed focusing attention on the causes of the incidents:

- *Risk Surveys and Audits*

- *Untoward Event Reporting*

- *Risk Register*

Analyse the causes, sorting out the differences between symptoms and the true causes. Usually there are several causes that require analysing and put in order of priority. This may well require further data collection which provides the facts needed rather than opinions:

- *Fault Tree Analysis*

- *Flowcharting*

- *Root Cause Analysis*

Generate potential improvements for which there are usually several options. The first idea is not always the best. 'Brainstorming' and 'building' on ideas are effective ways to find the right option.

- *Cause and Effect Analysis*

- *Further Data Collection and Analysis*

- *Bench-marking*

Select and plan the improvement to be implemented by ordering the options identified using cost-benefit analysis together with the timetable demanded by the severity and probability of the potential accident. A specific project plan should be prepared identifying the key activities with start and finish times and dates, and the named individuals who will carry them out. The proposed plan can then be presented for approval.

- *Cost-benefit / effectiveness Analysis*

- *Techniques for Deciding Priorities*

- *Force Field Analysis*

Implement the selected improvement ensuring there is regular review of the implementation to control progress and costs, and check benefits are being realised. Contingency plans may need to be activated to overcome practical difficulties arising.

- *Project Management*

Evaluate the improvement.

- *Accident and Untoward Event Analysis*

Figure 3.5.a – THE RISK MANAGEMENT PROCESS

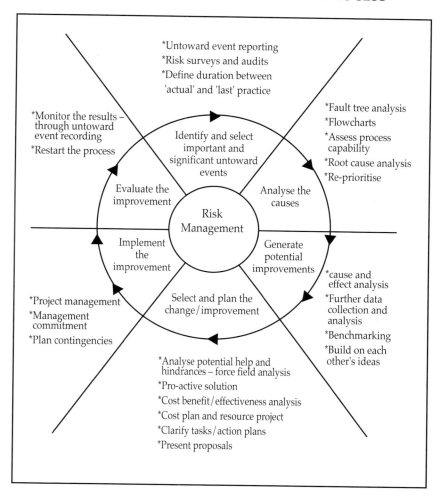

Figure 3.5.b – AMPLIFIER/FILTER PROCESS

The diagram illustrates risk management function on an 'amplifier – filter' basis to identify problems, present opportunities for change and improvement and select appropriate solutions.

HEALTHCARE PROBLEMS

STEP 1

GENERATE POTENTIAL CHANGE / SOLUTION

SELECT MOST SIGNIFICANT CHANGE OPPORTUNITY

STEP 2

IDENTIFY POTENTIAL CAUSES

SELECT MAJOR CHANGES

STEP 3

GENERATE POTENTIAL CONTINGENCY

SELECT SUGGESTIONS

CHANGE

3.6. METHODS FOR RISK IDENTIFICATION, ANALYSIS AND REDUCTION

The key questions in identification of risk are:

- what can go wrong?

- how can it go wrong?

- how frequently can it go wrong?

- what would be the effect(s)?

- what resources are available to assist (financial, manpower, expertise, time)

For example, cross-infection can happen in many ways – inadequate sterilisation, inappropriate ventilation, incorrect handling of bandages, swabs, etc. Inadequate sterilisation may be systematic and result in cross-infection very frequently; the mishandling of swabs may be a one-off carelessness by a trainee; inappropriate ventilation may be a regular problem with certain microbes. Harm may be incurred by one member of staff, many patients or everyone in a particular part of a hospital. One harmful incident may have one or series of risks associated with it. Risk management requires the use of a range of analytical tools and techniques to complement the six-stage process.

Paradoxically, risk analysis may be the least understood part of risk management. Nor may it be recognised as an activity in its own right. Too often identification of the risks is followed by a 'solution' to control, reduce or eliminate the risk (see Type III errors). However, an intermediate stage is desirable to analyse the outcome of the investigation in the light of the objectives, resources and so on. Risk management is essentially about identifying and defining problems which are worth solving within the resources likely to be available. Without analysis there is the real danger of designing and implementing solutions which cause problems in themselves.

There are several analytical tools and techniques for risk management, which help to ensure that people do not 'jump to solutions' without objective analysis, the most common of which are:

- Risk surveys and audits involving

- – structured observation;

- – risk audit;
- – checklists;
- – interviews;
- – questionnaires.
- Untoward Event Reporting including claims analysis;
- Fault Tree Analysis;
- Flowcharting;
- Root cause analysis
- Cause and Effect Analysis;
- Data collection, analysis and presentation;
- – check sheets;
- – graphs, scatter diagrams, histograms;
- Best practice bench-marking;
- Techniques for deciding priorities including
- – criteria analysis;
- – impact diagrams;
- – Pareto analysis;
- Force-field analysis;
- Project management especially error-proofing processes.

3.6.1. Structured Observation

As the actions and behaviour of people are a central aspect of all healthcare, an obvious risk identification technique is to watch what they do, to record this in some way and then describe, analyse and interpret what was observed. Structured observation, rather than 'participant observation', is a quantitative style of observation best suited to risk identification. A major advantage of observation is its directness: the risk manager watches what people do, how they interact with their environment and listens to what they say. This directness contrasts with, and can often usefully complement, information obtained by virtually any other technique.

Interview and questionnaire responses are notorious for discrepancies between what people say that they have done, or will do, and what they actually did or will do. Direct observation permits a lack of artificiality which is all too rare with other techniques.

This appropriateness to risk management does not imply that observation is an easy or trouble free option. There is a major issue concerning the extent to which an observer affects the situation under observation. How do we know what the behaviour would have been like if it had not been observed? Moreover, there are related methodological and ethical problems. There is also the very practical problem that observation tends to be time-consuming. Structured approaches involve a considerable time investment required in developing some kind of observation schedule or checklist. Even on those rare occasions when an existing checklist developed by another risk manager is suited to the task at hand, acquiring proficiency in its use can take much time and effort.

Once the observed persons know that they are being observed, then the observer is to some extent a participant in the situation, and the observation becomes potentially reactive i.e. potentially changing the thing observed. It is never logically possible to be completely sure that the observer has not in some way changed what is being observed, but there are several indicators which provide reassurance:

- the pattern of interaction stabilises over sessions;

- different observers code essentially identical patterns for different sessions;

- members of the group appear to accept the observer to the extent that they do not seek interaction;

- group members say that your presence does not affect what is going on.[3]

3.6.2.   Risk Audit

An examination of the risks presented by individual departments is essential as a benchmark in establishing a risk management programme. In order to do so a simple examination of the aims of the

---

3   It is helpful to check this with different 'constituencies' present. A surgeon may say that nothing has changed, whereas theatre nurses may claim he is better prepared.

department needs to be considered. The following is an aide-memoir for the process and may challenge the basis assumptions of those working in the department:

- what is the purpose of the unit or department?
- has the flowchart of the work process been prepared? If not, do so.
- what marks the success of the unit?
- what are the means by which failure is measured?
- what are the causes of failure?
- what action is taken following a failure?
- what corrective action is taken following a failure?

Is it the policy or inclination to blame individuals for failures of the system? If so, there is likely to be a significant under-reporting of errors. Any change in behaviour and safety will be made more difficult to assess.

Examples of a possible sequence for a risk investigation the risk research approach are shown in diagrams 3.6.2.a. and 3.6.2.b.

The outcome of the risk audit should be the preparation of a risk register which requires an action plan to be prepared with prioritised actions and risk owners.

3.6.3. Checklists

A checklist provides predetermined categories for recording what is observed and are based on:

- professional standards;
- statutory standards;
- local standards such as the Patient's Charter and local Charters.

These standards will differ from department to department and therefore separate checklists will be required for every specialty. Checklists provide a long series of items which can be recorded as present or absent.

A completed checklist provides confirmation that a process has been carried out according to a particular specification. Detailing the

Diagram 3.6.2.a. – POSSIBLE SEQUENCE OF A RISK INVESTIGATION

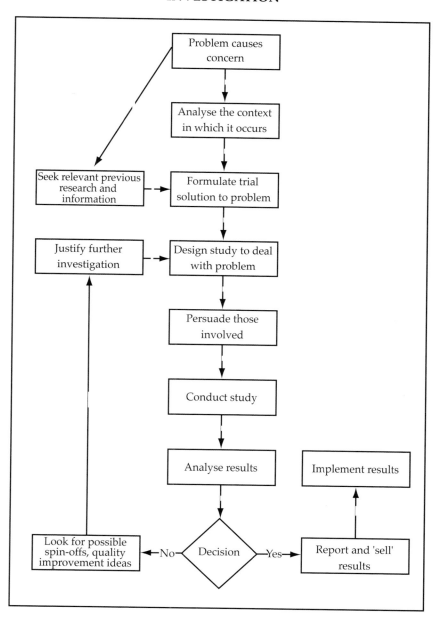

Diagram 3.6.2.b. – RISK RESEARCH APPROACH

Basis for Risk Analysis
Established Practice
Cross-Disciplinary Literature Search

*knowledge base

*project scanning
*environment scanning

Objectives of Risk Management
Determine Context, Methods, Content and
Organisation of Each Project

*knowledge
*competences
*skills
*concepts
*analytic criteria

DIAGNOSIS

What are they doing now?
Actors, Content, and Methods

*resources
*innovativeness
*skills
*objectives

DIRECTION SETTING
Evaluation Criteria
Comparators
Conceptual framework

Process

Individual Project Implementation
Identification of Risk
Analysis Within Appropriate Framework

*key milestones
*key effects
*key criteria
*major outcomes
*dissemination

How Do Practices Compare?
Best Practice in Delivery and Anticipation
Different Models of Applied Knowledge

*effectiveness
*measures

Shaping the Risk Management Strategy
Influencing professional practice
Initiating training and development
Encouraging innovation

specification of the process should ensure that it complies with appropriate statutory, professional and patient requirements.

Simple checklists may be prepared from an analysis of activity through flowcharting a process. By identifying each separate element of the process a checklist may be prepared to ensure that potentially harmful shortcuts have not been taken.

The Health and Safety Executive has prepared helpful checklists for audits to measure compliance with the statutory obligations on employers with respect for the safety of employees and members of the public. More detailed and specific checklists can be applied to clinical areas to take account of professional and patient centred requirements. High-risk areas with potential for patient harm include the operating theatres where unwitting assumptions of safety may be made unless the care process is constantly examined.

The safety of processes involving the patient in operative procedures may be enhanced by incorporating checklists into documentation. An operation on the incorrect side is a common and preventable cause of harm. In many hospitals the operating list is prepared from the admissions list. In effect this means that the clerk who prepares the admissions list dictates the side for operation through the accuracy of the entry to the admissions list. In all hospitals in the author's experience where this has been the procedure there have been incidents of wrong-sided operations.

Developing a checklist to audit activity is straightforward. An example is given diagram 3.6.3.a. Successful checklists are:

- simple to prepare;
- simple to use;
- sufficiently comprehensive for purpose;
- signed off as complete.

Checklists should be signed off by the person completing them, including date and time, to increase their reliability that the checks have been performed.

Particular areas where checklists may improve safety include the preparation of anaesthetic machines before surgical lists. The Association of Anaesthetists recommends machines should be checked

Diagram 3.6.3.a. – SAMPLE CHECKLIST FOR OPERATING THEATRE DOCUMENTATION

- [ ] patient identified on ward by identity bracelet and medical records
- [ ] operating list prepared by the admitting doctor after the patient has been seen
- [ ] operating list prepared after the patient has confirmed the side for operation
- [ ] side of operation spelled out in full on the operating list (not L or R)
- [ ] side for procedure marked with an indelible pen by person preparing the operating list
- [ ] pre-operative assessment by anaesthetist
- [ ] pre-operative assessment by surgeon
- [ ] patient sent for by name and number
- [ ] patient identified on arrival by name and number
- [ ] notes checked for identity, procedure and allergies
- [ ] operating list checked against patient
- [ ] patient asked to confirm side for operation
- [ ] handover completed satisfactorily mentioning side of operation
- [ ] positioning technique satisfactory

before each list by the anaesthetist and their assistant separately and has prepared a specific checklist for the purpose. A copy of the checklist should be attached to each machine for convenience. However, its use needs to be monitored through clinical audit if consistency of practice and approach between anaesthetists and operating theatres is to be achieved.

3.6.4. Interviews

Interviewing can be a most productive method of discovering what and how activities are being done, and uncovering risks. Not only do interviews provide facts, they enable the risk manager to verify facts and they provide an opportunity to meet staff and overcome resistance to change. Success will depend upon the interviewer's ability to work around, or avoid, resistance that may develop on the part of staff whose work habits will be altered by any changes that may be recommended.

Interviewing is a process of obtaining information by means of conversation. It entails being a good listener, keeping the conversation rolling and being able to keep the subject on the right lines. A certain amount of skill is required on the part of the interviewer; good preparation is essential. The risk manager should be impartial, tactful and, more positively, have skill in influencing others to accept advice they would prefer to ignore.

The success of the interview is determined by a number of variables including the prejudices of the interviewer and the interviewee. It is therefore important to supplement it with other means of fact finding not least observation and examination, often using checklists. However, an interview is usually the only way to understand the staff member's individual opinions and approaches. The higher in the organisation the more important this factor may be. Therefore it is important for the interviewer:

- to be aware of own bias;

- to reduce or eliminate that bias;

- not to have a pet solution;

- to be impartial and thorough;

- to be empathetic.

The wider the interviewer's experience, the greater becomes the temptation to recognise a risk, hazard or problem at a glance. In fact, very few of them are exactly similar, and the discovery of some apparent cause that is suspected to be operative is easily made. When the interview is passed and the collection of facts is complete is when experience is needed to work on what has been found. The value of self-discipline cannot be underestimated. Therefore, the risk manager must try to:

- refuse to guess;

- keep experience chained up;

- not prejudice the issue.

Many of the people to be interviewed will be enthusiastic and wholehearted about their work and may regard a visit by the risk manager as a suggestion that their work is not well done, and take this impression to heart.[4] Therefore, the risk manager must be fully prepared. The risk manager should know:

- the names of the people in charge and those with whom she is going to speak;

- what part the particular job represents in the work of the organisation, department or section and its purpose;

- the reason for selection of the particular person to be interviewed (is she/he outstanding, average, easy or difficult?).

The risk manager should also have ready a number of points upon which information is needed. As often as possible, the risk manager should formulate the actual questions required to gain information needed. A subsidiary part of the preparation is that of making arrangements for the visit: finding out, for example, a general announcement has been made about it, and if so, in what terms, or whether suspicion has been created by what has been said or left unsaid.

Interviews supplement more definite study of what is actually done, what questions should be asked to complete the story already discovered by watching the job, and what meaning to give to the

---

4   This will particularly so when the title of 'risk ' is combined with the title of 'quality manager'.

observations made or the answers received. To achieve this it is necessary to:

- make the interview impersonal;
- keep it objective;
- prepare for it beforehand.

When studying work methods it is necessary to:

- disclaim any association with grades or wages;
- confine questions and interest to the actual operations being carried out;
- avoid comparing one person to another;
- avoid asking anything which reflects badly upon the person being interviewed;
- encourage the staff member to go through the motions of the work in detail in order to get a factual picture of what is involved before listening to any account.

Following these preparations and the initial introductions, the first stage in the interview is to state the reason for the visit. If possible, the interviewer should also mention the method she is using. The staff member may have had little experience of being interviewed and may need help in explaining the work. The interviewer will not only have to study her own approach, but also guide the person interviewed without asking leading questions that suggest the answer to be given.

The following checklist may be helpful in preparing for and conducting an interview:

3.6.4.1. *Planning the Interview*

- clarify the problem and what is to be investigated.
- find out as much as possible about the subject area.
- prepare a list of main questions.
- ensure authority to interview has been obtained.
- choose the interviewees with care – especially if it is necessary to draw a sample.

3.6.4.2. Conducting the Interview

- ensure the interviewee is at ease before embarking on the main fact-finding.

- let the interviewee tell his or her story in his or her own words.

- do not ask leading questions.

- ask one question at a time.

- keep the sequence of questions logical.

- avoid the role as 'expert'.

- be straightforward and frank – avoid 'cleverness'.

- ensure the questions are fully understood.

- try to quantify vague references to percentages, etc.

- end the interview on a pleasant constructive note.

3.6.4.3. After the interview

- record the data at the earliest opportunity.

- check the facts as soon as possible.

- get agreement to the facts.

3.6.5. Questionnaires

Questionnaires are the least satisfactory method of fact-finding in healthcare risk management. Care must be exercised in designing the questionnaire, in field testing it and validating it before widespread use. The best use of them is to precede an interview when the respondent is given time to assemble the required information, thus saving time and focusing attention. The kinds of circumstances in which questionnaire surveys may be practicable are:

- where staff are located over a widely spread geographical area;

- when a large number of staff are required to furnish data;

- for verification of data found by other methods;

- when 100% coverage is not essential.

The basic design of a questionnaire falls into three sections:

1. *heading section* – describes the purpose of the questionnaire and contain the main references (name, date, etc.);

2. *classification section* – contains data for analysing and summarising the total data (age, job title, service provided, etc.)

3. *data section* – contains the data being sought.

The major problem in questionnaire design is that it is difficult to frame questions which are certain to obtain the exact data required. Also a feature of questionnaire surveys is that not all the forms will be returned. many people, particularly in the NHS, object to filling in another form while others delay completing them until they are eventually forgotten.

The aim in questionnaire design should be to formulate the questions so that no misinterpretation is possible and no bias is possible in the replies, even though this aim is virtually impossible to attain fully. A covering letter may be necessary to explain the purposes of the questionnaire in order to avoid misunderstanding and to help gain co-operation. The date by which the questionnaire should be returned should be stated.

If it becomes necessary to obtain a detailed story on the activities of all individuals in a section, a duties questionnaire may be used to collect the information. In the questionnaire each employee is asked to list duties and the average amount of time spent on each one. In many instances, the estimate of average time cannot be very accurate. This should not present difficulties as the risk manager knows that the use made of the questionnaire does not require high accuracy. It may be helpful to ask for the following additional information when considering duties:

- a list of all forms and reports connected with the work, together with information obtained and the operations performed upon them;

- a list of equipment used

- a list of unusual, out of the ordinary, duties that seldom occur and therefore cannot be conveniently listed among regular duties.

These 'duty lists' should be compared with any job descriptions which may exist.

3.6.6.   Untoward Incident and Claims Analysis

The value of structured investigation into the causes of medical misadventures is now undisputed. The consecutive *Confidential Inquiries into Peri-Operative Deaths*[5] (hospital deaths within 30 days of surgery) and the *Confidential Inquiries into Maternal Deaths* (deaths of women during pregnancy or within one year of childbirth) have been invaluable in providing information to improve practice. However, it is not necessary to have the death of the patient as the only outcome measure before recording and using information from non-fatal untoward events can be used to make improvements to the ways in which care is given. Two other Confidential Inquiries operate in the NHS:

- *Confidential Enquiry into Stillbirths and Deaths in Infancy* (CESDI) (stillbirths and infant deaths);

- *Confidential Inquiry into Suicides and Homicides by People with Mental Illness* (suicides within one year of contact with mental health services and homicides involving people who have been in contact with mental health services at any time).

The Health and Safety at Work etc. Act 1974[6] through The Reporting of Injuries, Diseases and Dangerous Occurrences Regulations 1995, (RIDDOR), places a statutory duty on every employer and employee to report events, injuries and diseases to the relevant enforcing authority. Failure to comply with these Regulations is a criminal offence.

Adverse events and reactions involving spontaneous adverse drug reactions from medicines have long been reported by clinicians under the Yellow Card Reporting Scheme which is handled by the Medicines Control Agency on behalf of the Committee on Safety of Medicines. The value of the scheme has been shown many times with the early recognition of untoward side effects from drugs. Anaesthetists have reported on the value of recording and reporting untoward incidents in clinical audit.

The collection of information can provide unexpected benefits. Inquiries into significant untoward problems, at Ashworth Hospital where instances of patient abuse occurred and at Grantham Hospital in

---

5   The origin and inception of the Confidential Enquiry into Maternal Deaths.

6   Health and Safety at Work etc. Act 1974, Chapter 37, HMSO 1974.

the Beverley Allitt Inquiry have both recommended that hospitals set-up untoward incident reporting systems. In the case of Beverley Allitt, an incident reporting system would have been likely to have identified her at an early stage as the only common link between events.

The Ashworth Inquiry also recommended that incidents should be graded for severity. The Mental Health Act Commission has since adopted this recommendation. Further development is required to translate the information needs of a Special Hospital to those of small community units and other clinical areas in acute hospitals. (see below)

An internal reporting system for health care providers is a useful addition to, and not a substitute for, statutory reporting mechanisms. Any fatal injury to an employee or other person, major injury or dangerous occurrence should be reported to the area office of the Health and Safety Executive on Form 2508. HSG(93)13 details reporting requirements for specific incidents relating to medical devices, food, non-medical equipment such as engineering plant, installed services, buildings and building fabric and medicinal products.

3.6.7.   Definition of an Untoward Incident

An untoward incident is an event which gives rise to, or has the potential to produce, unexpected or unwanted effects involving the safety of patients, users or other persons.[7] To improve the range of information collected this definition can usefully be extended to include all events which have or could result in a loss to the health care provider, such as theft or a breach in security.

Main Definitions

*   **Incident**

All occurrences, which have given rise to actual or possible personal injury to patient dissatisfaction or property loss or damage. This includes those incidents relating to clinical care, which have been described as:

---

7   *Reporting of Injuries, Diseases and Dangerous Occurrences Regulations 1995,* (RIDDOR)

Adverse Healthcare Event

An event or omission during clinical care and causing physical or psychological injury to a patient (An organisation with a memory)[6]

- ### Health Care Near Miss

A situation in which an event or omission, or a sequence of events or omissions, arising during clinical care fails to develop further, whether or not as the result of compensating action, thus preventing injury to a patient (An organisation with a memory).[8]

Sub Definitions

- ### Diagnosis and Treatment Related

Patient deaths, injuries or impairments in circumstances other than those related to the natural cause of illness, disease or proper treatment in accordance with generally accepted medical standards and that necessitate additional or more complicated treatment regimens or that result in a change in patient status (New York State Department of Health).

- ### Mental Health Act Commission Classification of 'Untoward Events'

Class A Incidents:

Incidents that result in death or cause such serious harm that they place the patient's life in jeopardy. They include, but are not limited to, homicide, attempted homicide, sudden or unexpected death and suicide.

Class B Incidents:

These are incidents that are not life threatening, but which acutely jeopardise the well being of the patient. They include, but are not limited to, allegations of patient abuse or neglect, sexual assault, racial incidents, attempted suicide, aggravated assaults, unexplained injuries and serious errors of medication.

Class C Incidents

These are incidents which seriously affect, or have the potential to

---

8 *An organisation with a memory*, Department of Health 2000 ISBN 011 322441 9

affect seriously, the health or the psychological well being of the individuals involved. They include, but are not limited to errors of medication (which may amount to Class B incidents), sexual improprieties, sexual, racial and gender harassment. Accidental injuries, assaults and acts of deliberate self-harm may amount to either Class C or Class D incidents depending on the severity of the outcome.

Class D Incidents

These are incidents which result in no injury, or in only very minor injury, and do not involved any blameworthiness on the part of any member of staff. They include, but are not limited to minor accidental injury, fights between patients without weapons and acts of deliberate self harm (Mental Health Act Commission).

Class E incidents

Any other untoward occurrence.

3.6.7.1. Incident Reporting

All members of staff, as employees, have a duty to see that all safety related incidents are reported in order to ensure that any trends may be identified at an early stage. This will allow other users to be alerted and prevent harm to others.

3.6.7.2. Introducing an Effective Reporting System

From experience, the introduction of an incident reporting system may be characterised by either early ownership and participation by clinicians, or suspicion and rejection by them. The difference between the two lies in the manner in which the system has been introduced and the degree of participation by clinicians in setting up the system.

Successful incident reporting starts from:

- staff participation, in particular stating their perceptions and the requirements of incidents which need to be reported;
- staff awareness training;
- feedback of the results;
- early action on reported incidents.

In order to encourage early reporting of incidents it is important that the reporting system should be as simple as possible. The report form should be concise and contain as many aids to easy completion as possible. The inclusion of tick-boxes for the type of incident and clear stipulation of the criteria to be reported will speed the completion of the forms and increase acceptability.

Forms should be completed at the time by the person who notices the incident. It does not matter whether the person was involved in the incident or not. It is also important that the reporting system is outside a disciplinary procedure, unless the incident is malicious or criminal.

Completed incident forms are disclosable in the event of litigation. It is therefore important that details are accurate and factual and do not contain opinions or apportion blame.

Completed forms should be assessed by the Consultant in charge of the patient, or by the Head of Department within 24 hours and appropriate remedial action taken. As an aid to indicating the priority for action, incidents may be graded for severity. A suggested risk rating system is detailed in Table 1. The forms should be sent to a central point for collation and placed on a database as soon as possible.

Reporting systems that comply with both statutory requirements and user needs can be implemented using a self-carbonned form with three copies. The first of these is sent to the Consultant or Head of Department, the second to the Occupational Health Department and the third retained in the report book to comply with the requirements for the payment of any compensation and statutory benefits. An analysis of incidents is reported to the Risk Management Committee of the provider.

It is perhaps a natural reaction for a new incident reporting system to be greeted with a degree of scepticism or mistrust. It is important not to judge the success or otherwise of a system too early. Incident reporting may typically start with the supply of information on equipment problems in the first instance. After a period, when the system has begun to prove its worth through effective feedback and the prompt rectification of defects, information on organisational problems may be supplied. After six months with an untoward incident reporting system information on clinical problems can be expected. Units using a criterion based reporting system have identified considerable savings from its use in the prevention of clinical accidents.[8]

Table 3.6.7.2 – IMPACT GRADING OF INCIDENTS

Severity	Grading	Effect on Health Objectives	Effect on Functional Capacity	Effect on Personal Safety
A	Dangerous	Patient care impossible	Physical plant destroyed	Death or potential death
B	Serious	Patient care significantly impaired	2 or more life support functions compromised	Major injury, but not life threatening
C	Moderate	Significant effect on quality of care	1 major function impaired	Moderate injury
D	Minor	Noticeable effect on quality	Minor	Minor injury
E	Other	No significant effect on quality	No noticeable effect	No apparent harm

FREQUENCY OF OCCURENCE

Hazard Rating
1. DAILY
2. ONCE PER WEEK
3. ONCE PER MONTH
4. ONCE PER YEAR
5. ONCE PER DECADE

COST OF PREVENTION

Hazard Rating
1. LESS THAN £5,000
2. £5K – £50K
3. £50K – £250K
4. £250K – £1M
5. GREATER THAN £1M

3.6.7.3. Information Details

The initial report of any incident should contain as much relevant information as is available. Dangerous occurrences should initially be reported by telephone with a written report made as soon as possible. The information should take the form of objective recording rather than subjective comment and opinion.

3.6.7.4. A Minimum Data Set for Incident Recording and Reporting

In order to create a meaningful database of incidents, consideration needs to be given to the extent of the information that the organisation requires. The following is suggested as a minimum data set for information:

- what happened
- who was affected
- who was involved
- where and when did it happen
- why did it happen
- what was the immediate cause
- what was the outcome of the incident
- additional requirements for diagnosis and treatment incidents
- additional requirements for mental health
- additional requirements for drug incidents
- additional requirements for medical devices
- additional requirements for security incidents
- information about who completed the form
- action taken
- costs

3.6.7.5. Analysis of Results

The analysis of untoward incident reports is able to offer a valuable insight into unexpected or unwanted effects on patients. As well as discharging statutory responsibilities for reporting accidents, a

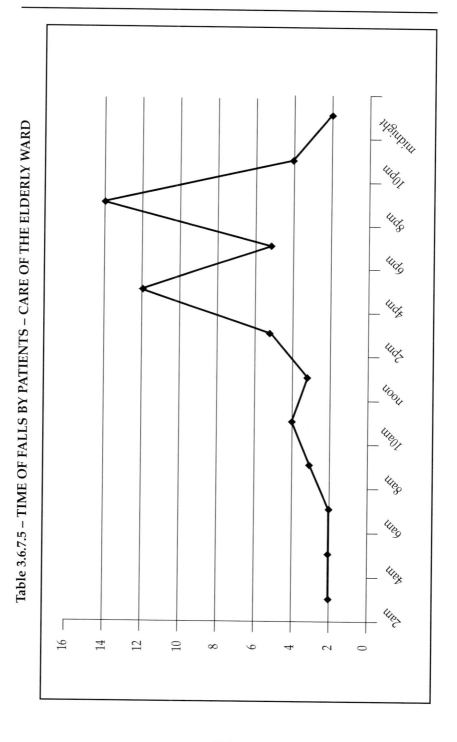

Table 3.6.7.5 – TIME OF FALLS BY PATIENTS – CARE OF THE ELDERLY WARD

Figure 3.6.7.6 – PRIORITISING RISKS

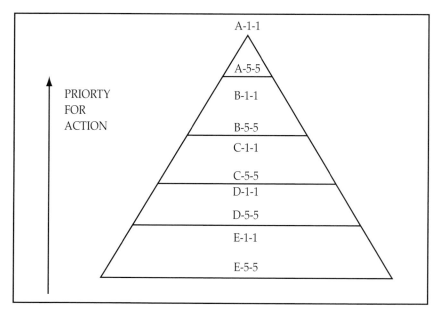

reporting system can provide valuable professional information. This is able to feed directly into clinical audit. A common criterion for reporting is falls, slips and trips. The results of recording incidents over a three-month period on one unit is shown in Table 3.6.7.5.

Investigation of the peak period for falls showed that they occurred when visitors were leaving the wards and the patient has tried to follow. Increasing the supervision on the wards during this time significantly reduced the incidence of falls.

3.6.7.6. Priorities for Action

The rating of risks may be expressed in terms of their actual or potential severity, frequency of occurrence and cost of prevention.

A hazard rating with the highest rating of A11 would merit immediate attention. One with an E55 rating, whilst noted, would not merit a particularly urgent action. This simple rating system may also be used to prioritise expenditure on projects involving investment in Health and Safety. An example of the risk priority triangle is shown in Table 3.6.7.6.

Whilst untoward incident reporting is an essential risk management tool, it is also important to try and gather information from other sources. For example, to enable relatives to express concerns which have yet to formalise in a complaint. To facilitate this, some Trusts have successfully introduced a simple form which is advertised and available throughout Trust sites for anyone, staff, patients, visitors or carers to complete with their concerns, suggestions or grumbles. The form is sent to the Chief Executive and actioned through the head of the particular service. It is important that effective action is taken within a short fixed timescale and the originator of the form informed of corrective action taken, unless the form is completed anonymously. From practical experience, this system makes an invaluable contribution to effective risk management in health care.

3.6.8. Special Reporting Requirements

Special reporting arrangements include:

3.6.8.1. Detained patients

Deaths of patients detained under the Mental Health Act should be reported to the Mental Health Act Commission within 24 hours of the death using form MHAC 3.

3.6.8.2. Medical Devices

All adverse incidents involving medical devices should be reported within the Trust using the untoward incident reporting system.

If the incidents involve or potentially could have involved:

- death;
- injury;
- deterioration in health;
- unreliable test results leading to inappropriate treatment or medication;
- minor faults or discrepancies which may be indicators of inadequate quality assurance on the part of the manufacturer or supplier;

should additionally be reported to the National Reporting and Investigation Centre of the Medical Devices Agency at the Department of Health.

Approximately 6,600 occurrences are reported each year.

Feedback to the health service from the Medical Devices Agency is through:

Hazard Notices which are used in the most serious cases, when either a patient's health or life has been put at risk, or staff safety has been compromised either by a device fault or operator error. They require immediate action when received by healthcare organisations;

Safety Notices when it is clear that a potential safety problem exists with a medical device. They call for action to avoid the risk, often involving alerting staff, or altering procedures either for use or maintenance of equipment;

Device Bulletins when device management changes are needed for safe and effective device use;

Pacemaker Technical Notes which are dedicated to advice relating to pacemakers and which are distributed directly to pacing centres.

In 1999, 6610 reports of adverse incidents were made to the MDA. These showed:

37% involved manufacturing problems (design, quality control, packaging etc.);

27% device faults which developed during use;

12% user error;

24% displayed no links to the device failure.

3.6.8.3. Recommendations Concerning Incident Reporting from the Allitt Inquiry:

- that in the event of the failure of an alarm on monitoring equipment, an untoward incident report should be completed and the equipment serviced before it is used again;

- that reports of serious untoward incidents to Local Health Authority and Regional Health Authorities should be made in writing and through a single channel which is known to all involved.

3.6.8.4. *Identifying and Understanding Medical Device Use Error*

The Human Factors Engineering Group[9] have identified some causes of errors in the usage of medical devices. Usually these arise from poorly designed systems leading to hazardous situations which cause patient or caregiver harm. Identifying and understanding errors that occur while using medical devices should be undertaken within the context of a complete understanding of the device use system. Essential components of this understanding include:

- device users – patients, family members, clinicians, professional caregivers;
- typical and atypical device use;
- device characteristics;
- characteristics of the environment in which the device will be used;
- the interaction between users, devices and the environments in which the device is used.

In examining the root cause of device incidents, the following questions will help:

- have problems occurred with the use of similar products? Why?
- is device use consistent with the user's expectations or intuition about the device operation?
- does the user understand the device operation?
- does the device require unexpected tasks or procedures to be performed?
- what are the critical steps in setting up and operating the device? Can they be performed adequately by users?
- how might the user set the device up incorrectly and what effects could this have?
- does the device adversely affect established processes or procedures?

---

9   *Medical Device Use-Safety: Incorporating Human Factors Engineering into Risk Management*, FDA September 2000

- is the user or environment likely to be different from originally intended? What effect could this have?

- does device use require physical, perceptual or cognitive abilities that exceed those of the user? How might the user's abilities affect their use of the device?

- can safety-critical tasks be performed incorrectly and what effects can this have?

- have all users been trained on the device? Can users operate the device safely and effectively if they don't have training?

- are storage and maintenance recommendations followed? What happens if they are not?

- do any aspects of device use seem complex? Can the operator become 'confused' when using the device?

- can the user see and hear all of the visual and auditory warnings?

- are device accessories expired, damaged, missing or otherwise different than recommended?

- has everyday handling of the device adversely affected it?

- does the device 'fail safe' or give the user sufficient indication of the failure?

3.6.9. Fault Tree Analysis (FTA)

In cases where an organisational or system failure can be identified from the beginning, fault tree analysis can be helpful in identifying possible causes. FTA starts at the system level and works down through the system, processes and sub-systems, equipment, supplies and so on, identifying all possible causes of failure. Standard symbols are used in the constructing the FTA chart to describe events and logical connections.

FTA can be used to calculate the frequency of an undesired event which may typically cause danger, expense and/or delay. The fault tree developed is a probabilistic diagram, similar to those used in decision analysis. The event of interest is known as the 'top event'. Below the top event, a fault tree can show sub-events and states that combine to produce the untoward event being examined. Alternative routes are

Figure 3.6.9.a – FTA STANDARD SYMBOLS

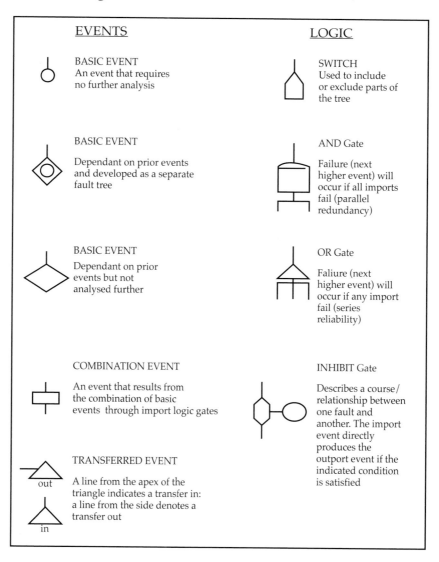

EVENTS

BASIC EVENT
An event that requires
no further analysis

BASIC EVENT

Dependant on prior events
and developed as a separate
fault tree

BASIC EVENT
Dependant on prior
events but not
analysed further

COMBINATION EVENT

An event that results from
the combination of basic
events through import logic gates

TRANSFERRED EVENT

A line from the apex of the
triangle indicates a transfer in:
a line from the side denotes a
transfer out

LOGIC

SWITCH
Used to include
or exclude parts of
the tree

AND Gate

Failure (next
higher event) will
occur if all imports
fail (parallel
redundancy)

OR Gate

Faliure (next
higher event) will
occur if any import
fail (series
reliability)

INHIBIT Gate

Describes a course/
relationship between
one fault and
another. The import
event directly
produces the
outport event if the
indicated condition
is satisfied

combined through 'or' gates, while events and states that are coincident are combined through 'and' gates. The tree is continued downwards to the level where reliable data are still available for the individual events or states being considered. FTA can also be used for design analysis, particularly for safety-critical systems in which multiple, simultaneous failure modes must be evaluated.

Figure 3.6.9.b – FAULT TREE EXAMPLE (INCOMPLETE)

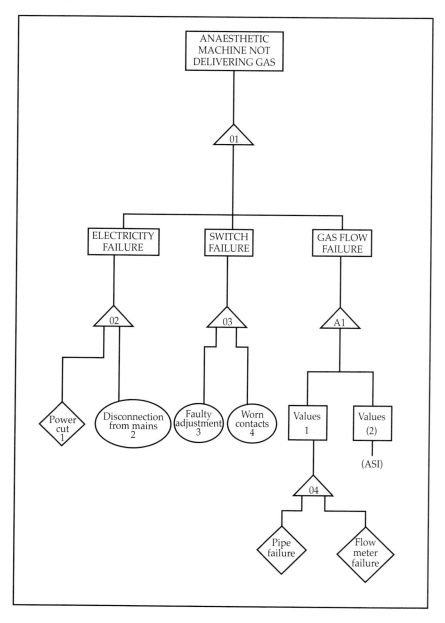

Figure 3.6.10.1 – STANDARD SYMBOLS FOR FLOWCHARTING

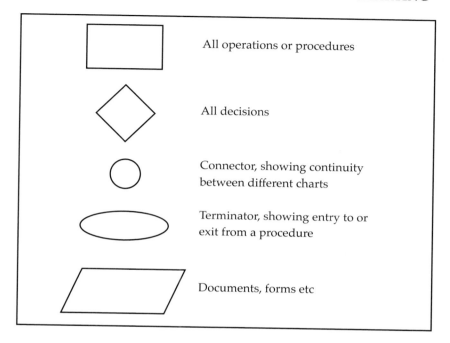

3.6.10. Flowcharting

Flowcharting is a common form of representing various processes. It is particularly useful in identifying concentrations of risk. Concentrations of risk may be readily identified through broad flow-charting of the care process and the pathway of information transfer. Identification of concentrations of risk is important to prevent a large number of patients from being harmed by a single error. Flowcharting can be carried out in various degrees of detail, but uses a set of standard symbols.

3.6.11. Level One Flowcharts

The purpose of level one flow-charting is to identify broad areas of risk which in turn indicate areas where additional quality control measures are required to prevent repetitive failures of the process. Two examples are given below. The first illustrates potential problems in the control of the reliability of specimens taken from cervical smears. All concentrations of risk require examination, assessment and risk control measures. Failures in the care and control of cervical smear specimens have been repeated in the UK in Liverpool in the mid-1980's, in Inverclyde in 1992 and Kent in the mid-90s. A similar failure of the recall system for cervical cytology occurred in London shortly after a review of the safety of cytology screening had been announced. A review of quality control had been undertaken, but did not include the reliability of recall procedures. A further example of the concentration of risk at a system point followed with a failure to recall women for further specimens as in diagram 3.6.11.a.

A further example is given in diagram 3.6.11.b. for patients referred to a single source of therapy.

There have been several examples to date of the vulnerability of single diagnostic and treatment sources to risk through basic assumptions of safety in the establishment of procedures. At one hospital, many patients received less radiotherapy dosage than anticipated through a single wrong assumption in the calibration of equipment. At another hospital many patients were affected and received a greater than planned dosage error which had been built in during the treatment planning phase. At another hospital, a failure in communication between the medical physicist and radiotherapist in respect of a new part of radiotherapy equipment again allowed a number of patients to receive the incorrect dosage.

Risk concentration planning shows a similar vulnerability in the handling of blood products and the need for quality control in the preparation of pharmaceutical and intravenous feeding preparations.

3.6.12. Level Two Flowcharts

Risks arising from care processes can be identified through the preparation and use of level two flowcharts. The accurate preparation of detailed flowcharts allows them to be used as the basis for checklists to audit compliance with recognised standards. An example is given in diagram 3.6.12.a. of the use of tourniquets in orthopaedic procedures.

The main principles to be observed in drawing flowcharts are:

1. *Make the flowchart clear, neat and easy to follow.* It will then make a good visual impact and communicate well. This implies:

   a. marking the logical start and end points;

   b. using standard flowcharting symbols;

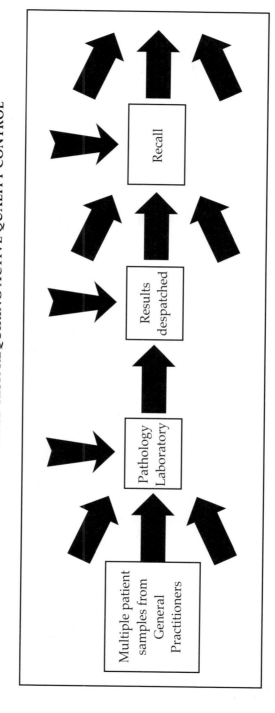

Figure 3.6.11.a – FLOWCHART OF CERVICAL RECALLS
AREAS OF CONCENTRATED RISK REQUIRING ACTIVE QUALITY CONTROL

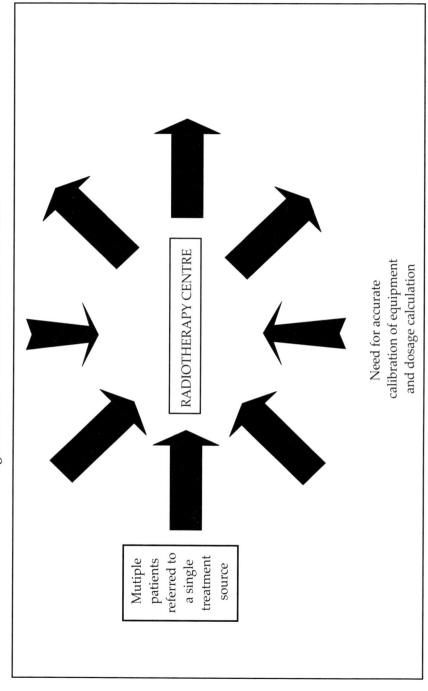

Figure 3.6.11.b – CONCENTRATION OF RISK

RADIOTHERAPY CENTRE

Mutiple patients referred to a single treatment source

Need for accurate calibration of equipment and dosage calculation

Figure 3.6.12.a – TOURNIQUETS IN OPERATING THEATRES

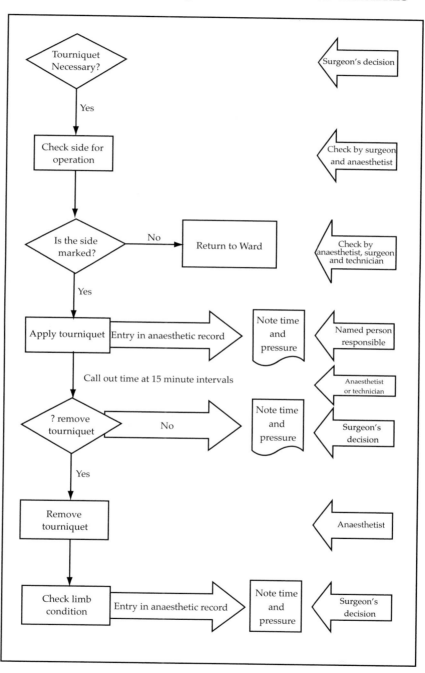

    c.   avoiding crossed flow lines;

    d.   using simple decisions, i.e. those giving yes/no or greater/equal/less than answers;

        • working in a consistent direction down or across the page.

2.   ***be logically correct.***

This implies:

    a.   no missed actions, all criteria branches accounted for;

    b.   no repeated actions;

    c.   a complete logical flow from start to end.

3.   ***work at a consistent level of detail.*** *Determine this level by reference to what* is being communicated and to whom. If a particular treatment, for example, implies a lot of actions at a lower level of detail, draw a separate flowchart to illustrate it.

4.   ***verify the validity of the flowchart by passing simple test data through it.***

It is often useful to draw a rough plan before starting the final chart so as to get the boxes arranged advantageously. A purposely incomplete example of a flowchart of a complaints procedure is shown in figure 3.6.12.b.

3.6.13. Root Cause Analysis

Root cause analysis is an analytical way of looking into the systemic cause of untoward events. The underlying principle is that a root cause can be determined by asking the question 'why?' five times to tease out the contributing factors.

These may be:

    • *Human resource issues*

        – *Are staff properly qualified and currently competent for their responsibilities?*

        – *Are staffing levels adequate?*

        – *Does planning account for contingencies to reduce effective staffing levels?*

Figure 3.6.12.b (compare with 5.2.7)
FLOWCHART (INCOMPLETE) FOR PATIENT COMPLAINT

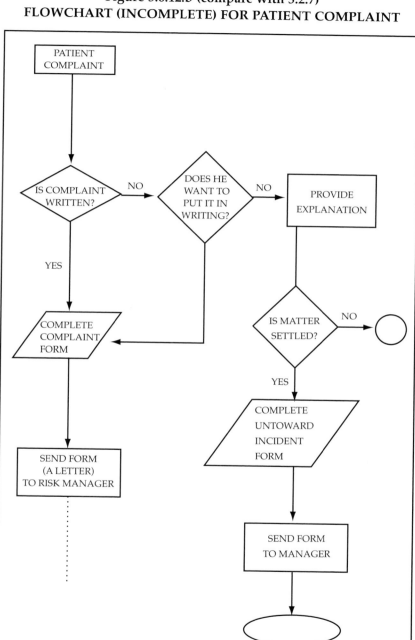

- – *Is staff performance in the operant process(es) addressed?*
- – *Can orientation and in service training be improved?*
- *Information Management issues*
  - – *Is all necessary information available when needed?*
  - – *Accurate and complete?*
  - – *Unambiguous?*
  - – *Is communication among participants adequate?*
- *Environmental management issues*
  - – *Was the physical environment appropriate for the processes being carried out?*
  - – *Are systems in place to identify environmental risks?*
  - – *Are emergency and failure mode responses adequately planned and tested?*
- *Leadership issues*
- *Corporate culture*
  - – *Is the culture conducive to risk identification and reduction?*
- *Encouragement of communication*
  - – *Are there barriers to communication of potential risk factors?*
- *Clear communication of priorities*
  - – *Is the prevention of adverse outcomes adequately communicated as a high priority?*
- *Uncontrollable factors*
  - – *How can we protect against these?*

The Association of Litigation and Risk Managers, together with the Clinical Risk Unit at University College,[10] have developed a protocol for the investigation of clinical incidents.

---

10 *How to investigate and analyse clinical incidents* BMJ 18 March 2000; 7237; 777-781

3.6.14. Cause and Effect Analysis

The 'Cause and Effect Diagram' or 'Fishbone Diagram' was first developed by Kaoru Ishikawa and the method is often referred to by his name. The principle aim of the technique is to identify and list all the possible causes that have given rise to a risk or hazard. The risk under discussion is placed in a box depicting the head of the fish.

A straight line describes the backbone and the rib bones, at 45 degrees, are used to identify every likely cause of the potential problem. Once that is done, spurs from the ribs can be used to represent further breakdowns of each cause. It does not matter if any particular cause appears more than once. On the contrary, it ought to be highlighted because it may prove to have some special significance.

The 'Fishbone Diagram' when completed resembles a skeleton of a fish. This diagram helps the risk manager and the team to separate causes from effects and to see an improvement opportunity in its totality. The following guidelines aid the construction of a Fishbone Diagram:

1. Write up the incident or accident, the effect, on the extreme right of a large piece of paper.

2. Draw in the main 'ribs' of the diagram and write a heading for each rib. The six dimensions risk management discussed above cover most problems.

3. Use brainstorming to list the causes on to the Fishbone Diagram. The brainstorming can be done in a free-style manner in which all the ribs of the diagram can be brainstormed simultaneously or the ribs can be taken one at a time and brainstormed in a more structured way.

4. Analyse the diagram to get a feeling as to the key causes of the problem.

5. In a more formal way, apply the Pareto principle to determine the 20% of the causes that contribute to 80% of the effect.

The Fishbone diagram can be prepared by a group and over a number of sessions. the whole process is a useful trigger point for further creative thinking. By building the diagram over more than one session additional benefits may accrue:

Figure 3.6.14.a – CAUSE AND EFFECT DIAGRAM – WRONG OPERATION

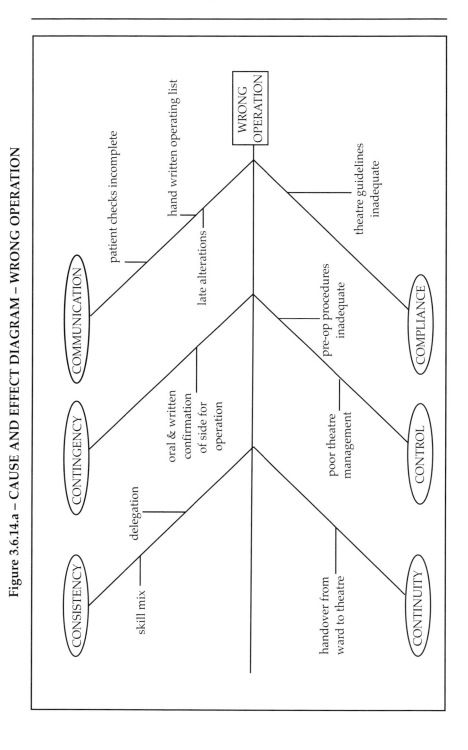

Figure 3.6.14.b – CAUSE AND EFFECT DIAGRAM – THE COMPETENT ORGANISATION

CO-ORDINATION AND COHESION

THE COMPETENT ORGANISATION

CONSISTENCY

CONTINGENCIES

CONTROLS

CONTINUITY

COMMUNICATION

COMPLIANCE

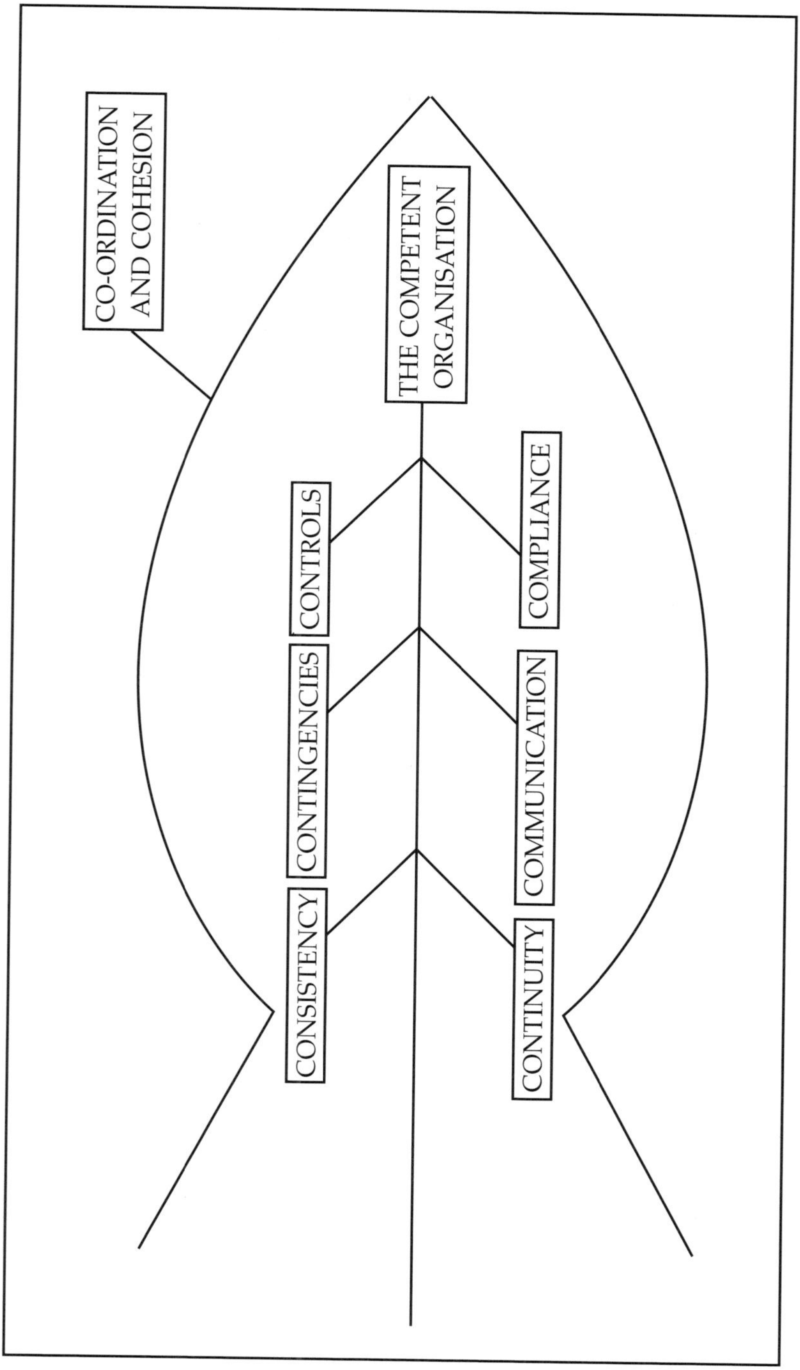

- fresh ideas regarding possible causes can arise during the interval;

- members will forget who originated every idea, thus making subsequent discussions less inhibited;

- encourages the group to continue to think about the issue and the underlying problems.

When the diagram is deemed to be complete each 'bone' or spur is discussed. The various causes are listed in ascending scale of complication. Obviously, if the cause of a problem is a simple one it is best to identify it first and remove it rather than grapple with the more complicated causes at the beginning of the cycle. Moreover, if during the discussion the group comes to the conclusion that one or more of the causes shown on the diagram are more important, circles are drawn around them. These are the causes that will receive more attention at the 'idea generation' stage of proceedings.

In a healthcare environment:

- it encourages the study of every angle of a problem before making a hasty decision as to what is wrong;

- it helps reveal the relationships and relative importance of parts of a problem;

- it focuses minds fully on the problem;

- it establishes a logical sequence for handling various parts of a problem in a systematic way;

- it prevents people concentrating on one cause or part of a problem;

- it forces the exploration of every possible solution and undermines excuses for further delay.

The effect of systematic consideration of these factors leads to the development of a tangibly competent organisation as illustrated in figure 3.6.14.b.

3.6.15. Further Data Collection and Analysis

Surveys or untoward event reporting may not identify all the data and information that is needed for establishing the root causes of a specific problem. More data may need to be collected and analysed.

3.6.16. Check sheets

Collecting the facts which demonstrate the dimensions of the 'causes' or point to potential solutions is important. The fact-based arguments developed are not only more powerful and likely to be accepted, they are also much easier to communicate. A common tool for collecting data is the 'check sheet' which is simply an organised way of recording information. The following guidelines will help in the design of check sheets:

1. Always state the full title of the data to be collected and the date or time period covered. For example:

    Partial title: 'drugs supply to and dispensing in the psychiatric unit'

    Full title: 'an analysis of the supply of drugs to and dispensing in the psychiatric unit each day over the four week period 1st May to 28th May 2001'.

2. Ensure the check sheets are uniform so that everyone uses the same form to collect comparable data.

3. Design the sheets in such a way that writing is kept to a minimum, with ticking of boxes preferred using the '5-bar gate'.

4. Collect only the amount of information needed to reduce the risk. Use statistical sampling rather than counting all items, for example.

5. Look out for things that can distort the data giving a biased result -

    –   seasonal influences;

    –   unusual events in the normal pattern of working;

    –   happenings on the outside that have an impact on the situation.

6. Aim to get a full picture by covering all the variables that occur in the situation.

3.6.17. Data Analysis

Where data has been collected it must be analysed, seeking to identify:

- trends;
- capability;
- performance;
- relationships.

Frequency tables can be created which show the most common measurements sampled and the spread, from which some conclusions can be drawn on the capability to reduce the risk.

Scatter diagrams can be used to transfer data collected which may be related or to demonstrate it has no relationship. From the grouping of two sets of data plotted on a chart, a strong or weak, positive or negative correlation can be established.

Figure 3.6.17.a – FREQUENCY TABLE

OBSERVED FACTOR	TALLY	FREQUENCY	RELATIVE FREQUENCY
A	IIII	4	4/125
B	HHI IIII	9	9/125
C	HHI HHI IIII	14	14/125
D	HHI HHI HHI HHI II	22	22/125
E	HHI HHI HHI HHI HHI HHI II	32	32/125
F	HHI HHI HHI HHI I	21	21/125
G	HHI HHI II	12	12/125
H	HHI IIII	9	9/125
I	II	2	2/125

No. of operations = 125

Figure 3.6.17.b – ANALYTICAL TOOLS AND TECHNIQUES

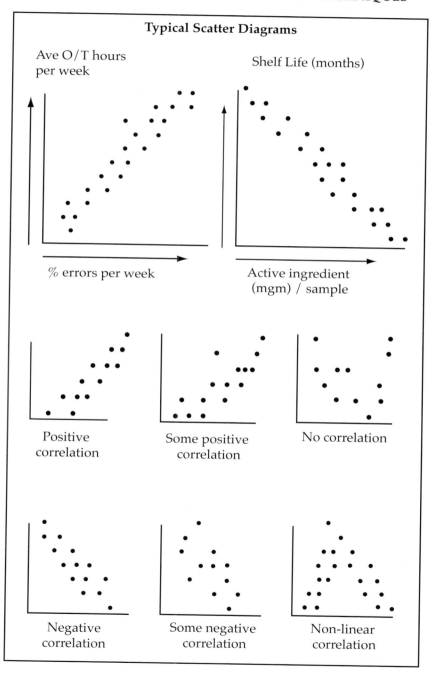

3.6.18. Bench-marking

Benchmarking is a process used to determine the best practice which will:

- indicate the opportunity for risk reduction;
- define the changes required to achieve the best practice.

The aim of bench marking is to improve standards to best practice in comparable institutions and can be applied to:

- services delivered;
- processes used;
- the people;
- organisational culture.

The means is by integration of the best practices from other organisations – not necessarily healthcare organisations – or from elsewhere within the same organisation. The process has six steps:

1. identify the aspects that should be benchmarked;
2. select the most appropriate measurements which will be used to determine risk reduction;
3. determine the current level of risk in the organisation;
4. decide who has the 'best' practice;
5. visit and determine the benchmark data, recording all relevant facts;
6. analyse and use the data to set targets and goals, and improve work processes to reduce risk and improve performance.

3.6.19. Deciding priorities – Criteria Analysis

Deciding the priority of different risk reduction options is a key step in several parts of the risk management process. As general guideline, an effective way of selecting the option which will have most impact is to rank the options using a range of criteria, i.e. the most important factors, which are selected in advance. Select up to five criteria, for example:

- benefit to patients

Figure 3.6.19.a

PRIORITISATION							
OPTIONS	CRITERIA					TOTAL POINTS	PRIORITY RANKING
	☐ POINTS	☐ POINTS	☐ POINTS	☐ POINTS	☐ POINTS		

- ease of implementation;

- resources required;

- time scale;

- urgency based on frequency and severity.

Such criteria analysis is best carried out using a form such that shown in diagram 3.6.19.a.

The ranking of the options can be determined as follows:

1. List the options in the first column.

2. List the criteria across the top.

3. Decide the relative weighting of each criterion by assigning a maximum score to each criterion, up to 10 points.

4. Consider each option in turn and allocate a score for that option under each criterion column, up to the maximum assigned for that criterion.

5. Total up all the points for each option.

6. Rank options according to the total points scored with the most important option having the highest score.

7. If the comparison does not 'feel' right, review the weightings and scores.

The approach will help objective decision-making but is time consuming.

3.6.20. Deciding Priorities – Impact Diagram

A less rigorous way of deciding which option to choose is to use an impact diagram which ranks the options against two criteria:

- high impact on what you are trying to achieve;

- ease of carrying it out.

The method requires the risk management team and manager to:

1. Identify each option with a number.

2. Plot the option on a chart by placing its number where it is judged most appropriate, relative to the other options.

Figure 3.6.20.a – IMPACT DIAGRAM

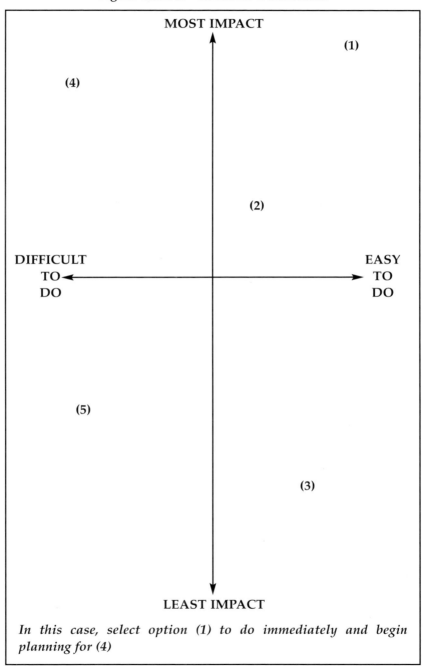

In this case, select option (1) to do immediately and begin planning for (4)

3. select the option which is easiest to do and which will have most impact on what is wanted to achieve.

3.6.21. Pareto Analysis

A Pareto diagram is a special form of vertical bar graph, or column graph, where data classifications are arranged in descending order from left to right. The only exception is a class referred to as 'others', which, if used, is always located at the extreme right of the diagram even if it is not the smallest of the classes. Pareto diagrams are used when attention needs to be directed to analysing data in a systematic manner, and when limited resources are available to apply to a number of potential risks or improvements. Thus when a risk or improvement is being selected a Pareto diagram can show which is the most significant. In other words, it can help to order priorities for what needs attention first.

The six steps to constructing a Pareto diagram are:

1. Decide how data should be classified (i.e. the major groupings) e.g.

   – by the time of day;

   – by type of incident;

   – by the equipment used;

   – by the staff group involved.

2. Use a check sheet to collect data for a specific time period.

3. Summarise the data from the check sheet:

   – arrange the data in order of sequence from largest to smallest and total them;

   – compute the percentages.

4. Construct a bar chart putting the largest bar to the extreme left.

5. Enter the cumulative percentage as line graph on to the bar graph.

6. Reference the diagram i.e. period covered, date, who prepared the diagram, the source of data.

Whenever possible a diagram showing cost should constructed. It is

Figure 3.6.21.a – PARETO HISTOGRAM

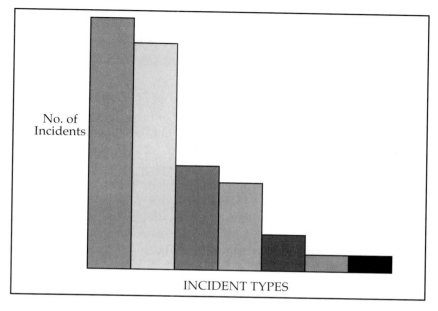

No. of
Incidents

INCIDENT TYPES

Figure 3.6.21.b – PARETO HISTOGRAM WITH CUMULATIVE %

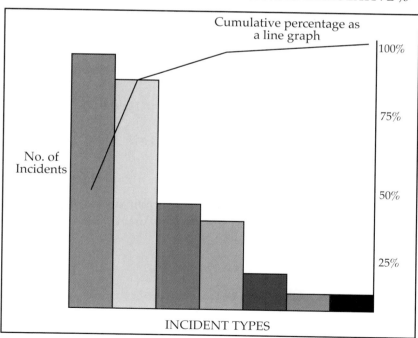

Cumulative percentage as
a line graph

100%

75%

No. of
Incidents

50%

25%

INCIDENT TYPES

often found that the position of each bar changes when comparing Pareto diagrams by cost against incident frequencies. When many types of incident are involved, the Pareto diagram becomes cumbersome. All minor categories should be grouped together under 'others' and put to the extreme right of the graph, making the diagram more manageable.

3.6.22. Force Field Analysis

Force field analysis is a technique for focusing on the factors involved in moving from a present state ('where we are now') to a future desired state ('where we want to be'). It can be used in risk management to assist in planning the implementation of a selected risk reduction option. Force field analysis consists of identifying those factors that will assist in achieving a successful implementation of the selected risk reduction measure and those which may prevent successful implementation. Once these forces have been identified and their relative strengths evaluated then ways can be found for increasing the 'helping' forces and reducing or eliminating the 'hindering' forces. The force field analysis should be based on the type of chart shown in Diagram 3.6.22.a.

The relative strengths of the forces involved can be shown by the length of the arrows used; to help in this a 1 – 5 scale can be applied to the force arrows.

3.6.23. Project Management

Project management involves planning to 'get it right' and provides:

- direction;
- control;
- support to the risk management prevention philosophy.

Risk management projects are no different from any other projects in their need to be managed properly. The degree of management required will vary depending on the size of the project, but all follow the same basic principles. Project management consists of four major areas:

- ensuring requirements for the project are agreed and understood;

Figure 3.6.22.a – FORCE FIELD ANALYSIS

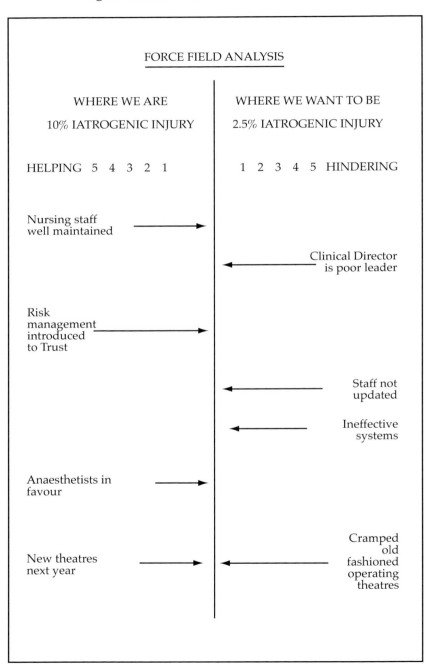

- planning the activities required;

- monitoring the progress of those activities and responding as necessary;

- reporting progress and outcomes.

Clear and agreed requirements are fundamental to producing a low risk or error free service and implementing a risk reduction project. The following needs to be known:

- who is going to benefit – patients, staff or visitors;

- where will the risk reduction be implemented;

- what level of training will be required;

- what documentation is required;

- when will it be required;

- what are the success criteria;

- does the implementation require support;

- what resources are required;

- are all requirements agreed and defined.

3.6.24. Project Planning

Match tasks and resources

- consists of assigning tasks to the people and equipment that are available. The people should have the necessary skills and training to perform the tasks assigned. Tasks may need to be rescheduled to match when a scarce resource becomes available or more resource requisitioned to cope with the project.

Decide on processes and procedures

- establish what processes and procedures the person and team will allow during carrying out the task and what standard the output from the task should meet. More complex tasks may require written procedures. Decide how the outcome of the task is to be measured and confirmed.

Identify risks and contingencies

- establish what risks there are in your plan and develop contingency plans where necessary to cope with their occurrence.

Figure 3.6.23.a – PROJECT DEVELOPMENT

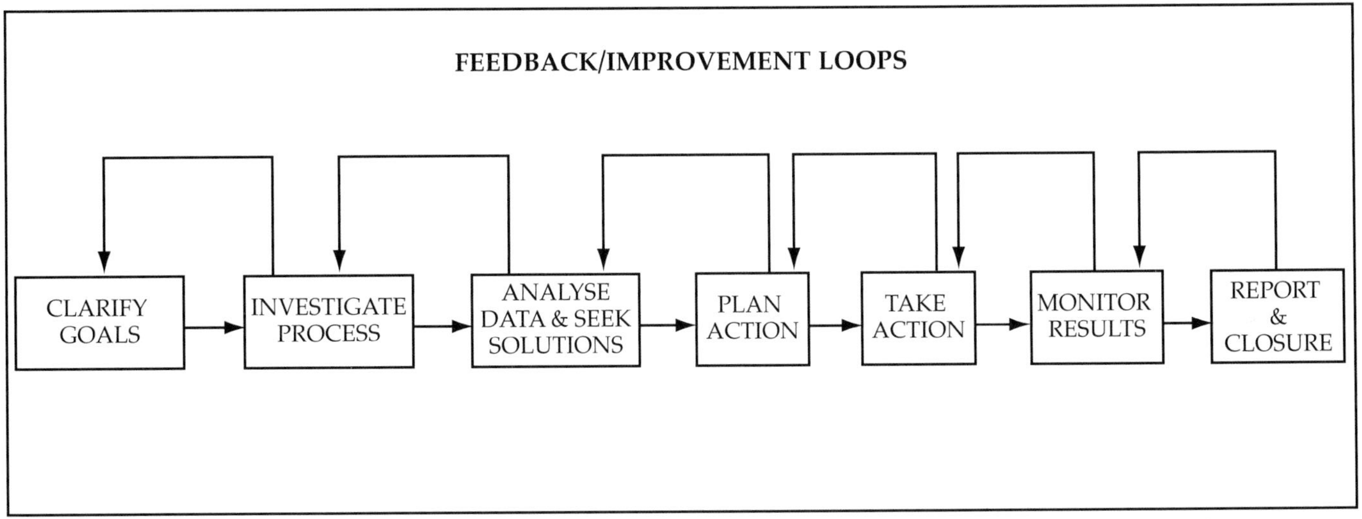

FEEDBACK/IMPROVEMENT LOOPS

CLARIFY GOALS → INVESTIGATE PROCESS → ANALYSE DATA & SEEK SOLUTIONS → PLAN ACTION → TAKE ACTION → MONITOR RESULTS → REPORT & CLOSURE

Table 3.6.24

PROJECT MANAGEMENT REFERENCES

Gill J. and Johnson P. (1991) *Research Methods for Managers* [London: Paul Chapman]

Martin J. and Spear R. (1985) *Project Manual, Block VI of Technology, A Third Level Course* [Milton Keynes, Open University]

Mayon-White, B. (ed) (1986) *Planning and Managing Change* [London: Paul Chapman]

Meredith J.R. and Mantel S.J. (1989) *Project Management – a managerial approach* 2 ed. [Wiley, Chichester]

Raimond P. (1993) *Management Projects* [London: Chapman & Hall]

Document and communicate

– not really a distinct step as it applies to all the above steps. All plans, assumptions, outcomes, risks should be documented and clearly communicated to all involved with the project.

3.6.25. Project Monitoring

Monitoring of the project is necessary to confirm that it is proceeding to the plan and to take any action necessary to cope with problems and slippage. The following is carried out during the monitoring phase:

checking progress against the plan

– as each task finishes the task can be recorded on the same form as the original plan. This allows the progress of the overall project to be seen at a glance and to determine the effect of slippage. External factors which may make an impact on the project should also be checked.

checking the outcome of tasks

– this is checking that the task has not only finished but that it has achieved the correct outcome. This may be accomplished by performing tests, trials and by reviewing. Record the results of whichever method used. Check effect of failures on the plan and re-schedule as necessary.

take appropriate action

- appropriate management action should be taken to keep the project proceeding to plan including calling for additional assistance.

3.6.26. Project Reporting

Reporting is necessary to communicate the progress and outcome of tasks both to the work group and to senior management. In addition there should be a central database of risk management projects. The central database is necessary to avoid duplication of risk management projects and to provide some means of organisation-wide co-ordination. It should be decided at the outset of the project at what frequency reports shall be produced and to what circulation. The simplest report may consist of just the up to date implementation plan. More complex reports may have written explanations of what is happening. There should be a final end project report to document any lessons learnt during the project.

3.6.27. Error Proofing a Process

Many of the risk management projects to be implemented involve trying to 'error-proof' various processes in order to eliminate faults or minimise the number or effect of mistakes. Working systems in health may be made less prone to error through a systematic identification of mistakes and using this information to identify less error prone procedures and, if necessary, restructuring the work environment and methods. This will involve asking key questions during the project, such as:

- what errors or mistakes occur at each process step?

- would changing the order of the steps prevent mistakes?

- if a step is often forgotten, would changing the order of steps make it more prominent?

- what less error-prone procedures are available?

- would changing a form prevent mistakes? Shading, giving different fonts and looks to a form, or different layout, making it easier to understand and complete can significantly affect safety.

- would using a checklist prevent mistakes?

- would clear directions, which were graphically illustrated and prominently displayed prevent mistakes? The less frequently a procedure is used, the more likely it is that operators will need easy to understand instructions to remind them how to perform the task. Even frequent procedures need instructions for the benefit of newcomers and temporary replacements

- does the work environment or layout require restructuring?

- does the work layout permit effective intervention for the patient's treatment? Examples where this fails is in the resuscitation rooms of some Accident and Emergency departments which are too small to allow access to the patient by all members of the resuscitation team.

- will the use of appropriate gadgets help reduce the propensity for error? Examples of these are the adoption of anaesthetic gas flow failure detectors and the use of pulse oximeters. Whilst not intended to be in any sense a substitute for clinical examination and judgement, they may provide a safe adjunct to observation and recording of a patient's condition under anaesthesia.

3.6.27.1. *Hazard Analysis and Critical Control Points (HACCP) PRINCIPLES*

HACCP is a systematic approach to the identification, evaluation, and control of food safety hazards based on the following seven principles:

Principle 1: Conduct a hazard analysis.

Principle 2: Determine the critical control points (CCPs).

Principle 3: Establish critical limits.

Principle 4: Establish monitoring procedures.

Principle 5: Establish corrective actions.

Principle 6: Establish verification procedures.

Principle 7: Establish record-keeping and documentation procedures.

These principles may easily be adopted as part of the error proofing process.

3.6.28. Outcome Matrices

Most risk taking situations involve options that, if selected, would eventually produce not just one outcome that matters but a number of them. As an example, imagine a patient who is trying to choose among a number of treatment options. Each of his/her potential treatments could be described with an 'outcome matrix' as in Figure 3.6.28.a.

OUTCOME MATRIX

Event		a	b	c	d	e	f	g
P	O							
O	U							
T	T							
E	C							
N	O							
T	M							
I	E							
A	S							
L								

For every time period there may be another collection of outcomes that are significant to the person or people involved.

The person's eventual satisfaction with their experience of a healthcare intervention would depend on which outcomes in the various categories are eventually realised, an eventual reality. Such an eventual reality can be seen as a collection or vector of outcomes. Outcome matrices help facilitate the discussion of losses as well as other loss issues.

The example used for the outcome matrix implicates two classes of reference:

- status quo references;
- non-status quo references.

A status quo reference is whatever a person presently has. ..... How is it determined what is a reference outcome and, by implication, what is considered a loss? In various situations, practitioners simply declare reference outcomes by fiat, so that they can get on with their work.

For instance in epidemiology, the implicit reference is sometimes the level of illness in a particular year. On other occasions, it is the level in another comparable country. "Objective risk" measures are then constructed from these standard reference outcomes. Such objectively defined references, losses and risk measures have been retained over the years because the analyses that rely on them have (e.g. perinatal mortality) been considered beneficial.

Most frequently, moreover, it seems that references are adopted for a variety of reasons. Hence most of them form the foundations of subjective rather than objective risk. (See figure 3.6.28.b.)

Figure 3.6.28.b – SUBJECTIVE OUTCOMES ASSESSMENT

Reference	Explanation
Personal Average (Adaption level)	Representative of those outcomes which have been experienced most often in the past and therefore reasonbly expected in the future
Situational Average	Applies to a situation rather than an individual; commonly employed in the risk measures used in finance, e.g. expected returns on investments
Target (Aspiration)	Outcome a person/group actually works to attain, e.g. iatrogenic injuries. Can be set internally or externally
'Best possible'	Most attractive outcome that is possible in given situations, e.g. 1% iatronic injury rate, established as a reference because cannot imagine any hospital doing better
Regret	Outcome that would have been attained, or thought would have been, if a competing option had been adopted

RISK MANAGEMENT SYSTEM – NHS CONTROLS ASSURANCE STANDARDS

November 1999

1 Board level responsibility for risk management is clearly defined and there are clear lines of accountability for risk management throughout the organisation, leading to the Board.

2 There is a Board sub-committee overseeing risk management

3 There is a Board-approved policy and strategy for managing risk that identifies accountability arrangements, resources available and contains guidance on what may be regarded as acceptable risk within the organisation

4 The risk management policy and strategy is communicated to all staff and is made available to the public and other stakeholders

5 There is a Board approved risk management plan that is reviewed by the Board at least annually

6 Individual directorates/departments have risk management policies and strategies which comply with the organisational risk management policy and strategy

7 Individual directorates/departments have risk management plans which are periodically reviewed and communicated to the Risk Management Committee

8 There is a designated complaints manager who is readily accessible to the public, and well-publicised arrangements are in place for making a complaint

9 Front line staff are empowered to deal with complaints on the spot

10 Independent review panels, when they are required, are established in full accordance with the NHS complaints procedure

11 There is a dedicated claims/litigation manager who is knowledgeable about health care law, civil litigation practices and procedures and the organisation's complaint procedure

12 Hazards are systematically identified, recorded, reported managed and analysed in accordance with agreed policy

13 Incidents, including ill health, are systematically identified, recorded and reported to management in accordance with an agreed policy of positive, non-punitive reporting

14 All reported incidents are graded according to severity and, where appropriate, investigated to determine underlying causes

15 All reported incidents are responded to and managed in accordance with agreed policy

16 All reportable incidents are communicated to the relevant external body in accordance with relevant reporting requirements

17 All reportable incidents are systematically analysed to identify trends and produce information for management review and action

18 All complaints are recorded, reported and managed in accordance with the requirements of the NHS Complaints Procedure

19 All recorded complaints are systematically analysed to identify trends and produce information for management review and action

20 Reports are published on complaints handling which includes patient's comments and suggestions and the results of surveys of patient satisfaction on the way in which complaints are handled

21 All reported claims are systematically managed in accordance with agreed policy

22 All claims are systematically analysed to identify trends for management review and action

23 There is an organisation-wide risk register that is populated by data representing all known risks

24 Risks are systematically identified and recorded on a continuous basis

25 All identified risks are systematically assessed and prioritised

26 The range of options for dealing with risk are assessed and risk treatment plans are implemented. Where appropriate, risk treatments are implemented in order of priority

27 All identified risks, and the effectiveness of implemented risk treatments are monitored and reviewed on a continuous basis

28 The range of options for dealing with risk are assessed and risk treatment plans are implemented. Where appropriate, risk treatments are implemented in order of priority

29 All relevant stakeholders are kept informed and, where appropriate, consulted on the management of significant risks faced by the organisation

30 An annual report is produced for the Board to demonstrate the risk management system's continuing suitability and effectiveness in satisfying the organisation's risk management policy and strategy

31 The organisation provides realistic resources to implement and support risk management

32 All employees, including managers and the Board, are provided, where appropriate, with adequate risk management information, instruction and training

33 Key indicators capable of showing improvements in management of risk and/or providing early warning of risk are used at all levels of the organisation, including the Board, and the efficacy and usefulness of the indicators is reviewed regularly

34 The risk management system is monitored and reviewed by management and the Board in order to make improvements to the system

35 The internal Audit function, aided as necessary by relevant technical specialists, carries out periodic audits to provide assurances to the Board that a suitable risk management system which conforms to this standard is in place and working properly

EMERGENCY PREPAREDNESS – CONTROLS ASSURANCE STANDARD
November 1999

1 Board level responsibility for emergency planning is clearly defined and there are clear lines of accountability throughout the organisation, leading to the board.

2 There is a documented major incident and service continuity plan, or plans, for the organisation

3 All feasible/realistic types of emergency are addressed in the major incident and service continuity plans

4 All scenarios in the major incident and service continuity plan(s) involve robust arrangements for the operational and financial recovery from such incidents

5 All internal and external stakeholders in the major incident and service continuity plan are consulted and collaborated with concerning their role in the plan(s)

6 Emergency preparedness tests are conducted as required to ensure the major incident and service continuity plan is enacted rapidly, and those named can be notified quickly

7 A review of the major incident and service continuity plan is undertaken regularly, leading where necessary to the identification of areas for improvement and implementation of such improvements.

8 Sufficient funding and resourcing is provided to ensure that the organisation can respond effectively to major incidents.

9 The organisation has access to up-to-date guidance relating to emergency planning.

10 All staff receive emergency preparedness training that is commensurate with their role in the major incident and service continuity plan.

11 Key indicators capable of showing improvements in emergency preparedness, and/or providing early warning of risk are used at all levels of the organisation, including the board, and the efficacy and usefulness of the indicators is reviewed regularly.

12 The system in place for emergency preparedness is monitored and reviewed by management and the board in order to make improvements to the system.

13 The Internal Audit function, aided as necessary by relevant technical specialists, carries out periodic audits to provide assurance to the board that a system of emergency preparedness is in place that conforms to the requirements of this standard.

4

ENVIRONMENTAL SAFETY AND HEALTH RECORDS

Environmental and organisational safety concerns for the risk manager in the healthcare field fall primarily under:

- health and safety;

- fire safety;

- security concerns;

- people;

- property;

- information – including health records and reports;

- disposal of waste and environmental pollution;

- ionising radiations.

4.1   STATUTORY FRAMEWORK

The principal legislation that forms the statutory framework in which the healthcare risk manager must operate is the Health and Safety at Work etc. Act, 1974. The Act seeks to secure the health, safety and welfare of persons at work and to protect members of the public from risks that might be created by the work of others. Crown immunity from the provisions of the Act was removed by amendment in 1987. The Health and Safety at Work etc. Act is the primary piece of legislation it has been extended to include, for example, any activity involving genetic manipulation or the keeping and handling of certain pathogens. As a result of new European Union Directives (nick-named the '6-pack'), new regulations came in to effect from the beginning of 1993. The current regulations and requirements on both employers and employees are the The Management of Health and Safety at Work

Diagram 4.1 –
EXAMPLES OF RELEVANT LEGISLATION COMPRISING THE
LEGAL FRAMEWORK FOR HEALTH AND SAFETY

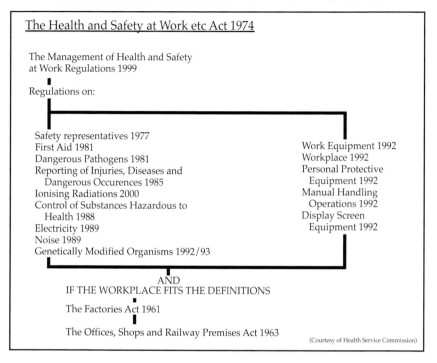

The Health and Safety at Work etc Act 1974

The Management of Health and Safety
at Work Regulations 1999

Regulations on:

Safety representatives 1977
First Aid 1981
Dangerous Pathogens 1981
Reporting of Injuries, Diseases and
   Dangerous Occurences 1985
Ionising Radiations 2000
Control of Substances Hazardous to
   Health 1988
Electricity 1989
Noise 1989
Genetically Modified Organisms 1992/93

Work Equipment 1992
Workplace 1992
Personal Protective
   Equipment 1992
Manual Handling
   Operations 1992
Display Screen
   Equipment 1992

AND
IF THE WORKPLACE FITS THE DEFINITIONS

The Factories Act 1961

The Offices, Shops and Railway Premises Act 1963

(Courtesy of Health Service Commission)

Regulations 1999[1]. Diagram 4.1. sets out examples of the relevant legislation for health and safety.

The Health and Safety Commission (HSC) requires NHS Trusts, the Health Commissions and the independent sector to establish effective systems to manage health and safety. Trust directors and managers, including clinical managers, alongside their budgetary responsibilities, have clear and defined responsibility for health and safety. Risk managers need to integrate the knowledge and skills into risk management systems of a broad range of staff – scientific (radiographers, laboratory workers, etc.) and technical (estate managers, electricians, plumbers, etc.) – who should be encouraged to understand in detail the implications of the specific regulations

1   1999 No. 3242 Health and Safety, *The Management of Health and Safety at Work Regulations 1999*

applicable in their work areas. The HSC together with the NHS Executive encourages the integration of health and safety measures within risk and business management because:

- the law requires it and individuals can be prosecuted if their organisation has broken the law through their wilful consent or neglect;

- the high cost of poor health and safety performance is a drain on resources (the Health and Safety Executive estimate that at least 5% of a hospital's annual running costs are taken up with accidents);

- efficiency savings can be gained by integrating health and safety management into the general process of business management;

- the NHS aims to become an exemplary employer (the aim is that, by 2004, health and safety performance across the health care sector will present a model for others to emulate);

- quality management is a seamless process and good health and safety practice will have effects on clinical care and the containment of medical mishap.

Section 2 of the Act sets out the general duties owed by employers to their employees. It is the duty of every employer to ensure, "so far as it is reasonably practicable", the health, safety and welfare at work of all his employees. This includes safety and risk in relation to:

- the provision and maintenance of plant and systems;

- arrangements in connection with the use, handling, storage and transport of articles and substances;

- information, instruction, training and supervision of employees;

- maintenance of premises or places of work and access to and egress from those places of work;

- the immediate working environment.

Section 3 sets out the general duties owed by employers to members of the public other than their employees. The duty is that persons not in the Trust's employment are not exposed to risks to their health and safety from the way the Trust conducts their business.

Section 4 covers the duties owed by people who have, to any extent, control of the workplace to persons who are not employees.

It is a criminal offence to fail to discharge any of the duties laid down in the Act and subsequent regulations, whether intently or by neglect.

Two sets of regulations are of particular importance – Reporting of Injuries, Diseases and Dangerous Occurrences Regulations (RIDDOR) and the Control of Substances Hazardous to Health Regulations (COSHH). The former stipulates the compulsory recording and reporting of accidents and incidents.

'Reportable accidents' include all fatal and major injuries and any that result in incapacity from carrying out normal work for more than three days. If a person at work has one of the diseases listed in the regulations and if he has engaged in the activity listed, that disease must be reported. The accidents and incidents covered by the regulations must be reported directly to the Health and Safety Executive, in a defined format (the Statutory Reporting Form). **It is important to realise that this applies to accidents involving patients and visitors as well as staff.** This statutory duty to record and report accidents and incidents can be used to establish a more extensive 'untoward event recording system' as a key tool of risk management (see Chapter 3). Many accidents and potentially dangerous incidents will occur that will fall outside the statutory reporting criteria, but can be used as a valuable source of information.

The COSHH regulations expand and clarify the duties in respect of hazardous substances to which employers, employees and others may be exposed. COSHH specifically requires that risk assessments are made of all hazardous substances likely to be encountered as a result of a work activity. Clinical waste falls within the scope of these regulations and it is essential that a written health and safety policy includes safe handling and disposal of clinical waste, e.g.,

- all staff including ancillary be suitably trained and protected;
- domestic and other waste collection should not be used for clinical waste;
- contaminated sharps and needles should be placed in a sharps container made to current European standards;
- all clinical waste must be clearly identified before it is removed for disposal. (See below for more detail).

4.1.1 The Management of Health and Safety at Work Regulations 1999

The Management of Health and Safety at Work Regulations 1999 set down procedures through which the risk manager is able to demonstrate compliance with the law by:

- assessing health and safety risks to patients, employees and visitors to identify preventive and protective measures required by law and performing risk assessments. (Visitors include patient's relatives and friends, contractors, employees provided by agencies and employees of other employers on multi-occupancy sites. Temporary workers are also covered);

- undertaking risk assessments in respect of new or expectant mothers;

- ensuring that young persons are protected;

- making arrangements for putting into practice the preventive and protective measures including planning, organisation, control, monitoring and review;

- providing appropriate health surveillance;

- appointing competent persons;

- setting up procedures to deal with serious and imminent danger;

- ensuring contact with external services for first aid, emergency medical care and rescue work;

- providing employees with understandable information;

- providing employees with adequate training and instruction;

- co-operating and co-ordinating with other employers where they share premises or workplaces;

- consulting with safety representatives.

(Courtesy of the Health and Safety Commission)

These procedures are compatible with risk programmes and offer a mechanism for integration with clinical risk management and general and business risk management.

Separate health and safety policies will need to be compiled for each department or directorate. Some of the regulations will be applicable in some areas, but not in others and necessarily local expert knowledge will be needed to adapt control measures more precisely to needs. Again the Health and Safety Commission has laid down guidelines as to what a directorate or departmental policy would need to demonstrate:

- the policy is clearly written;

- the policy sets out the people responsible and the procedures to be followed for identifying hazards, assessing risks and preventing or controlling them;

- all staff know about and understand the policy;

- the departmental or directorate policy is compatible with the overall organisation's policy;

- the policy is up to date and there is a mechanism for its regular review and amendment, if necessary;

- the policy lays down how performance is scrutinised and reviewed;

- the policy works and is effective.

The risk manager will have to ensure that appropriate policies and programmes are being promulgated, organised and implemented throughout the organisation. The risk manager cannot be expected to have responsibility for or in depth knowledge of how the policies are implemented.

Senior management, together with the risk manager, should ensure supportive health and safety culture, structure and systems are put into place in order to secure compliance. This entails:

- a central committee with responsibility for overall risk management and health and safety programmes led by a member of the Board of management and reporting to the Board;

- line management responsibility for health and safety;

- competent individuals appointed, with time, resources and authority, to monitor and review health and safety;

- involvement of employees and safety representatives in policy formulation and development including co-operation and co-ordination between employers on the same site and the statutory consultation with trade union appointed safety representatives;

- effective communication – e.g. written material, discussion, training, supervision – to ensure understanding and effective implementation;

- good personnel practices in recruitment, induction, deployment, training and so on to ensure competence in health and safety matters;

- competent people appointed to assist employers to comply with legislation.

The last point is a requirement of the Management Regulations. The Health and Safety Commission's *Management of health and safety at work: Approved Code of Practice (HSC, 1992)* helps to identify what 'competence' means in health and safety terms. The HSC has also published "Management of Health and Safety in the Health Services: Information for Directors and Managers" which is a useful guide to the main elements of health and safety management. It groups performance standards into three:

- performance standards for management action;

- performance standards for the assessment, prevention and control of risks;

- performance standards for documentation.

The first relates to the management process and the functions of control, co-operation, communication and competence. The second group is for the control of risks and the use of risk management methods (Chapter 3) for hazard identification and risk assessment. The standards take the form of outcome standards which should take the legal requirements as the minimum acceptable standard. The third group is necessary in order to demonstrate compliance with the minimum standards of performance. Compliance with the COSHH Regulations should also be routinely assessed and monitored through the Health and Safety procedures. Occupational exposure to chemicals such as medical gases and glutaraldehyde should particularly be assessed.

Safety of buildings and falls from windows

There have been 20 deaths directly as a result of falls in ten years in NHS hospitals and 13 in private nursing homes. 46 falls reported to the Health and Safety Executive resulted in either death or serious injury. A high proportion of cases have included psychiatric or confused elderly patients.

Regulation 14(1)(a) of the Workplace (Health, Safety and Welfare) Regulations 1992 states:

Every window....shall be of safe material or be protected against breakage...where necessary for reasons of health and safety.

Regulation 15 of the above states:

No window...shall be in a position when opened which is likely to expose any person in the workplace to a risk to his health and safety.

4.1.2   COSHH Evaluation

When performing a COSHH evaluation, the risk manager will need to separate chemicals and biological hazards into priority groups. This may be conveniently undertaken by following the Department of Health guidelines which separate:

Priority Group 1: High risk substances requiring extensive controls;

Priority Group 2: Recognised health hazard, but low exposure or low health hazard;

Priority Group 3: Little or no hazard.

The health effects of substances should be found on the hazard data sheets.

Control measures in place should include:

- training
- systems of work
- emergency procedures
- usage
- local ventilation
- general ventilation

- waste disposal

- provision of personal protective equipment

- air monitoring

An additional and perhaps unexpected hazard may arise from the use of rubber gloves, the use of which is designed to reduce the risks to staff of HIV, hepatitis B and hepatitis C. Rubber gloves are made with latex and accelerators as part of the manufacturing process. Both of these are allergens. The use of gloves with excess allergens, which arises from insufficient washing in the manufacturing process, may lead to sensitisation, contact dermatitis and systemic immune allergic response. It has been estimated that 10% of operating staff in the U.S.A. have developed allergies to rubber through the use of rubber gloves.

4.1.3   Aldehydes – Glutaraldehyde and Formaldehyde

Aldehydes are used extensively in health care as disinfectants and as a preservative. They are irritant chemicals for which special precautions must be taken to prevent harm to workers. All disinfectants and detergents should be stored in clearly labelled containers.

Glutaraldehyde is commonly used to disinfect surgical instruments, particularly on endoscopy units. It warrants special consideration as an irritant liquid. Skin contact may result in sensitisation dermatitis. Exposure to glutaraldehyde vapour may cause eye irritation, nasal irritation or precipitate an acute episode of bronchospasm.

Vapour is easily formed from the liquid and glutaraldehyde should therefore be used in enclosed fume cupboards fitted with adequate local exhaust ventilation. Goggles and gloves should be worn when the glutaraldehyde liquid is made up and disposed of. Latex gloves may give adequate protection for short periods of exposure. Longer exposure needs nitrile rubber gloves for better protection.

Glutaraldehyde has a Health and Safety Executive maximum exposure limit of 0.05 parts per million (short-term exposure limit, 15 minute reference period), although susceptible people will exhibit respiratory symptoms below this level.

Formaldehyde (known as formalin when in solution at 38-40% concentration) is used to preserve tissue in pathology, as a disinfectant in general use and to sterilise instruments in steam vapour. It is a potent irritant for which special precautions should be taken. Respiratory irritation has been seen at concentrations of 0.2-0.3 parts per million (ppm). Formaldehyde has a maximum exposure limit of 2ppm and a time weighted average exposure (TWA) of 2ppm.

Formaldehyde vapour is used to sterilise instruments in Sterile Supply Departments. The quality of the seals in the sterilising system need to be regularly checked under the Control of Substances Hazardous to Health inspections.

4.1.4   Latex allergies – the Implication for Clinical Risk

The use of latex gloves and other latex medical products has increased significantly in response to the AIDS threat and a growing recognition of bodily fluids as the source of transmitting infectious agents. This increase has been accompanied by a growing number of people with latex sensitivity. The risk needs to be managed, both in general practice and hospital settings. Although natural rubber products have been widely used for many years, allergic reactions have been recognised only relatively recently.

A significant proportion of the one million people working in the NHS is exposed to natural rubber or latex products and the risk of sensitivity to them. Additionally, a number of patients are also exposed to the risk. These include those with spina bifida and a history of multiple surgical and medical procedures. In one study, 60% of patients with spina bifida had latex allergy as defined by history, serological and/or skin prick tests. It is likely that 10% of patients with spina bifida will have clinical allergy and 50-60% will have circulating IgE antibodies specific for latex.

A further study of 224 hospital employees showed 17% tested positive for latex glove extracts. These included nurses, laboratory technicians, dental personnel, respiratory therapists and doctors. One French study of patients showed an allergy prevalence rate of over 36% in those patients with a history of both atopy and exposure to latex.

Individuals sensitive to avocado, chestnut or banana show an increased likelihood of sensitisation to rubber latex.

Types of Reaction to Latex

There are three different types of reactions to natural rubber latex and the accelerators used in product manufacture. These are irritation, delayed hypersensitivity (allergic contact dermatitis) and immediate hypersensitivity (anaphylaxis).

Irritation is classed as a non allergic condition. In most affected people the skin is dry and crusty and the symptoms subside when exposure and contact with latex ceases.

A delayed hypersensitivity response (type IV) typically occurs between six and forty eight hours after contact with latex. The area of skin in contact becomes dry, crusty with eruptions appearing as blisters and sores. Repeated exposure causes the reaction to extend beyond the area of contact. It is thought that the accelerators used in manufacture of gloves cause this reaction. In some cases the individual may become sensitive to latex in other products.

Anaphylaxis, or immediate hypersensitivity (type I), is mediated by the circulating immunoglobulin, IgE. It is a reaction to the natural protein residue found in natural rubber latex. An initial reaction of an itching rash is accompanied by systemic symptoms including itching of the eyes, swellings of the lips or tongue, breathlessness, dizziness, abdominal pain, nausea, hypo tension, shock and potentially, death.

POWDERED GLOVES

The use of powdered gloves increases the risk of latex allergy, not only to the user, but also to those in the surrounding area. Powdered gloves have a higher level of extractable protein than powder free gloves. When powdered gloves are used, the powder may be introduced into the patient's body or come into contact with mucous membranes causing sensitisation and allergic reactions. Glove powder is a well-documented cause of post-operative intra-abdominal adhesions. The protein residue in latex readily attaches to the modified starch powder used as a lubricant in gloves allowing airborne transmission and absorption.

MANAGING THE RISKS

As we have seen, all employers have a duty to carry out a risk assessment of the workplace under the COSHH Regulations (1999). The risk assessment needs also to include suitable control measures and necessary health surveillance. Specific information on latex allergy should be available at the workplace.

From July 1998 all medical gloves have been required to carry the CE marking under the provisions of the Medical Devices Directive (93/42/EEC). This marking indicates that the product complies with the Essential Requirements for safety and performance.

Latex gloves tend to fall into the following categories:

Surgical (sterile)

Examination (sterile or non sterile)

The risk assessment should take into account whether sterile gloves are being used unnecessarily and whether non-latex gloves, such as vinyl or neoprene, can reasonably be substituted. Sensitised staff should be initially advised to switch to powder free gloves with low extractable protein levels. If this is not effective the use of a non-latex glove between the latex glove and hand is recommended or switching to non-latex gloves.

RISKS TO PATIENTS

Staff should be aware of the dangers of latex allergy for patients. A clear history should be taken of allergies as part of the routine assessment. A pointer to latex allergy may be swelling of the lips or itching after blowing up balloons. Some patients may have experienced a reaction when being examined at the dentists or for internal examinations. Some may react to condoms or diaphragms.

Where a type I allergy is confirmed and surgical or other medical procedures are required, the patient must be treated in an environment where the risks are minimised and where anaphylaxis can be treated. Non-latex gloves should be used. Where a surgical procedure is required, placing the patient first on the list will minimise the risk of airborne powder exposure. In the event of anaphylaxis, it is well to remember that ordinary syringes contain latex. Glass syringes should therefore be used and the anaesthetic equipment checked for latex components.

NHS Controls Assurance Standards – Health and Safety November 1999

1 Board level responsibility for health and safety is clearly defined and there are clear lines of accountability for health and safety matters throughout the organisation, leading to the Board

2 There is a health and safety committee, constituted and working according to the requirements laid down in HSC98/064 and Section 2(7) of HASAWA, which facilitates consultation on all health and safety matters

3 The organisation has a health and safety policy that complies with the requirements of the HASAWA, HSAC guidance and HSG(97)6

4 Individual directorates and departments have health and safety policies, which are compatible with the organisation health and safety policy

5 All staff are made aware of the organisation's health and safety policy and, where appropriate, any directorate and departmental policy

6 Staff and safety representatives are properly consulted on health and safety matters

7 Compliance with health and safety legislation is routinely monitored

8 Health and safety hazards and incidents, including injuries, diseases and dangerous occurrences, are dealt with in accordance with the processes contained in the risk management system standard

9 Where two or more employers share the workplace, there is demonstrable evidence of co-operation and co-ordination of health and safety measures

10 Contractors are briefed on health and safety requirements and, where appropriate, contractual obligations are formally notified

11 Non-routine, new work and any foreseeable events of serious or imminent danger are dealt with in accordance with pre-determined emergency plans

12 The effectiveness with which management of health and safety responsibilities has been carried out is systematically assessed within individual performance reviews

13 All staff have access to a confidential occupational health service

14 Health and safety risks are systematically identified and recorded on a continuous basis

15 All identified health and safety risks are systematically analysed and prioritised

16 The range of options for dealing with health and safety risks are assessed and risk treatment plans are implemented in order of priority and, where appropriate, alongside other risk treatments which are necessary to deal with wider risks faced by the organisation

17 All identified health and safety risks and the effectiveness of implemented risk treatments are monitored and reviewed on a continuous basis

18 The Board is informed of and, where necessary, consulted upon all significant health and safety risks and associated treatment plans on a continuous basis

19 Other stakeholders are kept informed and, where appropriate, consulted on the management of health and safety risk

20 There are sufficient 'competent persons' to provide health and safety assistance to the organisation

21 There is access to up-to-date information on health and safety legislation and guidance, including NHS Executive guidance, to all within the organisation who require the information

22 Employees, including managers and the Board, are provided with adequate information, instruction and training on health and safety matters

23 Key indicators capable of showing improvements in health and safety management and/or providing early warning of risk are used at all levels of the organisation, including the Board, and the efficacy and usefulness of the indicators is reviewed regularly

24 The system in place for health and safety management, including risk management arrangements, is monitored and reviewed by the management and the Board in order to make improvements to the system

25 The Internal Audit function, in conjunction with a health and safety specialist, carries out periodic audits to provide assurances to the Board that a suitable system of infection control which conforms to this standard is in place and working properly

4.2   FIRE SAFETY

Fire safety within healthcare premises must be a priority for risk managers. A fire in a hospital poses major threats not only to patients and staff, but also the potential of the unit to continue to provide care.

In 1989 there were 4 deaths and 128 other casualties in 2,412 reported fires in U.K. hospitals. Of these, 29 spread beyond the room of origin and 102 were discovered later than 30 minutes of starting. Although 28.5 % were associated with smokers' materials, the highest number were deliberately started. This trend has continued with 25% of hospital fires reported as cases of arson. Waste material was the most common material first ignited (23.5%).

It is essential that any fire strategy is based upon the avoidance of fire.

If a fire occurs, there needs to be a means of:

- rapid detection;
- containment;
- control.

These contingencies in turn need to be supported by procedures for removing patients to a place of safety which are:

- reliable;
- rehearsed.

All units, both NHS Trusts and directly managed units are subject to the recommendations on fire safety which have been issued by NHS Estates under the title *Firecode*. This is a systematic approach to reduce the potential for fires in health service premises. The Code is laid out in a series of documents published by NHS Estates to formalise and set standards for the layout, design, construction and fire safety management of hospitals and other healthcare premises. The Code places an obligation upon the NHS Management Executive to monitor health service compliance with its provisions. In HSC 1999/191 the NHS Executive stated the aim that full compliance with fire safety must be achieved by 31 March 2003 and a 90% compliance with Health and Safety backlog by 31 March 2002.

4.2.1 Principle Statutes Relating to Fire Safety

The main Acts with a bearing on fire safety in NHS healthcare premises are:

- The Fire Services Act 1947;
- The Health and Safety at Work etc. Act 1974;
- The Fire Precautions Act 1971 as amended by the Fire Safety and Safety of Places of Sport Act 1987;
- The Building Act 1984;
- The Registered Homes Act 1984;
- The Housing Act 1985 as amended by the Local Government and Housing Act 1989.
- Fire Precautions (Workplace) Regulations 1997

Following the NHS and Community Care Act 1990, the Secretary of State retained powers of direction which require NHS healthcare premises, including NHS Trust premises, to comply with Firecode. Section 60 of the NHS and Community Care Act came into effect from 1st April 1991 which removed Crown immunity. No Crown immunities in respect of fire precautions apply to special hospitals. All NHS staff and its fire prevention advisers are now subject to the statutory enforcement of fire safety provisions.

The Fire Precautions (Places of Work) Regulations have been introduced following the EC Directives 89/391/EEC and 89/654/EEC and have been published by NHS Estates as the Health Technical Memorandum 86 and requires active fire risk assessments in hospitals.

4.2.2 Fire Certificates

NHS premises may or may not need a fire certificate to be issued by the local fire authority under the Fire Precautions Act 1971. The difference in requirements depends upon whether the area is put to a designated use and if the number of employees exceeds specified limits. Certificates are required for premises such as offices and factories where:

- more than twenty people are employed;
- more than ten are employed on other than the ground floor;
- there are two or more designated premises in a building and the aggregate number of people working within exceeds twenty, or ten elsewhere than on the ground floor;
- there are designated factory premises in the facility;
- explosives or highly flammable materials are stored or used.

Hospital wards and other parts of hospitals directly concerned with the nursing and treatment of patients are not subject to fire certificates, but may be inspected by the local fire authority which is able to issue, under Section 10 of the Act, requirements for improvements where there are serious risks of fire. As part of an escalation process, if the hospital does not comply, the fire authority is able to issue Prohibition Notices and appoint inspectors who have powers of entry and inspection. Prohibition Notices enable the facility to be closed.

Parts of a hospital activity which may be regarded as factory activity include:

- hospital maintenance workshops;

- ambulance maintenance workshops;

- laundries (with boiler houses);

- laboratories (having manufacturing processes);

- hospital sterilising and disinfecting units;

- catering production units (cook/freeze or chill meal production);

- electrical stations (including standby generation);

- boiler houses;

- industrial therapy units (providing work/employment for long-stay patients);

- central sterile supply departments;

- theatre sterile supply departments;

- pharmaceutical departments (manufacturing or bulk supply work);

- hospital medical photographic departments;

- radiotherapy shielding workshops (substantial manufacturing);

- radiological departments (X-ray processing and large units);

- renal units (maintenance and refurbishment areas);

- certain large stores/warehouses undertaking "factory processes".

An NHS Trust is able to apply for a fire certificate to the Head of the local fire authority in whose area the premises are situated.

4.2.3   Principles of Fire Safety in Health Care Premises

The key principles of fire safety in NHS premises are laid down in the 'Firecode Policy and Principles' as:

- *if at all possible, outbreaks of fire do not occur;*

- *fires that do occur are rapidly detected, an alarm is given and the fire brigade is called;*

- *there is a safe means of escape from all endangered areas to places of safety for everyone on the premises;*

- *the fire is extinguished as quickly as possible;*

- *first aid fire-fighting is attempted, if it is safe to do so;*

- *the development and spread of any fire is delayed and contained as long as possible by structural and other means;*

- *endangered areas are evacuated quickly to a pre-arranged and rehearsed procedure;*

- *evacuated areas are checked for the presence of patients and other persons and that a roll call for this purpose has been completed.*

4.2.4   Factors Contributing to Fire Safety

Fire safety is inevitably the product of a combination of human and physical factors. These include:

4.2.4.1 *Physical Factors:*

Careful building design and construction which complies with

- approved regulations
- approved codes of practice
- which are reviewed where the usage is changed

appropriate automatic fire alarms and fire detection systems which are:

- developed in liaison with the building designers
- properly installed
- adequately maintained
- activated as part of the evacuation training

appropriate first aid fire fighting equipment which is adequately maintained including:

- hose reels
- portable hand operated extinguishers
- fire blankets
- fixed fire fighting equipment

for industrial zones:

- sprinklers
- foam inlets
- total gas flooding (not Halon)

for special fire risks e.g. electrical or inflammable liquids:

- extinguishers of a non-water type

the usage of fire retardant materials, furnishings, fixtures and fittings including:

- electrical equipment
- mechanical equipment

4.2.4.2 *Human Factors:*

- effective local management
- fire safety policies
- staff training
- as part of induction training and on an annual basis

4.2.4.3 *Patient Factors*

The following groups of patients should be regarded as a particular risk of fire related incidents:

High risk

- those who cannot walk either with or without assistance;
- those with learning disabilities;
- those who suffer from mental illness.

Very high risk

- patients for whom clinical treatment or condition creates a high dependency;
- intensive therapy units;
- special care baby units;
- operating departments.

4.2.4.4 Organisation Responsibilities

4.2.4.4.1 Chief Executive

The Chief Executive of an NHS Trust is responsible for the fire safety of all premises belonging to, or occupied by, the Trust.

As such the Chief Executive must ensure that all premises have:

- a clearly defined fire safety policy;

- a programme, agreed with the local fire authority, for installing and satisfactorily maintaining an adequate level of physical fire precautions designed to prevent the occurrence of fire, ensure its early detection and warning, and to control and stop the spread of fire;

- an emergency evacuation plan to include means for raising the alarm in case of fire, first-aid fire fighting, methods for the movement or evacuation of patients, staff and other occupants in an emergency and appropriate, periodic and formally-recorded staff training in all these matters.

4.2.4.4.2 Board Director

The Chief Executive should be assisted by a Board level Director who may have tasks delegated to assist in the discharge of the duty for fire safety. These tasks may include:

- ensuring the implementation of all statutory and Firecode requirements in premises owned or occupied by the health care provider;

- ensuring that, for all premises which have a fire certificate, the requirements of the certificate are complied with;

- the health provider has appropriate fire policies;

- ensuring that a nominated officer together with a sufficient number of deputies are appointed;

- ensuring that an annual fire safety report is presented to the Board;

- ensuring that programmes of work for maintaining and improving fire precautions are prepared for all premises;

- ensuring that no-smoking policies are enforced in all premises;

- ensuring that a 'Certificate of Firecode Compliance' is returned by the Chief Executive to the Director of Estates Policy at NHS Estates at the end of each calendar year.

Additionally, all Board Directors are responsible for fire precautions and staff training within their own areas of responsibility.

4.2.4.4.3 Nominated Fire Officer

The Executive Director with responsibility for fire safety may appoint a nominated fire officer to undertake specified responsibilities to aid compliance with Firecode requirements. The appointment is strongly recommended by Firecode. Responsibilities of the nominated fire officer may include:

- co-ordination of fire safety management throughout the premises to ensure uniformity of standards;

- appointing deputies at each of the premises and maintain an up to date record of their names;

- ensure that all staff participate regularly in fire safety training and fire drills; attend major fire drills;

- maintain a record at all fire drills and training sessions;

- to prepare an annual report for the Executive;

- to receive and co-ordinate reports of all fire incidents.

4.2.4.4.4 Purchasing Officer

The purchasing officer is responsible for co-ordinating the health provider purchasing function and ensuring that all textiles and furniture obtained complies with the guidance given in the Health Technical Memorandum 87.

4.2.4.4.5 Specialist Fire Safety Adviser (Competent persons)

Under the terms of the Firecode a competent person is defined as:

a person recognised as having sufficient technical training and actual experience, or technical knowledge and other qualities both to understand fully the dangers involved, and to undertake properly the statutory and Firecode provisions referred to in this document.

The duties of a specialist fire adviser include:

- advising management of fire precaution measures generally;

- advising management of their initial and continuing responsibilities in respect of designated premises requiring a fire certificate;

- ensuring that applications for fire certificates are made;

- ensuring that the provisions of a fire certificate are met;

- preparing and witnessing training programmes for staff;

- assisting in the preparation of evacuation plans.

4.2.4.4.6 Annual Report on Fire Safety

An Annual Report on fire safety should be submitted to the Board which should include:

- a review of the Fire Safety Policy with recommendations on any amendments which are required;

- a summary of the extent to which fire training and fire drills have been undertaken in the previous twelve months;

- a record of the number and percentage of the staff by department that have attended fire training and drills during the previous twelve months;

- a list of the outstanding fire precautionary work in priority order including any outstanding recommendations by the local fire authority;

- a summary of fires which have occurred in the previous twelve months.

4.2.4.4.7 Emergency Arrangements and Contingency Planning

The basic principle of escape from a fire is that the occupants of a building should be able to turn their backs on a fire and proceed through circulation areas and stairways to a place of safety, firstly within the building and then, if necessary, outside the building.

An emergency evacuation plan needs to be prepared for all premises occupied by the service. Each plan should include:

- the means of raising the alarm in case of fire;

- methods of first aid fire-fighting;

- methods for the movement of the evacuation of patients, visitors and staff;

- the location of assembly points.

The fire evacuation plan should be prepared in conjunction with any professional adviser employed. In hospitals, particularly in patient access areas, the immediate and total evacuation in the event of fire may not be desirable or necessary. For example, some handicapped patients, patients in wheelchairs and bed-bound patients, cannot negotiate escape routes. Special facilities for decision making to evacuate will be needed for high dependency patients, particularly in intensive care.

4.2.4.4.8 Fire Notices

Fire notices should be displayed prominently throughout all premises. The purpose of a fire notice is to give concise instructions of the actions to be taken on discovering a fire and on hearing an alarm. Easy to understand notices can usefully include a local site plan which indicates where the notice is situated and the evacuation route to be taken.

4.2.4.4.9 Fire Drills

Fire drills should be undertaken at least once each year on all health premises. Fire drills are training sessions which should test the effectiveness of emergency plans and fire safety training. They should rehearse procedures and do not necessarily involve the evacuation of a whole building. Fire drills do not necessarily involve the movement of patients.

4.2.4.4.10 Contingency Planning

Whilst most health providers will have developed procedures to deal with the immediate effects of a fire, evacuation and fire control, the major risk to the provider may well arise from the aftermath of being unable to provide a service. Each health provider needs to consider what facilities would be available to remain in business following a fire – even small controlled fires which may adversely affect Information Technology or telecom facilities.

4.2.4.4.11 Reporting of Fires

All fires at premises within the control of, or contracted to, a Health Authority where the fire brigade has been called must be reported to the Director of Policy at the NHS Executive within 48 hours. Fires involving death or multiple injury must be reported to the Health and Safety Executive under the Reporting of Injuries, Diseases and Dangerous Occurrences Regulations 1985.

4.2.5   Fire Authority Powers of Enforcement

Fire authorities have powers of enforcement on health premises under two sections of the 1971 Act:

Section 10. The fire authority may prohibit or restrict the use of any health service premises, including patient areas of hospitals, by serving on the occupier a notice "a prohibition notice" in cases where:

the fire authority are of the opinion that the use of the premises involves or will involve a risk to persons on the premises in case of fire so serious that the use of the premises ought to be prohibited or restricted.

Section 9D. The fire authority may serve on the occupier a notice, an "improvement notice" in respect of premises covered by Section 9A (exempt from fire certificates) of the Act in cases where:

a fire authority are of the opinion that the duty imposed under Section 9 of the Act has been contravened in respect of any premises to which that section applies.

NHS Controls Assurance Standards – Fire Safety
November 1999

1 Board level responsibility for fire safety is clearly defined and there are clear lines of accountability throughout the organisation, leading to the Board

2 There is a documented fire safety policy that has been approved by the Board and has been communicated across the organisation

3 Fire safety roles and responsibilities are clearly defined when accommodation is shared with other organisations

4 An annual Certificate of FIRECODE Compliance is signed by the Chief Executive and returned to NHS Estates

5 Staff and safety representatives are properly consulted on fire safety matters

6   Fire hazards and incidents are dealt with in accordance with the processes contained in the risk management system standard

7   All applications for fire certification for premises designated by Order under the Fire Precautions Act 1971 have been made and certificates have been received

8   All premises controlled by the Housing Act 1985 have been notified to the local housing authority

9   Applications are made for all new building or renovation work covered by the Building Regulations 1991

10 The risk management process contained within the risk management system standard is applied to fire safety

11 Fire safety risk assessments have been completed for all occupied premises and are maintained up-to-date

12 The organisation's premises meet the minimum physical statutory requirements laid down in the Fire Precautions (Workplace) Regulations 1997 and the Health and Safety (Safety Signs and Signals) Regulations 1996

13 All occupied areas have suitable and up-to-date emergency plans in case of fire

14 The organisation's physical fire safety infrastructure is maintained and tested in accordance with legislation, Approved Codes of Practice, British Standards, and/or manufacturer's guidelines

15 The organisation has access to up-to-date fire safety legislation, Approved Codes of Practice, FIRECODE, British Standards, and other guidance relating to fire safety

16 All staff receive a level of fire-safety training that is appropriate for their individual responsibilities in the event of a fire and a record is made of all training received

17 Key indicators capable of showing improvements in fire safety and/or providing early warning of risk are used at all levels of the organisation, including the Board, and the efficacy and usefulness of the indicators is reviewed regularly

18 The system in place for managing fire safety, including risk management arrangements, is monitored and reviewed by management and the Board in order to make improvements to the system.

19 The Internal Audit function, aided as necessary by relevant technical specialists, carries out periodic audits to provide assurance to the Board

that a system of fire safety management is in place that conforms to the requirements of this standard

4.3   SECURITY

4.3.1   General

Maintaining security in the healthcare setting provides the risk manager with particular challenges. The traditional view has suggested that security is only concerned with personal and property safety. However, the increasing complexity of healthcare in a business setting means that the security of information, including clinical records, should attract the expertise of the risk manager to reduce risks.

The duties imposed on the organisation by statute means that security is necessarily a Board level concern with the Chief Executive having overall responsibility for compliance.

Central to the justification of expenditure on security measures is an accurate knowledge of the provider's assets and measurement of the extent of losses. The National Association of Health Authorities and Trusts (NAHAT) published an *NHS Security Manual* in 1992 which the risk manager will find helpful in considering elements of security. A supplement was issued in 1995.

Active control of security has been shown to be effective in reducing losses. Trusts which have taken active steps to reduce crime have reported a reduction of up to 80% of losses in one year.

This consideration of security is directed to:

- personal security
- for the patient
- for staff
- property security
- patients
- staff
- the organisation
- Information security
- patients

- access to information
- access to Health Records Act 1990
- access to Medical Reports Act 1988
- confidentiality
- compulsory and permissible breaches in confidentiality

Security Design

NHS Estates recommend the following security considerations in hospital design and operation:

- new hospital design should use space syntax analysis to identify and design out risk areas;
- departments should have their own car parks and entrances which should be locked at night;
- daytime access should be locked at night;
- the main circulation route of a hospital should be directed through working areas to allow informal policing.

Additional measures to these can include:

- using blue lighting in areas where drug misusers inject, such as the toilets in the Accident and Emergency Department (this makes veins for injection difficult to identify);
- decorative pastels colours and down lighting in areas where there are potentially violent patients;
- colour coding of carpets to define access.

Factors predisposing to crime include:

- flat roof construction;
- poor lighting
  - internal
  - external
  - alcoves to hide in.

Principle Acts affecting Physical and Personal Security

4.3.2   Health and Safety at Work etc Act 1974

The Health and Safety at Work etc Act 1974 imposes a duty on an employer to ensure that as far as is reasonably practicable there are:

- safe systems of work;
- safe working environments;
- safe premises;
- adequate training and instruction;
- the provision of information to allow employees to ensure their safety at work.

Employers are required to assess risks to security and to document them.

4.3.2.1 *Occupiers' Liability Act 1984*

The Act gives three areas of special responsibility:

- there is a duty on the organisation to ensure that visitors and property are reasonably safe;
- the organisation must be prepared for children to be less careful than adults;
- warnings affecting safety must be given where appropriate.

Simple examples of these are:

- a security policy has been established which is actively implemented;
- child access and egress is guarded and child access to danger areas on wards and in clinics is restricted;
- to warn of a wet floor during cleaning operations.

4.3.2.2 *Unfair Contract Terms Act 1977*

The purpose of the Act is to prevent onerous terms in contractual matters. In health provision, it means that disclaimers will be ineffective in cases which result in:

- death;
- personal injury.

4.3.2.3 *Children Act 1989*

All staff who will work with children must be vetted, including a police check.

4.3.3 Personal Security

Security in the provider setting necessarily needs to balance the needs of access with that of individual safety. It is important that staff receive training in security as part of their induction and that this training is continued on a regular basis. Where there has been a breach in security there is a further opportunity for relevant training.

Patients and visitors should be able to identify members of staff from their name badges. Not only is this a requirement of the Patient's Charter, but easily identified name badges enable staff **to challenge the presence of anyone who is not wearing appropriate identification in a clinical area who is not known to the member of staff.** This empowerment and expectation to challenge is an area which is uncommon in the culture of the NHS.

In balancing the needs of access for visitors with the need for security, it is important that a policy of safety is followed in the provider unit. Reference to a security policy and the ways in which this may affect users should be made in literature given to patients as well as the local press being informed. Clearly marked and simply designed name badges are much more easily identified as belonging to an organisation than small identity badges containing a photograph which could have been issued by any similar unit or organisation. A telephone number should be clearly stated to allow the patient (particularly in the community) to check the identity of the member of staff. Security in the issue of badges can be assisted by having a single supplier who only issues badges on receipt of an order from a known signatory.

Contractors should be required through a 'Permit to Work' system to wear clearly marked visitors badges. Similarly, 'official visitors' should be required to sign in and out of the premises and to wear suitably clear badges. A failure to have such a system in place may well have contributed to several well publicised breaches in hospital security, including the abduction of babies and the murder of patients. **In carrying out risk audits in special care baby units, the author has not yet failed to put himself in the position of being able to abduct a baby. This has been without the issue of identification by the host hospital.**

The wide variety of the types of provider means that security policies need to be tailored to individual unit needs. The risk manager must be involved in drawing up the policies which should be known to all staff. The local police crime prevention officers provide an invaluable advisory service upon request.

4.3.3.1 Security for the Patient

It is important that when considering a policy for the personal security of patients that a balance is struck between personal safety and individual rights and liberties. This is particularly relevant to patients with mental illness and those with learning disabilities. This balance can usefully be incorporated into the care plan and reviewed in the light of the experience of the individual patient.

Staff in units which contain patients who may demonstrate assaultative behaviour, such as the mentally ill and those with learning disabilities, need to carry out and act upon risk assessments of the behaviour. Establishing the boundaries of acceptable behaviour is part of good practice on these units. Seclusion facilities may need to be available – depending on the severity of illness – and the use of them needs to comply with the Mental Health Act Code of Practice.

4.3.3.2 Infant Abduction

There have been five infant abductions from hospitals in the U.K. 1990-1995. These have resulted in increasing security measures, the most popular of which are:

- closed circuit television;
- audio entryphones;
- electronic tagging of infants;
- hands free access control systems;
- to advise the timing of birth announcements after discharge from hospital;
- to advise mothers to refuse treatment if an identity badge is not worn;
- to provide tamper proof double tagging of the infant;
- to provide a visitors' reception area;

- to install a staff photograph Board to aid identification;
- to increase security awareness at antenatal clinics;
- to give mothers a discharge pass.

Additionally, the Maternity Services Patient's Charter requires:

- two identifying labels for the infant;
- that the mother be shown the labels as soon as possible to confirm the details.

Contingency plans are needed for abduction to cover the following areas:

- raising the alarm;
- closing the ward;
- calling security staff;
- calling the police;
- carrying out a local search;
- counselling support;
- public relations.

4.3.3.3 Security for Staff

All trusts should have in place an explicit 'zero tolerance' policy to attacks on staff. All assaults should be reported to the police. Fear of assault is a major concern to many staff, particularly those who work outside normal hours and in the community. The risk manager may find it helpful to survey staff attitudes to determine the extent of the concern and as an adjunct to good staff relationships.

Staff involved in the treatment of patients who may have a violent propensity, such as the mentally ill or those with learning disabilities, should all be trained in the 'breakaway' technique to enable them to detach from violent behaviour. Staff in residential facilities, such as an acute hospital for the mentally ill should be trained in C&R techniques. These are known as either 'Care and Responsibility' or 'Control and Restraint', but each allow for three members of staff to adequately restrain a violent patient. The techniques should not be used with less than three members of staff because of the risks of harm to the patient.

These risks include neck and back injury and strangulation.

Staff working with patients who may be violent should have access to personal alarms and panic button systems in the health facility. This applies equally to the Accident and Emergency Department as well as to a forensic psychiatric outpatient clinic. The system should alarm in a place which is staffed all the time that the member of staff is at risk. A remote answer telephone or intercom will improve security of access at night in Accident and Emergency Departments. It may well be helpful for any members of the security staff, or a police presence at times of high risk, to be based in the Department. The use of CCTV and protection screens has been shown to reduce incidents of violence.

A high level of lighting in hospital grounds after dark is a major deterrent to violence to staff. Staff working late may be reassured to be accompanied to their car by a member of the security staff or a colleague. Staff fears are real and it is for the risk manager to minimise the reality of their fears.

Staff need to be trained in the control and prevention of violence. This needs to be reinforced on a regular basis. Staff also need access to effective counselling after they have been subject to actual or potential violence.

Ulster Health and Social Services Trust further examined the parts of a violence prevention policy as follows:

Element1: staff members will plan and prepare appropriately for direct client contact.

- staff to ensure that they have detailed and accurate referral information prior to initial direct contact with the client;

- where a client is already known, the staff member should obtain information on their usual behaviour patterns;

- staff members should be aware of the process of risk assessment and undertake an assessment where possible.

Element 2: Staff members should be aware of how their own behaviour may trigger an aggressive outburst:

- staff members will be aware of the impact of their non-verbal communication during interactions with clients, e.g. body posture, gestures, facial expression;

- staff members should be aware of the impact of self-presentation on clients, e.g. manner of dress, badges, etc.

Element 3: Staff members will interact with clients in a manner which minimises the likelihood of an aggressive incident occurring:

- staff should be punctual for appointments with clients and will inform the client in advance if appointments have to be postponed or cancelled;

- staff members will accept the clients right to feel angry and will attempt to discuss the cause of the anger;

- staff members will use listening skills to show the client that they are being heard – and taken seriously.

4.3.3.4 *De-escalation* of Potential Violence

De-escalation, or defusion, is the term applied to a combination of verbal and non- verbal interactions which can, when used appropriately reduce the threat of violence, including the patient's anger and return them to a more calm state of mind. All staff working in mental health settings, irrespective of grade, who interact with patients should be provided with basic de-escalatory skills.

Summary of de-escalation skills:

- maintain adequate distance;

- move towards a safer place, avoid corners;

- explain intentions to patient and others;

- try to appear calm and self-controlled;

- ensure own non-verbal communication is non-threatening;

- engage in conversation, acknowledge concerns and feelings;

- ask open-ended questions;

- ask for any weapons to be put down (not handed over); and

- know how to call for help in an emergency.

The NHS has commend a zero-tolerance approach to violence in the workplace and issued specific advice for different work areas, including community and general practice and for the ambulance services.

4.3.4 Property Security

The NHS Risk Management Handbook identified two general principles in considering property security:

- **remove the target from sight**
  Use draws and lockers. Draw window blinds and curtains at night.

- **place the target behind barriers**
  Close doors and windows when the premises are not in use. Doors and windows should be maintained and of sufficient strength.

To these may be added:

- **restrict access to the premises**
  Review the number of access points available at night. Lock those which are not essential for service access.

- **know the extent of potential losses**
  Establish inventories of property including values.

- **accurate documentation**
  Records of the receipt of a patient's property should be clear and accurate. Staff need to be trained in the description of property. Staff who attend patients in other than central locations should keep an up to date diary of their movements available at their base and inform a central point when their duties have finished.

- **consider security at the design stage**
  Thieves do not like to be caught. Clear external lighting will deter theft. Vehicles parked in the line of sight of hospital receptions are much less likely to be stolen or vandalised.

- **staff training**
  Much of the fear of a breach in personal security can be alleviated through staff training and the use of personal alarms.

4.3.4.1 Property of Patients

Patients entering hospital on an elective basis should be encouraged to leave valuables at home. In any event, clear details should be taken and recorded at the time of the patient's admission. Property which is retained by the patient should also be noted. Patients should be encouraged to place any valuables which they insist on bringing in the custody of the hospital. Receipts should be issued to be matched against the property upon its return to the patient. It is only by having a system that is open to audit that the hospital may protect itself from allegations of and actual loss. Losses which do occur should be investigated immediately. Where these are significant or potentially criminal the police should be informed. The control of patients' property should be clearly stated in the unit's security policy. Because of the different requirements, there should be a distinct policy for patients who may be resident for considerable periods, such as the elderly and/or physically frail.

4.3.4.2 Property of Staff

Staff should be aware that the control and safety of their own property is their responsibility. Adequate lockers should be provided. Staff working in outpatient and Accident and Emergency departments should be particularly aware of the increased risks of theft. Staff who are at increased risk of violence, both in outpatient and inpatient settings should be advised not to wear expensive items of clothing, jewellery or spectacles.

4.3.4.3 Property of the Organisation

There has been an increase in theft from the health service which means that active steps need to be taken to reduce losses. Although most providers insure against loss from theft, a poor record will inevitably lead to increased insurance premiums. The most popular steps taken by Trusts are to:

- provide Closed Circuit television;
- lock down portable items;
- mark portable items;
- put portable items in protected areas;
- ensure 24 hour security presence;
- provide personal alarms;
- provide identity badges and require them to be worn;
- gain support and advice from the local police.

4.3.5   Fraud Prevention

Fraud is the deliberate misrepresentation of fact for the purpose of depriving someone of a possession. In 1998, prescription fraud was estimated to be £150M per year amounting to an evasion of prescription charges to over 6%.

In 1998, the Department of Health established a Directorate of Counter Fraud Services. The function of the Directorate is to lead the implementation of an anti-fraud strategy and to take responsibility for all policy and operational matters of fraud and corruption throughout the NHS.[2] All Trusts and Health Authorities are required to have in place fraud and fraud response policies and staff are required to have appropriate training in policy content and use.

4.3.5.1 NHS Anti-Fraud Strategy

The strategy sets out its aims which are to:

- reduce fraud to an absolute minimum within a set time scale;
- put in place arrangements to hold fraud at a minimum level permanently;
- target more NHS resources at providing better patient care.

The framework for implementing the stated aims comprises of:

- objectives;
- approach;
- tactics;
- standards;
- support.

4.3.5.2 Objectives of the Strategy

The creation of an anti-fraud culture through:

promoting the concept that fraud is an important waste of resources;

the promotion of a zero-tolerance culture to fraud;

---

2   *Countering Fraud in the NHS* – Department of Health 1998

joint responsibility to reduce fraud.

Maximum deterrence of fraud:

by ensuring that the totality of anti-fraud measures represents the strongest deterrent possible to those perpetrating or considering perpetrating fraud.

Successful prevention of fraud which cannot be deterred;

by developing the most effective preventative measures so that attempted fraud will fail;

Professional investigation of detected fraud:

by developing the levels of skills and techniques to allow investigations to be brought to a satisfactory conclusion.

Effective sanctions, including appropriate legal action against people committing fraud:

by developing the law and regulatory frameworks within the NHS to ensure they are concise and unambiguous

Effective measures for seeking redress in respect of money defrauded:

by the recovery of defrauded funds.

The Directorate of Counter Fraud Services has established offices in each NHS Region. Each Trust is required to appoint a Local Counter Fraud Specialist, LCFS. The responsibilities of the LCFS are to:

- report to the Trust's Chief Financial Officer;

- provide a written report, at least annually, to the Trust on counter fraud work undertaken;

- undertake proactive work to detect cases of fraud and corruption, particularly where systems weaknesses have been identified;

- report to the Directorate cases which promote fraud prevention;

- investigate and report on cases of suspected fraud.

Fraud may be perpetrated by an individual acting in isolation, or by two or more people acting in collusion. This latter method may be extremely difficult to detect.

Examples of fraud include:
by patients

- patients claiming exemption from prescription charges when they were not in fact exempt;

- a patient falsely claimed travel expenses to an out-patient clinic;

- patients have falsely stated that they have lost their prescriptions and obtained duplicates;

- patients have falsely registered with a number of doctors and obtained prescriptions from each.

by pharmacists

- conspiring with a GP, a pharmacist submitted bogus prescriptions for re-imbursement with a value of over £1M;

- pharmacists substituting an expensive drug with a cheaper alternative, but claiming for the more expensive drug;

- adding items to the prescription;

- altering the amounts of drugs;

- fraudulently generating fees for emergency opening.

by hospital consultants

- by falsifying employment agency worksheets while working full time for an authority;

- falsely recording private patients as NHS to avoid making appropriate payments to a hospital.

by staff

- claims for duty payments and hours worked with no evidence that the work had been done;

- forging the signatures of authorised signatories and submitting false invoices to support reimbursement requests;

- submitting false claims;

- accepting gifts in exchange for placing orders;

- colluding with suppliers to submit invoices for goods not delivered;

- misappropriation of catering and stationery supplies.

involving patients' income

- a community living scheme manager stole from two disabled patients whose incomes he was responsible for managing;

- a nurse stole from patients with learning disabilities having persuaded them to let him hold their building society books.

research fraud

- a senior consultant fraudulently claimed to have performed pioneering surgery and computer records were tampered with to falsify results.

NHS Controls Assurance Standards – Security
November 1999

1 Board level responsibility for security is clearly defined and there are clear lines of accountability for security matters throughout the organisation, leading to the Board

2 There is a Board-approved security policy and strategy, that has been communicated throughout the organisation and is, where appropriate supported by an agreed plan

3 A crime prevention programme is implemented and supported throughout the organisation.

4 There is proper and timely response to security incidents in accordance with appropriate response plans for specific security incidents

5 Security hazards and incidents are reported and analysed in accordance with the processes contained in the risk management system standard

6 The risk management process contained within the risk management system standard is applied to security risks

7 The organisation has access to up-to-date security-related legislation and guidance

8 Where appropriate, all employees receive security training that is commensurate with risks in their work area

9 The competency and performance of security personnel, whether employed internally or out-sourced, is monitored

10 Key performance indicators capable of showing improvements in security management, and the management of associated risks, are used at all levels of the organisation, including the Board, and the efficacy and

usefulness of the indicators is reviewed regularly

11 The system in place for managing security is monitored and reviewed by management and the Board in order to make improvements to the system

12 The Internal Audit function, aided as necessary by relevant security specialists, carries out periodic audits to provide assurance to the Board that a system of security management is in place that conforms to the requirements of this standard

4.4 HEALTH RECORDS

4.4.1 Principle Acts and Regulations

- Data Protection Act 1998

- Access to Personal Files Act 1987

- Access to Medical Reports Act 1988

- Access to Health Records Act 1990

The underlying principle in respect of information gained by a healthcare professional in the course of contact with a patient is that the information is to be treated as confidential. It is important to recognise that this is a basic ethical consideration, but also that confidentiality is not an absolute.

Patient information is required to be disclosed by statute for:

- the notification of infectious diseases to the local director of public health section 11 of the Public Health (Control of Diseases) Act 1984;

- poisoning under the Factories Act;

- poisoning under the Control of Substances Hazardous to Health;

- the notification of drug addicts under the Misuse of Drugs (Notification of Supply to Addicts) Act 1973;

- where patients are harmed by ionising radiation under the The Ionising Radiations Regulations 1999 (IRR 99) *Ionising Radiation (Medical Exposure) Regulations 2000 (IRMER 2000)*

- giving information which may lead to the identification of a driver under s.172(b) of the Road Traffic Act 1972;

- identifying terrorist suspects under the Prevention of Terrorism (Temporary Provisions) Act 1989;

- notification of births section 124(4) of the National Health Service Act 1977;

- termination of pregnancy para.4(1) of the Abortion Regulations 1991.

Notifiable diseases means any of the following diseases: acute encephalitis, acute meningitis, acute poliomyelitis, anthrax, cholera, diphtheria, food poisoning, leprosy, leptospirosis, malaria, measles, meningococcal septicaemia, mumps, ophthalmia neonatorum, paratyphoid fever, plague, rabies, relapsing fever, rubella, scarlet fever, smallpox, tetanus, tuberculosis, typhoid fever, typhus, viral haemorrhagic fever, viral hepatitis, whooping cough and yellow fever.

The NHS Trusts and Primary Care Trusts (Sexually Transmitted Diseases) Directions 2000 requires every NHS trust and Primary Care Trust to take all necessary steps to secure that any information capable of identifying an individual obtained by any of their members or employees with respect to persons examined or treated for any sexually transmitted disease will not be disclosed except:

(a for the purpose of communicating that information to a medical practitioner, or to a person employed under the direction of a medical practitioner in connection with the treatment of persons suffering from the disease or the prevention of the spread of the disease, and

(b) for the purpose of such treatment or prevention.

Where it is considered in the patient's best interests, it may be permissible to discuss details of treatment or prognosis with relatives. This should only be done where the relatives understand that the information is given in confidence. Particular care needs to be taken where the patient is mentally ill or terminally ill.

The ethical duty of confidentiality extends beyond the death of the patient. Requests for disclosure of information should only be made by or with the agreement of the executor, if the patient left a valid will, or the person granted letters of administration if they did not.

A judge may make an order for the disclosure of medical records if he/she considers them to be relevant for the purposes of litigation. If a health worker is asked to give details of a patient to a court when they do not have the patient's consent, they should ask to be directed by the judge to disclose the information.

There are rare instances where disclosure of confidential information is in the public interest, against the wishes of the patient. The risk manager needs to take individual advice in these circumstances. The Court of Appeal in the case of *W v. Egdell* gave the following clarification of disclosure on the grounds of public interest:

- *that the public interest defence justifies disclosure to the proper authorities;*

- *that a 'real' risk of danger to the public will be sufficient grounds to justify disclosure, even if the danger is not imminent.*

A possibility of serious harm, rather than a probability is sufficient to constitute a 'real risk'.

Health workers need to recognise that different professionals involved in the team care of patients have different responsibilities in respect of confidentiality. In child care, for example, the social worker has a clear responsibility to notify possible child abuse to their superiors.

4.4.2   Caldicott Guardians[3]

The Caldicott report was the outcome of a Review was commissioned by the Chief Medical Officer of England owing to increasing concern about the ways in which patient information is used in the NHS in England and Wales and the need to ensure that confidentiality is not undermined. It made 16 main recommendations which should be examined by any risk manager, to safeguard the identification of patient details within and outside the health system.

4.4.3   Caldicott Principles for Handling Patient Information

The Caldicott report identified the following principles for the handling and disclosure of patient information:

Principle 1 – Justify the purpose(s)

Every proposed use or transfer of patient-identifiable information within or from an organisation should be clearly defined and

---

3   The Caldicott Committee: *Report on the review of patient-identifiable information –* December 1997

scrutinised, with continuing uses regularly reviewed, by an appropriate guardian.

Principle 2 – Do not use patient-identifiable information unless it is absolutely necessary

Patient-identifiable information items should not be included unless it is essential for the specified purpose(s) of that flow. The need for patients to be identified should be considered at each stage of satisfying the purpose(s).

Principle 3 – Use the minimum necessary patient-identifiable information

Where use of patient-identifiable information is considered to be essential, the inclusion of each individual item of information should be considered and justified so that the minimum amount of identifiable information is transferred or accessible as is necessary for a given function to be carried out.

Principle 4 – Access to patient-identifiable information should be on a strict need-to-know basis

Only those individuals who need access to patient-identifiable information should have access to it, and they should only have access to the information items that they need to see. This may mean introducing access controls or splitting information flows where one information flow is used for several purposes.

Principle 5 – Everyone with access to patient-identifiable information should be aware of their responsibilities

Action should be taken to ensure that those handling patient-identifiable information – both clinical and non-clinical staff – are made fully aware of their responsibilities and obligations to respect patient confidentiality.

Principle 6 – Understand and comply with the law

Every use of patient-identifiable information must be lawful. Someone in each organisation handling patient information should be responsible for ensuring that the organisation complies with legal requirements.

4.4.4   Summary

A key recommendation of the Caldicott Report, published in December 1997, was the establishment of a network of 'Caldicott Guardians' of patient information throughout the NHS.

Each Health Authority, Special Health Authority, NHS Trust and Primary Care Group should appoint a 'Caldicott Guardian' by no later than 31 March 1999. Ideally the Guardian should be at Board level, be a senior health professional and have responsibility for promoting clinical governance within the organisation.

This action includes:

- a management audit of current practice and procedures

- annual plans for improvement that will be monitored through the clinical governance framework

- the introduction of registered access authorisation to certain patient information held outside of the organisation (i.e. through the NHS Strategic Tracing Service)

- the development of clear protocols to govern the disclosure of patient information to other organisations.

4.4.5   Retention of Health Records

The retention of health records is detailed in the Health Circular HC (89)20. The circular is open to local interpretation and implementation. It is important to note that the advice which it contains places the provider at risk in cases brought under the Consumer Protection Act 1987. The circular recommends the following retention periods:

- paediatric records – 25 years;

- psychiatric records – 20 years after discharge from the last episode of psychiatric care;

- all other health records – 8 years after the last episode of care.

The Consumer Protection Act allows for a case to be brought up to ten years after the event which has given rise to the claim. A further period of eight months should be added for the service of proceedings. Health records should therefore be retained for a minimum of ten years and eight months.

4.5   HEALTH INFORMATION SECURITY

4.5.1   Data Protection Act 1998

The Data Protection 1998 implements the EC Directive 95/46/EC on the protection of individuals with regard to the processing of personal data and on the free movement of such data. One of its purposes is to safeguard "the fundamental rights of individuals".

The Act defines personal data as that which relates to a living individual who:

- can be identified from that data or

- from that data and any other information which is in the possession of, or likely to come into the possession of the data controller.

The main provisions of the Act started to come into effect in 2000, but there are transitional arrangements until 2007. Up to date guidance is available at http://www.doh.gov.uk/dpa98/

Principles of Data Protection (Issued by the Data Protection Commissioner)

Compliance advice from the Data Protection Commissioner (2000):

4.5.1.1 The Rules Under the Data Protection Act

Anyone processing personal data must comply with the eight enforceable principles of good practice. They say that data must be:

- fairly and lawfully processed;

- processed for limited purposes;

- adequate, relevant and not excessive;

- accurate;

- not kept longer than necessary;

- processed in accordance with the data subject's rights;

- secure;

- not transferred to countries without adequate protection.

Personal data covers both facts and opinions about the individual. It also includes information regarding the intentions of the data controller towards the individual, although in some limited circumstances exemptions will apply. With processing, the definition is far wider than before. For example, it incorporates the concepts of 'obtaining', holding' and 'disclosing'.

4.5.1.2 Subject Access to Health Records

The Data Protection Act 1998 was implemented on 1 March 2000. Although there are periods of transitional relief during which certain provisions of the new legislation need not be complied with, the implementation of the new legislation will have an immediate impact in respect of subject access to health records.

The right of subject access allows the individual to gain access to personal data of which he is the subject. Typically this will involve supplying an individual with copies of records relating to him when asked to do so. For general information about the right of subject access see *The Data Protection Act 1998 – An Introduction.*

A request for access must be made in writing and no reason need be given. Subject to any applicable exemption, the applicant must be given a copy of the information and, where the data is not readily intelligible, an explanation.

Data controllers are entitled to satisfy themselves that the applicant is either the data subject or, if the applicant is applying on behalf of the data subject, that person has been authorised to do so.

Although the Act does not provide an express right to directly inspect records, it is permitted with the agreement of the data subject and data controller. It is stated Department of Health policy that such requests should be accommodated, unless the requests fall within the exceptions.

Requests for access should be dealt with promptly. The guidance states that this must be no later than forty days after the request and fee have been paid and received by the data controller. If it is not possible to comply with the timescale, the applicant should be informed in writing.

4.5.1.3 Rights of Rectification

If the data subject believes that data recorded about them is inaccurate the person may apply to the court for an order, or the Data Protection Commissioner for an enforcement notice, either of which may require that the inaccurate data, and any expression of opinion based upon it, is rectified, blocked, erased or destroyed.

Where the data is inaccurate but accurately records information given by the data subject or another person, the court or the Commissioner may instead order that the record should be supplemented by a statement of the true facts as approved by the court/Commissioner.

4.5.1.4 Refusing Access Under the Act

The Data Protection (Subject Access Modification)(Health) Order 2000 provides exemptions from the subject access rights in two situations:

- where permitting access to the data would be likely to cause serious harm to the physical or mental health or condition of the data subject or any other person (which may include a health professional);

- where the request for access is made by another on behalf of the data subject, such as a parent for a child, access can be refused if the data subject had either provided the information in the expectation it would not be disclosed to the applicant or had indicated that it should not be disclosed, or if the data was obtained as a result of any examination or investigation to which the subject consented on the basis that information would not be disclosed.

Before deciding whether the exemption in paragraph 1 applies the data controller who is not a health professional must consult the health care professional responsible for the clinical care of the data subject; or if there is more than one, the most suitable available health care professional. If there is none, a health care professional with the necessary qualifications and experience to advise on the matters to which the information requested relates must be consulted.

4.5.1.5 Health Record

A health record is defined in the 1998 Act as being any record which consists of information relating to the physical or mental health or condition of an individual, and has been made by or on behalf of a health professional in connection with the care of that individual.

It is clear, therefore, that many of the records being held by NHS Trusts, surgeries and other health care institutions will constitute 'health records' and will therefore fall within the scope of the 1998 Act's subject access provisions.

4.5.1.6 Relationship to the Access to Health Records Act 1990

This piece of legislation formerly gave individuals a right of access to manual health records – i.e. to the sort of non-automated records that the Data Protection Act 1984 did not apply to. However, the Access to Health Records Act 1990 has now been repealed except for sections dealing with requests for access to records relating to the deceased. Requests for access to records relating to the deceased will continue to be made under the Access to Health Records Act 1990. However, requests for access to health records relating to living individuals, whether the records are manual or automated, will now fall within the scope of the Data Protection Act 1998's subject access provisions and must be dealt with in the manner stipulated in that Act.

4.5.1.7 Charges for Granting Subject Access

A fee may be charged for the provision of copies of records under the Act, subject to a maximum charge. No fee may be charged where the subject access request is to be complied with other than by supplying a copy of the information in a permanent form – i.e. by allowing the applicant to inspect the record. This provision only relates to requests for access to non-automated records at least some of which was made after the beginning of the period of 40 days immediately preceding the date of the request. This provision broadly replicates the provision of the Access to Health Records Act 1990 that, in effect, allows patients to look at recently created records without charge.

The risk manager should be conversant with current fees payable. Up to date information on charges applicable are available on the Home Office website at:
http://www.homeoffice.gov.uk/ccpd/dpsafmsi.htm

4.5.1.8 Other Information has to be Given to the Data Subject

- a description of the data;
- a description of the purpose/s for which the data are being or are to be processed;
- a description of the recipients or classes or recipients of the data – i.e. persons to whom the data are disclosed

The data subject must also be given;

- any information available to the controller as to the source of the data;

- an explanation as to how any automated decision taken about the data subject has been made.

Definition of a 'health professional'

In interpreting the Data Protection Act 1998 "health professional" means any of the following;

a) a registered medical practitioner (a "registered medical practitioner" includes any person who is provisionally registered under section 15 or 21 of the Medical Act 1983 and is engaged in such employment as is mentioned in subsection (3) of that section.)

b) a registered dentist as defined by section 53(1) of the Dentists Act 1984,

c) a registered optician as defined by section 36(1) of the Opticians Act 1989,

d) a registered pharmaceutical chemist as defined by section 24(1) of the Pharmacy Act 1954 or a registered person as defined by Article 2(2) of the Pharmacy (Northern Ireland) Order 1976,

e) a registered nurse, midwife or health visitor,

f) a registered osteopath as defined by section 41 of the Osteopaths Act 1993,

g) a registered chiropractor as defined by section 43 of the Chiropractors Act 1994,

h) any person who is registered as a member of a profession to which the Professions Supplementary to Medicine Act 1960 for the time being extends,

i) a clinical psychologist, child psychotherapist or speech therapist,

j) a music therapist employed by a health service body, and

k) a scientist employed by such a body as head of department

(For more information about the transitional provisions see *The Data Protection Act 1998 – An Introduction available* at http://www.dataprotection.gov.uk.)

The Act is important as protection for individual rights of privacy.

4.5.2 Some Offences Under The Data Protection Act

4.5.2.1 Unlawful Obtaining Etc., of Personal Data

It is an offence for a person, without the consent of the data controller, knowingly or recklessly, to obtain or disclose personal data or the information contained in personal data, or procure the disclosure to another person of the information contained in personal data.

4.5.2.2 Unlawful Selling of Personal Data

If a person has obtained personal data in contravention of the provision referred to in paragraph 4.4.2.1 above it is an offence to sell or offer to sell the personal data.

4.5.2.3 Enforced Subject Access

Unless one of the statutory exceptions apply it is an offence for person to require another person or a third party to supply them with a relevant record

Risk Management Points

Complying with the Act is important and the risk manager should take account of the following:

- the health provider should be registered with the Data Protection Registrar, registration lasts for 3 years and may therefore unintentionally lapse registration;

- there should be a clear policy for the collection and retention of data;

- there should be a clear policy to cover requests for access to data;

- the computer system should be secure and include:

- checks on data integrity;

- back ups of data at least daily;

- secure storage of backed up data at a remote site;

- staff training;

- passwords should be used for system entry and regularly changed;

- screen blanking when not in use by authorised staff;

- secure terminal positions which cannot be overlooked by unauthorised people – particularly in out-patients and Accident and Emergency Departments;

- secure offices to house equipment;

- secure storage of printouts.

4.5.3 Access to Health Records Act 1990

The Access to Health Records Act 1990 was passed to correct the then anomaly that access was permitted to automated records, but not to manual 'hard copy' health records. Health records are defined as those made by or on behalf of a health professional in connection with the care of an individual. It now only applies to the records of deceased patients.

Health professionals who are defined under the Act as:

(a) a registered medical practitioner [including a person who is provisionally registered under section 15 or 21 of the Medical Act 1983 and is engaged in such employment as is mentioned in subsection (3) of that section];

(b) a registered dentist;

(c) a registered optician;

(d) a registered pharmaceutical chemist;

(e) a registered nurse, midwife or health visitor;

(f) a registered chiropodist, dietician, occupational therapist, orthoptist or physiotherapist;

(g) a clinical psychologist, child psychotherapist or speech therapist;

(h) an art or music therapist employed by a health service body; and

(i) a scientist employed by such a body as head of department.

'Care' is defined as:

"examination, investigation, diagnosis and treatment."

A request for access must be considered where it is made by:

- where the patient has died, the patient's personal representative and any person who may have a claim arising out of the death.

When an application to see the medical records is made, the holder – generally the health provider – is under a duty to consult with the 'appropriate healthcare professional' to ensure that disclosure will not cause serious harm to the applicant.

If the patient was treated within 40 days of the application, access should be given within 21 days. If the period exceeds 40 days since the last treatment, 40 days for access are allowed. If a copy is requested, the cost should not exceed that of preparing the copy and the cost of postage, if appropriate.

If the patient considers the record to be inaccurate, he/she may request that the record be changed. If there is further dispute on the accuracy of the record, it is open to the patient to apply to court. No sanctions are built into the Act, but a healthcare provider should expect to pay the costs of a court application if they have in any way acted unreasonably.

Risk Management Points

- there should be a clear policy for the implementation of the Access to Health Records Act and Data Protection Act;

- health records should be easily retrievable;

- records should be securely stored;

- parts of records such as CardioTocoGraphs and ElectroCardioGraphs should be securely stored within the record.

4.5.4   Access to Medical Reports Act 1988

The Act gives rights to patients where a medical report which has been written about them by a doctor involved in their care and which are for the use of a third party. It covers reports prepared for employment or insurance purposes. The act excludes reports which are based on an examination by an independent medical practitioner who will not have had access to the confidential information which forms part of the ordinary doctor-patient relationship. The prime purpose of the Act is to allow patients to see, and if necessary challenge, a medical report before it is sent to the employer or insurer.

Employment purposes are defined as:

the purposes in relation to the individual of any person by whom he is or has been, or is seeking to be, employed (whether under a contract of service or otherwise).

Insurance purposes are defined as:

the purposes in relation to the individual of any person carrying on an insurance business with whom the individual has entered into, or is seeking to enter into, a contract of insurance, and 'insurance business' and 'contract of insurance' have the same meaning as in the Insurance Companies Act 1982.

'Care' is defined as including:

"....examination, investigation or diagnosis for the purposes of, or in connection with, any form of medical treatment".

Where a patient is excluded from seeing a medical report under the Access to Medical Reports Act, they may still be able to obtain access under the Access to Health Records Act.

Where a patient has given notice that they wish to see a medical report, the doctor should not release the report for 21 days after being given notice. For practical reasons, the period of 21 days should run from the date of receipt of notification. This has yet to be tested in the courts. The doctor should retain a copy of the report for six months.

Disclosure of the report is not required where the doctor considers that this would be likely to cause **serious harm** to the physical or mental health of the patient or others nor if disclosure would reveal information about another individual, or the identity of another person who has supplied information about the person.

No charge should be levied for access to the report. If a copy is required, a reasonable fee may be charged.

In cases of factual dispute in the contents of the report, the patient may request correction. If the dispute is unresolved, it is open to the patient to apply to the courts for an order for compliance.

Risk Management points

- all medical staff should be aware of the Act and its consequences;

- a ready source of advice should be available to medical staff.

Controls Assurance Standards – Health Records
November 1999

1 There is an organisation-wide records management strategy which is endorsed by the Board

2 A senior manager is responsible for co-ordinating, publicising and monitoring implementation of the records management strategy

3 Local records managers are appointed and are accountable to the senior manager

4 A 'Caldicott Guardian' has been appointed and liases closely with local records managers

5 There is a comprehensive records management programme which includes cost-effective management of non-current as well as active records, the destruction of records when no longer required, and which takes account of the risk management policy and strategy

6 Managers in all directorates/departments ensure that staff are aware of the vital role that records play in delivering health care and are also aware of their personal responsibilities for any records they create or use

7 Records management services and controls are included in the organisation's information management and technology (IM&T) strategy(ies)

8 Employees, including managers and the appointed Caldicott guardian, are provided with adequate information, instruction and training on records management matters

9 Key indicators capable of showing improvements in records management and/or providing early warning of risk are used at all levels of the organisation, including the Board, and the efficacy and usefulness of the indicators is reviewed regularly

10 The systems in place for records management are monitored and reviewed by management and the Board in order to make improvements to the systems

11 Formal audits include, where appropriate, consideration of records management issues

4.6 WASTE DISPOSAL

4.6.1 Definition

Clinical waste is defined as in the Controlled Waste Regulations 1992 as: any waste which consists wholly or partly of:

- human or animal tissues
- blood or other body fluids
- excretions
- drugs or other pharmaceutical products
- swabs or dressings
- syringes, needles or other sharp instruments

which unless rendered safe may prove hazardous to any person coming into contact with it.

And:

any other waste arising from medical, nursing, dental, veterinary, pharmaceutical or similar practice, investigation, treatment, care, teaching or research, or the collection of blood for transfusion, being waste which may cause infection to any person coming into contact with it.

4.6.2 Principle Acts and Regulations Relating to Waste Disposal in Healthcare

4.6.2.1 Health and Safety at Work etc. Act 1974

A healthcare provider has a duty that, as far as is reasonably practicable, the health and safety of employees and others who may be affected by the storage, handling or disposal of waste products are protected.

4.6.2.2 Environmental Protection Act 1991

Section 33 imposes a duty that controlled waste must not be disposed of in a manner which is likely to cause harm to the environment or to human health.

Section 34 extends the duty of care so that those who dispose of waste must ensure that it is safely managed from production to final disposal.

Unintentional escape of waste must be prevented and the arrangement for waste transportation and disposal undertaken by an authorised person.

An authorised person is either:

- a person who is the holder of a waste management licence;

- a person registered as a carrier of controlled waste in accordance with the **Control of Pollution (Amendment) Act 1989;**

- a Local Authority which is a waste collection authority (in Scotland this is a Scottish Waste disposal authority).

4.6.2.3 *The Public Health (Control of Disease) Act 1984*

The Act prohibits placing matter exposed to infection from a notifiable disease in a dustbin or ashpit unless it has been disinfected. Notifiable diseases are detailed in section 4.3.5.1.

4.6.2.4 *Control of Pollution (Special Waste) Regulations 1980*

The regulations require that a consignment note be used at each stage of the disposal process and must be signed at each stage from the producer to final disposal.

Special waste includes prescription only medicines, controlled waste with a flash point below 21 degrees centigrade, corrosive chemicals and other chemicals likely to be found in hospital laboratories.

4.6.2.5 *Control of Substances Hazardous to Health Regulations 1999*

The regulations require healthcare organisations to make an adequate assessment of risk from clinical waste and to take measures which prevent or control exposure to the risks.

4.6.2.6 *Water Industry Act 1991*

The Act makes it an offence to discharge waste, e.g. drugs or chemical waste, into the sewer without the prior approval of the local sewerage provider.

4.6.2.7 Environmental Protection (Duty of Care) Regulations 1991

The regulations require the keeping of records of waste transfer and disposal. They are referred to in more detail below.

4.6.2.8 The Carriage of Dangerous Goods by Road Regulations 1996

4.6.2.9 Control of Substances Hazardous to Health 1999

4.6.2.10 The Producer Responsibility Obligations (Packaging Waste) Regulations 1997

These regulations impose obligations to recover and recycle a specific tonnage of packaging waste. The obligations are in line with the objectives set out in *EC Directives on Packaging and Packaging Waste (94/62/EC)*.

4.6.3 Categories of Waste

Waste should be categorised in order to minimise the risk of

- infection
- injury to individuals
- damage to the environment

Typical sources of waste in the clinical environment are typically:

- clinical
- non-clinical
- special
- confidential

The identification of the categories of clinical waste will help to determine the required strategies for waste management, including the method of final disposal.

4.6.4 Segregation of Waste[4]

Safe management and controlled disposal of waste requires proper segregation. This should be undertaken at the point of origin in order that appropriate routes can be identified for treatment and/or disposal.

---

4   NHS Estates *Healthcare Waste Management* HTM 2022 TSO 1997

The Health Service Advisory Committee (HSAC) has given guidance on colour coding for waste containers for the various categories of healthcare wastes and this means of segregation is endorsed by NHS Estates and the NHS Executive.

- Yellow – Group A waste, infectious waste for incineration
- Yellow and black stripes – non-infectious waste
- Light blue – potentially infectious waste for autoclaving before disposal. This includes laboratory cultures, human specimens and materials which are suspected of containing pathogenic agents.
- Black – non-clinical or household waste

4.6.5 Storage of Clinical Waste

Clinical waste should be separated from other waste and stored in yellow bags or containers in an area where people will not come into contact with it. The area should be clearly marked with warning signs, well lit and ventilated. Bags should be labelled with the source or origin of the waste for tracing purposes. The bags or containers should not be more than three quarters full to reduce the risk of breakage or spillage. Clinical waste should be collected as frequently as necessary. Waste which is placed in bags should be transferred as soon as possible into rigid containers. The containers should be of a sufficiently robust kind so that when closed they are vermin proof, leak proof, tamper resistant and will prevent penetration of the container by needles or other sharp objects.

Sharps should be stored in containers which comply with the British Standard BS 7320. These are closed containers which should securely closed when three quarters full. They should be stored safely out of the reach of children, both when in use and when awaiting collection.

Waste which should be autoclaved before disposal should be placed in a light blue plastic bag.

All waste which is awaiting collection for final disposal should be stored in a facility which is not prone to vandalism, theft or scavenging.

4.6.6   Disposal of Clinical Waste

4.6.6.1 Incineration

Two stage incineration is the preferred method of disposal of clinical waste. The HSAC in the guidance note *Safe Disposal of Clinical Waste* states that the following should be incinerated:

- soiled surgical dressings, swabs and all other contaminated waste from clinical areas;

- waste materials which pose a risk to staff handling them, such as waste from patients with infectious diseases;

- all human tissue, including blood, and related swabs and dressings;

- all sharps.

4.6.6.2 Autoclaving

Laboratory cultures, specimens and other materials which are suspected of containing pathogenic agents should be autoclaved before being transferred for final disposal. If it is not possible to autoclave these waste items, they should be securely placed in leak-proof containers which are suitably labelled and the containers transported directly to the incinerator.

4.6.6.3 Other waste

Drugs and similar chemical waste should be returned to the pharmacy. They should not be flushed into the drainage system without the consent of the local sewerage provider. Waste which does not pose a significant risk, such as stoma bags should be discharged to the sewer. If there is a significant risk of infection, they should be incinerated.

4.6.6.4 Radioactive Waste

Healthcare providers which accumulate or dispose of radioactive waste must apply to Her Majesty's Inspectors of pollution for permission. The application must state full details of the nature, types and activity of the waste, proposed disposal routes and include radiological assessments of the impact of disposal at the proposed limits.

4.6.7 Transfer of Waste

The healthcare organisation should ensure that the carrier who removes waste is an authorised person. If they are not, the responsibilities for final disposal of the waste rests with the organisation which is liable to prosecution if the waste is incorrectly managed.

4.6.8 Record Keeping

Environmental Protection (Duty of Care) Regulations 1991 require records to be kept of waste transfer and disposal. The transfer note with a description of the waste must be completed and handed to the authorised person disposing of the waste. The note should contain information about the parties to the transfer and be signed by both parties. The records should be retained for a minimum of two years. Repeated transfers of the same sort of waste may be included on one note, provided that the type of waste is identical in each case. In these circumstances the note is valid for one year.

The note should contain the following information:

- what the waste is;
- how much waste there is;
- the type of container;
- the time and date of transfer;
- the names and addresses of both parties;
- the category of authorised person each one is;
- the waste carrier's registration certificate number or waste licence number and the name of the issuing council;
- if there is an exemption from the requirement to register, the reason must be stated.

The test of the information is whether a third party could safely take over disposal of the waste if that became necessary.

Risk Management points

Correct disposal of clinical waste minimises risks of infection, sharps injuries and minimises the costs of inappropriate disposal

Risk management of waste disposal should include

- accountability arrangements;

- processes and contingencies;

- capability;

- outcomes;

- internal audit findings.

4.6.9   Further Information

Health Services Advisory Committee *Safe Disposal of Clinical Waste*

Health Technical Memorandum HTM 2065

**Controls Assurance Standards – Waste Management
November 1999**

1 Board level responsibility for waste management is clearly defined and there are clear lines of accountability throughout the organisation, leading to the Board.

2 There is waste management policy and strategy that is approved by the Risk Management Committee (or Board) and reviewed at least annually.

3 All waste is categorised in accordance with HTM 2065 and HSAC.

4 All waste is segregated in accordance with the guidance contained in HTM 2065 and HSAC.

5 All waste containers conform to legislative requirements

6 Prior to final disposal, all waste requiring storage is kept in accordance with HSAC requirements.

7 Staff who handle waste take all necessary safety precautions.

8 Transport of waste on-site or off-site is done in accordance with HSAC requirements.

9 Any on-site treatment of clinical waste complies with HSAC recommendations.

10 Waste hazards and incidents are dealt with in accordance with the processes contained in the risk management system standard and HSAC.

11 The risk management process contained within the risk management system standard is applied to the management of waste.

12 There is access to up-to-date waste management legislation and guidance.

13 All employees involved in handling waste receive appropriate information, instruction and training.

14 Key performance indicators capable of showing improvements in waste management and the management of associated risk are used at all levels of the organisation, including the Board, and the efficacy and usefulness of the indicators is reviewed regularly.

15 The system in place for waste management, including risk management arrangements, is monitored and reviewed by management and the Board in order to make improvements to the system.

4.7 IONISING RADIATIONS

The use of ionising radiation in healthcare is a unique feature of the service. The potential for patient or staff harm is such that the risk manager needs to be conversant with current statutes, regulations and practice. Many healthcare providers use ionising radiation as part of patient investigations or treatment, whether for a nurse ordering an x-ray in a cottage hospital or a neuro-surgeon carrying out a CT scan in a large teaching hospital. There are several statutes and regulations in respect for ionising radiation, but the common thrust is to minimise exposure for the patient and members of staff and to ensure the safe handling of materials.

4.7.1 Principle Statutes and Regulations

4.7.1.1 *The Ionising Radiations Regulations 1999 (IRR 99)*
Ionising Radiation (Medical Exposure) Regulations 2000 (IRMER 2000)

The principle regulations came into effect in 2000 and replaced the *Ionising Radiations Regulations 1985* (IRR85) and the related *Ionising Radiations (Outside Workers) Regulations 1993.*

The Health and Safety Executive is the regulating body for radiation exposure control in medical and dental practice. All health employers using radiation are required to comply with these regulations and are required to obtain HSE authorization before undertaking activities involving radiation. As such, health care providers are referred to in the regulations as 'radiation employers'.

4.7.1.1.1 Medical Exposure

Medical exposure is defined in the regulations as "exposure of a person to ionising radiation for the purposes of his medical or dental examination or treatment which is conducted under the direction of a suitably qualified person and includes any such examination or treatment conducted for the purposes of research".

4.7.1.1.2 Risk Assessment

Radiation employers are required to undertake prior risk assessments arising from the use of ionising radiation and to prevent and limit the consequences of identifiable radiation accidents. The quality of the assessment is described in the regulations as 'suitable and sufficient'. Contingency plans should be drawn up for any reasonably foreseeable accident.

The risk assessment should be able to demonstrate that:

- all hazards with the potential to cause a radiation accident have been identified: and

- the nature and magnitude of the risks to employees and other persons arising from these hazards has been evaluated.

Having identified a potential hazard, the radiation employer needs to take all reasonably practicable steps to:

- prevent any such accident;

- limit the consequences of any such accident which does occur; and provide employees with the information, instruction and training, and with the equipment necessary, to restrict their exposure to ionising radiation.

Risk managers will find the contingency planning proforma at Chapter Three useful to assist with this exercise.

4.7.1.1.3 Radiation Advisers

Radiation employers should have access to suitably qualified radiation advisers, Radiation Protection Advisers (RPA). The qualifications for this are:

- holding a valid certificate of competence from an organisation recognised by the HSE as an assessing body; or

- hold a National or Scottish Vocational Qualification (N/SVQ) level 4 in Radiation Protection Practice issued within the last five years; or

- under transitional arrangements up to the end of 2004, have held a formal appointment by an employer as an RPA under IRR85. From 2005, existing RPAs will need to hold either a certificate of competence or a N/SVQ.

The HSE produces *The Radiation Protection Adviser Newsletter* which provides key information on radiological protection issues.

4.7.1.1.4 Restriction of Exposure

Every radiation employer is under a duty to restrict, as far as is reasonably practicable, the extent to which employees are exposed to radiation. An annual exposure to a greater dose than 15mSv, (see below for units of measurement), should be immediately investigated. The maximum annual dosage for employees over 18 is 20mSv; below aged 18 it is 6mSv. Higher limits apply to particular exposure of the lens of the eye or small areas of skin. Where higher doses are suspected, the employer has a duty to inform the HSE.

Unsurprisingly, special arrangements are extremely important for pregnant and women who are breastfeeding. For an employee who is pregnant, the equivalent dosage to the foetus must not exceed 1mSv from the time of notification of the pregnancy for the rest of the pregnancy. Where an employee is breastfeeding, the conditions of exposure should be limited to prevent any significant body exposure to the employee.

The National Radiation Protection Board has issued guidance on the radiation exposure of pregnant patients during medical diagnosis. The main objectives are to minimise the exposure of the conceptus before the pregnancy is confirmed and to prevent unnecessary exposure of the foetus where radiological investigations are indicated during the pregnancy.

Detailed dosage limitations for different substances are detailed in the regulations.

Importantly, where a system has been put into effect to limit exposure, the employer has a duty to record the reasons for the decision and to ensure that the records are preserved for a period of fifty years from the making.

4.7.1.1.5 Information, Instruction and Training for Employees

All health employers have a duty to ensure:

- all employees who are engaged in work with ionising radiation are given appropriate training in the field of radiation protection and receive such information and instruction as is suitable for them to know:
  - the risks to health created by exposure to ionising radiation;
  - the precautions which should be taken; and
  - the importance of complying with the medical, technical and administrative requirements of the regulations.

- adequate information is given to other persons who are directly concerned with the work with ionising radiation carried on by the employer to ensure their health and safety so far as is reasonably practicable; and

- those female employees of that employer who are engaged in work with ionising radiation are informed of the possible risk from ionising radiation to the foetus and to a nursing infant and of the importance of those employees informing the employer as soon as possible:
  - after becoming aware of their pregnancy; or
  - if they are breast feeding.

4.7.1.2 Referrers, Practitioners and Operators

Referrers, practitioners and operators are defined in the regulations as:

Referrer: Person who refers a patient for x-ray

Practitioner: Person who justifies proceeding with the radiological examination

Operator: Person who carries out the radiological exposure.

All three groups should be trained adequately to undertake their jobs. A list of such suitably trained personnel should be kept by the employer together with details of qualifications and training undertaken. A continuous education programme should be in place for all practitioners and operators.

The employer needs to develop clinical criteria and radiation dosages relating to the radiological exposures and which is available to referrers. Copies of all legislation and accompanying documents must be available in the department.

4.7.1.2.1 Duties of Employees Under IRR99

It is the duty of any employee who is engaged in working with ionising radiations to exercise reasonable care while carrying out the work and to use any personal protective equipment provided. As well as making full and proper use of the equipment, there is an obligation to report any defect and to return the equipment to suitable accommodation for storage when not in use.

4.7.1.2.2 Regulation 32 – Equipment for Medical Exposure IRR99

Regulation 32 states that employers must ensure that equipment for medical exposures is designed, installed and maintained to ensure that the exposures are kept as low as reasonably practicable compatible with the clinical purpose of the examination.

Where practicable, equipment should include a suitable means of informing the user of the quantity of radiation produced during a radiological procedure. Importantly, the regulations require the health employer to have a quality assurance programme in place.

The quality assurance programme should include:

- adequate testing of new equipment or apparatus before it is first used for clinical purposes;

- adequate testing of the performance of the equipment or apparatus at appropriate intervals and after any major maintenance procedure to that equipment;

- where appropriate, such measurements at suitable intervals as are necessary to enable the assessment of representative doses from any radiation equipment to persons undergoing medical exposures.

The controls procedures should be audited to ensure that they take place and are of a suitable standard.

An administered radiation dosage which is much larger than intended must be investigated and reported to the Health and Safety Executive if it results from equipment malfunction or defect. There are specific time requirements to retain the investigation report or a copy. The immediate report should be kept for a minimum of two years; the detailed report or a copy must be kept for fifty years.

Whilst it would seem only common sense for checks to be made on the level of radiation emitted by machines, including CT scanners, a review by the National Radiological Protection Panel, published in 1992, indicated that only 7% of CT operators included periodic dose measurements as part of their quality assurance programme. It is important that departments review their compliance with current recommendations in order to comply with the regulations. CT scans account for approximately 2% of all x-ray examinations, but account for approximately 20% of the collective dose of radiation due to medical exposures.

Written protocols are required for all procedures carried out as part of radiological work. All functions within the department should be documented, from the patient's arrival to their departure. Diagnostic reference levels are required for standard sized patients and for each piece of equipment. This requires all practices to set levels of exposure for each type of examination.

4.7.1.2.3 Comforters and Carers

Comforters and carers are defined in the regulations as 'an individual who (other than as part of his occupation) knowingly and willingly incurs an exposure to ionising radiation resulting from the support and comfort of another person who is undergoing or has undergone medical exposure.' A dosage level should be set in the department's procedures. The Approved Code of Practice states that the level should not exceed 5.0 mSv in 5 consecutive years. 'Comforters and carers' applies to those looking after patients treated with implanted radiation sources as well as those holding patients during x-ray procedures.

4.7.1.2.4 Discharge to a Nursing Home

The regulations make it a requirement for the HSE to be informed as soon as it is known that a patient is to be returned to a nursing home following the administration of a radionuclide. This should be undertaken at the appointment stage. Whilst it is strictly the responsibility of the nursing home to undertake the notification, there is a responsibility on the Department of Nuclear Medicine to inform them.

4.7.1.3 Radioactive Substances Act 1993 (RSA 1993)

The Act provides for control in two areas by requiring those who keep or use radioactive materials to:

- register with Her Majesty's Inspectorate of Pollution (HMIP) who will issue a certificate of registration;

- be authorised and obtain a certificate of authorisation for the accumulation and/or disposal of radioactive waste.

The Act removed the exemption from registration by NHS facilities which previously existed.

In applying for registration the provider needs to state for each hospital:

- the address where the radioactive materials are to be kept;

- the name of the person responsible in law for ensuring compliance with the Act – normally the Chief Executive;

- the purpose for which the materials will be kept and used;

- a description of the materials (including the names of nucleotides);

- the maximum quantity and maximum radioactivity likely to be present on the premises at any time and likely to be used per week or month.

Provider units will need to state the name of the person who is competent to supervise the use accumulation and disposal of radiation materials. This person should be the Radiation Protection Adviser (RPA).

4.7.1.3.1 Record Keeping

Records of radionuclide stocks and the amounts of waste accumulated and disposed of need to be kept and made available when requested by the HMIP. Authorisation and registration stipulations need to be strictly complied with and will be inspected.

4.7.1.3.2 Employers' Responsibilities

Health providers need to be satisfied that:

- doctors and dentists employed by them and who are responsible for administering radioactive medicinal products (RMP) hold valid certificates for the procedures carried out;

- staff acting under the directions of a certificate holder can at any time check that the directing practitioner holds an appropriate certificate;

- the use of RMPs by staff is properly authorised when the certificate holder is absent.

The risk manager should check the systems are in place to monitor that:

- radioactive substances are being administered only by certificate holders or those acting on their direction;

- the activity administered to a patient is recorded.

4.7.1.3.3 Equipment Records

The employer has a duty to ensure that an inventory of radiation equipment is drawn up which includes enough information to identify either complete assemblies of equipment or individual items of ancillary equipment.

The inventory should include:

- name of the manufacturer;

- model number;

- serial number or unique identifier;

- year of manufacture;

- year of installation;

- service agent;

- maintenance history.

4.7.2 The Units of Measurement Regulations 1986 (SI 1986 No 1082)

The regulations recommend the adoption of standard European units of measurement.

The Becquerel (symbol Bq) is the SI of activity, the Gray (Gy) the SI of absorbed dose, the Sievert (Sv) the SI of dose equivalent and the unnamed SI of exposure is the Coulomb per kilogram. (Ckg-1).

4.7.3 The Medicines Act 1968

The Act covers the licensing provisions for the manufacture and supply of medicines, including radiopharmaceuticals. If a hospital produces radiopharmaceuticals, a manufacturer's licence is needed and the hospital will be subject to inspection by the Medicines Control Agency.

4.7.4 Retention of Hard Images

The retention of hard images is a matter for local interpretation of the Health Circular HC(89)20. Where a choice needs to be made between retaining the hard image and the x-ray report, the Royal College of Radiologists recommends that greater value lies in retaining the report. The x-ray report is considered to be the permanent constituent of the record and the x-ray film considered to be of a transitory nature.

4.7.5 Organisation Responsibilities

Health Service Guideline HSG(95)3 defines the duties of NHS authorities and Trusts to be fully aware of the statutory requirements concerning ionising radiation and to operate policies which meet them.

NHS authorities and Trusts should ensure that:

- HSG(95)3 is brought to the attention of all staff who deal with ionising radiation, and that it is effectively implemented;

- written statements of policy exist for the medical use of ionising radiation and make clear the responsibilities of specified staff members;

- arrangements exist for carrying those policies into effect, and for periodically reviewing the effectiveness of policies and arrangements;

- they are satisfied that their policies and implementation procedures are regularly reviewed and kept up to date;

- arrangements exist for the provision of advice on radiation protection to senior management and to employees;

- arrangements exist for the appropriate notification of incidents;

- records are available at the request of the Inspectorates.

4.8   ELEMENTS OF INFECTION CONTROL

"There is a managed environment, which minimises the risks of infection to patients, staff and visitors"[5]

4.8.1   Patients Affected by Hospital Acquired Infection

Studies have shown that approximately 10%[6,7] of patients at any one time have been infected in hospital. Infected patients stay longer in hospital, adversely affecting waiting lists and diverting resources which would be better used elsewhere.

In-patients are more susceptible to infection than the general population. Susceptibility is affected by age, by pre-existing disease and by the medical, surgical or immunosuppressive treatment the patient receives. Elderly patients and neonates are particularly vulnerable. In addition, the frequent need for antibiotics favours the emergence in hospitals of resistant bacteria.

Infections add to a patient's discomfort and length of stay in hospital. They may also adversely affect the management of the patient's other medical conditions.

It is possible that currently about 30% of hospital acquired infection could be prevented by the better application of existing knowledge and implementation of realistic infection control policies[8].

---

5   NHS Executive – *Controls Assurance Standard – Infection Control* Nov 1999

6   *Hospital Infection Control* – PHLS 1995

7   *The Management and Control of Hospital Acquired Infection in Acute NHS Trusts in England* – National Audit Office, February 2000

8   *Hospital Infection Control* – PHLS 1995

4.8.2   Antibiotic Resistance

The emergence of anti-biotic resistant strains of bacteria which readily spread to cause outbreaks has made efforts to control infections one of the main tasks for infection control staff. Highly resistant strains of Staphyllococcus aureus (e.g. methicillin resistant Staphyllococcus aureus (MRSA), Gram-negative bacilli and enterococci are present in many hospitals in the UK and most other countries.

Implementation of effective antibiotic policies and prevention of cross infection are necessary to reduce the emergence and prevent the spread of resistant strains.

High standards of sanitation and hygiene, especially in hospitals and old people's homes, are needed to stop outbreaks of resistant bacteria.

Using antibiotics carefully
The careful usage of antibiotics is central to reducing the opportunities for the emergence of anti-biotic resistant strains of bacteria. This can be assisted by:

- educating doctors and patients to discourage inappropriate prescriptions for antibiotics; most simple coughs, colds, sore throats and influenza are caused by viruses and an antibiotic won't help.

- advising patients, if they are prescribed antibiotics, to complete the course; stopping before the end of a course may make it easier for the resistant bacteria to take over. This is especially important in tuberculosis.

- reducing the use of antibiotics in farm animals, especially where these are used just to enhance their growth.

4.8.3   The Public Health Laboratory Service

The Public Health Laboratory Service (PHLS) protects the population from infection by detecting, diagnosing, and monitoring communicable diseases. It provides evidence for action to prevent and control infectious disease threats to individuals and populations.

The evidence comes from expert analysis and assessment of data generated from the PHLS's own microbiological and epidemiological investigations and from many other sources.

The PHLS is also represented on a number of professional groups, such as the Handwashing Liaison Group, as even very simple things like ensuring that staff wash their hands between contact with patients can have a huge impact. It is important that all concerned continue with and consolidate work such as this to minimize the spread of infections in hospital.

4.8.4   Legal Requirements

Hospital infection control is an important part of an effective risk management programme to improve the quality of patients' care and the occupational health of staff.

The Controls of Substances Hazardous to Health Regulations (COSHH) 1994 includes pathogenic organisms amongst the hazards covered and require a formal risk assessment. Hospitals have a legal obligation to comply with the provisions and requirements of food legislation. The Food Safety Act 1990 and subsequent regulations introduced increased penalties for non-compliance and a defence of 'due diligence'.

NOTIFICATIONS OF INFECTIOUS DISEASES (NOIDS) IN ENGLAND AND WALES

In order to maintain a national picture of infections, certain diseases are required to be notified. (See also chapter 4).

The statutory requirement for the notification of certain infectious diseases came into being towards the end of the 19th century. Diseases such as Cholera, Diphtheria, Smallpox and Typhoid had to be reported in London from 1891 and in the rest of England and Wales from 1899. The list of diseases has been increased over the decades and now stands at about 30. Originally the head of the family or landlord had the responsibility of reporting the disease to the local 'Proper Officer' but now this is restricted to the attending medical practitioner, either in the patient's home or at a surgery or hospital.

The prime purpose of the Notifications system is *speed* in detecting possible outbreaks and epidemics. Accuracy of diagnosis is secondary and since 1968 clinical suspicion of a notifiable infection is all that is required. If a diagnosis later proves incorrect it can always be changed or cancelled. Statistics were collected nationally at the Registrar General's Office, who already collected data on births, marriages and deaths. The Office was later known as the Office of Population Censuses and Surveys (OPCS) and now as the Office for National Statistics (ONS), but in 1997 the responsibility for administering the NOIDS system transferred to the Communicable Disease Surveillance Centre (CDSC).

Consultants in charge of infected or colonised patients or those at particular risk of infection have a common law duty of care for the health and safety of staff, visitors and other patients within the hospital. The infection control team should inform consultants of microbiological hazards arising from their patients.

4.8.5   Accountability and Process Framework

All trusts should have an established framework for Board level accountability for infection control, medicines management and catering. The Chief Executive is responsible for ensuring that there are effective arrangements for infection control.

There should be clear lines of accountability established throughout the organisation which includes defining the relationships between the risk management committee, clinical governance committee, medicines management committee, infection control committee and infection control team. The infection control committee should endorse all policies relating to infection control.

Prevention and control of infection should be considered as part of all service activity. This includes the input by the control of infection team into engineering and building works, the contracting process for hotel services and the purchase of medical devices and equipment.

The infection control team needs to develop and implement an annual infection control programme with clearly defined objectives and which is audited as part of the programme. The team should produce an annual report which is presented to the Board.

Surveillance of infection should be carried out as specified in the annual infection control programme and the results reported. Management and the Board should regularly review the systems in place for the control of infection in order to make improvements to the system.

All surveillance methods have the following key components:

- data collection using standard case definitions;

- collation of data;

- analysis and interpretation of data;

- dissemination of information for action to those who need to know.

Glenister et al[9] in 1992 compared selective methods for surveillance over an extended period of time against comprehensive standard methods designed to detect all infections in the study population. The researchers found the best general method was laboratory based ward liaison surveillance which involved follow up of positive microbiological reports with review of the patient's case records (nursing notes, medical notes, temperature charts and treatment charts) and, in addition, twice weekly visits to the wards to review the case records of all patients considered by the ward nursing staff to have infection. This method took 6.4 hours per 100 beds weekly and detected 71% of infections found by a much more time consuming, comprehensive survey which involved examination of all records of all patients three times weekly (18 hours per 100 beds).

The infection control team should provide education to all health care staff, including those working in support services.

4.8.6   Particular Problem Areas

4.8.6.1 Basic Hygiene Arrangements

Prevention and control policies for hospital acquired infection should be reviewed regularly for:

- MRSA

- patient isolation

- handling of sharps

- clinical waste management

- handwashing

- antibiotic usage

---

9   Glenister HM, Taylor LJ, Cooke EM, Bartlett CLR. *A Study of Surveillance Methods for Detecting Hospital Infection*, 1992 PHLS

- urinary catheters and usage
- intravascular devices.

4.8.6.2 Handwashing

Effective hand hygiene is possibly the most effective method of preventing hospital acquired infection.[10,11] Doctors who decontaminate their hands between patients reduce hospital acquired infection rates. Many observational studies in intensive care units show low rates of handwashing, especially among doctors.

Excuses given include:

- insufficient hand basins
- lack of supplies of liquid soap
- lack of supplies of paper towels

Handwashing – areas most frequently missed:

- thumb
- ring finger
- fingertips
- inter-digital surfaces

4.8.7 Highest Incidence of Surgical Site Infection (75th centile)

- large bowel surgery
- vascular surgery
- CABG
- knee prosthesis
- hip prosthesis
- abdominal Hysterectomy

---

10 Gould DJ, Wilson-Barrett J 1996. *Nurses infection control practices*. International Journal of Nursing Studies 33:143-160

11 Teare EL, Cookson B, French G, Gould D, Jenner E , McCullocjh J, Pallatt A 1999 *Handwashing. A Modest Measure with big effects* BMJ 318 686

Specialities with the highest risk of hospital acquired bacteraemia (75th centile)

- **Haematology**
- **Oncology**
- **Nephrology**
- **Gastroenterology**
- **General medicine**
- **Cardiology**
- **Infectious diseases**
- **Geriatric medicine**

4.8.8   Arrangements for the Control of an Outbreak in Hospital[12]

Outbreaks of hospital infection vary greatly in extent and severity, ranging from a few cases of mild urinary tract infection to a large outbreak of food poisoning affecting many people. There should be clear arrangements in place to cover emergency preparedness, communications and controls. The contingency planning tool outlined in chapter three can inform this process.

4.8.8.1 Recognition of an Outbreak

The rapid recognition of outbreaks is one of the most important objectives of routine surveillance. A severe outbreak may be easy to identify; outbreaks may however be more insidious and reach considerable proportions before recognition. This latter case may well occur if the infections are in out-patients, (e.g. adenoviral conjunctivitis), follow discharge from hospital (e.g. surgical wound infections), or have a long incubation period (e.g. tuberculosis, hepatitis). Whilst such outbreaks may be recognised by a laboratory, recognition may rely upon the vigilance of medical and nursing staff.

Steps to be taken in an outbreak exists

An initial assessment should be undertaken which determines:

- if the outbreak is likely to be of major importance

---

12 *Hospital Infection Control* – PHLS, March 1995

- if the outbreak appears confined to the hospital
- whether there may be implications for the community generally.

Outbreaks of limited extent should be dealt with by the Outbreak Control Group and infection control team together with appropriate advice to clinical staff. The CDSC should be informed.

Where the outbreak is not confined to the hospital, the Communicable Disease Consultant should co-ordinate action. Health authorities should have in place appropriate plans for community outbreaks drawn up together with the Local Authority.

Major outbreaks

Consideration as to whether a major outbreak has occurred requires an assessment of the number of people involved, the pathogenicity of the organism and the potential for spread within the hospital or community. A single case of diptheria on a paediatric ward would require all the procedures associated with a major outbreak, whereas many cases of a mild non-transmissable illness may be considered and treated as a minor outbreak.

However, if there is any doubt as to whether an outbreak is minor or major, the procedure for a major outbreak should be followed.

The Major Outbreak Control Group (MOCG)

Upon deciding that a major outbreak has occurred, the MOCG should be immediately convened by the Infection Control Consultant. The group should include the Outbreak Control Group together with the Director of Public Health, Public Health Laboratory Service, Regional Epidemiologist, Medical Director, Nursing Director Occupational Health staff and Chief Environmental Health Officer (if the infection is likely to be food or water-borne).

Functions of the MOCG

Once a major outbreak has been identified, the functions of the MOCG are:

- to take all necessary steps for the continuing clinical care of patients during the outbreak;
- to clarify the resource implications of the outbreak;
- to agree and co-ordinate policy decisions on the investigation

and control of the outbreak and ensure that they are implemented, allocating responsibilities to specific individuals who will be responsible for taking action;

- to consider the need for outside help and expertise;

- to ensure that adequate communication channels are established, nominating one person to be responsible for statements to news media;

- to provide clear instructions to ward staff and others, including contracted staff;

- to agree arrangements for providing information to patients and visitors;

- to ensure communication with the Department of Health;

- to meet frequently to review progress on the outbreak investigation and control;

- to define the end of the outbreak;

- to evaluate the lessons learned;

- to prepare a preliminary report, within 48 hours, interim reports as necessary and a final report. The reports are to inform others outside the hospital of lessons to be learned from the outbreak.

4.8.8.2 Major Outbreaks of Infection in the Community

Types of outbreak

There are two types of outbreak in the community which may have very significant implications for hospitals:

Acute outbreaks which develop quickly over a few hours. They are generally toxin mediated (e.g. staphylococcal food poisoning) and associated with a point source. The patients are not infectious and the symptoms are entirely due to the ingestion of microbial toxin.

Non-acute outbreaks develop over a period of days or even weeks. Salmonella food poisoning and influenza are examples. Salmonella infections may, on occasion, be so acute that they mimic toxin mediated illness. Milk and water borne outbreaks are likely to be extensive and involve large numbers of people spread widely both geographically and in time.

For acute outbreaks, the hospital should consider using the Major Incident Plan and involve the same team as for the MOCG and inform the Communicable Diseases Centre (CDC).

4.8.8.3 Sterilization or Disinfection of Medical Devices: General Principles[13]

The following principles are applicable to most questions CDC receives about sterilization or disinfection of patient-care equipment. However, these statements are not intended to be comprehensive.

- in general, reusable medical devices or patient-care equipment that enters normally sterile tissue or the vascular system or through which blood flows should be sterilized before each use. Sterilization means the use of a physical or chemical procedure to destroy all microbial life, including highly resistant bacterial endospores. The major sterilizing agents used in hospitals are:
  - moist heat by steam autoclaving,
  - ethylene oxide gas, and
  - dry heat.

  However, there are a variety of chemical germicides (sterilants) that have been used for purposes of reprocessing reusable heat-sensitive medical devices and appear to be effective when used appropriately, i.e., according to manufacturer's instructions. These chemicals are rarely used for sterilization, but appear to be effective for high-level disinfection of medical devices that come into contact with mucous membranes during use (e.g., flexible fibreoptic endoscopes).

- disinfection means the use of a chemical procedure that eliminates virtually all recognized pathogenic micro-organisms but not necessarily all microbial forms (e.g., bacterial endospores) on inanimate objects. There are three levels of disinfection: high, intermediate, and low. High-level disinfection kills all organisms, except high levels of bacterial spores, and is effected with a chemical germicide cleared for marketing as a sterilant by the Food and Drug Administration. Intermediate-level disinfection kills mycobacteria, most

---

13 Communicable Diseases Centre – Atlanta – 1999

viruses, and bacteria with a chemical germicide registered as a "tuberculocide" by the Environmental Protection Agency (EPA). Low-level disinfection kills some viruses and bacteria with a chemical germicide registered as a hospital disinfectant by the EPA.

- heat stable reusable medical devices that enter the blood stream or enter normally sterile tissue should **always** be reprocessed using heat-based methods of sterilization (e.g., steam autoclave or dry heat oven).

- laparoscopic or arthroscopic telescopes (optic portions of the endoscopic set) should be subjected to a sterilization procedure before each use; if this is not feasible, they should receive high-level disinfection. Heat stable accessories to the endoscopic set (e.g., trocars, operative instruments) should be sterilized by heat-based methods (e.g., steam autoclave or dry heat oven).

- reusable devices or items that touch mucous membranes should, at a minimum, receive high-level disinfection between patients. These devices include reusable flexible endoscopes, endotracheal tubes, anaesthesia breathing circuits, and respiratory therapy equipment.

- medical devices that require sterilization or disinfection must be thoroughly cleaned to reduce organic material or bioburden before being exposed to the germicide, and the germicide and the device manufacturer's instructions should be closely followed.

- except on rare and special instances (as mentioned below), items that do not ordinarily touch the patient or touch only intact skin are not involved in disease transmission, and generally do not necessitate disinfection between uses on different patients. These items include crutches, bedboards, blood pressure cuffs, and a variety of other medical accessories. Consequently, depending on the particular piece of equipment or item, washing with a detergent or using a low-level disinfectant may be sufficient when decontamination is needed.

Exceptional circumstances that require non-critical items to be either dedicated to one patient or patient cohort, or subjected to low-level disinfection between patient uses are those involving

- patients infected or colonized with vancomycin-resistant enterococci or other drug-resistant micro-organisms judged by the infection control program, based on current state, regional, or national recommendations, to be of special or clinical or epidemiologic significance

or

- patients infected with highly virulent micro-organisms, e.g., viruses causing hemorrhagic fever (such as Ebola or Lassa).

A protocol for the local decontamination of surgical instruments is available at:
http://www.doh.gov.uk/decontaminationguidance/index.htm

The risk manager should refer to local policies for immunisation of health care workers, needlestick injuries, measures for the control of transmission for new variant CJD, HIV and AIDS, Hepatitis B and other current issues of concern. These may be obtained at the PHLS website: **http://www.phls.co.uk**

The Chief Executive is responsible for ensuring that there are effective arrangements for the decontamination of medical devices. Arrangements should include a senior member of staff with defined responsibility, who is provided with the necessary resources and authority for the task. It is expected that this officer will report directly to the Chief Executive.

Clear lines of accountability, for all parts of the decontamination cycle should be established defining the relationships between users and the Risk Management, Clinical Governance, and Infection Control Committees and the Infection Control team.

An annual report on the efficacy of the decontamination process should be submitted to the Risk Management Committee for review. This committee which includes in its membership the Chief Executive, should present the report to the Board.

The scope of responsibility should also consider contractors and professional liability where the organisation either buys in or sells services to other organisations.

The Institute of Sterile Service Management recommends the following:

- personnel should be trained to handle, collect and transport contaminated medical devices/ equipment and should wear protective clothing in accordance with local safety policies and procedures

- reusable devices should be separated from clinical waste at the point of use by persons aware of the potential infection hazards.

- sharps should be removed and placed into approved containers conforming to BS 7320 at the point of use.

- re-usable textiles should be placed in soiled linen bags and returned to the laundry service (HSG (95)18).

- contaminated liquids should be placed into leak proof containers for disposal unless facilities exist for the user to empty them into a clinical sluice.

- contaminated medical devices should be confined and contained in closed leak-proof plastic bags or containers to avoid spills, the generation of aerosols or contact with staff and environmental surfaces. They should be transported as soon as possible after use to the decontamination area; the contents of the containers should be labelled to facilitate processing.

- used equipment should be bagged and transported to the decontamination area in enclosed containers where necessary, and records kept of vehicles and containers used.

- contaminated medical devices and equipment must be kept separate from clean medical devices/equipment during transportation. This is achieved by using separate containers to provide physical barriers between clean and dirty items.

- contaminated medical devices / equipment shall only enter the department through the decontamination area.

4.8.8.4 *Activities Reported to Have no Effect on Controlling Hospital Acquired Infection*

- routine use of disinfectants for ward cleaning

- use of overshoes in operating theatres

- use of masks and hats in outer operating theatre or for wound dressing

- use of gowns by visitors to theatre
- three dose antibiotic prophylaxis rather than single dose
- turning operating theatre ventilation off at night

SOME WARD FOOD HYGIENE POINTS FROM A TRUST WITHOUT WARD INFECTIONS FROM CATERING FOR TWENTY YEARS[14]

WARD KITCHENS – 10 POINT GOOD HOUSEKEEPING

Wash your hands

Use the wash hand basin provided, especially before handling food and always after using the w.c.

Over clothing

Always wear clean, disposable blue aprons when handling food.

Do not store personal clothing and effects in the kitchen.

Smoking

Do not smoke whilst handling food or in ward kitchens at any time.

Remember this is an offence for which an individual may be prosecuted.

Illness/First Aid

Tell your supervisor of any skin, nose, throat or bowel trouble.

Cover cuts or sores with a waterproof dressing.

Food Service

Always serve food promptly on arrival at the ward.

Refrigerator

Check the refrigerator daily and defrost weekly.

Inside temperature should not exceed 5°C.

---

14 WARRINGTON COMMUNITY HEALTH CARE (NHS) TRUST

- date and label patient's food for identification and do not keep for longer than 24 hours.

- do not store medicines in refrigerator

Cleaning

Keep tidy – Clean as you go and use the correct materials.

Only keep essential items and do not store cleaning equipment in the kitchen.

Refuse

Keep the container covered at all times.

Empty frequently.

Pests

Report any vermin immediately to the Pest Control Officer.

Usage

Use the kitchen for food preparation and service only and not as a rest room.

Visitors must not be allowed into the kitchens.

NEVER KEEP FOOD OVER FROM ONE MEAL TO THE NEXT

4.8.9 National Action Plan – Action by the NHS for the Management and Control of Infection in Hospitals in England

In response to the growing concerns about hospital acquired infections, the Chief Medical Officer issued guidance under the circular HSC2000/002 which set performance standards for the NHS. These are:

4.8.9.1 *Summary*

The Health Service Circular (HSC2000/002) sets out a programme of action for the NHS to:

- strengthen prevention and control of infection in hospital;

- secure appropriate health care services for patients with infection;

- improve surveillance of hospital infection;
- monitor and optimise anti-microbial prescribing.

It follows a recent analysis by Regional Epidemiologists, commissioned by the NHS Executive, of the management and control of infection in acute hospital Trusts and complements HSC 1999/049 *Resistance to Antibiotics and other Anti-microbial Agents* and the Controls Assurance framework.

Requirement: Strengthen prevention and control of communicable disease and infection control processes

- secure appropriate arrangements for the control of hospital infection
- ensure senior management and Board level commitment
- review service agreements on hospital infection control
- secure appropriate membership and functioning of Hospital Infection Control Committee
- secure appropriate composition and functioning of Hospital Infection Control Team, including support staffing and resourcing
- ensure that programmes for the control of infection are in place and working effectively
- ensure that appropriate infection control policies and procedures are in place, implemented and monitored
- ensure that education on infection control is included in induction and orientation programmes for health care staff

Requirement: Improve quality of service provision through clinical audit and continuing professional development (CPD)

- review the infection control content of clinical audit and CPD programmes for NHS Trust staff, including the Infection Control Team.

Requirement: Secure a safe clinical environment through:

- high standards of hygiene and general cleanliness of the hospital environment

- ensure appropriate contracts are in place and monitored
- consideration of infection control issues in service developments
- involve Infection Control Teams in service specification, including building works and purchase of equipment

Requirement: Secure appropriate health care services for patients with infection:

- secure appropriate provision of isolation facilities within each Trust
- undertake risk assessment to determine appropriate provision within the Trust and agree level and type of provision with Regional Office

Requirement: Improve surveillance

- ensure that microbiology services meet the infection control and public health surveillance needs
- ensure that appropriate and timely information is provided to the Infection Control Team.
- ensure that laboratories report regularly to the relevant Consultant in Communicable Disease Control and Public Health Laboratory Service Communicable Disease Surveillance Centre
- ensure appropriate staffing and IT support to undertake surveillance

Requirement: Ensure that appropriate surveillance is being undertaken

- implement programme for surveillance of infection

Requirement: Utilise surveillance data to guide the control of infection

- review information outputs at local and Trust level and ensure that clinicians, managers and CCDCs are provided with appropriate and timely information

Requirement: Monitor and optimise anti-microbial prescribing

- promote optimal prescribing to contain and control anti-microbial resistance

- continue implementation of actions set out in HSC 1999/049, and report at regular intervals to the Regional Office on progress

Risk managers will need to ensure that progress reporting against these targets are reported to the Risk Management Committee and Board.

Controls Assurance Standards – November 1999
CATERING AND FOOD HYGIENE

1 Board level responsibility for food hygiene, nutritional policy and catering services is clearly defined and there is a clear line of management accountability throughout the organisation up to the Trust Board

2 Food premises are registered with the Local Authority

3 All food preparation, processing, manufacturing, distribution and transportation, is carried out in hygienic conditions

4 All foods are stored in appropriate conditions and protected from contamination and deterioration, including protection against pests

5 All food handlers maintain a high standard of personal hygiene

6 All food ingredients are purchased in accordance with a standard purchasing specification which is used by all suppliers and catering staff

7 All foods, including raw materials, ingredients, intermediate products and finished products, are kept at temperatures which comply with the Food Safety (Temperature Control) Regulations 1995

8 Food safety assessments are carried out with the aim of identifying the critical food safety steps within the business and taking appropriate control measures to reduce any associated risks

9 All dietary needs and preferences are met through meals which provide the key elements of a balanced diet and which provide patients with a choice of dishes presented in a written menu

10 Meal availability and service delivery complies with the requirements laid out in Hospital catering: delivering a quality service

11 Food hazards, incidents and complaints are dealt with in accordance with HSG (93)13, and general requirements contained in the risk management system standard

12 Contingency arrangements are in place to ensure the delivery of safe and nutritious food in the event of total or partial failure of normal arrangements

13 All food handlers are given supervision, instruction and/or training in accordance with their level of work activity and responsibility and training records are kept

14 There is access to up-to-date legislation and guidance relating to food hygiene, nutrition and catering services

15 Key indicators capable of showing improvements in catering services and food hygiene, and the management of associated risk are used at all levels of the organisation, including the Board, and the efficacy and usefulness of the indicators is reviewed regularly

16 The system in place for food safety is monitored and reviewed by management and the Board in order to make improvements to the system

17 The Internal Audit function, in conjunction with a catering/food hygiene specialist(s), carries out periodic audits to provide assurances to the Board that a suitable system of catering and food hygiene which conforms to this standard is in place and working properly

INFECTION CONTROL – 1999

1 Board level responsibility for infection control is clearly defined and there are clear lines of accountability for infection control matters throughout the organisation, leading to the Board

2 There is an Infection Control Committee that endorses all infection control policies, procedures, and guidance, provides advice and support on the implementation of policies, and monitors the progress of the annual infection control programme

3 There is an appropriately constituted and functioning Infection Control Team

4 Prevention and control of infection is considered as part of all service development activity.

5 An organisation wide annual infection control programme with clearly defined objectives is produced by the Infection Control Team

6 Written policies, procedures and guidance for the prevention and control of infection are implemented and reflect relevant legislation and published professional guidance

7 There is an annual programme for the audit of infection control policies and procedures

8 Timely and effective specialist microbiological support is provided for the infection control service.

9 Surveillance of infection is carried out using defined methods in accordance with agreed objectives and priorities, which have been specified in the annual infection control programme

10 A comprehensive infection control report is produced by the Infection Control Team on an annual basis, reviewed by the Risk Management Committee and presented to the Board

11 The Infection Control Committee and Infection Control Team have access to up-to-date legislation and guidance relevant to infection control

12 Education in infection control is provided to all health care staff, including those employed in support services

13 Key indicators capable of showing improvements in infection control and/or providing early warning of risk are used at all levels of the organisation, including the Board, and the efficacy and usefulness of the indicators is reviewed regularly

14 The system in place for control of infection is monitored and reviewed by management and the Board in order to make improvements to the system

15 The Internal Audit function, in conjunction with the Infection Control Committee and Infection Control Team, carries out periodic audits to provide assurances to the Board that a suitable system of infection control which conforms to this standard is in place and working properly

MEDICAL EQUIPMENT AND DEVICES MANAGEMENT – 1999

1 Board level responsibility for medical devices management is clearly defined and there are clear lines of accountability throughout the organisation, leading to the Board

2 There is a broad-based medical devices group

3 A broad-based purchasing advisory group has been established in accordance with Medical Devices Agency DB 9801.

4 There is a comprehensive organisation-wide policy on the deployment, monitoring and control of medical devices

5 All medical devices and equipment are selected and acquired in accordance with a clearly laid down policy which conforms to MDA and NAO recommendations

6 All professional users and end-users have access to manufacturer's

instructions and users sign statements to the effect that they have received instructions on the safe use of devices or equipment.

7 Manufacturers automatically send copies of revised instructions to a named recipient and these are appropriately dealt with

8 All instructions supplied by the user organisation are evaluated for their adequacy

9 Acceptance checks are carried out on all new equipment, whether purchased, leased or on loan, brought in to the organisation

10 All devices and equipment new to the organisation are properly stored after delivery

11 All new devices are subject to an 'acceptance procedure' before being put into use

12 All prescribing decisions are made by staff with appropriate professional qualifications and suitable experience, backed by appropriate administrative and technical support

13 All necessary information required to properly manage the organisation's range of medical devices/equipment is recorded on a suitable system

14 All medical devices/equipment are properly maintained and repaired

15 The in-house maintenance department is externally accredited

16 All medical devices returned for servicing and repair are properly decontaminated

17 Medical devices/equipment are replaced in accordance with an agreed policy

18 Loan equipment is delivered and commissioned in accordance with agreed procedures

19 All loaned equipment is collected when no longer needed

20 All loaned equipment is properly checked and tested

21 Where appropriate, medical devices are decontaminated in accordance with HSC 1999/178 and HSC 1999/179

22 Decontamination equipment that does not meet the requirements of current standards and test methods is upgraded or replaced as soon as practicable in accordance with a planned replacement programme

23 Medical devices that cannot be easily cleaned are replaced with devices that are easier to clean as part of a planned programme

25 A complete record of hazard and safety notices issued by the Medical Devices Agency is maintained; notices are distributed to the appropriate people in the organisation; and recommendations contained in the notices are implemented

26 The risk management process contained within the risk management system standard is applied to the management of medical devices risk

27 Staff are made aware of and, where necessary, trained in adverse incident reporting requirements for medical devices

28 All professional users are trained in the safe operation of medical devices

29 All technical supervisors are provided with appropriate training

30 All end-users are given proper training in the safe and effective use of medical devices

31 All staff are provided with training in the safe use of equipment

32 Key indicators capable of showing improvements in medical devices management and/or providing early warning of risk are used at all levels of the organisation, including the Board, and the efficacy and usefulness of the indicators is reviewed regularly

33 The organisation participates in benchmarking its management of medical devices in accordance with National Audit Office recommendations

34 The system in place for medical devices management, including risk management arrangements, is monitored and reviewed by management and the Board in order to make improvements to the system

35 The Internal Audit function, in conjunction with medical devices specialist(s), carries out periodic audits to provide assurances to the Board that a system of medical device management is in place that conforms to the requirements of this standard

MEDICINES MANAGEMENT – 2000

1 Board level responsibility for the safe and secure handling of medicines is clearly defined and there are clear lines of accountability throughout the organisation, leading to the Board

2 Suitable controls are in place, which ensure that the principles of the Duthie Report are met

3 Medicines are stored and handled in a safe and secure manner

4 The organisation conforms to Regulation 5 (1) of the NHS (Charges for Drugs and Appliances) Regulations 1989 as amended

5 Unlicensed aseptic dispensing in hospital pharmacies complies with EL (97) 52

6 Prescription, supply and administration conform to the requirements of relevant legislation and best practice. Prescription, supply and administration of medicines is undertaken only by appropriately qualified, competent staff

7 Controlled drug records comply with the Misuse of Drugs (Safe Custody) Regulations 1985 and are reconciled on a regular basis

8 All medicines no longer required are destroyed or otherwise disposed of in accordance with safety, legal and environmental requirements

9 The supply of medicines for clinical trials is undertaken in accordance with relevant legislation and best practice guidelines

10 The organisation reports adverse incidents involving medicinal products and devices to the relevant agency, and appropriately manages any subsequent required action

11 A pharmacist supervises pharmaceutical dispensing activities. All dispensing is undertaken by persons suitably trained and competent to perform the task

12 All healthcare staff involved with medicines undertake continuing professional development, which is aligned to clinical governance requirements, to ensure the safe and secure handling processes

13 The risk management process contained within the risk management system standard is applied to the safe and secure handling of medicines

14 The organisation, through the Chief Pharmacist, has access to up-to-date legislation and guidance relating to the safe and secure handling of medicines

15 Adequate resources support the safe, secure and appropriate use of medicines

16 Key indicators capable of showing improvements in the safe and secure handling of medicines and the management of associated risk are used at all levels of the organisation, including the Board, and the efficacy and usefulness of the indicators is reviewed regularly

17 The system in place for the safe and secure handling of medicines, including risk management arrangements, is monitored and reviewed by management and the Board in order to make improvements to the system

18 The Internal Audit function, aided as necessary by relevant pharmacy and other specialists, carries out periodic audits to provide assurances to the

Board that a system of medicines management is in place that conforms to the requirements of this standard

DECONTAMINATION OF RE-USABLE MEDICAL DEVICES STANDARD – December 2000

There is a system in place that ensures as far as reasonably practicable that all reusable medical devices are properly decontaminated prior to use and that the risks associated with decontamination facilities and processes are adequately managed

1 Board level responsibility for decontamination of re-usable medical devices is clearly defined and there are clear lines of accountability for decontamination matters throughout the organisation, leading to the board.

2 Decontamination issues are considered prior to the purchase of re-usable medical devices and decontamination equipment.

3 All surgical instrument sets are tracked through the decontamination process.

4 The use of all surgical instrument sets on individual patients can be traced to the appropriate patient.

5 All contaminated re-usable medical devices are handled, collected and transported to the decontamination area in a manner that avoids the risk of contamination to patients, staff and any area of the healthcare facility.

6 Cleaning, disinfection, storage and use of flexible or rigid endoscopes is undertaken in accordance with MDA DB 9607 and current legislative requirements.

7 All other re-usable medical devices are decontaminated in accordance with legislative and best practice requirements.

8 Decontamination equipment is subject to validation, calibration, monitoring and maintenance by appropriately qualified persons.

9 Ethylene oxide sterilisers are operated and used in accordance with legislative and good practice requirements.

10 All medical devices, decontamination equipment and surfaces are properly dealt with after use on patients known to have or who are in a risk category for CJD.

11 All decontamination equipment that does not meet the requirements of current standards and test methods is upgraded or replaced as soon as practicable in accordance with a planned replacement programme.

12 All medical devices that cannot be easily cleaned are identified and, where

practicable, and in a planned programme, replaced with versions that are easier to clean.

13 Every location in which the decontamination of re-usable medical devices is carried out is properly designed, maintained and controlled.

14 The risk management process contained within the risk management system standard is applied to all aspects of decontamination of re-usable medical devices.

15 SSD facilities meet the requirements for the segregation of clean and dirty activities set out in HBN 13 and ISSM 2000.

16 Appropriately qualified key personnel are in place in accordance with HTM 2010 and HTM 2030.

17 All staff involved in decontamination processes have access to up-to-date legislation and guidance.

18 Education and training in relevant aspects of decontamination practice is provided to relevant healthcare staff, including those working in a clinical environment.

19 Key indicators capable of showing improvements in the safety and efficacy of the system in place for decontamination of re-usable medical devices and/or providing early warning of risk, are used at all levels of the organisation, including the board, and the efficacy and usefulness of the indicators is reviewed regularly.

20 The system in place for decontamination is monitored and reviewed by management and the board in order to make improvements.

21 The Internal Audit function, in conjunction with the designated individual and in consultation with the Infection Control Committee, carries out periodic audits to provide assurances to the board that the decontamination of re-usable medical devices conforms to the requirements of this standard.

5

COMPLAINTS, CLAIMS AND FINANCIAL CONTINGENCIES FOR LITIGATION

"Funding successful claims for negligence means that there is less cash available to treat patients" – Commons Public Accounts Committee, 2000

5.1   INTRODUCTION

The salient feature of the 1980s and 1990s in medico-legal matters has been the seemingly inexorable rise in the number of complaints and claims against the health service. Changes in the health service itself, especially in being more 'market driven', and in the social and legislative environment have contributed to this phenomenon. However, the causes and effects of the increases are difficult to disentangle. Additionally, there is an 'iceberg effect' in that the patients who do complain or make claims are a minority of those who have grounds for complaint. The minority is even smaller for those making claims for compensation. It may therefore be reasonably expected that the number of complaints and claims in respect of healthcare will continue to rise for the future.

New mechanisms are being put into place to manage complaints, claims and their financial consequences. This chapter discusses the resulting changes in handling complaints. Many of the methods and approaches recommended for the management of complaints can be applied to the management of claims, especially in the preliminary stages when information is being sought by the potential claimant. It is advisable that once litigation begins, the claim is put into the hands of a solicitor or claims manager who is experienced and knowledgeable in medico-legal issues, only a few relevant matters relating to the claims handling process, especially those relating to monitoring progress, are discussed.

The final part of the chapter discusses the Clinical Negligence Scheme for Trusts (CNST). This scheme was designed to assist provider trusts in England with a form of 'insurance' to allow them to build financial contingencies through pooling risks and contributions. Most English trusts have joined the CNST and Scotland and Northern Ireland implement their own schemes. The health service in Wales already operates a similar pooling scheme.

The CNST is designed specifically to protect against the adverse effects of large clinical negligence claims rather than smaller claims. Nevertheless, it is hoped that by raising risk and claims' management standards across the NHS and by promoting better understanding of and information on the nature and extent of medical mishap, the effects will be minimised. An important feature of medical negligence is the extended length of time between an incident occurring and a claim being settled. Improved claims handling may help to reduce delay, not least because delay in the conclusion of a claim leads to mounting costs. The CNST estimates that claim inflation for clinical negligence runs at approximately 5% per annum in excess of the Retail Price Index.

5.2   COMPLAINTS

5.2.1   Introduction

In 1998-1999 in the NHS there were:

86,013 written complaints made about hospital care
38,857 written complaints made about family health services
27,949 hospital complaints concerned aspects of clinical treatment
285 hospital and 313 family health services complaints were referred for independent review.[1]

There is no nationally held information on how many complaints are upheld. These numbers of complaints may reflect:

- deteriorating service;

- growing social intolerance of mediocre or poor service;

- an increasing preparedness to complain;

---

1   Department of Health 2000

- premature and over enthusiastic public presentation of advances in medical science;

- service keenness to search out criticism in order to improve performance;

- a new openness and the Patients' Charter.

Perhaps only a minority of patients with grounds to complain do so. Some reasons may be fear of recrimination, not being taken seriously, bureaucratic opacity or the hopelessness of redress. On the other hand, it could be said that if there were not such deterrents to complaints then the morale in the service would be devastated. A review by the NHS Executive into the working of the complaints procedures is due to report in 2001. However, there can be severe consequences with not dealing with grievances, even though the seriousness of complaints can vary enormously from the service of lukewarm food to the injury or death of a patient:

- the service does not hear about its failings;

- faith in the service is undermined;

- costly if the grievance is not resolved at an early stage.[2]

5.2.2   Dealing With Complaints

Under the Complaints Procedure Act NHS Authorities are required to establish a complaints procedure and investigate and respond to complaints. Complaints are able to make a significant contribution to the risk management programme of a Trust, if efforts are made to learn from the reasons for the complaints.

135 consecutive complaints made by patients and others against an NHS Trust were examined by a Community Health Council as part of the Trust's risk management programme. The analysis showed the following:

Most common causes for complaint:

- misunderstandings

---

2   The Citizens' Charter Complaints Task Force *Putting Things Right* [HMSO, June 1995]. The complaints task force estimated that 'front-line' review costs between £3 and £45; external review about £770; and full scale investigation by the Health Service Commissioner as £11,200.

- poor communications

- attitudes of staff

- thoughtlessness

The Ombudsman in a recent report stated in respect of communications:

"Inevitably, problems of communication between staff, and between staff, patients and carers are part of many complaints that I investigate. Good communication is an essential part of good clinical treatment. The experience of my office is that good communications often feature some or all of the following:

Clinical notes are written for the purpose of communication between professionals and with patients and carers. This means that consistent information can be given and built upon. The success of patient-held records in areas such as ante-natal care shows the benefits of such an approach. However, too often, notes seem to be written with medico-legal rather than communication purposes in mind.

Patients and carers are listened to. 'He's not usually like that' and 'it feels different from what it did before' are important signals, sometimes missed. Concerns which may appear insignificant to staff can be very significant for patients, and become increasingly so if left unanswered.

Staff provide information in terms which patients and carers can understand, and confirm that they understand what has been said. A full and perfectly sound clinical explanation expressed in the wrong terms can easily be either incomprehensible to, or misunderstood by, patients. At best they may be left no wiser and, at worst, with a mistaken view of what they have been told. Staff need to ascertain the patient's level of understanding.

Difficult issues are tackled. It can be tempting, especially for busy staff who may have had little training in communication, to avoid discussing painful or sensitive issues with patients or carers. For example, while the final decision about the merits of resuscitation is a clinical one, failing to take any opportunity to involve the patient or relatives before making such a decision often causes far more distress than tackling this sensitive issue.

Mutually respectful and co-operative communications between

professionals. This means that one member of staff who has misgivings about the care planned by a colleague (peer or senior) can raise the matter with confidence. It also means that information can be shared, appropriately, between practitioners and organisations, in the interest of patients. The aim of the Commission is to improve standards of care by focusing on the experience of those using the NHS as a way of restoring public confidence in the NHS.

5.2.2.1 What the Complainant is Looking for:

- easy access to the system
- to be listened to
- access when they need it
- honest answers
- all their concerns addressed
- understandable explanations
- a real commitment to change circumstances
- sensitivity
- to be kept informed
- trust and confidence in the person dealing with their complaint

5.2.2.2 What the Complainant Does not Want is:

- being passed on to someone else (no one prepared to sit and listen)
- staff being defensive
- jargon
- being talked down to
- staff taking on a superior professional manner

When dealing with a complaint, staff should record in detail the actions taken. The complainant should always be informed of the next stage of escalation of the complaints procedure. It is important that patients detained under the Mental Health Act are informed of their rights under the Act and of their right to complain to the Mental Health Act Commission. Patients remaining dissatisfied with the handling of their complaint or the outcome have the right to invite the Health Service Commissioner (Ombudsman) to investigate.

The philosophy of complaints management adopted here is that complaints can be used as a useful risk management tool in monitoring, correcting and anticipating mistakes. New complaints procedures recommended by the National Health Service Executive (NHSE)[3] provide a framework that accords with that philosophy. The way a healthcare organisation processes complaints from patients and others is of vital importance to public and professional perception of that organisation and the quality of its services. It is noteworthy that a quarter of the investigations by the Health Service Commissioner is initiated by complaints about the way in which a NHS complaints has been handled. The Wilson Committee[4] found that the NHS complaints procedures were:

- over complex;
- user-unfriendly;
- take too long;
- over-defensive;
- often explain conclusions unsatisfactorily.

Clearly it should not be necessary for a patient to place a formal complaint as their only means of recording dissatisfaction. Early intervention by health staff, with an apology, as appropriate should be part of the essential skills expected of staff. Equally, there should be an expectation by patients and of staff that patients are informed at an early stage where the treatment has not gone to plan. A survey of 227 patients and relatives who were taking legal action through 5 firms of claimant specialist medical negligence solicitors showed that the decision to take legal action was determined not only by the original injury, but also the insensitive handling and poor communication after the original incident.[5]

---

3   *Complaints, Listening, Acting, Improving,* Department of Health March 1996

4   Department of Health *Being heard: the report of a review committee on NHS complaints procedures* May 1994.

5   Vincent C, Young M, Phillips A (1994) *Why do people sue doctors?* A study of patients and relatives taking legal action. Lancet; 343: 1609:1613

5.2.3   Patients' Charter

The Citizens' Charter complaints task force noted in its report *Putting Things Right*[6] that a small number of complaints may reflect difficulties of service users have in getting access to the system:

We see a rising number of complaints in the short to medium term as an indication of improved access, clearer standards of service (and therefore higher expectations) and a willingness to uncover dissatisfaction so that things can be put right .... It also demonstrates that people believe it is worthwhile making a complaint.

An important part of an organisation's risk management and quality assurance is having clear and effective complaints policy and procedure. An effective complaints policy can have a number of benefits:

- improves the organisation's image and the marketing of its services;

- provides a more realistic idea of public satisfaction and improved awareness of the harmful effect of public dissatisfaction;

- better internal and external relationships;

- can be used to improve service quality.

It is well known in manufacturing and service industry, that the dissatisfied customer expresses his or her dissatisfaction to others to a far greater extent than a satisfied customer expresses satisfaction. However it should be recognised that the complainant reflects the dissatisfaction of a larger number of patients who have kept quiet. It is important therefore to create the opportunity for someone to complain so that dissatisfaction can be turned to satisfaction. In the health service, patients and others may not complain because:

- their complaint will not be welcome and will meet with hostility or suspicion and doubt;

- they do not know how to complain;

- they do not know who to complain to;

---

6   See also MORI "Complaints Handling in the Public Sector: report for the Citizens' Charter complaints task force." [London: HMSO, June 1995]

- complaining involves unnecessary difficulties for the complainant

- nothing will happen to improve the position or no one will take responsibility for the problem if a complaint is registered;

- the response to complaints is always very long in coming;

- their complaint may adversely affect the care and treatment they receive.

Where health care organisations have to negotiate and win contracts, it is important to have insight into how the organisation is perceived and without that insight the organisation may not be able to react to changes in demand. Barriers to complaints may be built into the organisation because:

- staff are not permitted in any circumstances to deviate from "the rules" and not empowered to make decisions;

- there is no clear complaints policy;

- staff are not trained in processing complaints effectively;

- managers are not patient-focused and do not consider complaints to be justified;

- staff are generally criticised if complaints are received and mistakes are swept under the carpet;

- organisational systems are designed for administrative convenience not patient satisfaction.

5.2.4 Complaints and Discipline

As with an untoward incident reporting system, it is important to separate the complaints policy and procedures from disciplinary procedures. Complaints management is not about apportioning blame amongst staff although some complaints will reveal circumstances which indicate the need for separate disciplinary investigation. The latter investigation should not be allowed to disrupt or halt the complaints procedure. The complainant can be informed in general terms of any disciplinary action taken in order to demonstrate action has been taken on the complaint.

Consideration as to whether or not disciplinary action is warranted is a separate matter for management, which falls outside of the complaints procedure and must be subject to a separate process of investigation.

5.2.5 Who may Complain

5.2.5.1 *Trusts and Health Authorities*

Complainants will be existing or former patients using a trust's or health authority's NHS services and facilities. Complaints may be made on behalf of existing or former patients by anyone who has the patient's consent.

If the patient is unable to act, e.g. is dead or not competent, then their consent is not needed for a complaint to be pursued. In this circumstance, where the complaints manager, or convenor at the Independent Review stage, is of the opinion that the person is not suitable to pursue the complaint, they may refuse to deal with the complainant, and may nominate another person to act on the patient's behalf.

5.2.5.2 *Family Health Services Practitioners*

Complainants will be existing or former patients of a practitioner who has arrangements with a health authority to provide family health services. Complaints may be made on behalf of existing or former patients by anyone who has the patient's consent. If the patient is unable to give consent the next of kin can bring a complaint.

Where the health authority's complaints manager, or convenor at the Independent Review stage does not accept the complainant as a suitable representative of the patient, they may either refuse to deal with the complainant, or nominate another person to act on the patient's behalf.

5.2.6 Role of the Chief Executive, Complaints Manager and Convenor

There must be a designated complaints manager who is directly accountable to the Chief Executive, although in some small Trusts the Chief Executive may be the designated manager. More often than not the designated manager will also manage claims for compensation and much of what follows applies to the handling of claims as well as complaints. The role of complaints handler is to direct the complaint to the appropriate person in the organisation, cutting through bureaucracy and not creating other barriers. He/she may also act as a "listening ear" and should be accessible to the general public.

The Chief Executive must respond in writing to all written complaints and all oral complaints which are subsequently put in writing and signed by the complainant. In the case of an oral complaint, where the complainant is dissatisfied with the initial response and wants to pursue the matter further, the complaint should be put in writing and signed by the complainant.

In addition, a non-executive director should be appointed as a 'convenor'. The convenor should consider complainants' requests for an independent review if local attempts at resolution are unsatisfactory.

5.2.7 Complaints Procedure

As part of its complaints procedure, the trust/health authority must establish a clear local resolution process. In the case of family health services, local resolution is the responsibility of the practitioner.

A good service response through a complaints policy and procedure is an important part of a risk management strategy for even the most effective processing of complaints cannot compensate for flaws and deficiencies in the health care services offered. Boards of Trusts and Health Authorities must have and must publicise their written complaints policy and procedures. They must comply with the NHSE's guidance, which stipulates arrangements for local resolution of complaints and an independent review process. A good complaints policy:

- publicises the policy to patients and others;

- demands a system that makes it easier for people to complain by making it clear where and how to complain:

- ensures that complaints are processed promptly;

- is known by everyone in the organisation;

- ensures that all staff with patient contact are trained to process complaints;

- empowers staff to make decisions in accordance with the

organisation's policies and principles for handling complaints. In some specific situations, an established rule may not make sense from the patient's or the organisation's point of view. In that situation, the staff are authorised to change it (if a change is necessary, the reason needs to be analysed because it may be an opportunity to adjust systems to ensure satisfaction in other areas and for other patients);

- demonstrates that it is more important to satisfy the patient than win the argument;

- ensures constant monitoring of patient satisfaction;

- registers in one place all complaints so that trends and causes can be analysed and changes made if necessary.

- appreciates effective handling of complaints and gives recognition to all employees who help to find, correct and anticipate mistakes;

- satisfies staff internally as well as the patient and the organisation.

5.2.8   Apologies

The process should be fair, flexible and conciliatory, with the complainant given the opportunity to understand what to do to pursue the complaint. The overwhelming motive of complainants is not to seek monetary recompense but to seek information, to improve the position for others and to obtain an apology.

An apology does not necessarily prevent litigation but it may be sufficient in some cases. When apologising it is necessary to:

- distinguish the situation where there is liability and where there is possible defence;

- avoid admissions of liability for error made;

- use non-emotive language.

Taking care to avoid admitting liability should not prevent full and honest explanations being given.

5.2.9   Time limits

Local good practice will lay down time limits in which patients will have their complaints resolved as soon as possible. The NHS Executive guidance lays down that this should be within six months of the complaint being made or within twelve months from the date of the incident, whichever is earlier. The time limits can be extended where it is unreasonable for it to be expected to have been made earlier and it is still possible to investigate the events. Reasons might include the patient may not feel robust enough until medical problems are resolved.

5.2.10   Local Resolution

The local resolution process should encourage speedy resolution by those on the 'front-line' which requires staff to be empowered to deal with problems. Staff should be able to deal with complaints rapidly and even informally where appropriate. Only where front-line staff cannot investigate or cannot give the necessary assurance should the complaints manager become involved. However, all complaints should be noted and included in the information system for monitoring complaints and claims.

5.2.11   Involving Staff

In order to turn negative criticism from a patient into a positive contribution to risk management and quality improvement, it is important that the organisation and all its staff know how to handle complaints effectively. The first prerequisite for handling complaints effectively is a positive attitude amongst managers and staff. People with patient contact tend to express the attitude of their supervisors or the organisation. A genuine interest in correcting mistakes underlies effective complaints processing.

What staff do is re-enforced by behaviour that the organisation rewards. The staff who have been the subject of complaints should be able to see that complaints form a basis for improvements within the organisation. Handling a complaint is not just a question of sending a 'trouble-maker' packing, but can be a real learning exercise. Most people prefer to avoid complaints or criticism, but by overcoming feelings of suspicion, guilt or irritation a lot can be achieved. In a sense there is a need for staff to put themselves in the patient's place.

Imagining that the same thing had happened to them or a relative will help them understand the patient's needs and expectations.

Responses to complaints concerning clinical matters need to be agreed with the healthcare professional concerned. A badly handled complaint may mar a professional's career and the professional and other staff must see that they are been dealt with fairly, promptly and openly with tact. This may mean assisting with the making of statements and involving staff in the drafting of letters of reply to complainants.

5.2.12 Oral Complaints

Oral complaints should be resolved on the spot or within two working days at the latest.

The person dealing with an oral complaint by way of local resolution should:

- explain why the complaint is appreciated;
- apologise for any mistake or the events that led to a misunderstanding;
- promise to do something about it immediately;
- ask for the necessary information;
- correct the mistake promptly;
- check whether the patient is satisfied;
- prevent future mistakes.

5.2.13 Written Complaints

A minority of patients will make the effort to make a formal written complaint. If they do so, by far the majority of those letters will be from patients who are dissatisfied. An organisation can expect to receive 10 letters of complaint for every one letter of thanks. In principle, the process should be the same for oral or written complaints. However, there are some special aspects which should be taken into account.

All written complaints must receive a response in writing from the Chief Executive, as established by the Patients' Charter.

If the problem cannot be solved immediately, it is important that the patient still receives a prompt and personal reply within two days containing the following as a minimum:

- a demonstration that the patient and the complaint is important;

- an explanation why the complaint is appreciated;

- a recognition of the patient's right to complain;

- an apology for any inconvenience;

- an assurance of prompt action and investigation.

The final reply should be given as fast as possible thereafter. The NHSE performance target is for investigation and resolution to be less than twenty days. An early, preliminary reply to a written complaint is necessary, but not sufficient to regain the patient's confidence and trust. The final reply should give a satisfactory answer and should be sent quickly. The directions below will help staff and the organisation to give those patients who complain in writing the kind of treatment that is acceptable both to them, the staff involved and the healthcare organisation.

Staff and the risk manager (or complaints manager/handler/officer) should correct the mistake promptly if possible and inform the patient of the result of the investigation of their complaint as soon as it is available. This should explain the changes in the organisation's actions, systems, policies, and procedures brought about by the complaint.

The health care provider should reject complaints only when totally unreasonable demands from patients who are obviously trying to exploit a situation. This should be done in such a way that the patient understands they have been seen through but without showing anger or resentment.

Responses should avoid standard letters. A personal letter of reply written using the patient's title and name, and the name of the person replying and signing the letter should be sent. As far as possible, use the patient's own wording and phrases. The letter should be easy for everyone to understand – minimising technical terms, clichés or organisational jargon. It is often worthwhile giving the patient better treatment than expected and always follow up to make sure the patient is satisfied. This shows that you and the organisation are committed.

Any letter concluding the local resolution procedure should include mention of the right to seek independent review. The request for independent review should be made within twenty working days by the complainant, orally or in writing, to the convenor.

5.2.14   Independent Review

If a complainant is not satisfied with the local trust/health authority's response, or a family health services practitioner's response, as a result of the Local Resolution process, then a request can be made to the non-executive convenor for an independent review panel. The request may be orally or in writing. The request should be made within twenty-eight calendar days from the completion of the Local Resolution process. Any request for an Independent Review Panel received either orally or in writing by any other member of or employee of the trust/health authority should be passed on to the convenor immediately.

The convenor should acknowledge such requests within two working days and must then obtain a statement signed by the complainant clearly setting out the continuing grievances and why they are dissatisfied with the outcome of Local Resolution. The convenor must then:

- ensure impartiality;
- ascertain whether the local resolution process was thorough and fully exhausted;
- decide whether to set up an independent review panel;
- determine the terms of reference for that panel.

For the two latter points, the convenor should consult with a lay chairperson from the regional list, and take appropriate clinical advice where the complaint relates to clinical judgement. The convenor should not take longer than twenty days to decide whether to set up a panel. The actions to set up the panel, once the convenor makes a decision can be delegated to the Chief Executive in order to avoid delay.

The convenor should not set up a panel:

- if further action is feasible in the local resolution process;

- if all practical action has already been taken;
- if any legal proceedings have started.

When the convenor has decided that an independent review panel should be established, it should sit formally as a committee of the trust/health authority.

5.3 CLINICAL ADVICE TO THE CONVENOR

Where a complaint appears to relate in whole or in part to action taken as a consequence of clinical judgement, the convenor must take appropriate clinical advice in deciding whether to convene a panel. The convenor should initially seek the advice of the medical or nurse director on the board.

5.3.1.1 Independent Review Panel

The independent review panel comprises three members:

- an independent lay chairperson nominated by the Secretary of State from a regional list;
- the convenor or other non-executive director;
- in the case of trusts, a representative of the health authority;
- in the case of health authorities, another independent person nominated by the Secretary of State from a regional list.

Where the convenor decides (after taking appropriate advice) that the complaint is a clinical complaint, the panel will be advised by at least two independent clinical assessors nominated by the regional office, following advice from the relevant professional bodies.

The panel should be established as a committee of the trust/health authority board and the assessors are to be appointed by the trust/health authority to advise the panel.

The aim is to have two members of the panel who have no previous formal links with the particular trust or authority.

The panel must investigate the complaint and make a report setting out its conclusions and recommendations. It is required that:

- proceedings are confidential;

- no recommendations are made for disciplinary action or referral to a professional body;
- the panel has no executive authority;
- the panel has access to all relevant records;
- the complainant must have reasonable opportunity to express their views;
- the person complained against also may express their view of the complaint;
- the complainant and the person complained against may be accompanied by a 'friend' who may not be a legally qualified person acting in a legal capacity.

5.3.1.2 Independent Review Final Report

Copies of the final report should be sent to the complainant, the patient (if different), the Board Chairperson, the Chief Executive and the clinical assessors. In addition:

- the report should be confidential and set out the results of the investigation, conclusions and recommendations;
- appropriate extracts should be sent to the person complained against;
- if relevant, the clinical assessors' reports must be attached to the panel's final report;
- if the panel disagrees with the assessors' conclusions, the reasons must be stated.

It is good practice to provide the complainant and any person complained against with a draft version of the report at least fourteen days before the formal issue. Checks for accuracy can then be made. Those receiving the draft should be reminded that the report is confidential to them and the panel members.

The panel's final report should be sent to:

- the complainant;
- the patient, if a different person from the complainant and competent to receive it;

- any person named in the complaint;

- any person interviewed by the panel;

- the trust/health authority chairman and Chief Executive;

- in the case of complaints against family health services practitioners, the practitioner concerned;

- the regional directors of public health and performance management;

- the chairman and Chief Executive of the independent provider, where the complaint is about services provided by the independent sector;

- the health authority chairman and Chief Executive or G.P. who commissioned the service.

The report will have a restricted circulation. The panel shall not send it to any other person or body. The panel chairman has the right to withhold any parts of the panel's report and all or part of the assessors' reports in order to ensure confidentiality of clinical information.

The Chief Executive must write to the complainant specifying any action to be taken following the panel's report, normally within four weeks. The letter must also advise the complainant of the right to complain to the Ombudsman.

5.3.2 The Health Service Commissioner (the Ombudsman)

The Ombudsman may investigate complaints from members of the public who claim they have suffered injustice or hardship as a result of failures or mal-administration.

The Health Service Ombudsman is an office established under the National Health Act 1977. The Ombudsman has a duty to investigate complaints which fall within his remit. Complaints must normally be submitted within one year of the day upon which the events came the notice of the aggrieved party. A complaint cannot be investigated by the Ombudsman unless it has been brought to the attention of the Trust or Health Authority and which has been given the opportunity to investigate and reply.

The Ombudsman's remit is to investigate cases of 'maladministration', except in cases involving clinical judgement, where it is not relevant.

Maladministration is not defined in the legislation and is widely interpreted. For example, it is interpreted to include bias, neglect, delay, incompetence, ineptitude, perversity, faulty procedures, arbitrariness and rudeness.

The Ombudsman role has been extended[7] to include complaints involving clinical judgement and complaints arising from primary care. The 1996 Act also gives staff involved in complaints the right to complain to the Ombudsman if they consider that they have suffered hardship or injustice through the complaints procedure.

The Ombudsman reports separately to the English and Scottish Parliaments and the Welsh Assembly.

The Ombudsman has the power of the High Court to compel the production of documents and the attendance and examination of witnesses. Following a detailed and thorough investigation, the Ombudsman either upholds a complaint and makes recommendations for corrective action, or does not uphold the complaint. His work is overseen by a House of Commons Select Committee which may call a Trust or Health Authority to account for failing to follow the Commissioner's recommendations. To date, very few Trusts or Health Authorities have failed to grant a remedy recommended.

The Health Service Ombudsman publishes reports to:

- account for the work of his office together with the Annual Report;

- provide material for use in education and training;

- expose reports to public and professional scrutiny and discussion;

- help promote good practice in the health service.

In the ten years 1990 – 2000, the number of complaints received by the Ombudsman has steadily increased from 800 per year to 2,500 per year for the whole of England, Scotland and Wales.[8] Most refer to inadequate handling of complaints at a local level.

Ombudsman website: http://www.health.ombudsman.org.uk

---

7   Health Service Commissioner (Amendment) Act 1996

8   *Annual Report of the Health Service Commissioner* June 2000

5.3.3 Mental Health Act Commission and Complaints

Psychiatric patients may register their complaints to the Mental Health Act Commission which is empowered to investigate them. As with the Ombudsman, the Commission does not look to intervene unless the local resolution process has been completed. Providers of mental health services need to identify complaints involving patients detained under a section of the Mental Health Act 1983 and have this information available for the Commission to inspect. The Act places a duty on hospital managers, usually but not exclusively non-executive directors, to nominate a complaints officer who should log complaints and communicate the outcome of investigations to the patient. This additional complaints procedure therefore provides an additional jeopardy for mental health providers.

Unresolved complaints may go to litigation. Before a detained patient may sue in connection with a claim arising out of the detention, he or she must first obtain leave of the High Court. The court must be satisfied that the claim justifies investigation and raises a prima facie case.

5.3.4 The Community Health Council CHC

The NHS Plan announced the abolition of Community Health Councils to take effect in 2002 and their part-replacement by Patient Advocacy and Liaison Services in each hospital. The CHCs and their successor services were established to act as the 'patient's friend'. Patients are helped to find out about services and to make formal complaints, as necessary. Normally such complaints do not involve claims for compensation.

5.3.5 'Consumer' groups

Sometimes complainants may be acting on behalf of a wider group and thereby have more extensive objectives or a greater knowledge base than is immediately apparent. It is essential to understand the context of the complaint and investigate the incident thoroughly in order to provide a thorough response to such groups.

5.3.6 Complaints information

Complaints must be reported quarterly to the Board which must produce an annual report on complaints handling. This report must be circulated widely including, if appropriate, purchasers and patient advocate groups.

Whether a patient's complaint is made verbally or in writing, it is of the utmost importance for the organisation to register the patient's opinion about the complaint and the way the complaint was handled. This can be done by interviewing the patient with a pro-forma or by sending the patient the pro-forma in order that the patient can complete it personally. The untoward incident reporting system can also be used to register complaints, oral or written and claims.

5.3.6.1 Implementation of a complaints procedure

Introducing effective complaint management into a health care organisation may contain the following elements. The contents and sequence may be adapted, in accordance with NHSE Interim Guidelines, to the organisation's culture, present situation and existing requirements.

5.4 PREPARATION:

- the current complaint system should be surveyed;
- the current complaint record should be surveyed;
- a team from management and different departments should manage the process of implementation;
- a preliminary plan of action should be prepared;
- an internal marketing exercise should be organised.

Management commitment:

- the Board should formally agree the complaint policy, and establish a system for monitoring and evaluating results at regular intervals;
- all managers should be briefed about the purpose and advantages of introducing the principles of effective complaint handling;
- a flexible preliminary plan should be presented and agreed adjustments made.

Complaints policy:

- the support procedures for the complaints policy should be set up by consulting with and involving staff in flowcharting and other methods of establishing procedures;

- the policy should clearly state the organisation's basic attitude and philosophy towards complaints;

Department level complaint processing:

- an overview of the most common complaints should be provided;

- reasons for complaints should be clarified;

- action plans should be prepared for ease and consistency of use;

- make it easy for patients to complain;

- make patients feel appreciated when they complain;

- process complaints and competently;

- set up training for current staff and any new staff in the future;

- monitoring and evaluation procedures should be established.

At all stages it is useful to construct flow charts which describes the process at various levels. The flowcharts should overlap with those for the management of claims and other litigation.

5.5   CLAIMS FOR COMPENSATION

5.5.1   Introduction

The Clinical Negligence Scheme for Trusts (CNST) defines a claim as:

Any demand, however made, but usually by the patient's legal advisor, for monetary compensation in respect of an Adverse Incident leading to personal injury.

In the previous sections, it was argued that claims would tend not to arise if an original complaint about an adverse incident is handled sympathetically. During the complaint process and often in the initial stages of a claim, the patient, their relatives or friends are mostly interested, not in the payment of damages, but in explanations as to what happened together with expressions of regret and sympathy, and assurance that avoidable mistakes will not be repeated.

The reaction of the healthcare organisations and professionals on receiving notice of a claim or of learning of a potential claim should not be negative or perceived to be negative. Even when notice of a claim is given, a hostile or defensive reaction may encourage a complainant to pursue the matter stubbornly and eventually to court. An open and sympathetic approach may satisfy the person when really their wish to take legal action is ambivalent. Many of the principles of effective complaint management should be applied to claims management.

5.5.2 Claim Frequency and Rates

The frequency of litigation has certainly increased in recent years. It is difficult to isolate the effects of various possible causes which include:

- an increase in the number of specialist solicitors dealing with medical negligence and the advertising of their services;

- changes in patient attitudes towards the health care professionals;

- increasing consumerism in health services.

It can be assumed that the rate of litigation will increase further. The effect of the conditional fee system where the claimant pays legal costs dependent on the outcome of the action will, it is believed, lead to a rise in claim frequencies.

5.5.3 Claims Manager

All staff should be trained in risk management techniques relevant to their area of work. This is especially the case for the claims manager. Important to success in claims (and complaints) control is early training and close collaboration between staff members. Pre-claim, the claims manager should be trying to improve the standard of note-taking and the reporting of untoward incidents. Post-claim, the claims manager should be adept at preliminary investigations and statement taking. Effective claims handling is part of good risk management and the avoidance of litigation in general by:

- maintaining reasonable standards of care in gathering and ordering information;

- keeping meticulous contemporary notes;

- ensuring good communication.

Recurring themes in poor claims management relate to delay, the cascade of un-managed events and lack of communication between the parties and professionals involved.

5.5.4   Claims Procedures

The civil justice procedure for clinical negligence claims was significantly altered by the adoption of the recommendation of Lord Woolf[9] who, in 1996, described the legal process as *too unequal, too expensive, too uncertain, too slow, too complicated, too fragmented and too adversarial.*

The intention to claim is now governed by a pre-action protocol which is aimed at:

- more pre-action contact between the parties;

- better and earlier exchange of information;

- better pre-action investigation on both sides;

- putting the parties in a better position where they may be able to settle cases fairly and early without litigation;

- enabling proceedings to run to the court's timetable and efficiently, if litigation becomes necessary.

5.5.5   Disclosure of Health Records[10]

The Data Protection Act 1998 gives a right of access to all health records of living patients. (see chapter 4.4.1)

Disclosure of clinical records to enable a patient to gain advice on the relative merits of a claim is an inherent part of the claim process. The claims manager will need to organise the disclosure of health records to the claimant or their adviser. Claimants most often instruct solicitors in order to be given access to their health records for the purposes of the claim.

---

9   *Access to Justice* – Lord Woolf July 1996

10 *A protocol for obtaining Hospital Medical Records* – Civil Litigation Committee, Law Society June 1998

Letters of claim should contain full details of the claimant, a clear summary of the facts, the nature of the injury and details of the financial loss. The defendant should acknowledge receipt of the letter within 21 days, failing which the claimant is entitled to issue proceedings. The defendant has a maximum of three months from the date of acknowledgement to investigate and provide a reply stating whether liability is admitted and if not, the reasons for the denial.

If liability is admitted, there is a presumption that it will be binding where the value of the claim is up to £15,000. Claims up to this amount are dealt with under the 'fast track system' where the date of the trial will be automatically fixed for not later than 30 weeks from the date of directions.

On receipt of a claimant solicitor's letter requesting disclosure of records, it is usually best to instruct the organisation's own solicitor and to agree to disclosure. Agreement to disclosure, which may be forced by court order anyway, demonstrates to the claimant a willingness to be helpful and a commitment to discovering what really happened. The overall procedure for clinical negligence favours the competent claimant's solicitor although the balance shifts at trial. The key points in disclosing medical records are:

check the applicant is in one of the recognised categories:

- the patient;

- a person authorised in writing by the patient;

- someone with parental responsibility for the patient;

- someone appointed by the Court of Protection;

- personal representatives, as with a deceased person.

In order to get an early idea of likely allegation in any proceedings, ensure the person making the request for disclosure gives reasons (an early idea of allegations can be invaluable in carrying out internal investigations):

- obtain the consultants comments and opinion regarding the exceptions to the need to disclose i.e. information likely to cause serious harm to the physical or mental health of the patient or any other individual

- information relating to or provided by an individual other than the patient who would be identified from that information.

The advantages of speed in complying with disclosure at this stage are:

- reduction of the period of worry for healthcare professionals and patient;

- cost savings.

5.5.6 Health Records and the Case File

The claims manager should open a case file on receipt of a solicitor's letter of claim or any other clear indication that litigation might be being contemplated. If disclosure of health records is requested, it is good practice to prepare an additional copy to be retained for reference. The records may be in disarray and it may be sensible to:

- organise them in chronological order;

- identify any missing documents;

- read the records in order to be able to instruct solicitors and experts sensibly;

- take statements of events from the main healthcare professionals involved (doctors may wish to seek advice from their defence organisation);

- monitor the progress of the case regularly.

5.5.7 Monitoring Information

Claims should be regularly analysed to identify any trends and problem areas. Information technology may help for storage and retrieval of data and information. The minimum data set suggested by the CNST, whether the Trust is a member or not, is a very useful start. Additional data fields, such as the equipment used, the availability of protocols or the drug involved could usefully be added. For Trusts which are members of the CNST the quarterly submissions of claims data required as a member can easily be done electronically by diskette. It is necessary to be in contact with the Trust's solicitor to ensure that all the necessary steps are being taken and in time, in order to be able to consider the merits of continuing the case.

5.5.8   Settlement of Claims

The introduction of NHS Indemnity in 1990 made the process of the settlement of claims easier since the health authority or the Trust has responsibility for payment of claims out of their budgets. Liability no longer has to be apportioned between the NHS and the defence organisations. Moreover, following the "Naylor decision"[11] it is a standard direction of a court for experts' reports on liability issues of negligence and causation to be exchanged well in advance of trial. It may be necessary either to admit liability or to negotiate if expert reports do not show adequate grounds for defence.

There are three preliminary questions that should be asked with respect to each claim:

- can the claim be defended in principle, taking into account all the relevant facts, i.e. was there any negligence?

- if the claim can be defended in principle, is it practicable to do so?

- is it the interests of the hospital, its staff and in the public interest to defend it?

Only when these questions are asked and answered can a view be taken on the strategy and tactics to adopted in defence or settlement of a case. There is little point in defending the indefensible. As soon as it is apparent that a claim is indefensible, an offer of settlement or payment into court should be made. To continue to defend such claims only serves to increase the costs of both sides which will fall to be paid by the defendant.

5.5.9   Witness Statements

Exchange of witness statements of fact relevant to liability and causation issues is also a standard direction of the court during the litigation process and one which encourages resolution. The purpose of statement-taking is to achieve an objective account of the incident and ideally therefore the statement should be taken by the claims manager rather than another member of the statement-maker's team or department.

---

11 *Naylor v Preston Area Health Authority* [19987] 2 All ER 353, [1987] 1 WLR 958, CA.

The statement should contain:

- name, address and occupation of the witness;

- position and qualifications;

- name of patient and condition (especially important where the patient's records are mislaid);

- names and status of other witnesses;

- treatment being carried out at the time of incident;

- who 'consented' the patient (again, especially important where the consent form is mislaid);

- the statement-maker's own chronological account of the claim events.

The facts narrated should be the facts within the narrator's own knowledge, "to the best of the witnesses own knowledge and belief".[12] No hearsay evidence or opinion should be included. It is best to order the account chronologically using numbered paragraphs. Any copy documents to which the narrator refers should be attached to the statement because this avoids hunting for them later. It should be remembered that internal enquiry notes and minutes are not legally privileged unless the purpose of preparing the documents is to gather evidence for contemplated litigation.

5.5.10   Choice of Expert

Evidence and reports may be required from a relevant expert on issues of:

- liability;

- causation;

- condition and prognosis.

The report on condition and prognosis is to establish what level of damages should be paid if liability is shown. Experts from whom opinions are to be sought should be of an appropriate speciality. It may be appropriate for a single specialist expert to deal with all three aspects but it will necessary to present separate reports for (1)

---

12 See Order 38 Rule 2A, Rules of the Supreme Court, 1981.

liability/causation and (2) condition and prognosis. These reports may be exchanged at different times and different purposes.

For liability issues, the expert chosen should have:

- knowledge of the specialty;

- knowledge of clinical practice at the time of the incident;

- equal or higher seniority than the doctors concerned with the treatment.

An expert with previous medico-legal experience is more likely to write and present reports more clearly and to understand how the legal system works. The expert should have no connection with the service in which negligence is alleged. The claims manager and solicitor should keep details of experts they have worked with previously or should be able to obtain a recommendation from others, such as colleagues or the CNST. The Medical Register and Directory should also be at hand. It should also be noted that medical negligence work is very different from providing reports on accident cases and that the doctor for one type of work may not be appropriate for the other.

5.5.11   Instructing Experts

It is important to ensure the medical expert is approached and instructed properly. The legal procedures should be explained, the expert's particular role specified and the time scale set up. Experts will be better able to fulfil their role if documentation is well-prepared and if instructions containing indication of the issues to be addressed and what will be done with the report are clear. Keep the expert informed of progress of the case and notify them if the case is settled, discontinued before trial or closed because no action has been taken for some considerable time.

5.5.11.1 Expert Reports

Expert reports should be considered critically especially to decide whether negative opinions should be accepted. If the first report does not support the defence of a claim, it has to be decided whether a conference with counsel and expert would be useful or a second medical expert opinion should be sought. Other issues to consider are:

- are there inconsistencies within the report and between reports?

- does the nature of the defence need to be reviewed?
- is the report in suitable form for exchange?

5.5.11.2 Expert Fees

Experts should be paid as promptly as possible. Unless the level of an expert's fees are known from previous experience, fee estimates should be obtained in advance and compared with past cases.

5.5.12 Access to Justice Act and Financial Support for Claimants

The Legal Services Commission is a new executive non-departmental public body created under the Access to Justice Act 1999 to develop and administer two schemes in England and Wales:

The Community Legal Service, which replaces the former civil scheme of legal aid, bringing together networks of sources of funding (e.g. Local Authorities) and suppliers into partnerships to provide the widest possible access to information and advice.

The Criminal Defence Service which from April 2001 replaced the old system of criminal legal aid and provide criminal services to people accused of crimes.

The claimant who has financial support from the Legal Services Commission may have little monetary disincentive to allowing a claim to proceed to trial. The health service as the defendant will only recover costs of successful defence if:

- the claimant has failed to beat a payment into court, i.e. is awarded a lower sum;
- the costs of an interlocutory hearing have been awarded in the defendant's favour.

In either case, damages awarded are reduced by the defendant's costs. The defendant is clearly at a disadvantage in a case where the claimant is financially supported. If the claimant loses at the trial the costs order in the defendent's favour will not be enforced without the leave of the court so that in practical terms the order is useless. In small quantum cases, it can be worthwhile considering an economic settlement, irrespective of the merits of the case. However, there is the danger that others will be encouraged to make similar unmerited claims.

A claimant who successfully recovers damages when supported by the scheme has to repay statutory costs to the scheme, if successful. For the first time, lawyers are asked to report to the scheme on the chances of winning a claim in terms of the likely damages and costs as a ratio against the chances of winning the case. Permission to proceed is only given if these pre-conditions are met.

As an aid to consistency in the quality of claims handling, the Legal Services Commission operates a franchising scheme which is open to external audit of adherence with the scheme requirements.

5.5.13 Contingency Fees

Contingency fee based litigation 'no win, no fee' is beginning to have an impact on the rates of litigation. There are two key aspects of contingency fees:

- if a court claim is unsuccessful, the claimant does not have to pay his or her solicitor, but the unsuccessful claimant may be liable for some or all of the defendant's costs;

- if the claim is successful, the solicitor may charge more than the usual fee as reward for taking the claim i.e. uplift

Legislation allows solicitors to act on a contingency fee basis in three instances: personal injury including death, insolvency and human rights. Examples of claims for personal injury and fatal accident, which might affect a healthcare organisation, are:

- clinical negligence claims;

- claims by visitors who slip or injure themselves on NHS premises;

- claims by staff with back, neck and leg injuries from lifting;

- occupational health and industrial injury;

- claims relating to defective products or malfunctioning equipment.

When contingency fees are involved negotiation of settlement may become difficult. For example, a well-timed settlement offer may provoke different reactions in the claimant's camp. The solicitor may want to settle to secure the fees whilst the claimant may want more since there may be little left after uplifted fees are paid. It is true that any settlement confronts the claimant with a dilemma: accept and go away with some money or hold out for more and see irrecoverable costs escalate. Expenses which are not part of the claimant's solicitors fees – e.g. expert fees, court fees, photocopying, faxes and so on – will most likely be payable by the claimant.

5.5.14 Mediation

Mediation is the process whereby both sides agree on the choice of a third party who assists in reaching an agreement, but has not power to impose a solution. A pre-action protocol for the resolution of clinical disputes was published by the Clinical Disputes Forum in 1998. Pilot schemes have been established by the department of health with mediators drawn from the London-based Centre for Dispute Resolution, the Resolve Scheme and the Bristol-based Alternative Dispute Resolution Network. There are related methods of dispute resolution such as:

- executive tribunal (mini-trial) involving a panel with decision-making powers;

- expert appraisal involving an authority who produces a persuasive, although non-binding opinion on a issue within the claim;

- judicial appraisal where a senior legal figure delivers an opinion on the merits of the parties' cases.

However, alternative dispute procedures are not suitable if new legal issues have to be dealt with or there is a lack of consent by one party or the other. The overall costs have yet to fully quantified particularly in terms of legal representation adding to costs and in the variance of preparatory work for each case. The advantages and disadvantages of alternative dispute resolution are summarised in table 5.3.13.[13]

5.6 THE CLINICAL NEGLIGENCE SCHEME FOR TRUSTS (CNST)

5.6.1 Introduction

Clinical negligence claims in England and Wales cost approximately £150 million in 1994/95 and the rates of claims and settlement levels are expected to continue to rise. For all Trusts the highest claims form

---

13 Health Service Journal Special Report pp.1-5, 16 November 1995

the majority of costs and the most infrequent and least predictable; for example an acute Trust may face more than one claim in excess £1 million in any one year. Similarly several claims over £50,000 would be just as damaging for smaller Community or Ambulance Trusts. Such large settlements may limit a Trust's ability to provide planned improvements in patient care. The National Audit Report, 2000, indicates that current increases in claims are 36% per annum on a worst case scenario basis.

5.6.2   Establishing Financial Pooling

In 1995 the Department of Health established a central fund to help NHS Trusts to spread the costs of clinical negligence. Until then, Trusts had to meet the costs of clinical negligence either through their own revenues or by borrowing from the Treasury against agreed limits, the so-called External Finance Limit (EFL). A loan under the EFL would remain a debt which had both be serviced and repaid. If the trust tries to recover such variable costs through their contracts with purchasers threaten their own viability. Under the Clinical Negligence Scheme for Trusts (CNST), Trusts pay annual contributions into a pooled fund in order to share the cost of substantial claims. Members will pay an annual contribution related to their size, the nature of their clinical work, and eventually their claims experience. Discounts related to the degree of development of risk management programmes are available. This provides an incentive for Trusts to operate satisfactory risk management procedures. This discounting also points to the three main non-financial benefits of the scheme, namely:

- the development of risk management;

- an educational programme for the improvement of claim management techniques, risk management and so on ;

- the creation of a national database from which information can be disseminated about common causes of clinical negligence.

The Scheme was created in response to the increasing incidence of clinical negligence litigation against NHS Trusts. Membership is voluntary and open to all Health Service bodies (not general practitioners or dentists) in England exposed to clinical negligence liabilities. Some 340 Trusts joined in 1995. The Scheme operates by pooling contributions from subscribing members. The objective is to collect only enough in contributions to meet the costs of payments in any one year, called "Pay As You Go" funding. This will mean that the initial costs of joining the Scheme are low but are expected to rise substantially over the next decade as liabilities currently being incurred fall due. This is consistent with Parliamentary cash accounting which provides moneys for in year expenditure only. Large amounts of public, NHS moneys will not be tied up in anticipation of future liabilities and remain in patient care.

5.6.3   Financial Equilibrium

The management of claims payments has become a significant concern, particularly in respect of serial claims, for many Trusts. NHS Indemnity was introduced in 1990, but the financing of claims through the EFL loan arrangement was from its inception considered to be a holding measure until more suitable scheme for managing liabilities could be introduced. Whichever method was designed and implemented the aim had to be to smooth payments so not to disrupt the provision of resources for the healthcare of patients.

5.6.4   High Value Claims

A report by one medical indemnity company, which analysed high value claims,[14] showed that although about 4% of claims were valued at over £100,000 those claims amounted to approximately 61% of total outstanding liabilities. The report states:

Even worse, claims valued in excess of £500,000 which represent 0.6% of all claims by number account for a massive 26% of liabilities. Overall, further analysis shows a pareto effect in clinical negligence claims, that is 80% of liabilities arise from 20% of claims.[15]

It follows that the vast majority of claims are of low value and that in the first instance attention should focus on managing the high value claims and risk management efforts should initially focus on the high risk specialties of obstetric, orthopaedics, gynaecology, accident and emergency and general surgery. However, the large number of low value claims should not be overlooked particularly with regard to effect on patient care and on finances of serial claims.

---

14 SELVADURAI, N. *Risks and Writs – an analysis of high claims* pp.7-8, CNST Review Issue 1 Spring 1995.

15 Ibid. p.7.

The CNST has defined three financial categories of claims, A, B and C.

Category A Claims: these are claims in which the trust does not expect to receive reimbursement from the CNST. These are claims valued up to the chosen excess of the member trust.

These claims should be reported after settlement or after closure.

Category B Claims: these are claims in which the trust expects to receive reimbursement from the CNST and which are valued above the individual trust's excess, but below £500,000.

These claims are further classed as:

- likely settlers
- defensible claims
- complex cases.

They are required to be reported four times a year to the CNST.

Category C Claims: these are claims in which the trust expects to receive reimbursement from the CNST and are valued at or over £500,000.

5.6.5   Creating Contingency Funds

The CNST is designed to protect the Trust specifically against the adverse effects of the larger and relatively infrequent clinical negligence claims and introduces a mechanism for smoothing the financial risk based on principles of mutuality. It is not designed to protect against small claims for which self-insurance is the recommended means of funding.

Equally, the CNST is not centrally funded and Trusts will, over a period of years meet the full costs of clinical negligence liabilities. However, the Scheme will allow for greater certainty in budgeting and planning by protecting against the impact of an extremely large settlement, or cluster of settlements in any single year. In a pooling arrangement the one contingency reserve is much less than the sum of all individual members' contingency reserves. Furthermore, the greater the number of Trusts involved, the more predictable are total costs and the smaller the collective contingency needs to be.

Unlike commercial insurance schemes, the scheme is non-profit making and funding is not tied up when it could otherwise be used for patient care. The scheme is based on the principle of mutuality in that it is owned by its members. Any surplus funds that are collected will be used to offset subsequent contributions. Members will be encouraged to adopt best practice in both risk management and claims handling and will be offered a range of educational materials and activities to help them improve performance.

5.7 THE NHS LITIGATION AUTHORITY

A special health authority, the NHS Litigation Authority (the NHS LA) will administer the scheme on behalf of the Secretary of State. The NHS LA has a part-time Chairperson and a full-time Chief Executive, who is supported by a number of Directors, support staff and non-executive members combining a broad understanding of NHS issues with relevant specialist expertise. The Authority is advised by a Policy Steering Group (PSG) made up of and nominated by its members. The method of election will be on either a regional basis or as representatives of different member groups. The PSG should came effect from April 1996. Directors of Trusts are not allowed by law to be non-executive members of the NHS LA. The Authority has the discretion to vary or extend the ambit of the Scheme in later years in the interests of members and with the agreement of the Secretary of State.

The fundamental role of the NHS LA is to administer the Scheme on behalf of the Secretary of State and to find the right way through complex roles of the interests of the Secretary of State – representing the public purse, the users of the NHS and the member Trusts.

5.7.1 Legal Advice

Responsibility for the management and handling of the great majority of clinical negligence claims will remain with the Trust. After the first year the Trust will be expected to use a specialist solicitor from a panel of solicitors who have met the appropriate standards set by the CNST. This panel of solicitors, meeting minimum expertise criteria, is to be established to guide members from 1996/97 onwards. This reflects the Law Society's initiative in setting up a similar panel of claimant solicitors. A further panel of more experienced solicitors to deal with high value claims may also be drawn up. Defence costs for members will be paid only if a panel solicitor is used.

The performance of these specialist legal advisers will be closely monitored. Trusts need only obtain prior approval for the settlement of claims in which the Scheme has a liability. This may be a nominal autonomy over the conduct of claims since the financial benefit of membership of the scheme will only be available if the NHS LA criteria are followed. The NHSLA will assist in the management of those claims which involve more than one Trust as a defendant and in the very small number of extremely high value claims or those which carry a special medico-legal significance.

5.7.2   Membership Rules

In addition to the aspects of the scheme discussed here the membership rules published by the CNST cover issues such as:

- contribution payment frequency (quarterly, six monthly or annually in advance);

- contributions should be set before 31st October of the previous year;

- principally eligibility which in the first years is limited to all Trusts in England

- an initial membership period of three years subject to a minimum of one year's notice of exit after this three year period;

- exit can only occur at the end of the CNST's financial year, currently 31st March each year;

- entry can only occur at the beginning of each financial year (1st April).

5.7.3   Claim Entitlement

If an incident occurs and a claim is made and settled during the membership period, then the claim will be covered. If the trust leaves the scheme before settlement then the Trust would not be entitled to any benefits from the CNST. Thus long rather than short-term membership will be encouraged through design of the scheme.

5.7.4   Benefits Structure

Each Trust member will retain a portion of the liability – the excess –

for each claim so that members will always contribute toward each settlement. Members will choose the level of excess which applies to each and every claim and their contributions will be calculated accordingly. In 1996, there were six excess levels ranging from £10,000 to £500,000. There is also linked to the excess an ultimate threshold above which the CNST will contribute 100% of the balance of any claim. There is no upper limit on the amount the CNST will pay out for an individual claim. For claims where settlement is below the excess, the Trust will meet the entire cost and expenses of settlement. In between, i.e. above the excess and below the ultimate threshold, the CNST will pay 80%. Payments include all the legal costs and disbursements as well as defence costs if the lawyer is appointed from the approved panel of solicitors.

Each member Trust decides the level of excess it will pay, that is, how much the Trust will pay of a claim before calling on the CNST. Linked to the excess is an ultimate threshold beyond which CNST will meet 100% of the costs. Above the excess level chosen, but below the ultimate threshold, costs are shared 80% for the CNST and 20% for the Trust.[16] The choice of excess should be determined by the level of risk each Trust is prepared to accept on its own account.

However, changing the choice of excess in a pay-as-you-go scheme can cause problems for a Trust because different rules will attach to a claim reported and settled in years with different excess levels. The excess attached to an individual claim will be that for the year in which the claim is settled or reported whichever is the higher. Therefore, it will be probably more advantageous to choose a lower excess initially and pay proportionally more in contributions while those contributions are relatively low. If it becomes clear that the individuals Trust's experience is better than expected the excess should be increased as contributions rise.

5.7.5   Serial Actions

Provision has also been made for serial claims or class type actions in which a large number of patients claim injury from a single incident or a series of related incidents. Recent years have seen patients adversely

---

16 Stop Loss benefit – i.e. a benefit for all payments made arising from **all** claims settled after a certain predetermined financial limit has been reached – has been excluded from the Scheme on the basis that in the early years of a "Pay As You Go" scheme it is technically very difficult to implement.

affected by the same repeated error in cervical smear testing and by miscalibration of radiotherapy equipment. An aggregate cover for serial and class type actions is built into the scheme and member Trusts would have to pay part of the total loss itself from its aggregate excess which would be a percentage of the Trust's income from all its activities. In 1996 the proposal was that this percentage be 5% of total income and the CNST would pay the remainder above the aggregate excess.

5.7.6   Contributions

In the first year of the CNST contributions to the pool were calculated on the basis of activity grouping. Contributions will be determined from actuarial assessments of the total costs of settling all claims for the year, plus a small sum to cover both the establishment of a fluctuation reserve to smooth variability in year on year contributions and the management of the scheme. In the first year of the scheme (1995/96), contributions were based primarily on the Trust's turnover and specialty mix. In the second and third years more detailed data on a Trust's activity such as the number of staff employed in clinical specialties has been included in the calculation. It is hoped that in later years enough consistent information on individual member's claims history will have been collected and that this data can be used for the contributions calculation.

The basis is now related to staffing. The major medical, nursing and professions allied to medicine specialties and disciplines are grouped according to risk profile and a contribution rate set per whole time equivalent (WTE) for each group (the Group Rate). An individual Trust's contribution will be determined by multiplying the number of staff it has in each group by the Group Rate and then aggregating the results to give the gross contribution. The gross contribution will then be adjusted to reflect the level of excess chosen and any risk management discounts to be applied.

In order to be able to calculate individual Trust contributions fairly it is very important to build up and maintain a complete and accurate database of claim histories for each member Trust.

5.7.7   Risk Management

The CNST aims to develop risk management throughout its membership. To encourage such development risk management will be promoted through an educational programme of risk awareness, financial incentives by awarding contribution discounts and by creating good practice protocols in co-operation with the healthcare professions. This promotion is underpinned by the production of basic, objective standards of risk management and the development of a scoring system to provide a contributions discount structure.

Members of the CNST have three levels to achieve for compliance with the standards. Level one compliance attracts a 10% reduction in membership cost, level 2 a 20% reduction and level 3 a 25% reduction.

Discounts in contributions are to be linked to performance in risk management through the use of standards dealing with:

- organisation

- systems

- training

- processes

5.7.8   Appraising Risk Management Implementation

A system comprising both self-assessment and assessment visits is used to monitor whether standards are being attained and maintained. The CNST risk management proposals aim set specific and achievable standards which will be inexpensive to meet, bring the benefits of discount, contain the rising costs of accidents, in the longer term, and help improve patient care.

The outline CNST standards are:

Standard 1: Clinical Risk Management – Strategy and Organisation.
The board has a written strategy in place that makes their commitment to managing clinical risk explicit. Responsibility for this strategy and its implementation is clear.

Standard 2: Clinical Incident Reporting.
A clinical incident reporting system is operated in all medical specialties and clinical support departments.

Standard 3: Response to Major Clinical Incidents.
There is a policy for the rapid follow-up of major clinical incidents.

Standard 4: Managing complaints.
An agreed system of managing complaints is in place.

Standard 5: Advice and consent.
Appropriate information is provided to patients on the risks and benefits of the proposed treatment or investigation, and the alternatives available, before a signature on a consent form is sought.

Standard 6: Health Records.
A comprehensive system for the completion, use, storage and retrieval of health records is in place. Record keeping standards are monitored through the clinical audit process.

Standard 7: Induction, Training and Competence.
There are management systems in place to ensure the competence and appropriate training of all clinical staff.

Standard 8: Implementation of Clinical Risk Management.
A clinical risk management system is in place.

Standard 9: Clinical Care.
There are clear procedures for the management of general clinical care.

Standard 10: Maternity Care.
There are clearly documented systems for management and communication throughout the key stages of maternity care.

Standard 11: The Management of Care in Trusts Providing Mental Health Services.
There are clear systems for the protection of the public and service users.

Standard 12: Ambulance Service.
There are clear procedures for the management of clinical risk in trusts providing Ambulance Services.

The standards are further sub-divided to reflect the appropriate level of compliance. Each sub-criteria has been weighted to assist Trusts is assessing the priority for implementation and monitoring.

For example:

Standard 8: Implementation of Clinical Risk Management.
A clinical risk management system is in place.
8.2.1 All clinical risk management standards and processes are in place and operational.
8.2.2 Risk management policy is implemented through the general management arrangements of the trust.
8.2.3 A trust-wide clinical risk assessment has been conducted.
8.3.1 There is evidence of progression and achievement of action points based on recommendations made in the risk assessment.

A full list of the summary criteria of the CNST is in Appendix 2.

Criteria for risk management should be measurable, reflect risk exposures, be attainable and be capable of progressive implementation.

Each member is visited regularly when technical support will be offered and risk management standards evaluated against a scoring system linked to the contribution discounts. None of this will prevent the use of independent risk management consultants to develop individual programmes.

5.7.9 Compiling a Database

Since the fragmentation of claims handling following the introduction of NHS indemnity in 1990, there has been a lack of national analysis and feedback given detailing information on clinical incidents and the subsequent claims for the NHS. This gap in information has resulted in NHS organisations not being able to identify trends in types and the causes of incidents and claims, in order for Trusts to assess the vulnerability in their own organisation and if necessary, put in place mechanisms to minimise re-occurrence, before an event occurs at a local level. In addition because Trusts may not have a large enough sample, clusters may in some cases only be identified nationally..

5.7.9.1 *The Use of Comparative Data*

A database of claim histories can be used not only for calculating contribution rates but also communicate anonymised statistical information to members for educational, risk management, bench marking and financial applications. Each member Trust will therefore report:

- all claims made against the Trust whether or not the CNST will have any liability;

- serious untoward incidents where 'serious' is defined as a resulting claim may be valued above £100,000 and in terms of particular types of injury e.g. brain damaged infants.

There are four quarterly reporting cycles per year for the following which have occurred in the preceding quarter:

- all new claims notified;

- updates on open claims in which CNST has a liability;

- all claims settled.

The minimum data set for the CNST includes:

- the details of the Trust member;

- employees' details including status, specialty and percentage liability;

- claimant's details including gender, marital status, occupation, number of dependants and their age range, age, date of birth and date of death (if appropriate);

- claimant's solicitor;

- other parties involved;

- location of incident;

- specialty which gave rise to injury;

- probability of claimant winning damages;

- a synopsis of the case and the primary cause of the injury;

- estimate of quantum and estimated percentage of liability;

- dates of incident, of claim, of claim opening by the Trust, of estimated settlement

Consistency in claim data recording and claim management techniques across all members will be important to the completeness, accuracy and relevance of the central database. The CNST will have a claims handling manual for all members supported a claims management educational programme of seminars and published articles.

5.7.10 Claims Management

All claims must necessarily be notified in sufficient detail and frequency. Expertise in the management of claims is mixed throughout the NHS, between large and small providers, and between types of provider such as maternity, ambulance, acute and community. The availability of support and advice in the handling of claims will be helpful not only to Trusts but also patients and relatives. Because the CNST is designed to protect against large claims the handling of smaller claims will be in the hands of Trusts. Nevertheless, both the NHS LA and the individual Trusts would want to be assured that the settlement or level of settlement of claims is not the result of poor claims management. Protocols will be issued giving guidance for best practice but importantly the CLA will need to be consulted at critical stages in the management of a claim in which the CNST has financial liability. Furthermore before any offer is made to settle the CNST will need to be consulted.

5.7.11   NHS Litigation Authority Claims Management

As discussed above, most of the schemes liabilities will be generated by a small number of very high value claims. In addition, there will be a small number of cases in which an important medico-legal principle will need to be decided. In order to develop the expertise necessary to minimise large losses and to argue new, complex or uncommon issues, the Litigation Authority will handle those cases in conjunction with the member's solicitor and claims manager. The criteria for these jointly handled cases will be:

- claims which have a net reserve above an upper limit (the proposal is the ultimate threshold or £500,000 whichever is the lower though this may vary according to the claims management capacities of individual members);

- claims in which there is a fundamental principle of wider importance at stake;

- serial claims.

In addition the Litigation Authority will offer an optional claims management service to members on a fee basis.

5.7.12   Claim Mediation

If there is disagreement between the CNST and the member over the claim settlement or other claims management issue, then there will be an appeal procedure to the Litigation Authority. If there is no resolution even then, the member will be able to manage the claim as it wishes if it is willing to bear full financial liability. If the member is proved right any final settlement will be paid by the CNST.

5.7.13   Extending the Role of the Litigation Authority

In April 1999 the NHS Litigation Authority commenced two further schemes to cover trust liabilities that previously had been commercially insured. The schemes do not cover motor vehicle, Private Finance Initiative schemes and some income generation schemes. Both schemes are funded on a 'pay as you go' basis and have individual member excesses.

5.7.14   Property Expenses Scheme (PES)

The PES provides for non-catastrophic losses to buildings and contents. The protection provided by the PES includes engineering breakdown and explosion, contract works, goods in transit and fidelity guarantee – covering loss of money, securities or other property through fraud or dishonesty by employees.

Increased costs of working cover in the event of damage to buildings or plant, bomb scare or failures of public utilities is included in the scheme. The level of cover is subject to a delegated limit.

5.7.14.1 Claims Reporting Under the PES

The scheme requires the following claims to be reported, as a condition of continuing membership:

- all cases where the potential will exceed the excess

- cases within 20% of the excess regardless of whether the trust wish the authority to sub-excess claims handle;

- cases reported which fall within the excess may be liable to a Loss Adjuster's fee being charged as a disbursement.

Additionally, cases where the potential develops to the extent that the excess will be breached will be handled by the Authority and cases where the potential reduces to a level within the excess will be handled by the Authority to a conclusion.

5.7.15   Liabilities to Third Parties Scheme (LTPS)

The purpose of this scheme is to provide mutual financial pooling arrangements for claims arising from exposures to Employer's Liabilities, Public and Product Liabilities, Professional Liabilities (other than provided under the CNST arrangements) and Directors' and Officers' Liabilities.

The scheme does cover the costs of an inquiry ordered under the Health and Safety Inquiries (Procedure) Regulations and legal expenses arising in respect of a breach under the Health and Safety at Work etc. Act 1974, but does not cover any fine payable as a result of a successful prosecution.

5.7.15.1 Claims Reporting Under the LTPS

The scheme requires the following claims to be reported, as a condition of continuing membership:

- all accidents where a letter of claim is received and the potential will exceed the scheme excess;

- all claims with an initial valuation within 20% of the excess figure;

- all accidents which have or are likely to result in the following:
  - fatal injuries;
  - amputation of any limb;
  - likely HSE prosecution;
  - head injury;
  - absence of 10 consecutive working days.

5.7.15.2 Sub-Excess Claims Handling

The NHS Litigation Authority offers an additional service to all trusts which have joined both schemes. The NHS LA will handle all sub-excess claims for trusts in addition to those where access to the pool is required.

6

HUMAN RESOURCE STRATEGIES FOR SUCCESSFUL RISK MANAGEMENT

"Mediocrity – you can't promote it, you can't fire it and you can't win with it."[1]

Employees represent the most important resource for the health services, and the most important resource for the risk manager. The organisation's attitude to its employees forms an important context of risk management. This attitude will be formalised in its overall human resources strategy and personnel policies. Such a strategy or policy will be a major factor in controlling risks of various kinds.

6.1 THE IMPORTANCE OF THE HUMAN RESOURCE FUNCTION

6.1.1 Human Resource Policies

The workforce represents a major investment in terms of what has been spent to acquire and develop. It costs a great deal to keep it functioning. More importantly people introduce more variability and uncertainty into an organisation than almost anything else. The Henley Centre for Employment Policy Studies developed a working definition of a good employment policy:

an overall employment strategy which integrates the organisation's various personnel policies and manpower plans. It should enable it to meet and absorb the changing requirements of technology and markets in the foreseeable future.[2]

---

1 Fred Decker – *Publisher's View, Insight, Issue 2, 2000*
2 See Rothwell, S *Integrating the elements of a company employment policy* **Personnel Management** [November 1984]

The definition relates corporate objectives and as such interrelates to the accomplishment of the risk management strategy. The risk management and human resource strategies should reflect each other in contributing to the major objectives of the organisation. Both risk management and human resource strategies must be formulated with each other in mind and reflect the objectives of each other within the context of the overall business strategy.

Personnel strategy and policies relate to:

- remuneration, including Maternity and Parental Leave
- recruitment and selection
- terms and conditions, including working time directives
- job evaluation
- personal development plans, appraisal and supervision
- merit ratings and incentives
- performance measurement
- related pay
- pension schemes
- sickness schemes
- holiday payments
- manpower planning
- training and development
- induction – including infection control
- career development
- retirement and redundancy
- discipline and dismissal
- skills and training
- staffing levels and assessment
- skill mix
- communications
- human resource strategies

6.2   HUMAN RESOURCES FUNCTIONS

6.2.1.1 Recruitment

The Trust will need to be able to demonstrate that it complies with all current requirements that apply to recruitment including the Sex Discrimination and Race Relations Act. To discriminate against applicants on grounds of colour or gender is actionable. Police checks should be made where staff will be working with children and references taken up. It is Government policy that organisations should employ the disabled to a quota of the workforce.

6.2.1.2 Induction

The Standing Committee for Post Graduate Medical Education has issued guidelines for induction training which can usefully be adopted as reasonable standards throughout the service. Their key recommendations are that induction training should be:

- available to all staff, including locums;
- recognised as an important educational event;
- a contractual obligation;
- started at the time of appointment;
- designed to lower stress;
- designed to build confidence;
- held in an environment which is conducive to learning;
- free from interruptions;
- designed to avoid information overload;
- designed to provide readable written material to be referred to later;
- updated to make full use of the expertise of experienced junior staff;
- subject to participant evaluation and feedback;
- part of a planned, continuing and systematic programme which provides for follow-on information and advice.

Induction training should also cover health and safety, employer/ employee obligations infection control and fire safety.

6.3 STAFF CREDENTIALING

6.3.1 Incompetence

Incompetence by professional staff will inevitably expose patients to unnecessary risks in their treatment. Any professional has a duty to inform their employer where they have particular concerns that a colleague may be a danger to patients. This may include addictive behaviour by the member of staff or mental or physical incapability of performing their duties.

6.3.2 Locum / Agency Staff

Particular concerns are often expressed in respect to the capabilities of locum and agency staff. Many of these arise from the inadequacy of arrangements for assessing competence prior to appointment or taking up duties. No locum should be expected to be familiar with the working environment at a new hospital. There should be a very clear introductory documentation available to enable the locum to know what is expected of them. There can be no excuse for a hospital to appoint a locum without taking up and considering references as to their competency. There can be no excuse for a hospital to appoint and allow a locum to work without assessing competence.

6.3.3 Professional Indemnity and Vicarious Liability

Risk managers pay lip service to personnel issues at their peril. The staff of a healthcare organisation is the organisation's single most valuable asset. In practice, far from working with and for staff, some risk managers try to largely ignore them and risk solutions are designed to eliminate the human element as much as possible. In this view, humans are seen as unreliable, prone to errors, unreasonably inflexible and, above all, expensive. Our previous chapter on risk management methods may have misled the reader into thinking that the skilled application of logical techniques would inevitably lead to clean, efficient and reliable systems. However the risk analyst in healthcare is not dealing with an easily defined system, or set of systems. The purpose of healthcare, the goals and the objectives are not necessarily clear cut, nor is the analysis and management of risk.

Healthcare organisations may be considered as associations of different occupational groups, pursuing both collective and individual goals that are not necessarily the same and may even be incompatible. Decision making can be compromised and made risky through uncertainties, objectives changeable, ill-defined and inconsistent. Healthcare organisations as 'human activity systems' are complex and controls are often difficult to establish. The risk analyst may react in several ways, for example:

- adopt a 'hard systems' approach and design human action and decisions out of the system as much as possible, given the technology and finance available;

- under-characterise staff relationships to the working environment as that of an isolated subject with biological limitations and use ergonomics to deal with human limits such as reach, strength, workload capacity, response time, memory and cognitive ability;

- take a strict legalistic view – "this is the law and we have got to comply" – assuming a single solution and taking no account of either people or resources;

- integrate much broader human factors into the work of risk management;

- what do the staff need to know to avoid risks.

Diagram 6.3.3.a. provides a conceptual picture of the social and organisational filters through which risk management techniques must be used in order to integrate risk management with these human factors. Of major concern will be the staff's attitude toward and definitions of risk management and its results. It is by no means the case that people have to accept the 'result' or 'solution' offered them. The range of possible solutions and consequences of a particular risk analysis should not be underplayed.

Diagram 6.3.3.b. illustrates a series of choices and compromises being made in the process of selecting, designing and introducing a solution. It is usually the case that certain people – for example, nurse managers – have the main say in what will happen and then hide behind the techniques as having 'determined' the decisions taken. This 'technical imperative' can sometimes be useful to defend change though it often stretches the credulity of affected parties.

Diagram 6.3.3.a. – SOCIAL AND ORGANISATIONAL RISK FILTERS

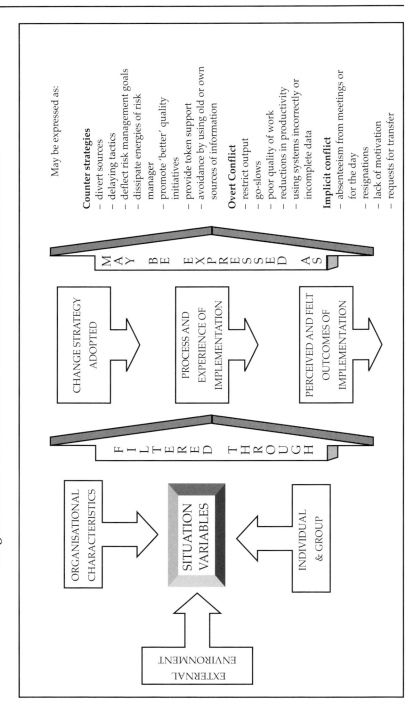

May be expressed as:

Counter strategies
– divert sources
– delaying tactics
– deflect risk management goals
– dissipate energies of risk manager
– promote 'better' quality initiatives
– provide token support
– avoidance by using old or own sources of information

Overt Conflict
– restrict output
– go-slows
– poor quality of work
– reductions in productivity
– using systems incorrectly or incomplete data

Implicit conflict
– absenteeism from meetings or for the day
– resignations
– lack of motivation
– requests for transfer

MAY BE EXPRESSED AS

FILTERED THROUGH

CHANGE STRATEGY ADOPTED

PROCESS AND EXPERIENCE OF IMPLEMENTATION

PERCEIVED AND FELT OUTCOMES OF IMPLEMENTATION

ORGANISATIONAL CHARACTERISTICS

SITUATION VARIABLES

INDIVIDUAL & GROUP

EXTERNAL ENVIRONMENT

Diagram 6.3.3.b.
DECISION AREAS IN RISK MANAGEMENT PROGRAMMES

CONSTRAINTS		
Finance • Service Patterns • Technology • Training		
Risk Management Process	⇐ Arena of choice ⇒	Main Influences
Research	• What shall we research? • Will finance be made available? • Is it worth pursuing?	Managers Accounts Professional NHSE Public

Perceived organisational needs	**Management**
	• Capital or labour intensive?
	• Who investigates and recommends?
	• What is the brief?
	  – limits to enquiry
	  – cost
	  – purpose, e.g. control, quality, savings
	  – effectiveness, efficiency, economy
		Managers
		Analysts
		Professionals

Investigation stage	• What are the evaluation criteria?
	  – economic
	  – medical
	  – organisational
	  – patient	

Results and introduction	**Reactions** • Acceptance by management • Modifications suggested and accepted • Negotiation with staff and/or patients	Managers Accounts Professional NHSE Public
Implementation	• Extent and influence of consultation • Speed of implementation • Level of diffusion	
Consequences	• Responses to feedback • Action as result of unintended consequences	

6.3.4   Staff, Objectives and Interests

Healthcare organisations are human activity systems and as such are political areas where a risk managers must take into account the objectives, viewpoints and interests of a range of people. Some typical interested stakeholders that need to be considered during any risk management programmes are:

- medical and nursing staff

- professions related to medicine

- administration / health records

- clinical audit

- patients

- boards of management

- other affected organisations e.g. voluntary bodies

- healthcare commissioners

- CNST

- CHI

- NHSE

Whatever the risk management ideas and changes being proposed, different groups and individuals will have different responses and reactions to them. Thus, in a laboratory the use of flowcharting may reveal redundancy or fears about their ability to use equipment. For others, it might show a new importance or enhanced status. Others may look forward to an improved service and safer handling of bio-hazard materials.

Reactions to specific changes can be predicted to some extent. This then enables these reactions to be planned for and permits the development of risk management changes and policies to reduce people's fears and resistance. One useful device is to examine the cost-effectiveness analysis that each individual and group is bound to make, albeit not always very consciously or formally whenever changes affecting them are pending. Only when such analyses are properly understood can policies to confront and change perceived losses be developed, and methods to weight such perceptions in the direction of benefits be implemented. This may not or cannot always be accomplished but it is a useful exercise.

6.4   OBJECTIVES AND OPINIONS

An organisation has many stakeholders. They do not necessarily share the same interests, values, beliefs and reasons for being connected with the organisation. In fact, it would be highly unusual if it were not so. It follows that stakeholders will not always pursue and support the same objectives either. For example, medical staff may want to retain the widest discretion of clinical opinion which may clash with perceptions that require as part of risk management the introduction of evidence based medicine. The demand of ward staff to keep drug stocks high so that any prescription may be dispensed easily may be opposed by the pharmacy department aim to keep stockholding costs down and reduce the danger of administering date expired drugs.

All this points in the direction of 'soft' systems thinking for analysing risk prevention and implementing damage limitation measures. A risk management process which is flexible and open to change is necessary, permitting interested parties to influence the design of programmes. Where this does not happen, and programmes are technically and economically oriented, immense problems can be stored up for the implementation stage. A risk management programme has little value if it cannot be implemented. A clash of objectives among stakeholders may be a crucial stumbling block which needs to be tackled by negotiation at an early stage.

The impact of risk management is summarised in diagram 6.4.a.

6.5   STRATEGIC OBJECTIVES

Senior managers have considerable organisational power and their objectives will have a crucial bearing on the shape and eventual operation of a risk management programme. Why then do managements introduce risk management? There are four main reasons:

- reduce financial uncertainty;
- comply with legal requirements;
- improve control over service delivery;
- raise quality and consistency of service.

Managers are also becoming aware of the increasing role risk management plays in changing the configuration of services and its

Diagram 6.4.a. – IMPACT OF RISK MANAGEMENT

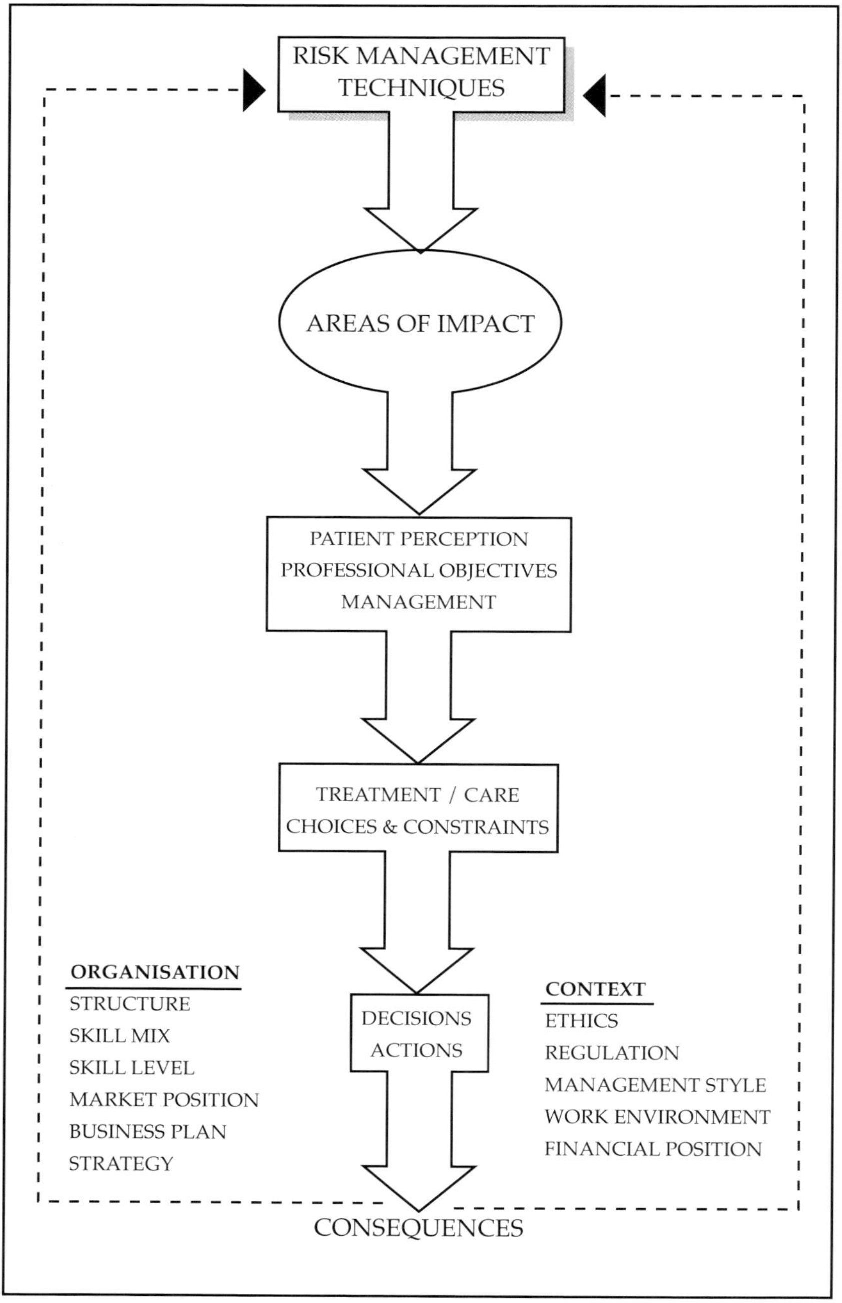

RISK MANAGEMENT
TECHNIQUES

AREAS OF IMPACT

PATIENT PERCEPTION
PROFESSIONAL OBJECTIVES
MANAGEMENT

TREATMENT / CARE
CHOICES & CONSTRAINTS

ORGANISATION
STRUCTURE
SKILL MIX
SKILL LEVEL
MARKET POSITION
BUSINESS PLAN
STRATEGY

DECISIONS
ACTIONS

CONTEXT
ETHICS
REGULATION
MANAGEMENT STYLE
WORK ENVIRONMENT
FINANCIAL POSITION

CONSEQUENCES

strategic potential for developing a response to purchaser and public demand ("competitive edge"). Often managers will not be able to state their aims so clearly and managers at different levels or in different functions will have different, sometimes conflicting, objectives for introducing risk management.

Frequently managers are also unclear and restricted in their view of what risk management can do for them. This makes the tasks of the risk manager, and the risk management consultant, easier in some ways, more difficult in others. The easy side is that such managers may be more open to the advice and preferences of those possessing expertise. This may not always be to the benefit to the organisation or the managers. The manager may find out a particular way of doing something is recommended regardless of organisational need or preferred technical fix, around which the organisation has to fit, rather than vice versa.

The difficult side is that the manager's – expressed as the healthcare organisation's needs and objectives must be clarified and met if the resulting solutions or recommendations are deemed to be successful or pertinent. Again this means an open-sided and flexible approach in the analysis and early stages.

It is common for managerial objectives to expand with increasing experience and understanding of what risk management can achieve. Many risk management programmes can be seen to develop in stages over time. Typically, at an initial stage, cost control limits a risk survey or audit to one department. In time, demands from other departments, for example, for the establishment of untoward incident reporting databases, may emerge as managers see the possibility of achieving objectives involving quality improvements, cost savings and faster information. Integration requirements for risk management is demonstrated in diagram 6.5.a

6.6   INFLUENCE IN ORGANISATIONS

Central to the understanding of influence within organisations is the concept of 'power' i.e. the capacity to make a difference.[3] Within an organisation there are divisions of labour, control structures, distribution of resources, ways of operating and rules, procedures and

---

3   Davison, S *Analysing organisations* London, Macmillan [1986]

Diagram 6.5.a. – INTERNAL AND EXTERNAL INTEGRATION OF RISK MANAGEMENT IN THE ORGANISATION AND WITH THE ENVIRONMENT

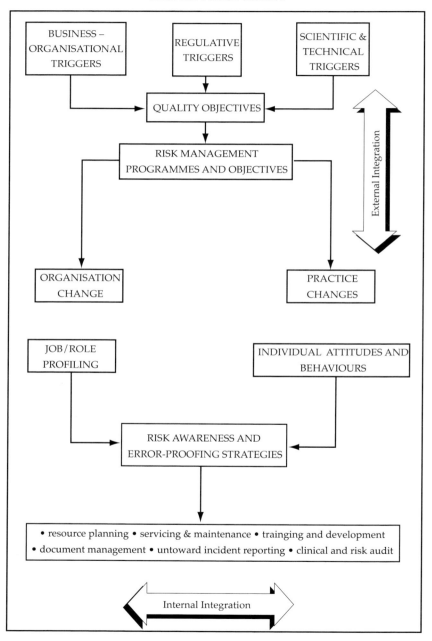

goals which will see some people favoured and others more constrained, in the exercise of power. The sources of power include:

- valued expertise;

- control over the provision of information;

- interpersonal skills and persuasiveness;

- control over rewards and punishments;

- physical force;

- position of individual or group in an organisation (*authority* – the right ceded by the organisation and inherent in a role, to act in certain ways, instruct people and commandeer resources);

- control of resources;

- *legitimacy* – the extent to which people share the values, norms and purposes of the exercise of power;[4]

- *control over the agenda* i.e. the exclusion or inclusion of certain items from / in discussion;[5]

- Networking.

Larger opportunities for achieving successful risk management and preferred outcomes when people operate in groups rather than as individuals. For example, groups are more likely to occupy strategic positions in the organisation relative to those whom they wish to influence. A *negative* power can arise where a group's activities are central to organisational functions are not substitutable by others, are immediate in their impact for other people's work, or involving coping with uncertainties on behalf of others. In such circumstances, dependence *on* implies influence *by* that group. As an example, the small number of consultants, apart from their expertise, have considerable bargaining power.

---

4 Here power comes from the capacity to manage the culture in an organisation. The importance of culture will be discussed later.

5 A problem of exclusion relates to employees at lower levels of an organisational hierarchy may be excluded from risk management decisions though they may be greatly affected by the decision outcomes. This may be detrimental in that they do not identify with, say, untoward incident reporting.

6.6.1 Case History

These considerations on organisational politics and their relevance to risk management may be illuminated by an example of a risk management survey in an acute hospital. Three prominent problems were identified in the particular department surveyed:

- inadequate organisation of medical records;
- flaws in the recording of information on progress of patient care by doctors;
- inadequate feedback about a patient's condition to nursing and professions related to medicine.

An underlying tenet of healthcare risk management is the requirement for communication within the healthcare team and continuity of care for the patient. At the hospital, the risk management recommendations were welcomed by nursing staff as providing more patient information and expanding their professional discretion.

Pharmacists, radiologists and other allied professions would have had their traditional roles expanded and more use made of their professional knowledge. Doctors were less positive as they argued that the recommended recording system was more time consuming, compromised patient care and disrupted current staff relations.

The real problem seemed to lie with the extent that risk management proposals impinged on the autonomy of the doctors and exposed their work to inter-professional scrutiny. Furthermore, some decision-making was shifted to other team members traditionally perceived as less knowledgeable.

The significant feature is the amount of control doctors have over the implementation of risk management. Doctors occupy senior formal positions in hospitals and in the institutional decision processes relating to Risk Management. Their expert knowledge means that their compliance is required in the development of risk management, especially clinical risk management. Medical knowledge is continually expanding and is difficult to incorporate in existing practice. It is doctors who can cope with and have a hold over this uncertain knowledge base. Doctors also gain power in their direct responsibility for patients undergoing procedures with high potential risk. Furthermore, doctors have a strong occupational organisation through, for example the Royal Colleges and their medical protection organisations. They can also exercise considerable control over the workplace and market conditions.

These factors provide some explanations for the slow reception of risk management into some healthcare institutions. Its acceptability will initially be low in hospitals and clinics which are hierarchically structured, with fairly rigid job demarcations and traditional relationships between doctors, nurses, professions allied to medicine, administration and ancillary staff. Risk management presupposes the creation of a healthcare team that through a problem- and patient-focused care:

- provides consistency and continuity of care;
- is less concerned with maintaining traditional roles;
- is dependent on shared expertise and information;
- follows a quality system.

Harrison[6] identified four cultures which can be in operation in any organisation.

The role culture:

This is a stable culture which has pre-determined rules and procedures and in which individuals know what is expected of them. It has a hierarchical structure enabling decisions to be controlled centrally. The objectives of the organisation are only understood by the power elite and understanding of the objectives diminishes downwards through thee organisation. This culture has a strong organisational identity.

Organisational template of a role culture[7]

- hierarchical structure
- rules, regulations and procedures important
- centralised decision making
- strong organisational identity
- maintenance of a stable environment

---

6 Harrison *How to describe your Organisation* Harvard Business Review Sept-Oct 1972

7 Donovan K *Hidden Forces* MA Thesis 1998 Plymouth Business School

Diagnostic personal identifiers of a role culture[8]

- you like a system which has a strong hierarchical structure making organisation- wide decisions centrally.

- you like regulation, procedures and policies.

- you have a strong organisational identity.

- you do not like to take risks.

- you prefer to have long term goals.

- you like to know what is expected of you.

- predictability and security are important.

The power culture:

A power culture is a risk taking culture where the decisions are made by the individual and based on outcome rather than procedure. Strategic direction and co-ordination is provided by a central power source which ensures that all parts have a common agenda. Individuals with a high need for power, a characteristic necessary for managerial success, will undoubtedly need to work in a power culture to avoid the mistrust they would engender in any of the other three cultures.

Organisational template of a power culture

- co-ordination from a central power source.

- little bureaucracy, few rules or procedures.

- objectives met quickly, but depend on a common under-standing by all concerned.

- total decision making power at an individual level.

- outward show of organisational identity.

- delivers change and is risk taking.

- typical identity of an executive director

---

8   op cit

Personal identifiers of a power culture

- you prefer co-ordination from a central power source, managing individual issues yourself.

- like to make your own decisions based on outcome, not procedure.

- you have an outward show of identity.

- you like to take risks.

- you are a driver of constant change.

- you continually seek to compete/improve performance and maintain influence.

- security is not important.

The task culture:

This is a team orientated culture which lends itself to technical expertise, rather than to organisational structure. It is advantageous in that it has the ability to adapt, promotes speed of decision making and encourages democratic freedom. However, it does have the tendency to lose sight/respect of the organisation's overall strategy.

Organisational template of a task culture

- influenced by expert rather than position power.

- autonomy and individual freedom evident.

- objectives are team, product or project orientated.

- a team rather than organisation identity.

- decision making is based on expertise.

- delivers change and is adaptable if that is part of the team's strategy.

- typical identity of a service manager

Personal identifiers of a task culture

- team relationships are of the utmost importance.

- you require professional autonomy.

- your allegiance is to the team rather than the organisation.
- you are willing to take risk if they are part of the team's strategy.
- you make decisions based on expertise.
- your performance is influenced by team acceptance.
- you require recognition from the team for a job well done.

The person culture:

In a person culture, the organisation exists for the needs of the individual. It emphasises personal growth, development and autonomous practice.

Organisation template of a person culture

- influenced by expert rather than position power.
- autonomy and individual freedom.
- individual objectives more important than the organisation's.
- individual decision makers.
- the individual is the central point.
- there is little allegiance to the organisation.
- adaptable only if beneficial to the individual.

Personal identifiers of a person culture

- you believe the organisation exists to serve you as an individual.
- you require personal autonomy.
- you identify with members of a collective group, but are motivated by your own needs.
- risk taking is dependent on whether it will help or hinder you as an individual.
- you are an individual decision maker.
- acceptance by respected peers is important.
- personal growth is the greatest importance.

6.6.2   Internal Organisational Analysis Tool

In assessing the internal environment to establish the most effective measures to promote risk management, the risk manager will be assisted by McKinseys Seven S framework in assessing potential conflicts and risks. These are:

- **Skills**

What is the preponderance of technically trained personnel whose perception is solely of personal autonomy?

- **Structure**

Is the structure hierarchical or flat, degree of central control?

- **Systems**

Are there conflicts of power, task or person cultures, pre-occupation with rules and procedures?

- **Shared values**

Is there variation in cultures across the organisation, lack of sense of vision?

- **Staff**

What is the type of cultural identity?

- **Style**

Is there a fear of failure, lack of recognition, lack of training opportunities, bureaucratic processes?

- **Strategy**

Is there a common values strategy or directed to favoured targets, e.g. research and development or politically dictated imperatives?

6.6.3 Resistance to Change

The above introduces the main strands of a broadened "human resources" perspective in designing, introducing and implementing risk management programmes. It recognises that the 'hard' techniques of risk analysis, identification, regulatory compliance and so on must be supplemented by an understanding of 'soft' approaches to human activity systems, in order to cope with resistance to change within complex healthcare institutions.

The attitude that 'resistance' is by definition wrong and should be overridden, ignored or suppressed must be eschewed in risk management. So must the response that the best thing to do is get the experts from the personnel department to handle 'people' problems. Certainly they can be asked to advise but responsibility should not be passed. The requirement within risk management is a more detailed analysis of the nature of that resistance.

There are many perspectives and they can be characterised in terms of four major views:

- unitarist
- technocratic
- pluralistic
- radical

6.6.4   Unitarist

- organisation is single team;
- interest and goals are shared;
- management leads the team;
- rational decisions ensure risk management employed efficiently to achieve objective;
- no room for conflict in implementation;
- 'resistors' are aberrant, misinformed or troublemakers;
- group resistance is explained by the presence of undue influence of 'resistors'.

6.6.5 Technocratic

- application of risk management is inevitable;
- often held by analysts and those skilled in risk management techniques;
- need to optimise risk management use to safeguard healthcare organisations;
- resistance due to misunderstanding, ignorance, reactionary attitudes or fear of the unknown.

6.6.6   Pluralistic

– resistance to change is to be expected rather than unusual;

– conflict due to individuals, groups and coalitions pursuing particular interests;

– compliance and co-operation are products of alliances between stakeholders to pursue specific interests;

– organisational stability is negotiated.

6.6.7   Radical

– resistance to change is normal;

– power resources are unequally distributed;

– fundamental divergence of interest between groups;

– in healthcare, managers want subordinates to work harder for less reward;

– order and co-operation are only temporary features and risk management used to perpetuate existing patterns of power;

– risk management could trigger organisational instability

These perspectives are possible ways in which organisational participants view change and resistance. In fact, in specific circumstances each could be fairly accurate picture of organisational reality. In the context of change, the nature and reasons for resistance need to be understood as a basis for handling risk management introduction and implementation. To achieve this, those responsible for risk management need to become aware of other people's perspectives, but also need to adopt an appropriate perspective, the one most closely approximating to the pattern of power relations and how specific organisation functions.

It is necessary to avoid the easy mistake of viewing resistance to change as an individual and psychological response. Figure 6.6.7.a. indicates how a number of variables which interact to produce often complicated patterns of resistance that need to be analysed carefully before and during the implementation of risk management. Resistance should not be seen merely as a problem to be solved so that risk management can be introduced as intended. In fact resistance is a good clue to what is going wrong and what can be done about it. Resistance

Figure 6.6.7.a.
ANTICIPTING RESISTANCE TO RISK MANAGEMENT

PERCEIVED LOSSES	PERCEIVED GAINS
1. Fears on economic grounds: • more work for some or reduced pay • fewer skills required means less pay in the long term	1. Economic gains
2. Fears about personal inconvenience: • less pleasant work conditions (environment, hours, locations, etc.) • more difficult work requires more effort	2. Hopes for more personal convenience
3. Concerns over decreased job satisfaction, etc.	3. Anticipated job satisfaction
4. Social fears	4. Social gains
5. Personal insecurity	5. More security
6. Dissatisfaction at handling of change	6. Satisfaction how change is handled

needs to be viewed in relation to the general results and outcomes required for risk management.

6.6.8 Individuals and Resistance to Change

A number of reasons can be put forward for individuals resisting risk management such as:

- feelings of inadequacy;

- fear of failure or of the unknown;

- disturbance of social relationships or loss of face;

- disturbance of psychological work habits related to established rules, policies, and procedures;

- lack of understanding of the purposes of change;

- lack of identification with changes;

- loss of personal control;

- no perceived need for risk management;

- redistribution of resources, authority, status, rewards and control;

- extra work related to bringing change;

- past resentment of individuals or organisations;

- change does really threaten.

Any or all these explanations may well apply. However, it is important not to assume but to analyse their applicability in specific circumstances. Analysis is important for any of the different strategies to be adopted in specific circumstances. For example, it cannot be assumed that a participative approach will always be successful, although this is the author's bias. Participation entails more interaction which can heighten and make more obvious the differences between people, rather than strengthen co-operation. The question is then whether or not the greater differences in opinion, and increased, more overt conflicts can be turned to constructive ends rather than damage risk management implementation.

We would be cautious about finding panacea in communicating with those affected by risk management programmes. All differences between organisational members are not necessarily eliminated by 'proper' communication with each other. Complete information and knowledge can make each party's self-interests fully visible and reveal any and all inequities. In this way, resistance against change is created in those who, with imperfect knowledge, might have gone along with the risk management programme.

6.6.9   Organisational Resistance to Change

A variety of organisational characteristics may hinder the reception of risk management, or create conflict as a result of it. These commonly include the reward systems, the custom and practice and machinery of collective bargaining, and the criteria used for assessing performance that prevail in the organisation.

6.6.9.1 Culture

Organisation culture is the set of shared norms, values, attitudes, myths and beliefs that evolve in, and within parts of, an organisation over a period of time. Culture can be a crucial factor in the reception of risk management. If senior management has created a culture of high trust throughout the organisation – if, for example, it deals with grievances, maintains open communications, rewards performance and provides job security – there is less likely to be resistance to risk management. However, if top management remains isolated or aloof, if class antagonisms are perpetuated at work, or if the organisational culture actively supports inflexible, conservative or 'safe' behaviour, the effective introduction may be hindered.

All organisational cultures are products of human investment in time, activity and precedent. They will also support a range of present activities and interests groups. Organisational members imbued in a culture may represent considerable obstacles to technological change, especially if that change process also necessitates the development of modified or cultures.

Handy[9] distinguishes between four types of culture in organisations:

- *power* (central power source, few rules and   procedures, precedent and whim important)

- *task* (project-oriented, flexible)

- *role* (rules, roles, procedures and predictability important)

- *person* (individual specialisms more important than organisation goals)

Such cultures can span the organisation or might be specific to a department or even group. Power and task cultures are probably more suitable for receiving risk management; the role culture more suited to continuing operation. Given the immense potential and flexibility of good risk management, the important thing is to develop the appropriate organisational culture. However, Handy's analysis suggests that task cultures tend to be more receptive to change, while the receptivity of power cultures tends to depend on the preferences and self-perceived interests of the power-holders at the centre. Role

---

9   Handy, C *Understanding Organisations* Pub Penguin 1993 ISBN 0-14-015603-8

cultures – typical of bureaucracies – tend to resist change, though this may be less so where risk management's potential for standardisation and using rules and procedures could be used to enhance bureaucratic functioning.

6.6.9.2 Sources of Stress

Stress as a major source of organisational risk is emerging in the form of morbidity and stress related claims. One major insurer has reported a 75% increase in the number of stress related claims.[10]

The company commissioned a survey by the University of Manchester Institute of Science and technology which used an Occupational Stress Indicator to sample staff attitudes through a questionnaire and focus groups. The results indicated that the five largest sources of stress arising at work came from:

- volume of work;
- lack of consultation;
- inadequate guidance;
- morale/organisational culture;
- being undervalued.

These results are similar to research undertaken on behalf of the Trades Union Council and are perhaps a guide to better practice for the NHS.

A survey undertaken by the Amalgamated Engineering and Electrical Union which involved 5,000 members indicated the following as major perceived sources of workplace stress:[11]

6.6.10 Lack of Control

- no control over work methods
- low pay
- shift work
- job insecurity
- unsocial hours

---

10 InfoRM July 2000 p16

11 op cit

- lack of promotion opportunities
- rigid supervision
- performance related pay

6.6.11   Lack of Social Support

- poor relations with supervisory colleagues
- sexism, ageism, racism
- impersonal treatment at work
- lack of communication

6.6.12   Poor Working Environment

- noise
- heat or cold
- poor lighting/ ventilation
- badly designed furniture
- inadequate work space
- poor seating, desks and keyboards

6.6.13   Poor Job Design

- too much or too little work
- new technology
- no control over workload
- concentration

6.7   A STRUCTURE FOR RISK MANAGEMENT

The wide range of potentially conflicting or competing elements within complex organisations means that the establishment of a structure for the implementation of a risk management strategy needs to give effective and credible representation for the participating constituents. These may typically comprise:

Clinical:

- Medical Specialties

- Diagnostic Specialties

- Nursing and Therapists

Non-clinical:

- Health and Safety

- Occupational Health

- Personnel

A primary purpose of the group is to establish the needs of the organisation in terms of:

- training

- health and safety

- safety of the workplace

- quality of staff

- procedures

Additionally, statutes place special responsibilities upon the Chief Executive and Directors of Trusts, such as the Health and Safety at Work etc. Act and Environmental Protection Act. The risk management process needs to have the overt commitment of the Chief Executive to its success.

The risk management forum for a health organisation therefore requires to be led at Board level. This is recognised in the Clinical Governance and Controls Assurance agenda with overt and explicit board level responsibility for implementation. As partially independent arbiters of the performance of NHS health organisations, the involvement of non-executive directors is important with direct reporting of the risk management forum to the Board. Every NHS board is required to have a risk management committee to co-ordinate and validate governance responsibilities.

Whilst individual health organisations will need to develop their own structure, diagram 6.7.a. illustrates one example which has been used successfully in an NHS Trust. The separation of clinical and non-clinical functions is artificial and illustrates a state of mind whereby health and safety and risk management is a function undertaken by a department rather than by all the individuals in an organisation as part of their routine.

6.8   THE ALLITT INQUIRY

Beverly Allitt was a nurse employed at the Grantham and Kestevan General Hospital. She was convicted for the murder of four child patients, the attempted murder of three child patients and for the grievous bodily harm of a further six child patients. She was sentenced to life imprisonment on every count. The Secretary of State established an Inquiry which reported and made various recommendations. Those relating to personnel functions and which should be incorporated in all personnel policies are as follows:

- that for all those seeking entry to the nursing profession, in addition to routine references the most recent employer or place of study should be asked to provide at least a record of time taken off on the grounds of sickness;

- that no candidate for nursing in whom there is evidence of major personality disorder should be employed in the profession;

- that nurses should undergo formal health screening when they obtain their first posts after qualifying;

- that the possibility be reviewed of making available to Occupational Health Departments any records of absence through sickness from any institution which an applicant for a nursing post has attended or been employed by;

- that procedures for management referrals to Occupational Health should make clear the criteria which should trigger such referrals;

- that consideration be given to how General Practitioners might, with the candidate's consent, be asked to certify that there is nothing in the medical history of a candidate for employment in the National Health Service which would make them unsuitable for their chosen occupation.

Diagram 6.7.a. – ORGANISATION CHART

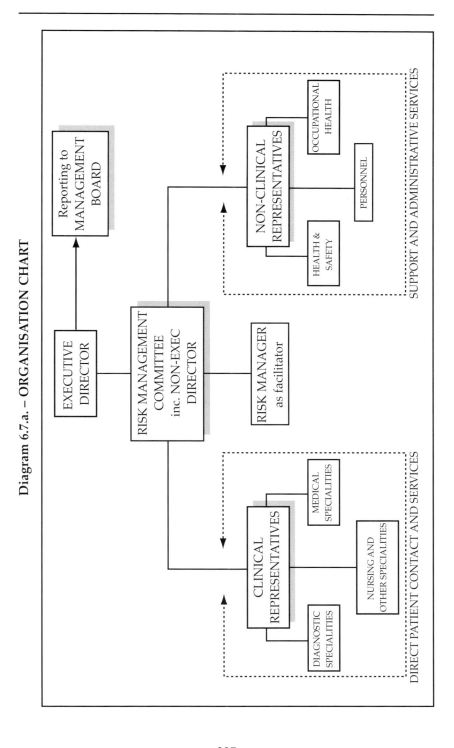

6.8.1 NHS Guidance on 'whistle blowing' (Protected Disclosure of Issues of Concern)

The Public Interest Disclosure Act 1998 was passed to enable people who have legitimate concerns for public safety or malpractice to air those concerns in confidence to a senior manager or non-executive director who is out the usual line management chain.

HSC 1999/198 gives the following guidance from the NHS Executive:

The fear of being labelled a trouble-maker, the fear of appearing disloyal and the fear of victimisation by managers and colleagues are powerful disincentives against speaking up about genuine concerns staff have about criminal activity, failure to comply with a legal duty, miscarriages of justice, danger to health and safety of the environment, and the cover up of any of these in the workplace.......

Every NHS Trust and Health Authority should:

Have in place local policies and procedures which comply with the provisions of the Public Interest Disclosure Act 1998. The minimum requirements of local policies should include:

- the designation of a senior manager or non-Executive Director with specific responsibility for addressing concerns raised in confidence which need to be handled outside the usual line management chain;

- guidance to help staff who have concerns about malpractice to do so reasonably and responsibly with the right people;

- a clear commitment that staff concerns will be taken seriously, and investigated;

- an unequivocal guarantee that staff who raise concerns responsibly and reasonably will be protected against victimisation.

The policy should cover the protected disclosure of all issues of concern that relate to:

- dangers to patients and carers;
- dangers to the environment;
- unlawful conduct;
- financial malpractice.

Further NHS information on Human Resources

HSC 1998/64 *Management of Health, Safety and Welfare Issues for NHS Staff*

HSC 1998/204 *Working Time Regulations: Implementation in the NHS*

HSC 1999/53 *For the record: managing records in NHS Trusts and Health Authorities*

HSC 1999/60 *Tackling racial harassment in the NHS: A plan for action*

HSC 1999/154 *Continuing Professional Development: Quality in the new NHS*

HSC 1999/156 *Implementing Section 21 of the Disability Discrimination Act 1995 across the NHS*

HSC 1999/162 *Working together – Securing a quality workforce for the NHS: A framework for managing Human Resources in the NHS*

6.8.1.1 NHS Controls Assurance Standards – Human Resources

Criteria November 1999

1 Board level responsibility for human resources is clearly defined and there are clear lines of accountability for human resources matters throughout the organisation, leading to the board.

2 The organisation supports the local Health Improvement Programme (HImP) with a comprehensive human resources and organisational development plan.

3 A workforce plan is produced annually and meets NHS Executive requirements.

4 All staff are recruited in accordance with relevant statutory employment legislation and mandatory NHS requirements.

5 Policies and practices on racial harassment are in accordance with the requirements of HSC 1999/060.

6 Staff sickness rates are recorded and monitored.

7 Workplace accidents and violence against staff are recorded and monitored.

8 There is a locally managed system of Continuing Professional Development, which is based on the criteria and principles contained in HSC 1999/154.

9 Training and development plans are in place for the majority of health professional staff.

10 Training and development plans are in place for the majority of non-health professional staff.

11 All staff have access to a confidential occupational health service.

12 All staff have access to a confidential counselling service.

13 Staff are involved in planning and delivering health care.

14 Acceptable standards of food and accommodation are provided for on-call staff and are agreed with the local workforce.

15 Induction arrangements for staff are subject to continuous review and improvements are agreed with local staff, with particular reference to doctors on rotational training.

16 An annual staff attitude survey is undertaken to measure the quality of working life.

17 The organisation has an adequately resourced human resources function.

18 The human resources function has access to up-to-date information on employment and related legislation and guidance.

19 Key indicators capable of showing improvements in human resource management and/or providing early warning of risk are used at all levels of the organisation, including the board, and the efficacy and usefulness of the indicators is reviewed regularly.

20 The system in place for human resources is monitored and reviewed by management and the board in order to make improvements to the system.

21 The Internal Audit function, in conjunction with the Human Resources function, carries out periodic audits to provide assurances to the board that a system of human resources management is in place that conforms to the requirements of this standard.

7

PROTECTION FOR CHILDREN AND VULNERABLE ADULTS

All Children deserve the opportunity to achieve their full potential[1]

7.1 CHILD PROTECTION

Approximately 160,000 children are the subject of investigation for possible abuse each year. Of these, some 24,500 will be placed on the social services register of children recognised as being at risk of abuse or the subject of abuse. Many will have been in contact with health care providers prior to referral. Over half the cases of abuse are reported to care professionals in the first instance. It is therefore important that health professionals and managers are familiar with child protection procedures and the need for vigilance and understanding of the subject.

The highest contribution that risk management can bring to the protection of children and vulnerable adults is to ensure that awareness of the possibility of abuse is present in each health professional who has contact with patients, and that sufficiently robust and known procedures are in place to be followed each time that the possibility of abuse needs to be acted upon. The risks from missed or mishandled abuse are high.

Risks include death or harm to the child, potential for future harm to others and damage to the reputation of the professionals and the institution. For this reason, child protection and protection for vulnerable adults is dealt with at some length. The first investigation and review carried out by the Commission for Health Improvement involved allegations of abuse against elderly patients.

---

1   Working together to Safeguard Children – Department of Health, Home Office and Department for Education and Employment 1999 The Stationery Office

Good practice calls for effective co-operation between different agencies and professionals; sensitive work with parents and carers in the best interest of the child; and the careful exercise of professional judgement, based on thorough assessment and critical analysis of the available information.

Child protection is concerned with the legal and social protection of children. The legal framework for this stems from The Children Act 1989. The Act defines a number of clear principles and duties in respect of child protection. These include:

- the child's welfare shall be the court's paramount consideration, section 1(1);

- delay is likely to prejudice the welfare of the child, section 1(2);

- the Court shall have regard to matters set out in the welfare checklist, section 1(3);

- the Court shall not make an order unless it considers that doing so would be better for the child than making no order at all, section 1(5).

As with other multi-agency care provision, risks are generated or controlled by the quality of any investigation, decision making and communication between parties.

The statutory care agencies involved in child protection include the police, social services departments and the National Society for the Prevention of Cruelty to Children. However, many cases of abuse will come to the attention of health care workers. A familiarity by health workers with the procedures to be followed in the child's interest is vital to the success of child protection.

Primary responsibility for the care and protection of children is placed upon the social services department of the local authority. The duty arises under Section 27 and Section 47 of the Act. The social services department has a responsibility to investigate reports of children who may be at risk of significant harm. The department is able to take action to protect and promote the welfare of the child in each case. This duty of care by the social services department applies whether the child is living with its parents, or living with another person or is in the care of a foster parent, residential home or school.

The Children Act 1989 places two specific duties on agencies to co-operate in the interests of vulnerable children:

7.1.1   Section 27

Section 27 provides that a local authority may request help from:

- any local authority;
- any local education authority;
- any local housing authority;
- any health authority, Special Health Authority or National Health Service Trust; *and*
- any person authorised by the Secretary of State in exercising the local authority's functions under Part III of the Act.

This part of the Act places a duty on local authorities to provide support and services for children in need, including children looked after by the local authority and those in secure accommodation. The authority whose help is requested in these circumstances has a duty to comply with the request, provided it is compatible with its other duties and functions.

7.1.2   Section 47

Section 47 places a duty on:

- any local authority;
- any local education authority;
- any housing authority;
- any health authority, Special Health Authority or National Health Service Trust; *and*
- any person authorised by the Secretary of State to help a local authority with its enquiries in cases where there is reasonable cause to suspect that a child is suffering, or is likely to suffer, significant harm.

The duty to investigate includes obtaining access to the child. If access is denied, or if information is withheld, the Authority must take sufficient steps to ensure that it receives sufficient information. General Practitioner services and Health Services have a duty to make services available to the Local Authority to discharge their functions. These arise from the National Health Services Act 1977 and the Health Services Act 1984. The child protection process is illustrated in diagram 7.1

7.1.3   Area Child Protection Committee (ACPC)

The Area Child Protection Committee is the key group for child protection, representing all relevant agencies and professionals.

7.2   THE CONCEPT OF SIGNIFICANT HARM

The Children Act 1989 introduced the concept of significant harm as the threshold that justifies compulsory intervention in family life in the best interests of children. The local authority is under a duty to make enquiries, or cause enquiries to be made, where it has reasonable cause to suspect that a child is suffering, or likely to suffer significant harm (s.47). A court may only make a care order (committing the child to the care of the local authority) or supervision order (putting the child under the supervision of a social worker, or a probation officer) in respect of a child if it is satisfied that:

- the child is suffering, or is likely to suffer, significant harm; *and*

- that the harm or likelihood of harm is attributable to a lack of adequate parental care or control (s.31).

There are no absolute criteria on which to rely when judging what constitutes significant harm. Consideration of the severity of ill-treatment may include the degree and the extent of physical harm, the duration and frequency of abuse and neglect, and the extent of premeditation, degree of threat and coercion, sadism, and bizarre or unusual elements in child sexual abuse. Each of these elements has been associated with more severe effects on the child, and/or relatively greater difficulty in helping the child overcome the adverse impact of the ill-treatment.

7.2.1   Significant Harm Section 31

'A court may only make a Care Order or Supervision Order if it is satisfied

(a) that the child concerned is suffering, or is likely to suffer significant harm and

(b) that the harm or likelihood of harm is attributable to

  (i) the care given to the child, or likely to be given to him if the order were not made, not being what it would be reasonable to expect a parent to give to him or

(ii) the child's being beyond parental control.'

Sometimes, a single traumatic event may constitute significant harm, e.g. a violent assault, suffocation or poisoning. More often, significant harm is a compilation of significant events, both acute and long-standing, which interrupt, change or damage the child's physical and psychological development. Some children live in family and social circumstances where their health and development are neglected. For them, it is the corrosiveness of long-term emotional, physical or sexual abuse that causes impairment to the extent of constituting significant harm. In each case, it is necessary to consider any ill-treatment alongside the family's strengths and supports.

To understand and establish significant harm, it is necessary to consider: the family context;

- the child's development within the context of their family and wider social and cultural environment;

- any special needs, such as a medical condition, communication difficulty or disability that may affect the child's development and care within the family;

- the nature of harm, in terms of ill-treatment or failure to provide adequate care;

- the impact on the child's health and development; and

- the adequacy of parental care.

It is important always to take account of the child's reactions, and his or her perceptions, according to the child's age and understanding.

Under s.31(9) of the Children Act 1989:

'harm' means ill-treatment or the impairment of health or development;

'development' means physical, intellectual, emotional, social or behavioural development;

'health' means physical or mental health; and

'ill-treatment' includes sexual abuse and forms of ill-treatment which are not physical.

Under s.31(10) of the Act:

Where the question of whether harm suffered by a child is significant turns on the child's health and development, his health or development shall be compared with that which could reasonably be expected of a similar child.

7.2.2   The Mental Illness of a Parent or Carer

Mental illness in a parent or carer does not necessarily have an adverse impact on a child, but it is essential always to assess its implications for any children involved in the family. Parental illness may markedly restrict children's social and recreational activities. With both mental and physical illness in a parent, children may have caring responsibilities placed upon them inappropriate to their years, leading them to be worried and anxious. If they are depressed, parents may neglect their own and their children's physical and emotional needs.

In some circumstances, some forms of mental illness may blunt parents' emotions and feelings, or cause them to behave towards their children in bizarre or violent ways. Unusually, but at the extreme, a child may be at risk of severe injury, profound neglect, or even death. A study of 100 reviews of child deaths where abuse and neglect had been a factor in the death, showed clear evidence of parental mental illness in one-third of cases. In addition, postnatal depression can also be linked to both behavioural and physiological problems in the infants of such mothers.

A Supervision Order may include requirements that a child submit to medical or psychiatric treatment, provided that the child consents, if they have the capacity and understanding to make an informed choice.

7.2.3   Confidentiality

The Government has given very clear advice on the limits to confidentiality. Working Together under the Children Act states that:

'In child protection work the degree of confidentiality will be governed by the need to protect the child. Social Workers and others working with a child and family must make clear to those providing information that confidentiality may not be maintained if the withholding of the information will prejudice the welfare of the child'

At all stages of child protection work professionals must be prepared to divulge any relevant information to keep a child from harm. There is no breach of confidentiality if the person consents to disclosure. Where the person is reluctant, they may be persuaded by the professional to disclose. The interests of the protection of the child is paramount, even when disclosure is contrary to the parent's wishes.

Parties to any arrangement to sharing information should be aware that The Data Protection Act 1998 requires that there is a "legitimate basis" for disclosing sensitive personal data. The introduction of special controls on the processing of sensitive data (including holding and disclosing them) is one of the major innovations of the new Act. Under section 2,"sensitive data" includes information as to the commission, or alleged commission, by the data subject of any offence; and criminal proceedings involving the data subject as the accused, and their disposal. The definition of "sensitive data" also includes information about the data subject's sexual life. It should also be made clear to all parties that information received under the arrangement is to be used only for the specified purpose(s). Thus, there should be a restriction on secondary use of personal data received under any information sharing arrangement *unless* the consent of the disclosing party to that secondary use is sought and granted.

If a public body acts *ultra vires* or outside its powers, then it may, at the same time, breach the lawfulness requirement of the first data protection principle. Section 115 of the Crime and Disorder Act 1998 may provide the parties with the lawful power they need provided the requirements of that section are met. This provides that any person can lawfully disclose information, where necessary or expedient for the purposes of any provision of the (1998) Act, to a chief officer of police, a police authority, local authorities, Probation Service or health authority, even if they do not otherwise have this power. This power also covers disclosure to people acting on behalf of any of the above named bodies. The "purposes" of the Act referred to in Section 115 include a range of measures such as local crime audits, youth offending teams, anti-social behaviour orders, sex offender orders, and local child curfew schemes. It should also be noted that Section 17 of the Act places a statutory duty on every local authority to "exercise its various functions ... with due regard to ... the need to do all that it reasonably can to prevent ... crime and disorder in its area".[2]

---

2   Data Protection Commissioner's Checklist for setting up Information Sharing Arrangements

Consideration must be given to whether the personal information can be disclosed lawfully and fairly. In terms of *lawfulness,* an agency will need to consider whether personal information is held under a *duty of confidence.* If it is, then it may only be disclosed:

(a) with the individual's consent; or

(b) where there is an overriding public interest or justification for doing so.

It will not always be the case that the prevention and detection of crime or public safety constitutes an overriding public interest for the exchange of personal information.

7.2.4 Quality Decision Making

The quality of decisions made in relation to child protection will be assisted if the following parameters are taken into account:

- there must be a full and fair investigation of the facts of each case;

- a person accused of abuse must be given an opportunity to answer the allegations and be given adequately detailed information of the allegations to enable them to do so;

- additional information, including that obtained at a Child Protection Conference should be disclosed to an alleged abuser;

- information can be disclosed to others who may come into contact with an alleged abuser:

- where it is intended to promote the welfare of a child and;

- the information is honest and fairly assessed and;

- the damage which may be caused to the individual does not outweigh the benefit of disclosure for child protection.

7.2.5 Schedule 1 Offenders

There is special responsibility on the prisons, probation service and social services departments in respect of persons convicted under section 1 of the Children and Young Persons Act 1933. The social services department must be informed by the prison prior to the release of a convicted prisoner. Similarly, the probation service should be involved.

Where a schedule one offender under supervision is seeking or who has found work which brings them into contact with children, the supervising probation officer has a duty to inform the employer. The same duty exists in relation to leisure activities. If the offender is living in or moves to accommodation where there are children, the probation officer needs to inform the social services department.

A list of Schedule 1 offences is at the end of the chapter.

7.2.6　Definition – Abused child

An abused child is a boy or girl, 17 years or under, who has suffered from, or is believed to be at significant risk, of physical injury, neglect, emotional abuse or sexual abuse. Somebody may abuse or neglect a child by inflicting harm, or failing to act to prevent harm. Children may be abused in a family or in an institutional or community setting; by those known to them or, more rarely, by a stranger.

Recognition of abuse depends upon the child's welfare being the paramount consideration. A number of factors aid recognition. These include:

- being fully aware of the signs and symptoms of abuse;
- awareness that abuse can occur in any social class;
- an index of suspicion that any injury could be non-accidental;
- lack of consistency between the history and the injuries;
- patterns of injuries which occur over time;
- an index of suspicion that an illness could be avoidable;
- awareness that children with learning and physical disabilities are vulnerable to abuse;
- sensitivity to a change in the child's behaviour;
- abuse to another child in the house;
- the presence of a known abuser in the house.

Additional factors which increase the suspicion index include:

- refusal of access to a child;
- refusal of examination of a child;

- disguising refusal to access by alleged or actual absence of the child;

- collusion by the non-abusing parent.

7.2.7 Physical Abuse

Physical abuse can lead directly to neurological damage, physical injuries, disability or – at the extreme – death. Harm may be caused to children both by the abuse itself, and by the abuse taking place in a wider family or institutional context of conflict and aggression. Physical abuse has been linked to aggressive behaviour in children, emotional and behavioural problems, and educational difficulties.

It is not necessary for the child to present with severe injury. Clinical concern may be aroused by:

- bruises or marks on a child;

- observations of the child's behaviour

- indications of family stress;

- mention of injury by a child, the parents, relatives or friends.

Unusual injuries in children

- back injuries in children who have yet to learn to walk;

- accidental head injuries are unusual in children under 6 months of age;

- bite marks – human teeth can leave clear oval or crescent shaped marks;

- burns with clear outlines;
    - cigarette burns are circular
    - linear burns from hot metal rods or electric fire elements
    - water line marks from scalds
    - uniform burns over large areas
    - splash marks above the main burn area from thrown liquid
    - friction burns from flooring
    - old untreated burn scars

- repeated or multiple bruising to the head;

- two simultaneous black eyes without bruising to the forehead;

- bruising with the imprint of belts, hand prints;

- bruising or tears around the earlobe;

- bruising in the mouth or under the tongue.

Fractures cause pain, swelling and usually discolouration over a bone or joint. The pain caused is distressing for the child and it is unlikely that parents can be unaware that the child has been hurt.

- any fracture in a child under 1 year is suspicious.

- any skull fracture in a child under 4 is suspicious.

Consideration should be given to a full skeletal survey if the explanation of the injuries leads to the suspicion of non-accidental injury **and**:

- the injury or history of injury suggests physical abuse;

- in all children under 18 months with evidence of trauma;

- in older children with severe bruising;

- in children with previous skeletal injury;

- in children who have died in unusual or suspicious circumstances.

7.2.8   Neglect and Failure to Thrive

Neglect is the persistent failure to meet a child's basic physical and/or psychological needs, likely to result in the serious impairment of the child's health or development. It may involve a parent or carer failing to provide adequate food, shelter and clothing, failing to protect a child from physical harm or danger, or the failure to ensure access to appropriate medical care or treatment. It may also include neglect of, or unresponsiveness to, a child's basic emotional needs.

Children who present and who may the subject of neglect and failure to thrive may show signs of:

- failure to grow within normal expected patterns and showing evidence of pallor, weight loss and signs of poor nutrition;

- listless, apathetic and unresponsive with no apparent medical cause;

- failure to meet the basic essential needs such as adequate food, clothes, warmth, hygiene, medical care and supervision;

- thriving when away from the home environment;

- failure of the parents or carers to provide adequate love and affection in a stimulating environment.

7.2.9 Emotional Abuse

Emotional abuse is the persistent emotional ill-treatment of a child such as to cause severe and persistent adverse effects on the child's emotional development. It may involve conveying to children that they are worthless or unloved, inadequate, or valued only insofar as they meet the needs of another person. It may feature age or develop-mentally inappropriate expectations being imposed on children. It may involve causing children frequently to feel frightened or in danger, or the exploitation or corruption of children. Some level of emotional abuse is involved in all types of ill-treatment of a child, though it may occur alone.

Emotional abuse can take many forms such as coldness, hostility, constant denigration, extreme inconsistency in behaviour towards the child or distorted emotional demands. The abuse may result in the child exhibiting symptoms of:

- low self-esteem;

- apathy;

- unduly aggressive behaviour;

- attention seeking behaviour, whether disruptive or over friendly;

- fearful or withdrawn "frozen watchfulness".

7.2.10 Sexual Abuse

Sexual abuse involves forcing or enticing a child or young person to take part in sexual activities, whether or not the child is aware of what is happening. The activities may involve physical contact, including penetrative (e.g. rape or buggery) or non-penetrative acts. They may include non-contact activities, such as involving children in looking at, or in the production of, pornographic material or watching sexual activities, or encouraging children to behave in sexually inappropriate ways.

Suspicion of sexual abuse often stems from the child's circumstances and behaviour, accompanied by symptoms described and physical signs observed or from a statement made by the child.

Experience from social service departments shows that children of both sexes are abused at all ages, that abuse may continue for several years before it comes to light and that abusers use their authority over the child to gain their co-operation.

Most children who are the subject of sexual abuse are abused by someone that they know. It may be a member of the family or someone known to the family. Many children feel guilty and responsible about their involvement and are put under pressure not to reveal the abuse.

The size of the list of symptoms and signs of possible abuse is an indicator difficulties in making an accurate diagnosis. The following list is of potential findings suggestive of abuse, but is not exhaustive:

- vaginal bleeding in pre-pubescent girls;

- genital lacerations or bruising;

- sexually transmitted diseases;

- abnormal dilation of the vagina, anus or urethra;

- faecal soiling or retention;

- itching, soreness, discharge or unexplained bleeding;

- unexplained recurrent urinary tract infections;

- semen in the vagina, anus, external genitalia or on clothes;

- recurrent abdominal pain;

- pregnancy, where the identity of the father is vague or secret;

- difficulty in walking or sitting.

7.2.11 Behavioural Indicators

There are many behavioural indicators associated with sexual abuse. These include:

Sexual

- sexually provocative relationships with adults;

- displaying more knowledge of sexual matters compared with peers;
- engaging in sexualised play with other children;
- engaging in sexualised behaviour with other children;
- excessively preoccupied with sexual matters;
- inappropriately asks for contraception, perhaps as a cry for help;
- hints at sexual activity through words, play or drawings.

General

- lack of trust in, or demonstrating fear of, familiar adults;
- child psychiatric problems including:
  - onset of soiling or wetting;
  - severe sleep disturbance;
  - changes in eating patterns;
  - changes in the pattern of behaviour;
  - social isolation;
  - withdrawal;
  - role reversal in the home e.g. daughter taking over the mothering role;
  - inappropriate physical contact between parent and child.
- School problems including:
  - learning difficulties;
  - poor concentration;
  - poor peer group relationships;
  - inability to make friends;
  - school used as a haven, arriving early and reluctant to leave;
- reluctance to take part in physical activity;
- reluctance to change clothes for physical education;
- truancy or running away from home;
- self-harm, self-mutilation or suicide attempts;
- dependence on drugs or alcohol;
- anti-social behaviour including promiscuity or involvement in prostitution.

Sexual abuse is usually committed by someone known to the child. This may result in considerable pressure being applied to the child not to report what has been happening. The closeness of the relationship can result in the child feeling guilty and responsible for what has happened. The diffuse nature of the presenting symptoms of behaviour increases the risk of faulty decision making. These risks can be reduced by adopting a thorough and systematic approach to investigating allegations of abuse.

7.2.12 Organised Abuse

Organised or multiple abuse may be defined as abuse involving one or more abuser and a number of related or non-related abused children and young people. The abusers concerned may be acting in concert to abuse children, sometimes acting in isolation, or may be using an institutional framework or position of authority to recruit children for abuse.

Organised and multiple abuse occur both as part of a network of abuse across a family or community, and within institutions such as residential homes or schools. Such abuse is profoundly traumatic for the children who become involved. Its investigation is time-consuming and demanding work requiring specialist skills from both police and social work staff. Some investigations become extremely complex because of the number of places and people involved, and the timescale over which abuse is alleged to have occurred. The complexity is heightened where, as in historical cases, the alleged victims are no longer living in the situations where the incidents occurred or where the alleged perpetrators are also no longer linked to the setting or employment role.

A paedophile is an individual whose conscious sexual desires and responses are directed partially or exclusively towards children to whom he/she may be directly related, incest or not. (Burgess et al 1978.)

Sex rings are operations organised by adults for illicit purposes. (Burgess 1984.) They are divided into the following types:

solo ring – adult operates alone with a group of children;

transition ring – the adult has begun to exchange or sell pornographic photographs of children and tries to pressure the child into the syndicated ring;

syndicated ring – a well-structured organisation formed for recruiting children, producing pornography, delivering direct sexual services and establishing a network of customers.

7.2.13   Children Involved in Prostitution

Children involved in prostitution and other forms of commercial sexual exploitation should be treated primarily as the victims of abuse, and their needs require careful assessment. They are likely to be in need of welfare services and – in many cases – protection under the Children Act 1989. The problem is often hidden from view. Area Child Protection Committees should actively enquire into the extent to which there is a local problem, and should not assume that it is not a local issue.

7.2.14   Child Pornography and the Internet

The Internet has now become a significant tool in the distribution of child pornography. Adults are now using the Internet to try to establish contact with children with a view to 'grooming' them for inappropriate or abusive relationships.

As part of their role in preventing abuse and neglect, ACPCs may wish to consider activities to raise awareness about the safe use of the Internet by children, for example, by distributing information through education staff to parents, in relation to both school and home-based use of computers by children.

7.2.15   Abuse of Disabled Children[3]

The available UK evidence on the extent of abuse among disabled children suggests that disabled children are at increased risk of abuse, and that the presence of multiple disabilities appears to increase the risk of both abuse and neglect. Disabled children may be especially vulnerable to abuse for a number of reasons. Some disabled children may:

- have fewer outside contacts than other children;

- receive intimate personal care, possibly from a number of carers, which may both increase the risk of exposure to abusive behaviour, and make it more difficult to set and maintain physical boundaries;

---

3   *Working together to safeguard children* HMSO 2000.

- have an impaired capacity to resist or avoid abuse;

- have communication difficulties which may make it difficult to tell others what is happening;

- be inhibited about complaining because of a fear of losing services;

- be especially vulnerable to bullying and intimidation; and/or

- be more vulnerable than other children to abuse by their peers.

Safeguards for disabled children are essentially the same as for non-disabled children.

There should be particular attention paid to promoting a high level of awareness of the risks and high standards of practice, and to strengthen the capacity of children and families to help themselves. Measures include:

- making it common practice to help disabled children make their wishes and feelings known in respect of their care and treatment;

- ensuring that disabled children receive appropriate personal, health, and social education (including sex education) ;

- making sure that all disabled children know how to raise concerns if they are worried or angry about something, and giving them access to a range of adults with whom they can communicate. Those disabled children with communication difficulties should have available to them at all times a means of being heard;

- an explicit commitment to, and understanding of all children's safety and welfare among providers of services used by disabled children;

- close contact with families, and a culture of openness on the part of services; and guidelines and training for staff on good practice in intimate care; working with children of the opposite sex; handling difficult behaviour; consent to treatment;

- anti-bullying strategies; and sexuality and sexual behaviour among young people living away from home.

Where there are concerns about the welfare of a disabled child, they should be acted upon in the same way as with any other child. The same thresholds for action apply. It would be unacceptable if poor standards of care were tolerated for disabled children which would not be tolerated for non-disabled children. Where a disabled child has communication difficulties or learning difficulties, special attention should be paid to communication needs, and to ascertain the child's perception of events, and his or her wishes and feelings.

In every area, social services and the police should be aware of non-verbal communication systems, when they might be useful and how to access them, and should know how to contact suitable interpreters or facilitators. Agencies should not make assumptions about the inability of a disabled child to give credible evidence, or to withstand the rigours of the court process. Each child should be assessed carefully, and helped and supported to participate in the criminal justice process when this is in the child's best interest and the interests of justice.

ACPCs have an important role in safeguarding disabled children through:

- raising awareness among children, families and services;

- identifying and meeting inter-agency training needs, which encourage the 'pooling' of expertise between those with knowledge and skills in respect of disabilities, and those with knowledge and skills in respect of child protection;

- ensuring that local policies and procedures for safeguarding children meet the needs of disabled children.

7.2.15.1 Abuse by Children and Young People

Work with children and young people who abuse others – including those who sexually abuse/offend – should recognise that such children are likely to have considerable needs themselves, and also that they may pose a significant risk of harm to other children. Evidence suggests that children who abuse others may have suffered considerable disruption in their lives, been exposed to violence within the family, may have witnessed or been subject to physical or sexual abuse, have problems in their educational development, and may have committed other offences. Such children and young people are likely to be children in need, and some will in addition be suffering or at risk of significant harm, and may themselves be in need of protection.

Children and young people who abuse others should be held responsible for their abusive behaviour, whilst being identified and responded to in a way which meets their needs as well as protecting others. Work with adult abusers has shown that many of them began committing abusing acts during childhood or adolescence, and that significant numbers themselves have been subjected to abuse. Early intervention with children and young people who abuse others may, therefore, play an important part in protecting the public by preventing the continuation or escalation of abusive behaviour.

Three key principles should guide work with children and young people who abuse others:

- there should be a coordinated approach on the part of youth justice, child welfare, education (including educational psychology) and health (including child and adolescent mental health) agencies;

- the needs of children and young people who abuse others should be considered separately from the needs of their victims; and

- an assessment should be carried out in each case, appreciating that these children may have considerable unmet developmental needs, as well as specific needs arising from their behaviour.

ACPCs and Youth Offending Teams should ensure that there is a clear operational framework in place within which assessment, decision-making and case management take place. Neither child welfare nor criminal justice agencies should embark upon a course of action that has implications for the other without appropriate consultation.

7.2.16 Female Circumcision

Female genital mutilation (FGM) is an offence created by the Prohibition of Female Circumcision Act 1985, unless it is performed on specific health grounds. A child who is believed to be at risk of undergoing circumcision should be considered under the category of physical abuse. A local authority is able to use its powers under s.47 of the Children Act 1989 if it has reason to believe that a child is likely to be or has been the subject of FGM.

7.3 ROLE OF STATUTORY ORGANISATIONS

7.3.1 Child Protection Procedures

A child thought to be at risk should be brought to the attention of the relevant social service department. The full range of potential professionals, members of the public, who may report anonymously, means that clear procedures need to be established. The methodology for these is simple, but needs to be comprehensively known. The simpler the procedure, the less likely it is for errors to be made.

After a full investigation of the allegations, there needs to be a meeting of all relevant professionals to consider whether the child should be placed on the Child Protection Register. The Child Protection Register is held by the Social Services Department. The criteria for the decision by a Child Protection Conference to place a child on the Register are:

- there has been significant harm leading to the need for a child protection plan **and/or**

- there is likely to be significant harm leading to the need for a Child protection plan.

In deciding whether harm is significant, a comparison must be made 'with that which could reasonably be expected of a similar child'.

The police have the responsibility to interview any alleged suspect of child abuse, whether the suspect is a young person or adult. If the alleged suspect is a child, consideration will need to be given to both criminal proceedings and child protection procedures for the suspect. If the child suspect is thought to be the subject of abuse, separate child protection investigations need to be undertaken.

A flowchart for child protection procedures is given in figure 7.3.1[4]

7.3.2 Video Recorded Interviews

Video recorded interviews of a child may be required, with their consent, where criminal proceedings are contemplated. In particular, where there are grounds to believe:

- a child under 17 years of age has been the subject of sexual abuse;

---

4   Appendix 5 op cit

Figure 7.3.1 – CHILD PROTECTION – FLOWCHART OF KEY STAGES

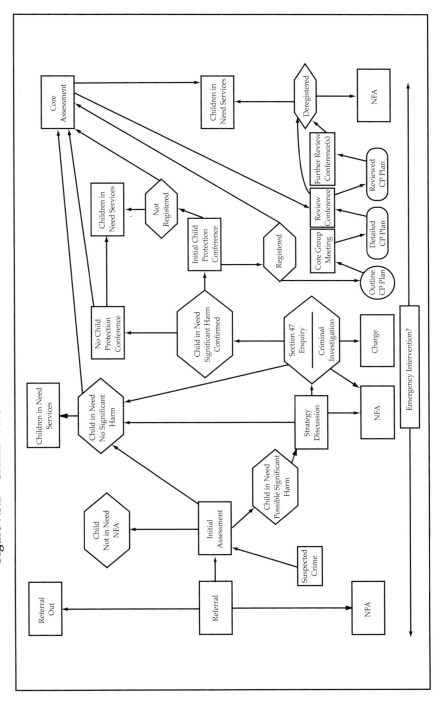

- a child under the age of 14 years has been the subject of physical abuse.

The interviews should only be undertaken by suitably trained police and social workers.

7.3.3   Local Authority

Local authorities, acting in order to fulfil their social services functions, have specific legal duties in respect of children under the Children Act 1989. They have a general duty to safeguard and promote the welfare of children in their area who are in need, and – provided that this is consistent with the child's safety and welfare – to promote the upbringing of such children by their families, by providing services appropriate to the child's needs (s.17). They should do this in partnership with parents and in a way which is sensitive to the child's race, religion, culture and language.

7.3.4   Guardians Ad Litem

The *Guardian Ad Litem* and Reporting Officer (GALRO) service is currently provided by local authorities as a statutory responsibility. Its function in care and related proceedings under the Children Act 1989, and many proceedings under adoption legislation, is to safeguard and promote the interests of individual children who are the subject of the proceedings by providing independent social work advice to the court. In care-related applications where the child is a party to the proceedings, the *guardian ad litem* appoints a solicitor to represent the child and is responsible for instructing the solicitor.

The *guardian ad litem*'s role as an officer of the court is limited to the duration of the court proceedings, including any appeal that might be lodged. In each case the guardian ad litem should exercise discretion over how best to undertake enquiries, assess information, consult a range of professionals and report to the court at interim hearings, directions appointments and at the final hearing.

The *guardian ad litem* has a statutory right to access and to take copies of local authority records which relate to the child concerned and any application under the Child Protection Act 1989. That power also extends to other records which relate to the child and the wider functions of the local authority or records held by an authorised person (i.e. the NSPCC) which relate to that child.

7.3.5   Education Services

All those working in the education services can contribute to the safeguarding of children and child protection processes. All schools and colleges have a pastoral responsibility towards their pupils. They can play a part in the prevention of abuse and neglect, through their own policies and procedures for safeguarding children, and through the curriculum. All schools and colleges should create and maintain a safe environment for children and young people, and should be able to manage situations where there are child welfare concerns.

7.3.6   Health Services

7.3.6.1 *Health Professionals*

All health professionals, in the NHS, private sector, and other agencies, play an essential part in ensuring that children and families receive the care, support and services they need in order to promote children's health and development. Because of the universal nature of health provision, health professionals are often the first to be aware that families are experiencing difficulties in looking after their children. The involvement of health professionals is important at all stages of work with children and families:

- recognising children in need of support and/or safeguarding, and parents who may need extra help in bringing up their children;

- contributing to enquiries about a child and family;

- assessing the needs of children and the capacity of parents to meet their children's needs;

- planning and providing support to vulnerable children and families;

- participating in child protection conferences;

- planning support for children at risk of significant harm;

- providing therapeutic help to abused children and parents under stress (e.g. mental illness);

- playing a part, through the child protection plan, in safeguarding children from significant harm; and

- contributing to case reviews.

There will always be a need for close co-operation with other agencies, including any other health professionals involved.

7.3.6.2 Health Authorities

The health authority should take the overall strategic lead for health services in local inter-agency working on child protection matters. It should co-operate with other agencies, especially the local authority, in planning services for vulnerable children and their families, and ensuring that local health agencies and professionals contribute fully and effectively to local inter-agency working to safeguard children and promote their welfare. This responsibility includes ensuring that there is suitable health service involvement in, and commitment to, the work of the ACPC. This involves ensuring the provision of advice and support to the ACPC in respect of a range of specialist health functions e.g. primary care, mental health (adult and child and adolescent) and sexual health. It also includes co-ordinating the health component of case reviews. To the extent that they commission health services, health authorities should ensure that service specifications should include clear service standards for safeguarding children and promoting their welfare, consistent with local ACPC procedures.

7.3.6.3 Hospitals and Community Health Services

NHS Trusts and Primary Care Groups/Trusts (PCG/Ts) are responsible for providing acute and community health services in hospital and community settings, and a wide range of staff will come into contact with children and parents in the course of their normal duties. Staff should be trained to be alert to potential indicators of abuse or neglect in children, and know how to act upon their concerns in line with local ACPC procedures.

Each NHS Trust – including PCG/Ts – should identify a named doctor and a named nurse or midwife who will take a professional lead within the Trust on child protection matters. The named doctor and nurse should have expertise in children's health and development, the nature of child maltreatment, and local arrangements for safeguarding children and promoting their welfare.

7.3.6.4 Medical Assessment

An early medical assessment may well be important as part of a multi-disciplinary child abuse investigation which should include a full family and social history. Management decisions should never rely solely on medical evidence or advice. Appropriate consent to a medical examination must be obtained. All examinations should take place in a child-centred environment.

The presence of a police surgeon should be requested when advice on forensic evidence is required. Bite marks may require identification and should be examined immediately that they are noted. A Home Office recognised Forensic Odontologist may be required to assist.

7.3.6.4.1 Physical Abuse

The child must be taken for medical assessment within 24 hours. A suitably experienced doctor must be alerted to the possibility of physical abuse and informed of the details of the examination.

7.3.6.4.2 Emotional Abuse/Neglect/Sexual Abuse

An immediate medical examination may not be necessary. Decisions concerning medical intervention should be taken in conjunction with the care manager. Consideration should be given to the need for the presence of a police surgeon.

7.3.6.4.3 Failure to Thrive

Children referred for failure to thrive may be the subject of current medical supervision and admission to hospital may be considered as part of the medical investigations. Consideration should be given to the presence of a police surgeon at the examination.

7.3.6.4.4 Consent for Medical Examination

Examination without consent is an assault. For consent to be valid it must be:

- informed – i.e. the person giving consent is aware of what he or she is consenting to and the possible consequences:

- freely given – i.e. without fears, threats, fraud or coercion.

Consent is therefore required for any medical procedure. Where the obtaining of consent is not practicable in an emergency, any medical procedure to deal with the emergency is justified. However, when the emergency has been dealt with, any further medical procedures require consent.

Where a child is 16 years or over, the child's consent is necessary. The consent of the parents is not necessary, nor is the parent's consent an alternative to the child's.

Where a child is under 16 years, the consent of the child alone is sufficient provided that the child truly understands what is proposed and is capable of appreciating the consequences. The child's capacity should be judged by the doctor and recorded. In the case of any other child, the consent of the parent, guardian or person with legal custody is required. Where parents disagree over giving consent, the consent of only one of them is necessary.

7.3.6.5 *Primary Care Groups and Primary Care Trusts*

Primary Care Groups are bodies covering groups of GP Practices and are responsible for improving the health of their combined practice population, developing primary and community health services, and commissioning hospital and community health services. All PGCs are expected to become Primary Care Trusts (PCTs), free-standing statutory bodies responsible for commissioning hospital and community health services, or in some circumstances, providing community health services directly themselves. The health authority should, through agreement with PGC/Ts, ensure that the local health service contribution to inter-agency working is discharged. Service specifications drawn up by PCG/Ts as commissioners needs to include clear service standards for safeguarding children and promoting their welfare, consistent with local ACPC procedures.

7.3.7 Statutory Powers of Protection for Children

7.3.7.1 *Emergency Protection Orders*

The court may make an emergency protection order under s.44 of the Children Act 1989 if it is satisfied that there is reasonable cause to believe that a child is likely to suffer significant harm if:

- he is not removed to accommodation; or

- he does not remain in the place in which he is then being accommodated

An emergency protection order may also be made if s.47 enquiries are being frustrated by access to the child being unreasonably refused to a person authorised to seek access, and the applicant has reasonable cause to believe that access is needed as a matter of urgency.

An emergency protection order gives authority to remove a child, and places the child under the protection of the applicant for a maximum of eight days (with a possible extension of up to seven days).

7.3.7.2 Child Assessment Order

The Child Assessment Order (C.A.O. Section 43) does not provide emergency protection. It is intended to be used where there is reasonable cause to suspect the child is suffering or likely to suffer significant harm, which is not so urgent as to justify the use of an E.P.O., i.e. cases of "suspicion". It is designed to deal with the situations where professionals agree a full assessment of the child is required, the parents are uncooperative, but there is no sense of emergency. The Child Assessment Order will be applicable in those small number of cases where a Court Order is necessary to gain further information.

The Court may make a Child Assessment Order if it is satisfied that:

- the applicant has reasonable cause to suspect that the child is suffering, or is likely to suffer, significant harm;

- an assessment of the state of the child's health or development, or the way in which he/she has been treated is required to enable the applicant to determine whether or not the child is suffering, or is likely to suffer, significant harm;

it is unlikely that such assessment will be made, or be satisfactory, in the absence of an order under this section.

7.3.7.3 Care Proceedings (SECTION 31)

Care proceedings are the only method by which the Local Authority can apply for children to be placed in their care, i.e. it is the only way for the Local Authority to obtain parental responsibility.

7.3.8 Care Orders

The Court may only make a Care or Supervision Order if it is satisfied:

- that the child concerned is suffering, or is likely to suffer, significant harm; and

- that the harm, or likelihood of harm, is attributable to:

- the care given to the child or likely to be given to him/her if the order were not made, not being what it would be reasonable to expect a parent to give him/her; **or**

- the child being beyond parental control.

Even when the grounds for an order are established, it does not necessarily follow that a Care or Supervision Order must be made. The order must be shown to be in the child's best interests in line with the child's welfare being the Courts paramount consideration.

The Court will also consider the Welfare Checklist:

- the ascertainable wishes and feelings of the child concerned (considered in the light of his age and understanding);

- his physical, emotional and educational needs;

- the likely effect on him of any change in his circumstances;

- his age, sex, background and any characteristic of his wish the Court considers relevant;

- any harm which he has suffered or is at risk of suffering;

- how capable each of his parents, and any other person in relation to whom the Court considers the question to be relevant, is of meeting his needs;

7.3.8.1 *Police Protection Powers*

Under s.46 of the Children Act 1989, where a police officer has reasonable cause to believe that a child would otherwise be likely to suffer significant harm, s/he may:

- remove the child to suitable accommodation and keep him or her there; or

- take reasonable steps to ensure that the child's removal from any hospital, or other place in which the child is then being accommodated is prevented.

No child may be kept in police protection for more than 72 hours

7.3.8.2 *The Protection of Children Act 1999*

The Protection of Children Act requires child care organisations to refer the names of individuals considered unsuitable to work with children to a Department of Health list, together with 'List 99' maintained by the Department for Education and Employment. It requires child care organisations not to offer work to individuals on the list and provides rights of appeal against inclusion on the list to an independent tribunal.

7.3.9   Problems and Barriers in Child Protection

In 1995, the Department of Health published *Child Protection: Messages from Research*, which summarised the key findings from 20 research studies commissioned by the Department through its child protection research programme. A number of important themes emerged about the operation of child protection processes during the period covered by the research:

- some professionals were using s.47 enquiries inappropriately, as a means of obtaining services for children in need;

- over half of the children and families who were the subject of s.47 enquiries received no services as the result of professionals' interest in their lives. Too often, enquiries were too narrowly conducted as investigations into whether abuse or neglect had occurred, without considering the wider needs and circumstances of the child and family;

- enquiries into suspicions of child abuse can have traumatic effects on families. Good professional practice can ease parents' anxiety and lead to co-operation that helps to safeguard the child. As nearly all children remain at, or return home, involving the family in child protection processes is likely to be effective. Professionals could still do more to work in partnership with parents and the child;

- discussions at child protection conferences tended to focus too heavily on decisions about registration and removal, rather than focusing on future plans to safeguard the child and support the family in the months after the conference;

- while inter-agency work was often relatively good at the early stages of enquiries, its effectiveness tended to decline once child protection plans had been made, with social services left with sole responsibility for implementing the plans;

- there was inconsistent use made of the child protection register, which was not consulted for 60% of children for whom there were child protection concerns.

7.3.10 Quality of Decisions in Child Protection

7.3.10.1 *Improving the Quality of Decision Making in Child Protection*

The quality of decisions made in relation to child protection will be assisted if the following are taken into account:

- there must be a full and fair investigation of the facts of each case;

- the facts of the case are reviewed as objectively as possible;

- a person accused of abuse must be given an opportunity to answer the allegations and be given adequately detailed information of the allegations to enable them to do so;

- additional information, including that obtained at a Child Protection Conference should be disclosed to an alleged abuser;

- information can be disclosed to others who may come into contact with an alleged abuser:

- where it is intended to promote the welfare of a child **and**;

- the information is honest and fairly assessed **and**;

- the damage which may be caused to the individual does not outweigh the benefit of disclosure for child protection.

- the examination of the parents or carers should include considering the need for a mental state assessment examination. A review of fatal child abuse and parental psychiatric disorder showed mental illness to be present in 35 of 100 cases reported to the Department of Health under "Part 8" reviews. Predominant amongst these were middle aged women in the recovery phase from a depressive illness.

7.3.10.2 *Detractors from Quality Decision Making in Child Protection*

Collaborative working between agencies involved in child protection is required for effective outcomes. Common detractors to impair or prevent this include:

- friction with tasks, priorities or role confusion;
- unrealistic or incompatible ideas on individual responsibilities;
- territorial disputes between professional groups;
- power, status and resource dependency incompatibilities.

The key way to prevent these problems is to increase multi-disciplinary training and mutual understanding of the organisational and individual roles in child protection.

7.3.11 Schedule 1 Offences

Schedule one offences include:

Common Law Offences

The murder of a child or young person under 18.

Offences Under the Offences Against the Person Act 1861

s5 Manslaughter of a child or young person under 18.

s27 The abandonment or exposure of a child under two so as to endanger its life or health.

s42 Common assault on a child or young person under 18.

s43 Aggravated assault on a female child or young person under 18 or on a boy under 14.

Offences Under the Infant Life (Preservation) Act 1929

s1 Child destruction

Offences Under the Children and Young Persons Act 1933

s1   Cruelty to a person under 16

s3   Allowing a person under 16 to be in a brothel

s4   Causing or allowing a person under 16 to be used for begging

s11 Exposing a child under 12 to risk of burning

s23 Causing, procuring or allowing a person under 16 to take part in a dangerous performance

Offences Under the Infanticide Act 1938

s1   Infanticide

Offences Under the Sexual Offences Act 1956

s1   Rape (or attempted rape) of a girl under 18

s2   Procurement of a girl under 18 by threats

s3   Procurement of a girl under 18 by false pretences

s4   Administering drugs to a girl under 18 to obtain or facilitate intercourse

s5   Intercourse with a girl under 13

s6   Intercourse with a girl between 13 and 16

s7   Intercourse with a mentally deficient girl under 18

s10 Incest (or attempt to commit incest) by a man where the victim is under 18

s11 Incest (or attempt to commit incest) by a woman, where the victim is under 18

s12 Buggery (or attempt to commit buggery) with a person under 18

s13 Indecency between men where one or both is under 18

s14 Indecent assault on a girl under 18

s15 Indecent assault on a male under 18

s16 Assault with intent to commit buggery

s19 Abduction of an unmarried girl under 18 from the parent or guardian

s20 Abduction of an unmarried girl under 16 from the parents or guardian

s22 Causing the prostitution of a girl under 18

s23 Procuration of a girl under 18

s24 Detention of a girl under 18 in a brothel or other premises

s25 Permitting a girl under 13 to use premises for intercourse

s26 Permitting a girl between 13 and 16 to use premises for intercourse s28 Causing, or encouraging the prostitution of, intercourse with, or indecent assault on, a girl under 16

Offences Under the Indecency with Children Act 1960

s1   Indecent conduct towards a girl under 14

Offences Under the Suicide Act 1961

s2   Aiding, abetting, counselling or procuring the suicide of a person under 18

Offences Under the Protection of Children Act 1978

s1   Taking, permitting to be taken, distributing or showing any indecent photograph of a person under 16.

Having such indecent photographs with a view to their being distributed or shown; publishing or causing to be published any advertisement likely to be understood as conveying that the advertiser distributes or shows such indecent photographs or intends to do so.

Offences Under the Child Abduction Act 1984

s1   Taking or sending out of the United Kingdom a child under 16 by a person connected with the child without the appropriate consent (abduction of the child by a parent etc)

s2   Without lawful authority or reasonable excuse, detaining or taking a child under the age of 16 so as to remove him from the lawful control of the parent or so as to keep him out of the lawful control of any person entitled to lawful control of the child (abduction of the child by other persons)

7.4   PROTECTION OF VULNERABLE ADULTS

The absence of specific legislation to protect the interests of vulnerable adults is perhaps an indicator that abuse of this group of people has not had a sufficiently high profile in the past. With the production of the paper, No Secrets,[5] the protection of vulnerable adults is now a concern for the risk manager.

---

5   *No Secrets – Guidance on developing Multi-agency Policies and Procedures to protect vulnerable adults from abuse –* Department of Health 2000

In order to properly address and fulfil a commitment to protecting this client group, it is important to obtain a commitment from local relevant health and social care agencies to determine:

- individual agency responsibilities;
- resource commitment;
- joint working agreements;
- joint assessment of needs;
- a commitment to equal opportunities;
- a commitment to quality improvement.

7.4.1.1 Abuse Definition

"The mistreatment of a vulnerable adult – physical, emotional or financial – which may take the form of physical assault, threatening behaviour, neglect, abandonment or sexual assault".[6]

7.4.1.2 Vulnerable Adult

"A person aged 18 years or over who is or may be in need of community care services by reason of mental or other disability, age or illness and who is or may be unable to take care of him/herself, or unable to protect him/herself against significant harm or exploitation".[7]

7.4.1.3 Recognition of Abuse

An increase in the dependency of a vulnerable person may result in progressively deteriorating circumstances. This may present in the following ways:

- physical disability or illness which affects the person's intellect or memory, control of their bladder and/or bowels, and/or severely limits their mobility;
- difficulties in communication; e.g. loss or difficulty with speech and understanding; dementia/Alzheimer's disease, loss of memory and concentration; deafness;

---

6 Amended from Mervyn Eastman – *Old Age Abuse* – Age Concern 1984

7 *Who Decides? Making Decisions on Behalf of Mentally Incapacitated Adults*, HMSO 1997

- mental health difficulties;

- visual disability;

- deaf-blindness.

7.4.1.4 *Predisposing Factors to Abuse*

The following areas of concern are pointers to the circumstances which may increase the likelihood of abuse.

- the person has a behaviour disorder or there are major changes in personality and behaviour;

- there is a history of disturbed family relationships;

- there is a history of abuse or violence within the family;

- family/carer stress due to low income or poor housing;

- role reversal;

- unplanned or enforced change in carer lifestyle;

- isolated carers (emotionally or socially);

- physical or mental illness in carers;

- alcohol or drug misuse by carers;

- unresolved problems of carers, despite seeking help.

7.4.1.5 *Physical Abuse*

7.4.1.5.1 Definition

The physical maltreatment of one person by another, who may be in a position of power over the victim. This may take the form of beating, pushing, slapping, rough handling, unreasonable confining, burning, pinching, physical coercion and misuse of medication.

7.4.1.5.2 Indicators

The following may be indicators of physical abuse:

- evidence of injury – unexplained or inconsistent with the explanation given and the person's medical circumstances;

- refusal to discuss injuries and/or fear of medical help or intervention;

- bruising
    - in well protected areas e.g. inside of thighs, inside of upper arms;
    - on soft parts of the body – not over bony prominences;
    - clustered as from striking;
    - In a 'pepper pot' formation

- finger marks;

- burns in an unusual location or of an unusual type, including friction burns;

- injuries to head/face/scalp – including bruises around the eyes and mouth – black eyes;

- injury shape similar to object;

- injuries/bruises found at different states of healing or such that it is difficult to suggest an accidental cause;

- ulcers, bed sores, cracked lips, being left in wet clothing, lack of clothing or acute or chronic health needs which are persistently ignored by carers and remain untreated to the point of suffering;

- excessive repeat prescriptions;

- under use of medication;

- unusual weight gain or loss;

- subdued personality in the presence of the carer;

- multiple provider moves – agency 'hopping';

- reluctance to seek assistance.

7.4.1.6 Emotional Abuse

7.4.1.6.1 Definition

A concerted action against the person's sense of self and self-esteem. Although it has a chronic, non-physical form, emotional abuse can exist in the absence of other forms of abuse. It is often the precursor to physical injury, sexual abuse, physical neglect and financial abuse. It is always present in any other form of abuse.

Emotional abuse may take the form of the threat of institutional care, provoking fear of violence, threats to withdraw care or support, not treating with respect, denying opportunities for privacy, constant humiliation or ridicule, harsh orders, shouting, swearing, betrayal of trust, discriminatory remarks, denial of access to religious and cultural observations and to a skilled interpreter.

7.4.1.6.2 Indicators

The following may be indicators of emotional abuse:

- symptoms of stress, e.g. bed wetting/soiling;
- insomnia or need for excessive sleep;
- change in appetite;
- unusual weight gain/loss;
- excessive and inappropriate craving of attention from individuals/agencies;
- agitation;
- anxious/tearful;
- resignation/low self-esteem;
- compulsive behaviour;
- inappropriately dressed or change in self-presentation;
- unexplained paranoia;
- withdrawn;
- lack of eye contact.

7.4.1.7 Sexual abuse

7.4.1.7.1 Definition

The involvement of vulnerable adults in sexual activities or relationships which either they do not want and have not consented to, which they cannot understand, or which takes place within a family, care giving authority or other power relationship.

This may include the perpetrator exposing his/her genitals and encouraging the subject to handle them; the perpetrator touching the subjects body; full sexual intercourse; rape; abuse of power to obtain sexual gratification; offering rewards for sexual acts; taking advantage of a lack of informed consent; not allowing the right of the subject to express their own sexuality; using personal care tasks as an opportunity for the care giver's sexual gratification; using offensive or suggestive language; withholding appropriate education or information.

7.4.1.7.2 Indicators

The following may be indicators of sexual abuse:

- a change in usual behaviour;
- withdrawal to isolated behaviour;
- overt sexual behaviour or language;
- self-inflicted injury;
- disturbed sleep patterns;
- difficulty in walking or sitting;
- torn, stained or bloody underclothes;
- 'love bites';
- bleeding or torn rectal or vaginal areas;
- bruising to inner thighs and/or genital area;
- high levels of stress or anxiety;
- self-mutilation;
- abuse of alcohol, drugs or solvents;
- low self-esteem.

7.4.1.8 Legal and Financial Abuse

7.4.1.8.1 Definition

The deliberate exploitation or manipulation of the person's legal or civil rights including misappropriation of monies or properties.

This may include:

- embezzlement;
- theft of property by direct and indirect methods;

- withholding pension books;

- misuse of benefits;

- prevention of entering long-term care for personal gain;

- misuse of personal allowance;

- misuse of legal powers for personal gain:
  - appointeeship;
  - power of attorney;
  - denial of legal advice or representation.

7.4.1.8.2 Indicators

The following may be indicators of legal and financial abuse:

- unexplained or sudden inability to pay bills or purchase necessities;

- unexplained or sudden withdrawal of money from accounts;

- disparity between assets and satisfactory living conditions;

- excessive interest by family members in the vulnerable person's assets;

- loss of property.

7.4.1.9 Neglect

7.4.1.9.1 Definition

Behaviour on the part of carers which results in serious impairment or development of the person cared for.

This may include:

- not giving personal care;

- failure to use risk management procedures;

- withholding the provision of aids, e.g. hearing aid, spectacles, false teeth, walking aids, incontinence aids;

- withholding food, drink, heat, light, clothing;

- not providing access to medical services;

- inadequate furnishings, bedding, appliances;

- abandonment;
- denial of social or cultural contact;
- denial of access to services or advocates.

7.4.1.9.2 Indicators

Indicators of neglect may include:

- neglect of accommodation;
- inadequate heating or lighting;
- poor physical condition, e.g. ulcers, bed sores;
- clothing in poor condition, e.g. unclean, wet;
- malnutrition;
- dehydration;
- failure to give medication;
- failure to access appropriate medical care;
- failure to ensure appropriate privacy and dignity;
- inconsistent or reluctant contact with health or social services.

7.4.2 Legal Context Relevant to the Mistreatment of Vulnerable Adults

Risk managers will find the current law relating to the mistreatment of vulnerable people fragmented, complex and out-of-date.

The mere fact that a person is a vulnerable or dependent adult does not of itself allow other persons to take decisions on their behalf. A close relative has no legal power to dictate to a vulnerable or dependent adult where they should live or how they should administer their finances. Until such a time as the person becomes mentally incompetent, their legal rights are the same as any other individual.

Vulnerable or dependent adults should always be advised of their right to discuss mistreatment with the police and/or an independent legal adviser. This advice should be recorded in writing.

7.4.2.1 *Capacity*

An individual is presumed to have the mental capacity to enter into a particular transaction until the contrary is proved. Once it has been proved that someone lacks capacity this state of affairs is presumed to continue until the contrary is proved.

A person should be regarded as having capacity if at the time of the decision they can:

- understand the situation and information presented;
- make a decision on the basis of the information or situation and the implications of their decision;
- communicate their decision.

The vulnerable adult should be enabled to the fullest extent to receive and communicate information and decisions in the manner in which they are most accustomed.

7.4.2.1.1 National Health Service and Community Care Act 1990 (Section 47)

This legislation provides the framework for all assessments of vulnerable adults living in the community. The local authority is required to carry out an assessment of need where a person appears to be in need of community care services. The Act makes provision for multi-agency assessment in appropriate and complex situations and a process of monitoring and review.

7.4.3 Assessment/intervention – Situations of Ongoing Risk – Legal Background

7.4.3.1 *Chronically Sick and Disabled Person's Act 1970*

- Section I requires each Social services authority to gather information on how many disabled persons are living in its area and to inform itself as to how it should plan to meet their needs.
- it also places a duty on the authority to publicise general information about services for disabled people and to ensure that anyone who uses its services is given information about other services which may be relevant to his/her needs.

- Section 2 creates a duty to provide a wide range of services as set out in the section.

7.4.3.2 National Assistance Act 1948

This provides the statutory definition of persons to whom a duty is owed under the chronically Sick and Disabled persons Act. The definition is wider than generally realised but is nonetheless poorly defined. Such persons are 'persons aged 18 or over who are blind, deaf or dumb, or suffer from mental disorder of any description and other persons aged 18 and over who are substantially and permanently handicapped by illness, injury or congenital deformity or such other disabilities as may be prescribed by the Minister'.

Residential and other services can or may be provided under sections 21,26 and 29. Further Directions from the secretary of State are contained in Approvals and Directions released in May 1993 in relation to both sections 21 and 29.

Under Section 47 a local authority has the power to seek an order from a magistrates court authorising removal of a person at severe risk. The application must be supported by a certificate from a community physician that the person is either;

- suffering from a grave and chronic disease, or
- is aged, infirm or physically incapacitated and living in unsanitary conditions and is unable to look after themselves and is not receiving proper care and attention from others.

7.4.3.3 National Assistance (Amendment) Act 1951

Allows for an application to be made without notice being given if it is certified by the Medical Officer of Health and another registered medial practitioner that in their opinion it is necessary to arrange for removal without delay.

7.4.3.4 Public Health Act 1936 Section 287

Local authorities have powers under Public Health legislation to enter and cleanse premises which constitute a public health risk.

7.4.3.5 *Powers Under the Mental Health Act 1983 – Mental Health Situations*

(see also Chapter 8)

The words 'person' and 'patient' can be interchanged throughout this section.

7.4.3.5.1 Sections 2,3,4

Make provision for compulsory admission to hospital or treatment respectively and in emergency situations.

7.4.3.5.2 Section 7

Deals with Guardianship. The Local Authority or a private individual may be appointed guardian to a person whose mental disorder is one of a specified kind, including mental illness, where guardianship is considered necessary for his/her own welfare or for the protection of others.

However, unless the patient is mentally ill or psychopathic, he must be suffering from 'mental impairment'. The legal definition of this requires the presence of 'abnormally aggressive or seriously irresponsible conduct' in addition to severe or significant impairment of intelligence and social functions. Thus, guardianship may not be appropriate merely because a person has a learning disability.

An application, supported by two doctors must be made to the local Social Services Authority by an approved social worker or by the patient's nearest relative. No application can be made if the nearest relative objects, but an application can be made to a County Court for any other person including the local authority to act in his/her place as the nearest relative, on the grounds that he/she is objecting unreasonably or is him/herself incapable by reason of mental disorder or illness; the guardian has power to require the patient to live at a specified place, or to attend for medical treatment, occupation or training, and can require access to be given at any place where the patient is living to doctors or social workers.

However, it must be noted that Guardianship does not provide the power to transport or transfer someone to specified accommodation in the first instance. Therefore, for the arrangements to be successful, a degree of co-operation or compliance would be necessary on the part of the person to whom the order applies. In addition, a guardian cannot compel the patient to undergo medical treatment without his/her consent. Guardianship lasts for six months but can be renewed and people placed under guardianship have a right to apply to a Mental Health Review Tribunal.

7.4.3.5.3 Section 115

An approved social worker may enter and inspect, at all reasonable times, any premises within the area of his/her Local Authority (but not in hospital) in which a mentally disordered patient is living, if he/she has reasonable cause to believe that the patient is not under proper care.

Forcible entry is not permitted but obstruction of the social worker without reasonable cause would be an offence under Section 129. Proceedings under this Section may be instituted by the local Social Services Department.

7.4.3.5.4 Section 127(2)

It is an offence for any individual to ill-treat or wilfully to neglect a mentally disordered person in his/her guardianship or 'otherwise in his custody or care (whether by virtue of any legal or moral obligation or otherwise)'. As this is a criminal offence, the standard of proof is 'beyond reasonable doubt'. There is no need for the victim to be receiving treatment for his or her mental disorder. At the time of the offence, the subject could, for example, be living in his/her own home, with relatives or friends. Proceedings may be instituted by the local Social Services Department with the consent of the Director of Public Prosecutions (Sections 127(4) and 130).

7.4.3.5.5 Section 135

An approved social worker can apply for a warrant to search and remove a patient (for up to 72 hours) believed to be suffering from a mental disorder and who is being neglected, ill-treated or not kept under proper control or who is living alone and is unable to care for themselves. A police officer exercising this power must be accompanied by an approved social worker, and also by a medical practitioner, when entering the property to execute the warrant.

7.4.3.5.6 Section 136

Section 136 includes powers to remove a person who appears to be suffering from a mental disorder in a public place to a place of safety for up to 72 hours. Only a police Constable can exercise this power.

7.4.4 Financial Protection

7.4.4.1 *Court of Protection*

The Court of Protection operates under Part V11 of the Mental Health Act and the Court of Protection Rules 1984.

It has jurisdiction where it is satisfied, after considering medical evidence, that a 'person' is 'incapable by reason of mental disorder of managing and administering his property and affairs'. Anyone meeting these criteria is known as a 'patient'. The Court has wide powers to administer and manage the patient's property and affairs but it has no power to decide questions relating to the care of the patient's person, except indirectly through control of his money.

In most cases, a receiver will be appointed to manage the patient's financial affairs under the supervision of the Court. Although a receiver will often be a relative, another person may be appointed if a relative is unsuitable. The Public Trustee can be appointed in the last resort. The Director of Social Services may also be appointed as a receiver.

Applications are made by completion of standard forms and most applications are made by post. The powers of the receiver are limited and specified in the order appointing him/her and a further direction or authority of the Court is required for matters outside the scope of the order. The powers of the receiver are terminated by the death of the patient.

7.4.4.2 *Power of Attorney*

This is an arrangement by which one person gives to another, authority in financial matters, to act on his/her behalf. It can confer on the donee, general or specific authority to act on the donor's behalf. The power can be time limited. An ordinary power of attorney cannot continue to be used after the donor loses capacity. To achieve this continuity, the power must be created as an enduring power of attorney before capacity is lost. The power of attorney has no application to a local authority.

7.4.4.3 Enduring Power of Attorney

Created by the Enduring Power of Attorney Act 1985 and operational since 1986, the Act provides a procedure whereby a power of attorney, if made in the prescribed form, can continue after the donor loses capacity. If the attorney has reason to believe that the donor is becoming incapacitated, he/she must apply to the Court of Protection to register the power and notify the donor and his/her closest relatives of the application.

The power lapses for most purposes until the registration procedure and other necessary formalities have been completed. The scope of an enduring power of attorney is limited to dealing with 'property and affairs' and it cannot be used in any other area. An enduring power of attorney can validly be granted only by someone who has sufficient capacity at the time of execution. It is, therefore, likely to be of particular value to older people, but only if they are properly advised and the need is perceived in time. However, a person who lacks capacity in relation to one issue is not necessarily prevented from executing an enduring power of attorney, provided he/she has then capacity to understand the meaning and effect of such a power.

7.4.4.4 Department of Social Security Agent

For situations where the person has capacity and requests that a named person collects their Social Security benefits. The responsibility to keep the Department of Social Security informed of changing circumstances remains with the service user.

7.4.4.5 Department of Social Security Appointee

For situations where the person is unable to make the decision regarding benefits for themselves. Application is made to the Department of Social Security for a named person to become an appointee to collect benefits. The responsibility to keep the Department of Social Security informed of changing circumstances rests with the appointee. It may be possible for a Social Worker to persuade the Department of Social Security to revoke an appointment if this exercise is being abused.

7.4.5   The Provision of Services

7.4.5.1 Contract Compliance

Standards of care are imposed on residential care and nursing homes registered under the Registered Homes Act 1984 by both that Act and by contracted obligations between the local authority and each home. These contractual obligations may require a greater standard of care than the minimum standards in the Registered Homes Act and it is therefore through these contracts that local authorities can develop and improve the standard of community care. Local authority officers should ensure contractual obligations are being complied with by the home. Contracts should contain remedies for failure to perform the contractual obligations and on occasion it may be necessary to use these remedies either independently or at the same time as powers under the Registered Homes Act.

7.4.6   Residential and Nursing Homes

7.4.6.1 Registered Homes Act 1984

Requires all residential care homes to be registered with the local authority and nursing homes with the health authority. The Act gives powers to authorised staff to enter and inspect premises where vulnerable adults are living.

Section 10 The grounds for cancellation are wide and one of these does relate to convictions for non-compliance with regulations. It is, however, necessary to first obtain a conviction relating to the service of a Regulation 20 Notice of non-compliance.

Section 11 If officers consider there is serious risk to the 'life, health or well being' of residents then they may obtain an order for immediate closure of the home. The legislation confers duties upon registered homes as to the proper management of residents monies and belongings.

7.4.6.1.1 Mental Health Act 1983

o Section 127(1) This refers to the ill-treatment of wilful neglect of a mentally disordered patient by a member of staff of a hospital or mental nursing home. This includes after-care supervision.

7.4.7 Civil Law

7.4.7.1 Family Law Act 1996- Part IV Family Homes and Domestic Violence

Sections 33 to 41 – Occupation Orders. Such orders decide who is allowed to occupy the home and can direct another party to the leave the home. The terms of the order and the factors to be considered will vary according to whether or not the applicant is entitled to occupy the property and their relationship to the other party or parties. If the applicant has the right to occupy the property, they can get an occupation order against anyone with whom they are 'associated' – not just spouses and cohabitants. The order might include other 'associated' persons such as relatives and joint tenants. If the applicant does not have right to occupy the property then they can only apply for an order against a spouse/former spouse/ cohabitant/former cohabitant.

Section 42 – Non-molestation Orders Sets out provisions for non-molestation orders. Such orders are defined as containing either or both of the following;

- provisions prohibiting the respondent from molesting another person who is associated with the respondent (e.g. spouse or former spouse or cohabitant).

- provisions prohibiting the respondent from molesting a relevant child. Further guidance is available in circular LAC (97)15

7.4.7.2 Injunctions Available Under the Law of Tort

The principle purpose of the tort system is to provide financial compensation but injunctions may be available in respect of the torts of assault, battery, nuisance, false imprisonment or trespass. These may be useful in cases involving people who are not covered by the legislation, although their scope is more limited.

Injunctions may not restrain conduct that is no more than harassment and a person may not be excluded from a home which he has a right to occupy. In Egan V Egan (1975) Ch 218 a woman who suffered continual physical assaults by her adult son was granted an injunction restraining him from trespassing on her property and from assaulting or molesting her. A similar order was obtained in Patel V Patel (1988) 2

F.L.R. 179 by a man whose son-in-law had been trespassing on his home and threatening him. These are all private law remedies upon which an individual will need to seek their own legal advice.

7.4.7.3 The Housing Act 1996

This Act introduced amendments to the 1985 Act and greatly increased a Local Authority's powers in relation to anti-social behaviour. Whilst this may not be directly relevant to a social worker's activities it may nonetheless be a possible solution to some situations.

Grounds 2 and 2a These relate to Orders of Possession of Council dwellings being made by the Court.

Section 1 52 (i) Allows the local authority to obtain injunctions against persons engaging in anti-social behaviour

7.4.7.4 Harassment Act 1997

Section 3 This creates a statutory tort of harassment and the victim can apply for an injunction under this section.

Although targeted at stalkers the scope of the act is much wider and may be applied to a very wide range of situations such as :

- domestic incidents
- bullying at school or work
- racial and sexual harassment
- political demonstrations
- intrusive news reporting

This Act also creates several new criminal offences and criminal courts now have the power to control offenders' behaviour after conviction by means of the restraining order- breach of which without reasonable excuse is also an arrestable offence.

7.4.8   Intervention Responsibilities

The lead responsibility in investigations will usually rest with the social services department. However, the Registration and Inspection Unit of the Health Authority also has statutory duties and responsibilities.

7.4.9   Referral Procedures

Any person who has knowledge of or suspicion that a vulnerable adult is being abused has a responsibility to refer to the Department of Social Services.

The safety and welfare of the individual is the primary objective. When emergency action is required this should not be delayed by the need to refer the case to investigating agencies.

Preserving evidence in situations where there is the possibility of a crime having been committed is vital to assist the police in an investigation. Any examination of the person to decide if medical attention is required should be kept to a minimum. If at all possible nothing should be moved, touched, or cleaned. Nothing should be thrown away even though articles may be damaged.

Ethical and statutory codes concerned with confidentiality and data protection are not intended to prevent the exchange of information between different professional staff who have a responsibility for ensuring the protection of vulnerable adults.

A considered decision to share information and act to protect a vulnerable adult currently at risk of abuse may have to be made. However, this must take into account the individual's wishes regarding such disclosures.

Where possible the confidentiality of the referrer will be respected when that person is a member of the public, or from a voluntary agency. However, it is considered good practice to be as open as possible with individuals and where the referrer is a member of an agency signed up to the Joint Policy Agreement on Adult Abuse, in most cases it would be appropriate to acknowledge the agency responsible for the referral.

It should be acknowledged that staff reporting allegations of abuse may require support both during and after the process.

All information, processes, actions and reasons/evidence for decisions must be recorded.

7.4.10   Risk Assessment in Vulnerable Adults

7.4.10.1 Introduction

The main function of Adult Services is to assess the needs of individuals and to arrange or provide services which meet these assessed needs. In both determining the individuals needs, and in deciding which services may be most effective in meeting their need, a key consideration should be an evaluation of the level of risk posed to the individual by both their circumstances and by the Authority's decisions in these areas. It is important to note that risk assessment should be a part of the assessments undertaken.

7.4.10.2 Who Requires a Risk Assessment ?

Anyone who is subject to an assessment (other than a self assessment) should be the subject of a risk assessment as part of the broader assessment process. The degree and depth of both the general assessment process and the risk assessment process will be guided by an initial appraisal of the individual's circumstances and their presenting need.

7.4.10.3 Undertaking a Risk Assessment

Assessing risk and choosing a course of action based on this assessment is something all professionals do, all of the time. At its most simple, risk assessment involves weighing up the advantages and disadvantages of a particular course of action so that we can make a decision whether the potential benefit to be gained from that action outweighs any possible harmful consequences.

It must be noted that not all risk taking is harmful and should be avoided. Individuals may choose to accept a certain level of either short or long term risk in order that they may achieve other aspirations (personal development, independence, increased level of self respect etc.) The decision to undertake risk behaviour should always be respected when such behaviour is the result of an informed choice on the part of an individual who is capable of making such a choice.

7.4.11   The Wider Assessment Process

As part of the Assessment and Care Management process professionals need to recognise and acknowledge that risk assessment is a fundamental part of the wider assessment process. In order for the assessment process to be of value to both the Authority and the service user, a fully rounded picture needs to be constructed of the individual and the circumstances which surround them.

The purpose of the assessment is to acquire as much knowledge as is reasonably possible about both the individual's current situation and about their wishes and aspirations for the future in order that what issues and risks they face can determined and evaluated. The views of other agency workers and/or the individual's carers, family and friends need to contribute to this process. It is important to identify and build on positives as well as to identify risk areas.

As the assessment unfolds, and a care plan for the individual is developed, a view needs to be taken on to how the provision of specific services will stabilise, reduce or eliminate risk. The professional needs to be clear that the outcomes they expect from the provision of specific services are closely linked to the perceived risks and that all services should be commissioned on the basis that they will impact on specified risk areas.

It is also important that the basis on which decisions were made is clearly recorded in order that any course of action may be properly explained and justified. Those undertaking risk assessments must document and record all the significant circumstances they have discovered documenting and recording which circumstances were considered most important and which were given greatest weight in determining the final course of action.

The reasons for deciding on a particular course of action, such as the provision or withdrawal of a specific service, should always be clearly stated to the service user and should always be recorded. It is also important to document instances when a decision to take no action was decided upon as the most appropriate outcome.

7.4.11.1 A Structured Approach to Risk Assessment

In exploring the circumstances which surround the individual, it must be recognised that some of the factors that need to be taken into account may sometimes appear both confusing and difficult to untangle. The following prompts may be helpful in order to clarify what are the most important issues that should be considered in order to determine the individual's current level of risk.

7.4.11.1.1 Identifying Risk Elements

The following questions are intended to act as an aide memoire to assist the professional undertaking the risk assessment to ensure that they have not missed any area which in retrospect would have been regarded as 'obvious' area of proper concern. They are not intended to be a substitute for professional judgement.

7.4.11.1.1.1 Is There a Risk of Physical Harm ?

- does the individual pose a risk of harm to themselves? for example:

- the individual may have injured themselves in the past;

- the individual may misuse alcohol or other substances or may misuse or be unable to use prescription medication effectively;

- has the individual a medical condition, which if not managed appropriately, may put them at risk?

- does the individual pose a risk of harm to others ? – this may be harm to strangers or may be harm to those close to them, family / carers, care workers etc.

- is the individual vulnerable to any form of pressure or influence which would make them open to physical exploitation – are they subjected to aggression, bullying or violence?

- what is the potential level of foreseeable harm?

7.4.11.1.1.2 Is There a Risk of Psychological or Emotional Harm?

- does the individual pose a risk to their own psychological or emotional well-being?

- is the individual vulnerable to any form of pressure or influence which would make them open to psychological or emotional exploitation?

- are they subject to emotional pressures which are detrimental to their mental health or well-being;

- what is the potential level of foreseeable harm?

7.4.11.1.1.3 *Is There a Risk of Sexual Harm?*

- is the individual vulnerable to any form of pressure or influence which would make them open to sexual exploitation – are they subjected to any form of inappropriate sexual behaviour or behaviour to which they are unable to give informed consent?;

- what is the potential level of foreseeable harm?

7.4.11.1.1.4 *Is There a Risk of Financial Exploitation?*

- is the individual vulnerable to any form of pressure or influence which would make them open to financial exploitation?

- are their finances properly organised, controlled and accounted for?

- what is the potential level of foreseeable harm?

7.4.11.1.1.5 *Is There a Risk of Neglect by Others?*

- is the individual at risk from others, family members/carers, care workers, neighbours, strangers, etc.? This risk may be the result of a deliberate act or it may be the result of a failure to act e.g. not ensuring that the individual is fed or warm;

- what is the potential level of foreseeable harm?

7.4.11.1.1.6 *Is There a Risk From the Individual's Immediate Environment or Surroundings?*

- is the individual at risk from their environment? The evaluation of risk from the individual's immediate environment or surroundings will depend on the way in which the environment and the individual's ability to cope with it inter-act. For example, an individual who forgets they have left an electric cooker on is at less risk than an individual who forgets to light a gas cooker, an individual who wanders is at less risk if they live in a contained environment such as sheltered accommodation than if they live next to a main road;

- what is the potential level of foreseeable harm?

7.4.11.1.1.7 *Health and Safety Risks*

Any service provider commissioned to provide services to an Authority have a statutory responsibility to take into account the Health and Safety risks posed to their staff in undertaking this service provision. The contract between the service provider and the Local Authority should detail the nature of the services to be provided. From this description the service provider will be able to judge what Health and Safety issues their staff will, potentially, be faced with. It is then the service provider's responsibility to ensure that these Health and Safety risks are recognised and overcome.

It is important when undertaking a risk assessment that any obvious or unusual Health and Safety hazards are noted, e.g. vicious dog, worn flex, loose carpet etc., and that these are documented and brought to the attention of the Service Provider, both verbally and in writing when commissioning or arranging for the service.

7.4.11.1.1.7.1 Identifying Future Risk

While undertaking a risk assessment the stability of the circumstances on which decisions are based need to be considered, looking at what has happened in the past and seeking to project what may happen in the foreseeable future. When assessing particularly volatile situations key factors should be identified, if possible, which are critical in order to sustain the position determined as being an appropriate response to the service user's circumstances.

For example, the risk assessment might identify that the care package to be in place may be dependent on the input of an informal carer, without this input the care plan may no longer be viable. (The clearest example of this is a service user who is dependent on medication to stabilise their condition but who will only accept medication from a specific individual. If this individual is incapacitated in some way and cannot administer the required medication the service user's care plan may collapse).

All complex or volatile risk assessments should contain an element which comments on the future stability of the service user's situation (as far as this can be foreseen) identifying issues which may influence this degree of stability. The risk assessment should, where appropriate, specifically detail key issues or circumstance which, were they to change, would jeopardise the care plan. Where possible such 'trigger points' should be clearly identified and if possible a contingency plan to deal with the more immediate results of the failure of key elements should be determined and recorded (for example, interim arrangements which may be necessary in the period before a full assessment can be undertaken).

When undertaking a risk assessment, the assessor should be mindful of the pivotal part informal carers often play in ensuring the success or failure of the care plan. The Carers (Recognition and Services) Act, 1995 states that carers should be offered the opportunity for a formal assessment in their own right under Section 47(1)(a) of the NHS and Community Care Act, 1990.

7.4.11.1.1.8 Determining Levels of Risk

In each of the risk categories above the professional needs to establish the potential level of harm presented by the risk or risk behaviour identified. He/she must also seek to establish the probability of this risk or risk behaviour occurring. For example: an individual may live near a main road and may occasionally wander. He/she should seek to establish what level or degree of harm may come to the individual should, for example, they wander onto the road. He/she will also need to determine, in this case by examining the pattern of previous incidents, how often this behaviour seems to occur (does it happen frequently, infrequently or rarely).

Following the risk assessment understanding of the impact of the risk or risk behaviour (the degree or amount of harm it may cause) and the probability of its occurrence (how frequently might it happen) should be drawn together in order to determine which risk category should be used.

To facilitate this, two particular considerations should be made:

- what is the highest level of risk indicated?
- is it possible to foresee circumstances under which a number of risk elements, currently identified as low or medium risks, may come together in such a way as to create a situation where the risks accumulate and lead to an increased level of risk?

7.4.11.1.1.9 Risk Categories

It is important that all agencies providing and contributing to services for vulnerable adults share and agree an interpretation of risk categories. The following are an example of agreed categories in use between agencies.

7.4.11.1.1.9.1 *Risk Category One – Those at Highest Risk*

People who are highly vulnerable and for whom there is an acute risk of death or serious injury should services not be provided.

This category will include, those who have refused to accept residential provision following an assessment which recommends such provision and it has been determined that the level of support available to them in the community does not/cannot meet their needs in full if those who are unable to care for themselves; those who are subject to serious abuse or exploitation and/or who pose a serious risk to themselves or to others. This category may include those who are at risk because they do not themselves recognise or accept the need for service.

7.4.11.1.1.9.2 *Risk Category Two – Those at High Risk*

People who are threatened with a loss of independence such that they would require residential or other forms of institutional care.

This category would include those who pose a significant risk to themselves or to others.

7.4.11.1.1.9.3 *Risk Category Three – Those at Medium Risk*

Those who are currently living independently with significant support services but for whom a change in circumstances would threaten their ability to continue to live independently.

7.4.11.1.1.9.4 *Risk Category Four – Those at Low Risk*

Those who receive services which either enhance the quality of their lives or further their aspirations towards independence and, for whom, a change in circumstances would threaten or reduce their quality of life.

7.4.11.1.1.10 Documenting the Risk Assessment

The risk assessment process should be clearly grounded in the wider assessment process. As such, it should be recorded:

- as a part of the assessment 'narrative'.

- in summary on a risk assessment proforma. This summary should state that all areas of risk have been examined and should specifically detail the level of risk determined (The service user is Risk Category One/four). A separate section should follow this summary detailing any identified Health and Safety risks posed to the service provider;

- by completing a pro-forma. Each section should be completed in full (giving a Not Applicable response where appropriate). Ensure that the reasons for your actions are clearly specified and, where service provision is recommended, that the outcomes anticipated from this service provision are clearly stated.

7.4.11.1.1.11 Next steps

If significant risks are identified, the assessor will need to call a case conference. The purpose of the conference is to:

- exchange information in a multi-disciplinary forum;

- determine the needs of the vulnerable adult and the degree of risk;

- formulate a plan, as necessary to address the well-being of the adult;

- clarify the roles and responsibilities of the agencies involved;

- make arrangements for monitoring and reviewing the care plan.

Key participants are:

- the vulnerable adult or nominated advocate;

- the primary carer, with the vulnerable adult's agreement;

- any professional involved with the vulnerable adult;

- any other professional with information and/or advice;

- any appropriate non-professional with information and/or advice.

7.4.11.1.1.12 Monitoring and Reviewing

In all cases where a care plan is implemented in respect of a vulnerable adult, monitoring and reviewing arrangements must be identified.

The minimum requirement for review is within six weeks of the implementation of the care plan and three monthly thereafter until the risk of abuse is eliminated.

A case conference should be convened where there are changes in the situation of the vulnerable adult and/or the care plan is failing to protect.

When the risk of abuse has been eliminated a case conference should be convened to address any changes to the care plan and monitoring and reviewing arrangements.

7.4.11.2 Bibliography and References for Child Protection

Working Together to Safeguard Children – Department of Health, Home Office, Department for Education and Employment 1999 – ISBN 011 322309

Department of Health. *Framework for the Assessment of Children in Need and their Families*. London: The Stationery Office, 2000.

HSC 1999/237 : LAC (99)3 *THE QUALITY PROTECTS PROGRAMME – 2000/01 TRANSFORMING CHILDREN'S SERVICES*

Department of Health. *Local Authority Circular LAC(93)17 Disclosure of Criminal Background of Those with Access to Children*. London: Department of Health, 1993.

Department of Health. *Local Authority Circular LAC(97)17: Guidance to the Children (Protection from Offenders) (Miscellaneous Amendments) Regulations SI 1997/2308*. London: Department of Health, 1997.

Department of Health. *Local Authority Circular LAC(99)33, Health Service Circular HSC 1999/237, DfEE Circular 18/99: The Quality Protects Programme: Transforming Children's Services 2000-01*. London: Department of Health, 1999.

The Department of Health, *Working Together under the Children Act 1989*. (HMSO 1991)

Home Office, Memorandum on *Good Practice on Video Recorded Interviews with Child Witnesses for Criminal Proceedings*. (HMSO 1992.)

Department of Health, *Protecting Children – A Guide for Social Workers undertaking a Comprehensive Assessment* (HMSO 1988.)

ABC of Child Abuse, Roy Meadow (editor) – (British Medical Journal 1989.)

A Guide to the Children Act 1989 – Richard White, Paul Carr and Nigel Leive (Butterworths 1990.)

Child Protection Guidelines – Dept. of Social Workers Studies, University of Southampton, 1990

Child Pornography and Sex Rings, Burgess 1984

Department of Health. *Child Protection: Messages From Research.* London: HMSO, 1995.

Cleaver H, Unell I, Aldgate J. *Children's Needs – Parenting Capacity: The impact of parental mental illness, problem alcohol and drug use, and domestic violence on children's development.* London: The Stationery Office, 1999.

Adcock M, White R (eds.) *Significant Harm: Its Management and Outcome.* Croydon: Significant Publications, 1998

7.4.11.3 Bibliography for Vulnerable Adults

Rotherham Joint Services Adult Protection Procedures

Old Age Abuse, Mervyn Eastman, Age Concern 1984

No longer Afraid, At home with dementia Social Services Inspectorate Reports Mistreatment of Older People – Association of Directors of Social Services

Who Decides – Lord Chancellor 1996

8

MENTAL HEALTH

8.1   INTRODUCTION

8.1.1   Prevalence of Mental Health Problems

The prevalence of people with mental health problems is difficult to calculate in detail. Methodologies are rarely comparable and information can be variable in quality. Prevalence data often uses different denominators. Some report rates for the general population others for the adult population (age 18-65).

The publication 'Keys to engagement[1]' indicates a prevalence rate per 100,000 general population per year of:

- 10,000 – 25,000 in contact with services, mostly primary care

- 2,000-4,000 with severe mental illness

- 300-1,500 with severe and enduring mental illness

- 14-200 with severe and enduring mental illness who are difficult to engage.

Substance misuse is a growing problem and highly associated with severe and enduring mental illness. Over one third of all people with a diagnosis of severe mental illness who were in contact with mental health services also had a problem related to the use of drugs or alcohol in a study in South London. Against this background, it is for the risk manager to advise on a safe care environment.

The care of patients who suffer from mental illness is a particular challenge because of the complexity of statute, regulations and guidance which cover standards of practice. There is a need to ensure that the standards of care comply with:

---

1   *Keys to Engagement* – The Sainsbury Centre for Mental Health 1998 ISBN 1 870480 36 8

- the standards laid down by statute;

- current accepted good professional practice;

- associated regulations and recommendations

whilst preserving the civil liberties of patients and at the same time protecting the public.

This was reflected in a Court of Appeal ruling, *(R. v. Secretary of State for the Home Office, ex p. K [1990] All E. R. 562, 570)* which stated that the policy and objects of the Act are:

to regulate the circumstances in which the liberty of persons who are mentally disordered may be restricted and, where there is a conflict, to balance their interests against those of public policy.

There is a public perception which equates mental illness with a measure of dangerousness. However misconceived this perception may be, it immediately poses risks to those who care for the mentally ill. The risks can be managed and risk control measures need to concentrate upon accurate assessment of patients, sound clinical documentation and an examination of working practises to determine areas of risk concentration.

Patients may be admitted to a psychiatric hospital or registered psychiatric nursing home either as voluntary patients or involuntary patients through the compulsory admission procedures of the Mental Health Act.

8.2   STATUTORY FRAMEWORK

The compulsory care of the mentally ill has in recent times fallen under the Mental Health Act 1959 which was substantially replaced by the Mental Health Act 1983. The Acts impose duties upon the mental health services which reflect the vulnerability of the patient group. An example of this is found in Section 128 of the 1959 Act, which is still current. This creates statutory offences of unlawful sexual intercourse with female patients for:

(1) a man on the staff of, or employed by, a hospital or mental nursing home to have extramarital sexual intercourse with a woman who is receiving treatment for mental disorder in that hospital or home either as an out-patient or an in-patient, and

(2) a man to have extramarital sexual intercourse with a woman who is subject to his guardianship or who is otherwise in his custody or care.

No offence is committed under S. 128 if the man did not know, and had no reason to suspect, that the woman was a "mentally disordered" patient.

8.2.1   The Mental Health Act 1983

The 1983 Act forms the main statutory framework for the delivery of care to patients who fall within the Act's definitions. According to the Court of Appeal, the "policies and objects" of the Act are "to regulate the circumstances in which patients who are mentally disordered may be restricted and, where there is conflict, to balance their interests against those of public policy".

The Act has been supplemented by the Code of Practice issued under S.118 of the Act which provides detailed guidance about how to protect the rights of patients detained under the Act. The Mental Health Act Commission was set up under the 1983 Act and has a statutory obligation to visit places where patients may be detained. It provides an important regulatory function of inspection and provides for the investigation of complaints.

The provisions of the Act have effect with respect to the reception, care and treatment of mentally disordered individuals, the management of their property and other related matters.

Under the Act:

"mental disorder" means mental illness, arrested or incomplete development of mind, psychopathic disorder and any other disorder or disability of mind and "mentally disordered" shall be construed accordingly;

"severe mental impairment" means a state of arrested or incomplete development of mind which includes severe impairment of intelligence and social functioning and is associated with abnormally aggressive or seriously irresponsible conduct on the part of the person concerned and "severely mentally impaired" shall be construed accordingly;

"mental impairment" means a state of arrested or incomplete development of mind (not amounting to severe mental impairment) which includes significant impairment of intelligence and social functioning and is associated with abnormally aggressive or seriously irresponsible conduct on the part of the patient concerned and "mentally impaired" shall be construed accordingly;

"psychopathic disorder" means a persistent disorder or disability of mind (whether or not including significant impairment of intelligence) which results in abnormally aggressive or seriously irresponsible conduct on the part of the person concerned.

Importantly, the Act states:

Nothing ...... shall be construed as implying that a person may be dealt with under this Act as suffering from mental disorder, or from any form of mental disorder described in this section, by reason only of promiscuity or other immoral conduct, sexual deviancy or dependence on alcohol or drugs.

Interpretation of the meaning of terms used in the Act is covered under S. 145.

Neither the Act nor the Code of Practice defines mental illness. This may lead to confusion over the appropriateness of admissions. The Report of the Committee of the Royal Commission on the Law Relating to Mental Illness and Mental Deficiency 1954-1957, Chairman Lord Percy (Cmnd. 169), considered that:

the term 'mental illness' would be used in the same sense as at present, including the mental infirmity of old age.

Guidance on interpretation from the Department of Health includes:

"Mental illness means an illness having one or more of the following characteristics:-

(i) *More than temporary impairment of intellectual functions shown by a failure of memory, orientation, comprehension and learning capacity;*

(ii) *More than temporary alteration of mood of such degree as to give rise to the patient having a delusional appraisal of his situation, his past or future, or that of others or to the lack of any appraisal;*

(iii) *Delusional beliefs, persecutory, jealous or grandiose;*

(iv) *Abnormal perceptions associated with delusional misinterpretations of events;*

(v) *Thinking so disordered as to prevent the patient making a reasonable appraisal of his situation or having reasonable communication with others.*

The mental illness should be of a nature or degree which warrants the detention of the patient in the interest of his health or the safety for the protection of others."

It is important to appreciate that the Act and compulsory admission for assessment or treatment can only apply where it is necessary and where there is a risk of harm:

- in the interests of his own health, or
- in the interests of his own safety, or
- for the protection of other people.

Only one of these criteria need apply in the individual patient's case, in addition to those relating to the nature of the patient's mental disorder.

Compulsory admission under any section of the Act may only proceed at the request of the patient's nearest relative or at the request of an Approved Social Worker. Approved Social Worker status is granted by the Local Authority under the terms of the Act. Detailed guidance is contained in DHSS circular No. LAC (86) 15 – Approved Social Workers.

An application under Section 2 provides for compulsory admission for assessment and may last for up to 28 days beginning on the day of admission. An application under Section 3 provides for admission for treatment, and may last for up to six months. Section 3 is renewable and the patient may be allowed on leave (Section 17) as part of their treatment plan. However, it is unlawful to recall a patient to hospital merely for the purposes of renewing the Section. An application for admission under Section 3 has to satisfy three criteria under the Act. These are:

1. *he is suffering from mental illness, severe mental impairment, psychopathic disorder or mental impairment and his mental disorder is of a nature or degree which makes it appropriate for him to receive medical treatment in a hospital; and*

2. *in the case of psychopathic disorder or mental impairment, such treatment is likely to alleviate or prevent a deterioration of his condition; and*

3. *it is necessary for the health or safety of the patient or for the protection of other persons that he should receive such treatment and it cannot be provided unless he is detained under this section."*

An application under Section 4 provides for compulsory admission in cases of urgent necessity. The applicant may be an Approved Social Worker or the patient's nearest relative. The medical examination may be carried out by a single practitioner who preferably has previous knowledge of the patient. The Section lasts for a maximum of 72 hours from the time of admission to hospital.

A completed application under the Act is sufficient authority for the patient to be removed to hospital. The responsibility for conveying the patient rests with the social services department.

Patients who are detained under the Act have restrictions placed on their civil liberties which are central to the seriousness with which health professionals must approach the question of whether a person should be the subject of compulsory detention. For example, patients detained on a section of the Act are not entitled to have their names placed on the Register of Electors. Doubts may be cast upon their ability to consent to marriage. Yet, Article 12 of the European Convention of Human Rights states:

Men and women of marriageable age have the right to marry and to found a family, according to the national laws governing the exercise of this right.

Detailed guidance on the subject was issued by the Department of Health in Circular HC (84) 12. This advice currently is that anyone who considers that a party to a marriage may not be capable of consenting to the marriage may inform the Superintendent Registrar to enter a caveat before the proceedings. There is an appeal process for the patient to follow if the Superintendent Registrar refuses to issue a certificate following the placement of a caveat.

Special responsibilities are placed on doctors if a Member of Parliament is subject to compulsory detention. The Speaker of the House of Commons must be informed and the Member examined by doctors appointed by the President of the Royal College of Psychiatrists; continuing detention and illness may result in the Member's seat being declared vacant. There is no similar removal of right of attendance for members of the House of Lords, but there is a requirement under the Department of Health Memorandum on the Mental Health Act for the Clerk of the Parliaments to be informed.

Once subject to compulsory admission for admission or treatment, the patient has a right of appeal against their detention under a section of the Mental Health Act. The patient must be informed of their right of appeal. The patient may appeal to a hearing by the Hospital Managers (see 8.2.3). This should be held within a reasonable time and allow for evidence to be given which accurately reflects the patient's mental condition and social needs. The registered medical practitioner in charge of the patient's treatment is defined as the 'Responsible Medical Officer' who should prepare a medical report for the hearing which refers to:

- the patient's current mental state;

- the history of the patient's mental illness including relevant social requirements;

- the reasons for a recommendation of continuing detention.

The patients must be informed of the outcome at the end of the hearing. If the detention under the Act is overturned by the decision of the Managers, the patient must be free to leave the hospital immediately.

Following a review by an expert committee of the Mental Health Act[2], the Government have issued proposals for consultation. The law and issues relating to people with mental health problems is likely to change significantly with new powers of compulsory community treatment[3].

8.2.1.1 Capacity and Detention

The case of R v Bournewood Community and Mental Health Trust ex parte L[4] concerned a 48 year old autistic man who was unable to speak and was incapable of consenting either to admission or medical treatment. He was an informal patient and his carers wished him to be returned to their home, but this was refused by the consultant. The carers applied for a writ of *habeus corpus* to secure his release. This was refused by the judge at the high court, but the Court of Appeal held that L was unlawfully detained. The House of Lords disagreed. The

2   *Review of the Mental Health Act* 1983-Department of Health, November 1999

3   *Reform of the Mental Health Act* 1983-Proposals for consultation Cm4480 November 1999

4   [1998] 3 AER

House of Lords found admission as an informal patient applied equally to patients who positively consented to admission and those who had not dissented.

8.2.2 Mental Health Review Tribunals

Independently of the process of an appeal against detention to the Hospital Managers, the patient may appeal to a Mental Health Review Tribunal. Mental Health Review Tribunals were set up following the 1959 Act. Current law and regulations which apply to Tribunals stems from the 'Mental Health Review Tribunal Rules 1983 (S.I. 1983 No. 942). A written application needs to be made to the Tribunal signed by the applicant or someone authorised to act on their behalf. Although there is no prescribed form for the application, forms have been produced and are available from Tribunal offices. (D.H.S.S. Circular No. HC (83) 17 para. 10). A Tribunal sitting to hear an appeal is normally comprised of a legal member, who is usually the Chairman and is appointed by the Lord Chancellor, a medical member and a lay member.

8.2.3 Mental Health Hospitals

Hospitals recognised for the compulsory admission and detention of patients under the Act are the responsibility of Hospital Managers. The duties and responsibilities of the Hospital Managers are recognised by Statute. Within NHS Trusts the Hospital Managers are now the non-executive directors of the Trusts and lay people appointed for the purpose. Where lay people have been appointed, they should be given honorary contracts which are subject to annual review. The discharge of all statutory responsibilities for the care of in-patients falls to be undertaken by Managers.

In particular, Managers are responsible for ensuring that the detention of any patient is lawful. Appointing Associate Managers may spread the workload of Managers. In order for them to properly discharge their duties, it is imperative that Managers and Associate Managers receive training to ensure their knowledge of the law and procedures is current and comprehensive.

Managers may, by formal resolution, delegate certain of their duties for the day-to-day care of the service whilst at the same time retaining overall responsibility for compliance with the Act and Code of Practice.

Patients may require to be detained using the doctor's or nurse's holding power both with a psychiatric hospital setting and an acute hospital. It is particularly important in the latter case, where the procedure is unlikely to be frequently used, that medical staff and staff authorised to receive documents are fully familiar with the law. Article 5 of the Human Rights Act gives the right to liberty and security of the person. A failure to follow correct procedures will expose the staff and organisation to an action under this article.

8.3 GUIDANCE FROM THE CODE OF PRACTICE

8.3.1 Powers of Hospital Managers Which may be Delegated

The following functions need specific officers to be nominated where the statutory powers and authority of Mental Health Act Managers is to be delegated:

- receipt of admission documents;
- scrutiny of admission documents;
- rectification of defective admission documents;
- medical scrutiny of admission documents;
- the duties of the patient record inspection Officer who ensures compliance with information requirements;
- the duties of patient information Officer (this must be different from the patient medical record inspection Officer);
- the duties of detained patient tribunal Officer;
- establishment and monitoring a system to review consent to treatment;
- receipt of reports on the use of restraint;
- the duties of complaints Officer;
- inspection and withholding of post;
- providing assistance to patients at Mental Health Review Tribunals;
- exclusion of visitors;
- the duties of complainant assistance Officer;

- the duties of complaints procedure compliance Officer;

Health Authorities have the responsibility to nominate a person whose duties include informing the courts, in compliance with section 39 of the Act, of the range of facilities available for patients.

To assist staff with the implementation of a current and consistent standard of care, the Code of Practice stipulates that the following explicit Guidance and Policies should be available for use:

8.3.2 Guidance for Staff Which Should be Drawn up and Issued with Appropriate Training by NHS Trusts:

- use of interpreters
- use of section 5(2)
- use of section 5 (4)
- care of young people

8.3.3 Policies Which Should be Available

- Section 136 jointly with social services and the police
- aftercare
- conveying patients to hospital
- manager's information policy
- use of restraint
- use of seclusion
- use of time out
- absence without leave
- complaints
- interception of mail (section 134)
  - Special Hospitals
- searching patients and belongings
- children visiting hospital

8.3.4 Guidance for Staff Which Should be Drawn up and Issued with Appropriate Training by Local Authorities

- requests from a nearest relative
- requests by way of general practitioners
- use of interpreters
- care of young people

8.3.5 Policies to be Issued by Local Authorities

- repeated requests for assessment
- Section 136 – jointly with NHS Trusts, directly managed units and the police
- conveying patients to hospital
- guardianship
- absence without leave
- aftercare

8.3.6 The Mental Health Act Commission

The Mental Health Act Commission is a Special Health Authority established to oversee the compliance of hospitals with the Mental Health Act and Code of Practice. The creation of the Commission follows implementation of s.56(1) and s.(11) of the Mental Health (Amendment) Act 1982 which was brought into force through the Mental Health (Amendment) Act 1982 (Commencement No 1) Order 1983 (S.I. 1983 No. 890).

Members of the Commission are appointed by the Secretary of State and comprise a Chairman and Vice-Chairman and a variable number of members. Commissioners work on a part-time basis and visit and report on hospitals where patients may be detained. The Commission publishes a biennial report and has published specific guidance on:

- Review of Treatment – Section 61
- Practice Note 1 – Administration of Clozapine
- GN 2/2001 (formerly Practice Note 2) – Nurses, The Administration of Medicine for mental disorder and the Mental Health Act 1983
- Practice Note 3 – S.5(2) of the 1983 Mental Health Act (Doctor's holding power)

- Practice Note 4 – Issues surrounding Section17 & 18 of the Mental Health Act 1983 (Leave of patients on Section and absence without leave)

- Practice Note 5 – Guidance on issues Relating to the Administration of the Mental Health Act in Registered Mental Nursing Homes

- Guidance note 1 – Guidance to Health Authorities

- Guidance note 2 – GPs and the Mental Health Act (revised 2000)

- Guidance note 3 – Guidance on the treatment of Anorexia Nervosa under the Mental Health Act

- GN 1/2001 – Use of the Mental Health Act 1983 in General Hospitals without a psychiatric unit

The functions of the Commission are to:

1. keep under review the exercise of the powers under the Mental Health Act;

2. visit and interview patients detained in hospitals and nursing homes;

3. investigate complaints that come within the Commission's remit;

4. appoint medical practitioners and others for the purposes of providing a second opinion and verifying consent to treatment;

5. receive and examine reports on treatment given under the consent to treatment provisions;

6. submitting proposals under the Code of Practice issued under s.118 of the Mental Health Act;

7. submitting proposals for the purposes of medical treatment which in the opinion of the Commission give rise to particular concern;

8. review decisions by Hospital Managers to withhold correspondence.

The Commission can be directed by the Secretary of State to review the care and treatment of informal patients.

It is important to appreciate the extent of the Commission's powers. Section 129 of the Mental Health Act states that a criminal offence will be committed by anyone who obstructs a person authorised by the Commission to carry out a review under subsection 4.

Mental Health Act Commission website: http://mhac.trent.nhs.uk

8.4   RISKS TO PATIENTS

8.4.1   Accident and Emergency Departments

Many patients attend Accident and Emergency Departments following episodes of self-harm, such as taking an overdose of drugs. If they are inadequately assessed, for example by an inexperienced junior doctor, the patient may successfully commit suicide before they are seen and assessed by an experienced psychiatric team member. Self harming patients should be seen and assessed as soon as practicable.

8.4.2   During the Admission Process.

The main risks which occur during the admission process arise through misunderstandings which may flow from the multi-agency approach to patient care. For compulsory admission, unless in an emergency, the patient must be seen and assessed by an Approved Social Worker, a doctor with prior knowledge of the patient and a doctor approved under S. 12(2) of the 1983 Act. Where a doctor with prior knowledge of the patient is not available, the social worker must make reference to the reasons for this.

The risks of inappropriate admission are minimised with a joint and common approach and clear and established policies. The introduction of any changes in practice should be accompanied by joint training of members of staff of the various agencies involved. Misunderstandings between potential patients and their advisers may arise through simple language difficulties. These may be eliminated with the use of an appropriate interpreter. A list of interpreters should be available to both social services and the admitting hospital.

8.4.3   Mentally Disordered Offenders

Special problems may arise for patients who are suspected of committing criminal offences. Members of the public who are suspected of committing offences and are suspected of being mentally ill may be taken to a place of safety by the police. This removal to a place of safety is contained under S. 136 of the 1983 Mental Health Act. Traditionally, the local police station is regarded as the place of safety. Under the Police and Criminal Evidence Act, 1984, the police have a duty to give the assessment of the person from the mental illness aspect priority over the potential criminal transgression.

Although the police surgeon is regarded by many police as their first source of medical advice, the most appropriate person to initially assess the possible mentally illness is the on-call Approved Social Worker. It is for the social worker to invite subsequent medical opinions to support an application for compulsory admission. For this reason, a locally negotiated and implemented policy specific to the handling of this group of patients should be agreed between the police, social services and the local health care provider.

Prison hospitals are not recognised as hospitals for the mentally ill under the Mental Health Act. This places important restrictions on the treatment available to the mentally ill in prisons. Treatments are limited to those to which the patient consents and treatment under common law which may be necessary to save the life of the prisoner. Treatment without the prisoner's consent is unlawful, even though it may be considered to be in their best interests.

Key risk areas from inquiries into homicides

- is there a system agreed between health services, social services and the police for the care of mentally disordered offenders?

- are policies regulating the outcome for mentally disordered offenders subject to automatic audit?

- is there sufficient secure provision for mentally disordered offenders?

- is there adequate housing provision for mentally disordered offenders?

- is there adequate and audited information flows between agencies?

- are all relevant staff trained in the law and therapeutic needs of mentally disordered offenders?

- is the role of the social worker as an 'appropriate adult' monitored?

8.4.4 During In-patient Treatment.

Patients are exposed to a number of risks of harm when an in-patient, not least from other patients. Control of the care environment is key to preventing episodes of patients harming each other or staff. Care needs to be exercised to ensure that patients do not receive over-stimulation due to overcrowding, noise and general disruption. Patient provocation, aggression and antagonism should be controlled. Boredom and a lack of environmental stimulation may be contributing factors which could be countered by the design of individual treatment programmes and a named nurse approach to care.

Section 18 of the Code of Practice provides a helpful summary of compliance with current approaches to in-patient care. A weighted risk indicator, assessing the likelihood of self-harm, neglect and harm to others, such as the use of the Royal College of Psychiatrists *Health of the Nation Outcome Scores*, (HoNoS), will be helpful in establishing a patient's dependency and severity of illness.

Major problems may occur associated with the difficulties of achieving consent to treatment. Compulsory admission or detention does not necessarily mean that a patient is unable to consent to treatment. Patients who are subject to Section 3 detention may be given treatment without consent, but these treatments are limited to those for the mental illness.

These are areas which pose significant potential risks to the civil liberties of patients. Civil liberties must be safeguarded through discussion with the patient and supported by accurate documentation which supports the decision making process. The registered medical practitioner responsible for the patient's treatment (the Responsible Medical Officer, R. M. O.) must complete the recognised statutory form for treatment without consent if no consent is given or it is not considered to be valid. When a patient passes to the care of another R. M. O., a further form must be completed.

To ensure compliance with the Act, provision has been made for access to a second medical opinion for treatments of specific types; these include the administration of medicine beyond a three month time limit and electroconvulsive therapy (ECT), when the patient does not consent to the proposed treatment. The second opinion is given by a doctor appointed by the Mental Health Act Commission.

The Mental Health Act Commission must be consulted for agreement to proposed treatment under Section 57 of the Act. This covers cases where it is proposed that the patient undergoes psychosexual surgery and the surgical implantation of hormones for the reduction of male sexual drive.

A more detailed consideration of the law relating to consent may be found in standard reference texts such as *Speller's Law relating to Hospitals*. It is important that risk management professionals are conversant with the current interpretation of the law relating to the treatment and care of mentally ill patients. It is not surprisingly a field of continuing development in the light of Court rulings and advice from the Mental Health Act Commission.

Risk considerations from inquiries

Is there an agreed policy for the management of difficult to place patients?

Are all major changes in the treatment of disturbed or potentially violent patients communicated to all nursing staff who have contact with the patient?

Are there adequate liaison arrangements with all agencies?

Are acutely and seriously disturbed patients nursed with other acute patients?

Is there a written policy on the handover of seriously disturbed patients?

Is there a system in place to ensure that all front line staff have received training in managing individuals who may be

- disturbed
- aggressive
- troubled
- distressed?

If a member of staff is threatened or attacked, are any immediate changes in the treatment plan made by other staff?

Are separate services provided for patients requiring different levels and types of nursing care such as:

- acute admission wards?

- severe behavioural problems?

- frail elderly mentally infirm patients?

- young people with substance misuse?

8.4.5 Risks Following Discharge.

The main risks arise from the balance between providing continuing care to individual patients in the community, maintaining their civil liberties and protecting members of the public. The continuing care of patients is most effectively provided by the various agencies involved in the patient's care meeting regularly to review their state of health and progress and formally setting out a Community Care Plan or Community Management Plan. This approach follows from the NHS and Community Care Act 1990 which outlines how continuing care in the community should be provided.

8.4.6 The Care Programme Approach

Structured Care Planning to record and monitor care intentions is recommended for all patients. The original guidance follows the recommendations of the Royal College of Psychiatrists, which was issued by the Department of Health in the Circular HC (90)23/LASSL(90)11 to provide a framework for effective mental health care.

The Care Plan should include specifying a named care co-ordinator to take the lead in maintaining regular contact with the patient. The patient's severity of dependency may be graded as Standard or Enhanced, according the patient's needs and risk.

A key factor in determining the success of post-discharge arrangements is the involvement of the patient and carers. Where appropriate, the patient should be able to choose the care co-ordinator. The patient must be informed that the details of the care programme will be circulated to other disciplines when his consent has been obtained. The CPA must comply with the requirements of the Carers (recognition & services) Act 1995.

The characteristics of people on standard CPA will include some of the following:

- they require the support or intervention of one agency or discipline or they require only low key support from more than one agency or discipline;

- they are more able to self-manage their mental health problems;

- they have an active informal support network;

- they pose little danger to themselves or others;

- they are more likely to maintain appropriate contact with services.

People on enhanced CPA are likely to have some of the following characteristics:

- they have multiple care needs, including housing, employment etc., requiring inter-agency co-ordination;

- they are only willing to co-operate with one professional or agency but they have multiple care needs;

- they may be in contact with a number of agencies (including the Criminal Justice System);

- they are more likely to require more frequent and intensive interventions, perhaps with medication management;

- they are more likely to have mental health problems co-existing with other problems such as substance misuse;

- they are more likely to be at risk of harming themselves or others;

- they are more likely to disengage from services.

Significant risks to the patient or the public may arise when the patient defaults from or refuses treatment. The response of the service to this will determine whether there are satisfactory risk control measures in place. Any care plan should define what is meant by default. The definition of default may include:

- where the patient fails to attend an appointment with a community worker and fails to give any adequate reason;

- discharging himself from an in-patient unit against medical advice.

Patients at risk of failing to take necessary medication, which may be accompanied by a deterioration in their condition, may be followed up by assertive outreach working. This provides for regular supervision and response to deterioration in the medical condition prior to acute exacerbation of the condition. The assertive outreach technique is particularly helpful for patients with severe and enduring mental illness.

A number of medicines used in the long term treatment of mental illness may have particular toxic effects. These require continuing monitoring of blood levels to ensure therapeutic levels are maintained without toxicity. In particular, lithium salts used in the treatment of manic depression may become toxic if used with diuretics or if the patient develops acute sickness and diarrhoea. Patients should be warned of these effects before leaving hospital and the need for regular blood samples to be taken.

Service users on enhanced CPA require, as part of their care plan, crisis and contingency plans. These plans form a key element of the care plan and must be based on the individual circumstances of the service user.

8.5   RISKS TO HEALTHCARE PROFESSIONALS

8.5.1   During the Admission Process

Incomplete documentation may invalidate the legality of the admission. Admission documents need to be checked for completeness. This may be undertaken by an administrator who has formally had the job delegated to him by the Managers. The admission forms should also be checked by a medically qualified person to ensure that the medical recommendations fulfil the criteria for admission under the Act. Failure to adequately complete the documentation means that the requirements of the Act have not been fulfilled and that the patient has an unanswerable case of false imprisonment.

8.5.2   Violence in In-patient Units

Risks of the effects of patient violence are reduced where all clinical staff have received training in the use of control and restraint. This method of control is only safe where at least three trained members of staff are present. Less than three staff involved in the process may result in injury to the staff or patient. Claims for compensation arising from injuries sustained in these circumstances, either by patients or staff, would be difficult to resist.

All staff who come into contact with patients suffering from mental illness should be trained in the use of 'Breakaway' techniques to enable them to escape from immediate danger. Remote hand held alarms should be provided and carried by staff at all times to help them summon assistance. The source of assistance should be centrally located and separately manned during the time that staff are exposed to the risk.

Risk Assessment pointers – lessons from inquiries

Is there a risk management procedure in place for both in-patients and community services which:

- assesses and takes account of all overt threats of harm to self or others, absconding, substance misuse, criminal record, family history of suicide?

- provides for a new risk assessment on presentation or transfer to another team?

- informs staff of the individual's propensity to violence?

- assesses environmental risk, both to patients and staff and which includes equipment?

- takes account of who may be harmed and how?

- evaluates the adequacy of current arrangements and the need for additional measures?

- records in writing the nature of the risks?

- is supported by a systematic incident reporting system?

- has a regular review system to reassess the risks?

- has a system in place to ensure that the risks are communicated to all relevant persons and agencies?

- includes arrangements for the escort of patients on leave?

- assesses risk in decisions on granting leave?

- includes the circumstances of personal searches?

- an assessment of risks is included in the discharge summary?

- provides a contingency for patients discontinuing treatment or contact with services?

- includes signs and symptoms of impending relapse?

- provides a contingency for missed appointments?

- has a contingency in place for patients who refuse admission, but are not compulsorily detainable?

- has a continuing programme of staff development in the assessment of risk, including resuscitation?

8.5.3 Good Practice in the Clinical Environment[5] – Reducing the Risks of Violence

Hospital wards are unnatural environments. They should be made:

- comfortable;

- safe;

- private when appropriate;

- homely.

All areas should look clean and friendly and reception areas should be well planned. Separate areas should be provided for patients with a police escort.

Crowding should be avoided and there should be a perception of space. Noise levels should be controlled, non-smoking and smoking areas provided together with a safe 'time-out' area. Privacy should be available for both patients and staff. Facilities should be provided for the safe and secure storage of patients' belongings.

Possible antecedents of violence include:

- increased restlessness, bodily tension, pacing and arousal;

- increased volume of speech and erratic movements;

- facial expression tense and angry and discontented;

- refusal to communicate and withdrawal;

- thought processes unclear and poor concentration;

---

5   *Management of Imminent Violence* – Royal College of Psychiatrists 1998

- delusions or hallucinations with a violent content;
- verbal threats or gestures;
- warning signs from earlier episodes;
- service users self-reporting angry or violent feelings;
- carers reporting users' imminent violence.

Tactics for de-escalation include:

- maintaining adequate distance;
- moving to a safe place and avoiding corners;
- explaining intentions to the patient and others;
- appearing calm, self-controlled and confident;
- ensuring that verbal communication is non-threatening;
- engaging in conversation, acknowledging concerns and feelings;
- asking for the facts of problems and encouraging reasoning;
- asking for a weapon to be put down;
- considering methods of sedation, e.g. medication;
- awareness of methods of summoning assistance.

8.5.4 Risk of Violence and Mental Disorder

Any homicide (or other serious violence) by a mentally disordered person is profoundly worrying, and it is essential to learn lessons from such disastrous events. Recent research has perhaps helped us to define more clearly whether and in what circumstances mentally disordered people may behave in a dangerous way. It may be reasonable to summarise the state of current knowledge in five statements:

a) the great majority of mentally ill people and those with learning disability present no increased danger to others;

b) the best predictors of future offending among mentally disordered people are the same as those for the rest of the population – previous offending, criminality in the family, poor parenting etc.;

c) people with a severe mental illness such as schizophrenia or manic depressive disorder, may present an increased risk to others when they have active symptoms;

d) people suffering from severe mental illness who have active symptoms and also misuse drugs or alcohol may present a seriously increased risk to others;

e) people with psychopathic disorder, by definition, present an increased risk to others.[6]

8.5.5 Deaths of Detained Patients

The deaths of all detained patients must be notified to the Coroner and the Mental Health Act Commission on form MHAC 3 within 24 hours of the death. Following a review by the Mental Health Foundation of deaths of detained patients published in December 1995, the Foundation recommended:

- Mental Health Professionals should have training in the high risk of suicide amongst patients diagnosed as suffering from schizophrenia or a related disorder;

- all mental health units should have a clinical risk management policy;

- units with a high level of absconding are advised to review the physical environment and care policies in the unit;

- the absence of patients who have absconded, or who have failed to return from leave at the agreed time, should lead to an immediate search by unit staff. The police should be alerted at once in cases of high risk;

- all units should ensure that staff are trained in the use of a Section 17 leave policy. The policy should conform to the guidelines in the Code of Practice for the Mental Health Act;

- all mental health units should have an agreed clinical protocol for the management of patients with seriously disturbed behaviour;

- all sudden deaths where a prescribed medication or health care intervention could have played a causal role in the death

---

6   Reed J British Journal of Psychiatry (1997) 170 (suppl 32) 4-7

should be the subject of an internal review and multi-disciplinary audit.

The Mental Health Act Commission has reviewed causes of death of detained patients.[7] 253 deaths of 1,471 cases reviewed resulted in an inquest. The most common causes of death were as follows:

Hanging	34%
Jumping from a height	14.2%
Being hit by a train	11.5%
Drowning	8.3%
Overdose	5.1%

24% of deaths occurred while the patients were being observed at least every 15 minutes. The majority of deaths, 41%, took place in a public place while the patient was on approved leave or absent without leave. This emphasises the need for review of observation and risk assessment procedures.

Whilst many of the deaths were reported as due to hanging, a closer review shows that strangulation, rather than a fracture of the second cervical vertebra was the cause of death. This means that closer attention to identifying potential ligatures and ligature points needs to be made to improve ward safety.

8.5.6   Lessons From Safer Services for In-patient Suicides[8]

Report findings:

- 4% of all suicides were psychiatric in-patients;

- around one third of in-patients suicides took place on the ward;

- in-patient suicides, particularly those on the ward, were most likely to be by hanging;

- suicide on the ward was most common in the evening and night;

---

7   Deaths of Detained Patients in England and Wales, Mental Health Act Commission, February 2001

8   *Safer Services* – National Confidential Inquiry into suicide and homicide by people with mental illness 1999, Department of Health

- around one quarter of in-patient suicides were under special observation;

- in almost a quarter of cases there were difficulties in observing patients because of ward design;

- in a quarter of in-patient suicides, there were nursing shortages on the ward.

Recommendations for risk reduction

- all services should review the physical structure of wards to identify

  - (1) any obstruction to the observation of high-risk patients and

  - (2) structures which could be used in suicide by hanging or strangulation

- wards in which these cannot be removed should not be used for the admission of acutely ill patients;

- alternatives to intermediate level observations should be developed for patients at risk;

- services should increase and monitor the observations of patients in the evening and night;

- risk assessment should always be carried out prior to granting leave in patients who are recovering from illness.

These findings were refined in the second report of the Confidential Inquiry, Safety First.[9] This emphasised that clinical services should place priority for suicide prevention and monitoring on:

- in-patients under non-routine observation

- in-patients who are assessed to be at high risk or who are detained and in the first seven days of admission

- in-patients who are at high risk and who are sufficiently recovered to allow home leave but whose circumstances lack support (particularly those who live alone)

---

9   Safety First – Five Year Report of National Confidential Inquiry into suicide and homicide by people with mental illness, Department of Health, 2001

- recently discharged patients who are at high risk or who were recently detained

- patients who become non-compliant while under enhanced CPA.

8.5.7   The Use of Seclusion

Seclusion is the supervised confinement of a patient in a room, which may be locked to protect others from significant harm. Its sole aim is to contain severely disturbed behaviour which is likely to cause harm to others.[10]

Seclusion should be used only when violence is uncontrollable by any other means (i.e. de-escalation techniques, physical interventions or medication) and therefore presents further hazards to the patient and staff. There should be a clear policy in place about its use which details amongst other things:

- when seclusion is to be used;

- when it should be reviewed;

- an observation schedule;

- effects on outcome of treatment; and

- a record of its use.

Further detailed guidance on the use of Seclusion can be found in Chapter 19 of the Mental Health Act 1983 Code of Practice; the Mental Health Act Commission's 8th Report; and in the Royal College of Psychiatrist's Management of Imminent Violence.

8.5.8.   Reporting and Recording Systems

Staff working in the NHS must report every incident of violence or abuse when it occurs or as soon as possible thereafter.

Managers must therefore ensure that all staff know how to report a violent incident, and should establish robust, uncomplicated reporting and recording systems to encourage staff to record details of all incidents of violence. This means systems that are easy to use and not too time-consuming. As a minimum, the following information should be recorded in the event of a violent incident:

---

10 *Code of Practice* – Department of Health and Welsh Office 1999

- details of the individuals involved;
- the cause of the incident and when/where it happened;
- any injury(ies) suffered by the victim and any resulting absence; and
- the action taken by managers to prevent the incident occurring again.

The NHS zero tolerance campaign resource pack contains further information on the Criminal Justice System and explains what happens after an incident has been reported to the police.

When a violent incident occurs

Staff should not feel that they have to cope alone when a violent incident occurs. Managers should support staff when they report an incident. Support should include:

- post trauma support such as counselling and debriefing (but only after an assessment is made to its likely benefit- evidence suggests that poor services or those inappropriately used can do more harm than good) and/or practical assistance such as medical attention;
- supporting staff when they are dealing with the police and during any prosecution that may follow;
- helping staff apply for compensation (a police crime number will be needed) through the Criminal Injuries Compensation Authority (CICA) or the NHS Injury Benefit scheme; and
- dealing with any press enquiries and ensuring that the member of staff's privacy is maintained.

Managers should ensure, following an incident, that safety measures are reviewed and staff training refreshed if necessary to improve the safety of staff in the future.

References

NHS zero tolerance zone Resource Pack 'We don't have to take this' (1999) published by the Department of Health and is available on the zero tolerance website www.nhs.uk/zerotolerance or by telephoning the NHS Responseline on 0541 555455.

Safer Working in the Community: a guide for NHS managers and staff on reducing the risks from violence and aggression by the Royal College of Nursing and the NHS Executive, September 1998. Copies are available from RCN Direct (Reorder No. 000 920) by telephoning 0345 697064.

Management of Imminent Violence – Clinical practice guidelines to support mental health services by the Royal College of Psychiatrists, March 1998. Copies available by telephoning 020 7235 2351.

Mental Health Act 1983 Code of Practice. 1999 edition Copies available from the Stationery Office by telephoning 0870 600 552.

The Mental Health Act Commission's 8th Report. Copies available from the Stationery Office by telephoning 0870 600 552.

NACRO (National Association for the Care and Resettlement of Offenders)

Mental Health Unit
169 Clapham Road
London SW9 0PU.
Telephone 020 7582 6500.

The Code for Crown Prosecutors

Home Office Circulars: No. 66/90 'Provision for mentally disordered offenders' & No. 12/95 'Mentally Disordered Offenders: Inter-Agency Working'. Copies available from Home Office publications on 020 7273 2066.

British Institute of Learning Disabilities (BILD)
Wolverhampton Road
Kidderminster
Worcestershire

DY10 3PP.

8.6   REFORM OF THE MENTAL HEALTH ACT[11]

8.6.1   Guiding Principles

The Green Paper on the reform of the Mental Health Act 1983 states

---

11 *Reform of the Mental Health Act 1983 – Proposals for Consultation* Cm 4480 November 1999

that in common with most UK legislation, there is nothing specifically within the 1983 Act to describe the principles that underpin it. However, the Family Law Act 1996 does include guiding principles, as well as the Children Act 1989. The key principles for a new Mental Health Act are:

Informal care and treatment should always be considered before recourse to compulsory powers;

Patients should be involved as far as possible in the process of developing and reviewing their own care and treatments;

The safety of both the patient and the public are of key importance in determining the question of whether compulsory powers should be imposed;

Where compulsory powers are used, care and treatment should be located in the least restrictive setting consistent with the patient's best interests and safety and the safety of the public.

8.6.2 The Benefits of the Proposed Changes

The key reforms and benefits are:

- formal assessment procedures to apply to all patients for whom a compulsory treatment order is sought. Entry to compulsory care and treatment to be through one gateway;

- all patients subject to compulsory care and treatment beyond 28 days to have their case automatically considered by an independent mental disorder tribunal;

- the care team must demonstrate that the criteria for making a compulsory order are met, unlike the previous Mental Health Review Tribunal process where it is for the patient to prove that they should no longer be detained;

- compulsory treatment orders to apply in the community for the first time, as well as in hospital;

- the legislation governing the provisions of care and treatment to be based on principles explicitly contained in it.

9

COMMON AND AVOIDABLE RISKS IN HEALTHCARE

The identification, assessment and control of particular risks may be aided by an examination of previous errors and assessing a particular area of activity for susceptibility to similar failures. The lists and illustrations built into this chapter are compiled from common system errors found in healthcare. They are not intended to be exhaustive, but provide assistance from using established risk management techniques. The reader should be able to use them to examine their own working practices and environments.

Clinical Area
Figure 9.1 Accident and Emergency

Risk – Unwanted Outcome	Preventative Measure/Damage Limitation	Notes
Patient access restricted – poor signposting	Dedicated shortstay car parking with adequate width parking spaces for the disabled	Easy to read sign posts reduce patient anxieties
Communication failure – Emergency Services	Written handover by ambulance crew	Failure to pass information has resulted in the death of patients
Violence/abuse to reception staff	Secure reception area	May improve with decoration detail Security staffing
Excessive assessment waiting times	Triage on entry to department	Skill mix of patient severity to medical/nurse staffing can be helpful – a pure operational research problem
Inadequate assessment of patients	Structured training with assessment	Training should be recorded
Missed fractures	Review of X-rays by consultant	Review using clinical audit to monitor missed fracture rate
Missed flexor tendon injuries	Fixed protocol for treatment including review by senior medical staff	

Clinical Area

Figure 9.1 Accident and Emergency

Preventative Measure/Damage Limitation (*cont.*)

Risk – Unwanted Outcome	Preventative Measure/Damage Limitation (*cont.*)	Notes
Missed scaphoid fractures	Initial four view X-rays with plaster application and review at ten days	Protocols need to be introduced with training and their effectiveness reviewed through audit. The date of review should be noted. Copies of all previous protocols and guidelines should be securely kept for future reference
Injury to patient in the department	Supervision, particularly of the frail or disabled during transfer for investigations	All injuries should be recorded
Delay in disposal of patient	Structured discharge and admission procedures	A multi-disciplinary and multi-departmental problem – needs to be resolved by a team
Faulty follow-up e.g. lost to review	Review discharge arrangements and documentation – overdoses and need psychiatric referral and risk assessment	
Missed child abuse	Raise index of suspicion through training	Health visitor with responsibility for child health and follow-up should be appointed

Clinical Area

Figure 9.1 Accident and Emergency

Preventative Measure/Damage Limitation *(cont.)*

Risk – Unwanted Outcome	Preventative Measure/Damage Limitation *(cont.)*	Notes
Fatal accident survivors	Bereavement counselling skills to be taught to staff – facilities for relatives	Record of counselling should be kept
Inadequate major accident response	Regular staff training	Advanced Trauma Life Support training for all senior staff
	Regular review of the major accident (MAJAX) procedure. Simple action cards available at a central point for each member of staff	Does the MAJAX plan ensure that the right skilled person is in the right place to treat the right grade of injury at the right time with the right facilities?
		Mortuary facilities may limit the number of casualties which can be accommodated

Clinical Area

Figure 9.2 Operating Theatres and Anaesthesia

Risk – Unwanted Outcome	Preventative Measure/Damage Limitation	Notes
Wrong operation – wrong side, wrong procedure	Adequate checking and marking procedures	Ensure that checks are not merely confirmations of previous errors in the procedure
	Clear operating lists with the side marked in full	Lists should be prepared after the admitting doctor has confirmed the side for operation with the patient
	Adequate agreement with the patient in respect of breast operations	An individual breast lump should be marked and the site agreed with the patient
	Check of patient by the operating surgeon	Ideally, the operating surgeon should be responsible for the patient on admission
	Adequate swab and instrument checks for number and the integrity of instruments	A system is required to identify and correct faulty instruments
Swab or instrument retained after procedure	Staff training to emphasise the importance of not rushing patient cavity closure	

Clinical Area
Figure 9.2 Operating Theatres and Anaesthesia

Risk – Unwanted Outcome	Preventative Measure/Damage Limitation (*cont.*)	Notes
Equipment failure	Adequate maintenance	Visual inspection before use. Testing of anaesthetic apparatus before use. Audit of staff equipment usage
Equipment contamination e.g. Tuberculosis	Adequate diagnosis – adequate sterilisation procedures	
Diathermy Burns	Staff training. Equipment checking. Equipment maintenance	
Endoscopic, minimal access (keyhole) procedure errors	Accredited training of staff – applies to all new technical procedures including the use of lasers	Clinical audit can be used to deter the "seen one, done one, teach one" approach
Operating department explosions	Safe storage of anaesthetic gases	COSHH review should determine safe storage
Excess exposure of staff to medical gases	Monitor air levels of gases and flow rates of fresh air ingress	Should be regularly monitored

Clinical Area

Figure 9.2 Operating Theatres and Anaesthesia

Risk – Unwanted Outcome	Preventative Measure/Damage Limitation (*cont.*)	Notes
Oesophageal intubation Failed intubation	Examination of patient Failed intubation drill for assistant	Training Fibre optic laryngoscope will help
Malignant hyperpyrexia	Patient selection – adequate family history Malignant hyperpyrexia drill	
Malignant hyperpyrexia	Ready supply of Dantrolene – sufficient for a loading dose – based on 80mgms/kilo	Expiry dates need to be clearly marked on the box
Death in Theatre	Patient selection	Eliminate unnecessary out of hours surgery
	Pre-operative Resuscitation	Needs to be adequately assessed
	Staff skill levels	Training, pre-operative consultation
	Death in Theatre policy	Needs to cover informing the Coroner and relatives

Clinical Area

Figure 9.2 Operating Theatres and Anaesthesia

Risk – Unwanted Outcome	Preventative Measure/Damage Limitation (*cont.*)	Notes
Product liability exposures	Regularly out-date stock, including sutures and drugs	Stock control affects financial risks and viability of usage of resources Stock usage numbers should be recorded and records kept for 10 years and eight months to allow for the extended service of a writ
Over-run Operating lists Out of hours Surgery Utilisation of Theatre Resources	Effective Theatre organisation	Operating Theatre Committee – Membership to reflect usage – Seniority to increase effectiveness
Fire	Fire hazard inspections	
	Fire alarm siting and inspection Ventilation inspection	
	Fire evacuation training	Should be carried out in theatre, not as a remote activity

Clinical Area
Figure 9.3 Intensive Care

Risk – Unwanted Outcome	Preventative Measure/Damage Limitation	Notes
Equipment faults Intracardiac and intravascular catheters can cause ventricular fibrillation with a current leakage of microamps	Inspection before use Report faults to technicians Report faults as untoward incidents	Adequate maintenance Pre-acceptance testing of appliances Care when unplugging and plugging in to minimise risks of damage
	Adequate alarms	Alarms tested before use
Equipment usage errors	Equipment set up in line of sight	Reduces errors in settings of equipment
Equipment malfunctions	Maintenance in accord with manufacturers instructions	Particularly applies to sterilisation of ventilator valves Particular care and training needed for syringe pumps
	Controlled use of high radio wave emitters e.g. mobile telephones, wireless communications by emergency services	
Drug usage errors	Adequate checking	Clarity of drug charts

Clinical Area
Figure 9.3 Intensive Care

Risk – Unwanted Outcome	Preventative Measure/Damage Limitation (*cont.*)	Notes
Inadequate staffing	Management which supports the function of the department	
Inadequate staff	Selection and training – skill mix assessment	
	Clinical supervision procedures	Regular skills updating
Inadequate observations/recordings	Review charts	Charts should record: General observations Fluid balance Prescribed drugs Neurological observations as appropriate
Patient/relative stress	Reduce sleep deprivation	Control of care environment Observe diurnal light variations Apparently unconscious patients may be able to hear
	Full explanations of condition and prognosis	

Clinical Area
Figure 9.3 Intensive Care

Risk – Unwanted Outcome	Preventative Measure/Damage Limitation (*cont.*)	Notes
	Pre-operative visit for elective admissions	Unrestricted visiting, but observe secure access
	Waiting area for relatives	
	Overnight area for relatives	
Self-poisoning	Referral for psychiatric opinion	
Dialysis – failure of drainage	Accurate diagnosis of the problem Obstruction of tubing Excessive leakage Patient's position Catheter blockage	Accurate diagnosis of the problem is paramount in deciding corrective action

Clinical Area
Figure 9.4 Obstetrics and Gynaecology

Risk – Unwanted Outcome	Preventative Measure/Damage Limitation	Notes
Discontinuity of care during labour	Planned handover	Morning and evening ward rounds by a senior member of the medical staff
		Adequate documentation
Birth asphyxia	Adequate selection of cases for appropriate delivery method	
	Adequate supervision during labour	
	Adequate trained staff	Clinical audit of activity and outcomes
	Adequate monitoring	Equipment current and maintained
Delay in performing emergency procedures	Adequate numbers of trained staff	Dedicated anaesthetic cover
	Adequate facilities	Dedicated operating theatre and recovery facilities – blood availability

Clinical Area
Figure 9.4 Obstetrics and Gynaecology

Risk – Unwanted Outcome	Preventative Measure/Damage Limitation (*cont.*)	Notes
Aspiration of stomach contents	Antacid policy	Staff training in use of policy
	Resuscitation facilities	
Post Natal Depression	Ante Natal awareness for expectant parents	May reduce severity, if not frequency
	Availability of treatment resource	e.g. Referral to Community Mental Health Team
	Staff awareness	Training

In Vitro procedures

Sperm mix up	Adequate record keeping	
	Adequate housekeeping	Cleaning pipette between specimens

Clinical Area
Figure 9.4 Obstetrics and Gynaecology

Risk – Unwanted Outcome	Preventative Measure/Damage Limitation (*cont.*)	Notes
Gynaecology		
Inadequate specimens	Training in techniques	
Perforation during intra-uterine procedures	Training/supervision	Clinical audit
Drug dosage errors	Training and checking	
Sterilisation failure	Pre-operative counselling at time of consent	Adequate recording of discussion in the medical records
Inadequate specimens	Operative technique	
Ureteric damage during hysterectomy	Operative technique and/or pathology	Not necessarily negligent, but care of follow up and diagnosis important to the defence of claims
Allegation of operation without consent e.g. hysterectomy or hysterectomy whilst pregnant	Documentation in medical records	A full menstrual history is advisable and recorded – lack of menstruation may mean pregnancy undiagnosed

Clinical Area

Figure 9.5 Laboratory Medicine

Risk – Unwanted Outcome	Preventative Measure/Damage Limitation	Notes
Mixed specimens between patients	Housekeeping procedures	Record keeping
Cleaning of microtome between patient specimens
Incorrect Blood Group	Housekeeping and checking procedures	
Blood contamination	Adequate checking	
Blood contamination
Faulty storage containers	Avoid reliance on one supplier	
Blood contamination
Faulty storage facility	Adequate alarms on storage facility	
Blood contamination
Infected donor	Screening of donors	Screening programme needs regular updating in the light of epidemiological evidence
Nosocomial infections	Hygiene training	All health institutions should have a formal and known Control of Infection Policy

Clinical Area

Figure 9.5 Laboratory Medicine

Preventative Measure/Damage Limitation *(cont.)*

Risk – Unwanted Outcome	Preventative Measure/Damage Limitation *(cont.)*	Notes
Infection rate monitoring		Clinical audit activity
MRSA policy		Needs compliance testing and review
Effective use of Control of Cross Infection		Control of Infection Committee with adequate professional input

Figure 9.6 Other Clinical Areas

Risk – Unwanted Outcome	Preventative Measure/Damage Limitation	Notes
Paediatrics		
Abduction from in-patient area	Security measures – limited access	Staff awareness of potential
Drug dosage errors	Paediatric pharmacopoeia	Staff training Induction training for junior medical staff
	Clear prescription sheets	Pharmacy audit and control of drugs – **EXTREME CARE IS REQUIRED WITH VINCA COMPOUNDS TO PREVENT INTRATHECAL ADMINISTRATION – DEATH OR PARALYSIS IS AN INEVITABLE COMPLICATION**
Missed epiglotitis	Adequate index of suspicion and training	
Missed hip dislocation in new born period	Staff training in examination technique	Findings should be recorded

Figure 9.6 Other Clinical Areas

Risk – Unwanted Outcome	Preventative Measure/Damage Limitation *(cont.)*	Notes
Paediatrics *(cont.)*		
Missed abuse	Adequate index of suspicion and training	May be physical, neglect and failure to thrive, emotional or sexual
Child abuse	Child protection procedures	Needs staff training and updating in the light of experience
Radiotherapy		
Non-therapeutic dosage	Adequate calibration of equipment on installation and after operational changes Adequate calculation of dosage with quality control – multidisciplinary	These two simple measures would have prevented the two largest series of incorrect applications of radiotherapy in the UK
Post-irradiation tissue damage	Adequate explanations to patient when obtaining consent Patient support and referral	Adequate pain relief Access to pain relief service

Figure 9.6 Other Clinical Areas

Risk – Unwanted Outcome	Preventative Measure/Damage Limitation (cont.)	Notes
Mental Health		
Lithium toxicity/brain damage	Adequate monitoring of blood levels	Patients and carers should be informed of the importance of regularly attending for blood level monitoring and the risks of dehydration
Monoamine oxidase inhibitor toxicity	Information to patients on dietary restrictions	Patients should be given an information booklet
Suicide	Adequate assessment of risk	Nursing observation policies need to be clear and recorded – clear AWOL procedures
	Preventative assessment of suicide opportunities	Hanging is the most common method of suicide for in-patients – eliminate hanging and suffocation points

Figure 9.6 Other Clinical Areas

Risk – Unwanted Outcome | **Preventative Measure/Damage Limitation** *(cont.)* | **Notes**

Mental Health *(cont.)*

Risk – Unwanted Outcome	Preventative Measure/Damage Limitation	Notes
Assault	All clinical staff trained in breakaway and de-escalation techniques	Training should be recorded and repeated regularly
	All nursing staff trained in control and restraint methods	Training should be recorded and repeated regularly
	Assistance alarms	Training in usage and regular testing of systems
Arson	Control of opportunities by observation and control of combustible materials	
Patient lost to follow up	Adequate and audited Care Programme Approach with contingency plans	See Chapter 8

Figure 9.7 Other Areas of Risk

Risk - Unwanted Outcome	Preventative Measure/Damage Limitation	Notes
Back Injury	Lifting and Handling Training	Training should be structured and recorded with staff given certificates of competency
Falls	Assessment of workplace risks	At least annual assessment
	Assessment of workplace risks	At least annual assessment
	Assess patient risks	Use standard risk assessment tools – falls analysis through incident reporting
	Assess staffing levels	Assess skill mix requirements for patient dependency needs
Fire	Staff training	
	Control of combustible materials	
	Contingency plan	
Motor vehicle accidents	Defensive driving training	

Figure 9.7 Other Areas of Risk

Risk - Unwanted Outcome	Preventative Measure/ Damage Limitation *(cont.)*	Notes
IT failure	Adequate backup of information	
	Contingency plan	
Telecoms failure	Contingency plan	
Flooding	Adequate site preparation	
	Contingency plan	

Appendix 1

CONTROLS ASSURANCE STANDARDS

The following standards are those not included in the text, but which were also introduced in 1999

BUILDINGS, LAND, PLANT AND NON-MEDICAL EQUIPMENT

1 A suitably qualified professional has been designated to manage the estate.

2 Board level responsibility for buildings, land, plant and non-medical equipment is clearly defined and there are clear lines of accountability throughout the organisation, leading to the board

3 The organisation has a board-approved policy and strategy for the management of its land, buildings, plant and non-medical equipment that meets the requirements of its business plan and service strategy.

4 An up to date operational estate policy and up to date operational procedures are in place

5 An annual review is undertaken to assess the capability of the Estate to meet the needs of the organisation and legislative requirements

6 The organisation's asset base is managed systematically, based on an agreed approach.

7 All property management issues are evaluated, considered, and dealt with to achieve optimum customer satisfaction, utilisation and financial control

8 The risk management process contained within the risk management system standard is applied to Healthcare Estates

9 The organisation has access to up-to-date legislation and guidance relating to Healthcare Estates.

10 Relevant staff receive training and instruction on the safe operating and maintenance of Healthcare Estates.

11 The competency and performance of Healthcare Estates personnel to meet legislative requirements and perform regular duties is evaluated.

12 Key performance indicators capable of showing improvements in Healthcare Estates, and the management of associated risks, are used at all levels of the organisation, including the board, and the efficacy and usefulness of the indicators is reviewed regularly.

13 The organisation benchmarks itself against other organisations.

14 The system in place for managing Healthcare Estates, including risk management arrangements, is monitored and reviewed by management and the board in order to make improvements to the system.

15 The Internal Audit function, aided as necessary by relevant technical specialists, carries out periodic audits to provide assurance to the board that a system of managing Healthcare Estates is in place that conforms to the requirements of this standard.

CONTRACTS AND CONTRACTORS CONTROL

1 Board level responsibility for control of contracts and contractors is clearly defined and there are clear lines of accountability throughout the organisation, leading to the board.

2 There is a policy and strategy for the control of contracts and contractors that complies with the requirements of the NHS Executives Finance Manual for NHS Trusts and Health Authorities.

3 There is a procurement strategy that is reviewed at least annually.

4 All suppliers of goods or services are covered by a contract or agreement.

5 A current contractor/contract register is maintained and reviewed regularly.

6 Clear and detailed specifications are followed for all purchases.

7 The purchase of all products and services conforms with required methods of procurement specific to the type of product or service.

8 Criteria are developed and used to select all suppliers and contractors.

9 All suppliers and contractors are selected and approved based on agreed procedures.

10 All contracts to supply goods or services are regularly monitored and reviewed.

11 There is access to up-to-date legislation and guidance relevant to the control of contracts

12 All relevant staff receive training on the organisation's procurement and contracting processes.

13 Key performance indicators capable of showing improvements in the control of contracts and contractors, and the management of associated risks, are used at all levels of the organisation, including the board, and the efficacy and usefulness of the indicators is reviewed regularly.

14 The system in place for control of contracts and contractors is monitored and reviewed by management and the Board in order to make improvements to the system

15 The Internal Audit function, aided as necessary by relevant technical specialists, carries out periodic audits to provide assurance to the board that a system of managing contracts and contractors is in place that conforms to the requirements of this standard.

ENVIRONMENTAL MANAGEMENT

1 Board level responsibility for environmental management is clearly defined and there are clear lines of accountability throughout the organisation, leading to the board

2 The organisation has an effective policy and strategy for environmental management which is endorsed by the Board and adopted throughout the organisation

3 A thorough environmental review has been carried out to establish a register of significant environmental risks

4 There are agreed environmental targets and objectives which are fulfilled by an ongoing programme

5 The risk management process contained within the risk management system standard is applied to the management of environmental risk

6 There is access to up-to-date information on environmental legislation and guidance, including NHS Executive guidance, to all within the organisation who require the information

7 Education and training on environmental management issues is provided for all relevant staff.

8 Key indicators capable of showing improvements in environmental management and the management of associated risks are used at all levels of the organisation, including the board, and the efficacy and usefulness of the indicators is reviewed regularly.

9 The system in place for environmental management, including risk

management arrangements, is monitored and reviewed by management and the board in order to make improvements in the system

10 All aspects of the system in place to manage environmental risk, including risk management arrangements, are subject to independent verification by internal audit, in conjunction with relevant environmental specialists on a periodic basis

INFORMATION MANAGEMENT & TECHNOLOGY

1 The Board takes responsibility for the organisation's IM&T system, including IM&T technology projects and the use and management of information.

2 The Chief Executive or a named Executive Director takes responsibility for all aspects of IM&T and is accountable to the Board.

3 An IM&T Group, or equivalent, oversees, takes decisions and is accountable to the Board for all matters in relation to IM&T.

4 There is a qualified IM&T Manager, or equivalent.

5 There is a comprehensive IM&T policy that is agreed by the Board and links into the organisation's overall strategic plan.

6 There is an IM&T strategy designed to achieve the objectives outlined in the organisation's IM&T policy.

7 An agreed IM&T procurement process is adhered to throughout the organisation.

8 An agreed IM&T project management process is adhered to throughout the organisation.

9 In the design and implementation of any IM&T project, a consistent set of control processes are always followed.

10 All patient information, either electronic or paper-based, is validated as authentic.

11 All patient information, either electronic or paper-based, is protected through the application of robust security measures to ensure confidentiality.

12 All patient information, either electronic or paper-based, is always treated by staff as private.

13 The risk management process contained within the risk management system standard is applied to all aspects of IM&T.

14 The organisation has access to up-to-date legislation and guidance relating to information management and technology.

15 The IM&T function is staffed with appropriately skilled IM&T specialists.

16 All IM&T stakeholders are appropriately trained to perform their duties with the information technology that is provided to them.

17 All IM&T stakeholders are trained to manage the information that they produce and use within their role.

18 Key indicators capable of showing improvements in the management of IM&T and/or providing early warning of risk are used at all levels of the organisation, including the board, and the efficacy and usefulness of the indicators is reviewed regularly.

19 The system in place for managing IM&T, including risk management arrangements, is monitored and reviewed by management and the board in order to make improvements to the system.

20 The Internal Audit function, aided as necessary by relevant technical specialists, carries out periodic audits to provide assurance to the board that a system of managing IM&T is in place that conforms to the requirements of this standard.

21 Communication and consultation takes place with all IM&T risk stakeholders

TRANSPORT

1 Board level responsibility for environmental transport issues is clearly defined and there are clear lines of accountability throughout the organisation, leading to the board.

2 The organisation has undertaken a review of its current transport arrangements.

3 The organisation has identified targets for reducing environmental pollution from transport and has associated timescales for achievement.

4 The organisation's targets and timescales for achieving reduced pollution levels from transport are communicated throughout the organisation.

5 The organisation has taken into consideration travel by contractors and suppliers in its review, and subsequent targets for reducing environmental pollution from transport.

6 The organisation has developed its targets and plans to reduce environmental pollution from transport, in partnership with relevant stakeholders.

7 The risk management process contained within the risk management system standard is applied to transport.

8   The organisation has access to up-to-date legislation and guidance relating to requirements and risks associated with transport.

9   Key indicators capable of showing improvements in reducing the environmental effects of transport are used at all levels of the organisation, including the board, and the efficacy and usefulness of the indicators is reviewed regularly.

A model action plan for the implementation of controls assurance is available from:

http://www.geoffroberts.com

Appendix 2

CLINICAL NEGLIGENCE SCHEME FOR TRUSTS – SUMMARY STANDARDS

The weighting (H High, M Medium and L Low) is given at the end of the standard

Standard 1: Clinical Risk Management – Strategy and Organisation

The board has a written strategy in place that makes their commitment to managing clinical risk explicit. Responsibility for this strategy and its implementation is clear.

1.1.1.   There is a written clinical risk management strategy that has been approved by the trust board. H

1.1.2   An Executive Director has been charged with responsibility for clinical risk management throughout the trust. This is clearly stated in the policy. H

1.1.3   One or more persons is charged with the responsibility for co-ordination of clinical risk activities. H

1.1.4   The person(s) responsible for co-ordinating clinical risk is accountable to the nominated executive director. M

1.2.1   The strategy has been distributed to all clinical staff. M

1.2.2   The strategy is available to the public and other stakeholders. L

1.2.3   The trust can produce documentary evidence demonstrating that the board's strategy is being implemented. M

1.2.4   A formal risk management forum exists in which clinical risk related issues are discussed. H

1.3.1   The trust can produce documentary evidence demonstrating that the board's strategy is being implemented and is subject to continuing review. H

Standard 2: Clinical Incident Reporting

A clinical incident reporting system is operated in all medical specialties and clinical support departments

2.1.1   Clinical incident reporting is operating in 10% of all specialties. H

2.1.2   The incident form gathers significant data about the event. M

2.1.3   The incident report form contains clear guidance. M

2.1.4   Summarised clinical incident reports are provided regularly to relevant bodies for review and action. H

2.1.5   The trust has a policy on the relationship between incident reporting and disciplinary action. H

2.2.1   Clinically related events are reported as they occur and before claims are made. M

2.2.2   There is evidence of management action arising from clinical incident reporting. H

2.2.3   Clinical incident reporting is operating in 25% of all specialties. H

2.2.4   The person receiving clinical incident reports has written instructions on the action to be taken. Incidents are graded for their degree of risk upon receipt of the form, and guidance on this is given. M

2.2.5   In the interests of patient safety, openness and constructive criticism of clinical care is actively encouraged. M

2.3.1   Implementation of clinical incident reporting is operating in all specialties. H

2.3.2   All clinical staff receive training in clinical incident reporting. M

Standard 3: Response to Major Clinical Incidents

There is a policy for the rapid follow-up of major clinical incidents.

3.1.1   The policy covers responsibility for management of the incident. H

3.1.2   The policy is explicit about responsibility for informing patient(s) and/or relatives. H

3.1.3   The policy covers record keeping about the incident. M

3.1.4   The policy is explicit about which individuals in the trust must be informed. M

3.1.5   The policy details which other interested parties need to be informed of the event. M

3.1.6   The policy makes it explicit that the patient must be informed before the media. M

3.1.7   The policy covers media relations and who will be responsible for them. M

3.1.8   For serial incidents there is a strategy for dealing with multiple enquiries, such as "hotline arrangements". M

3.2.1   There is in place a process for the detailed investigation of major clinical incidents. M

Standard 4: Managing complaints

An agreed system of managing complaints is in place.

4.1.1   The method of dealing with complaints is clear and meets NHSE guidelines. H

4.2.1   Examples of two changes which reduce risk as a consequence of complaints can be demonstrated. M

4.3.1   Examples of five changes which reduce risk as consequence of complaints can be demonstrated. M

Standard 5: Advice and consent

Appropriate information is provided to patients on the risks and benefits of the proposed treatment or investigation, and the alternatives available, before a signature on a consent form is sought.

5.1.1   There is patient information available which includes reference to the risks and benefits of ten common elective treatments. H

5.1.2   All consent forms used comply with NHSE guidelines for design and use. H

5.2.1   There is patient information showing the risks/benefits of common elective treatments. H

5.2.2   There is a policy/guideline stating that consent for elective procedures is to be obtained by a person competent and capable of performing the procedure. H

5.3.1   There is a clear mechanism for patients to obtain additional information about their condition. M

5.3.2   The consent policy is audited for compliance. H

Standard 6: Health Records

A comprehensive system for the completion, use, storage and retrieval of health records is in place. Record keeping standards are monitored through the clinical audit process.

6.1.1   There is a unified health record which all specialties use. H

6.1.2   Records are bound and stored so that loss of documents and traces are minimised for in-patients and out-patients. M

6.1.3   The health record contains clear instructions regarding filing of documents. M

6.1.4   Operation notes and other key procedures are readily identifiable. M

6.1.5   CTG and other machine produced recordings are securely stored and mounted. M

6.1.6   There is a computer system, or other, for identifying and retrieving x-rays. L

6.1.7   The storage arrangements allow retrieval on a 24 hour/ 7 day arrangement. L

6.1.8   There is clear evidence of clinical audit of record keeping standards for all professional groups in at least 25% of specialties, including any high risk specialties, within the 12 months prior to the assessment. H

6.1.9   There is a mechanism for identifying records which must not be destroyed. L

6.2.1   A&E records are contained within the main record for patients who are subsequently admitted. L

6.2.3   Nursing, medical and other records (e.g. physiotherapy notes) are filed together when the patient is discharged. M

6.2.2   There is a system for ensuring that the GP is sent a copy of the A&E record. L

6.2.4   There is a system for measuring efficiency in the recovery of records for in-patients and out-patients. L

6.2.5   The health record contains a designated place for the recording of hyper-sensitivity reactions, and other information relevant to all healthcare professionals. H

6.2.6   There is clear evidence of clinical audit of record keeping standards for all professional groups in 50% of the specialties, within the 12 months prior to the assessment. H

6.3.1 An author of an entry in a health record is clearly and easily identifiable. H

6.3.2 There is clear evidence of clinical audit of record keeping standards for all professional groups in all of the specialties, within the 12 months prior to the assessment. H

6.3.3 There is a computer based Patient Administration System. L

Standard 7: Induction, Training and Competence

There are management systems in place to ensure the competence and appropriate training of all clinical staff

7.1.1 All clinical staff (including all grades of medical staff) attend a mandatory general induction course on joining the trust. H

7.1.2 All clinical staff (except Doctors) attend a specific induction appropriate to the specialty in which they are working. H

7.1.3 The trust has a written policy which requires relevant clinical staff to be competent to perform basic life support whenever called upon to do so, and can demonstrate that there is a system in place to fulfill the policy, and training records are maintained. H

7.1.4 There is a procedure to verify the registration of clinical staff. M

7.1.5 There is a system which identifies any equipment for which the operator is required to have specialist training. H

7.2.1 All medical staff in training attend a specific induction appropriate to the specialty in which they are working. H

7.2.2 Clinical risk management is included in the general induction arrangements for all healthcare staff. M

7.2.3 The trust has clear policies for addressing shortfalls in the conduct, performance and health of clinical staff and staff are made aware of it. L

7.2.4 The trust has an induction system covering all temporary (locum, bank or agency) clinical staff to ensure that such employees are competent to perform the duties of their post. H

7.2.5 Medical staff in training can demonstrate that they are technically competent to undertake their duties. H

7.2.6 The trust has a clear policy requiring a Consultant to have attended a relevant training programme before embarking upon techniques which are new to him or her and which are not part of an Ethical Committee approved research programme. M

7.2.7   Training programmes are in place to ensure that staff operating diagnostic or therapeutic equipment can do so in a safe and effective manner. M

7.3.1   90% of eligible staff have attended basic life support training in the last 12 months. M

7.3.2   There is a section on clinical risk management in the medical staff handbook incorporating key policies and procedures. M

7.3.3   Staff who operate diagnostic or therapeutic equipment are formally trained to do so safely and effectively. M

Standard 8: Implementation of Clinical Risk Management

A clinical risk management system is in place

8.2.1   All clinical risk management standards and processes are in place and operational. H

8.2.2   Risk management policy is implemented through the general management arrangements of the trust. M

8.2.3   A trust-wide clinical risk assessment has been conducted. H

8.3.1   There is evidence of progression and achievement of action points based on recommendations made in the risk assessment. H

Standard 9: Clinical Care

There are clear procedures for the management of general clinical care.

9.1.1   All specialties have in place an integrated policy that identifies and addresses the needs of the patient prior to, and in preparation for, discharge from the hospital. M

9.1.2   There are appropriate systems in place for the safe storage and administration of human blood and blood products. M

9.2.1   The trust applies the advice in the National Confidential Enquiries. H

9.2.2   Clinical areas admitting emergencies are appropriately staffed at all times. H

9.2.3   There are clear lines of accountability and responsibility for staff working in another organisation's facility. M

9.2.4   The trust's policy on procedures for the discharge of patients is subject to ongoing monitoring. L

9.3.1   Emergency surgery out of hours is reduced to a minimum. H

9.3.2   There are specific clinical procedures, pathways or guidelines for each specialty. H

Standard 10: Maternity Care

There are clearly documented systems for management and communication throughout the key stages of maternity care.

10.1.1   The arrangements are clear concerning which professional is responsible for the woman's care at all times. H

10.1.2   There are referenced, evidence-based multi-disciplinary policies for the management of all key conditions / situations on the labour ward. These are subject to review at intervals of not more than three years. H

10.1.3   There is an agreed mechanism for direct referral to a Consultant by a Midwife. H

10.1.4   There is a personal handover of care when medical shifts change. H

10.1.5   There is a labour ward forum or equivalent, to ensure that there is a clear documented system for management and communication throughout the key stages of maternity care. M

10.1.6   All Clinicians should attend six monthly multi-disciplinary in-service education/training sessions, on the management of labour, and CTG interpretation. H

10.2.1   There is a Lead Consultant Obstetrician and Clinical Midwife Manager for labour ward matters. M

10.2.2   The labour ward has sufficient medical leadership and experience to provide a reasonable standard of care at all times. H

10.3.1   Emergency Caesarean Section can be undertaken rapidly and in a short enough period to eliminate unacceptable delay. M

10.3.2   There is a personal handover to obstetric locums, either by the post-holder or senior member of the team, and vice versa. H

Standard 11: The Management of Care in Trusts Providing Mental Health Services

There are clear systems for the protection of the public and service users.

11.1.1   All service users are assessed for the possibility of self harm or harm to others. H

11.1.2   All staff undertaking assessments of service users have received appropriate training. M

11.1.3   Appropriate control measures are in place to reduce the risk of self harm or harm to others by service users. M

11.1.4   There is a multi-disciplinary care programme approach. M

11.2.1   The trust has a mechanism for ensuring that there is detailed provision of care and supervision of service users following their discharge from hospital. M

Standard 12: Ambulance Service

There are clear procedures for the management of clinical risk in trusts providing Ambulance Services.

12.1.1   Records are made of patients who refuse to travel or refuse treatment. M

12.1.2   Decision making regarding discontinuance of resuscitation attempts. H

12.2.1   Patients suffering trauma or accident are transported to a location appropriate to their clinical needs. M

Index